Dramatic Revisions of
Myths, Fairy Tales and Legends

Dramatic Revisions of Myths, Fairy Tales and Legends

Essays on Recent Plays

Edited by VERNA A. FOSTER

McFarland & Company, Inc., Publishers
Jefferson, North Carolina, and London

LIBRARY OF CONGRESS CATALOGUING-IN-PUBLICATION DATA

Dramatic revisions of myths, fairy tales and legends : essays on
   recent plays / edited by Verna A. Foster.
         p.   cm.
   Includes bibliographical references and index.

   ISBN 978-0-7864-6512-5
   softcover : acid free paper ∞

   1. American drama — 20th century — History and criticism.
   2. Mythology, Classical, in literature.   3. Myth in literature.
   4. Fairy tales in literature.   5. Legends — History and criticism.
   6. Classical drama — Adaptations — History and criticism.
   7. Fairy tales — Adaptations — History and criticism.
   8. Literature — Adaptations — History and criticism.   I. Foster,
   Verna A., 1946–
   PS352.D72 2012
   812'.5409—dc23   2012033848

BRITISH LIBRARY CATALOGUING DATA ARE AVAILABLE

Front cover image © 2012 Shutterstock

Manufactured in the United States of America

McFarland & Company, Inc., Publishers
   Box 611, Jefferson, North Carolina 28640
   www.mcfarlandpub.com

For Gareth and Rebecca Foster

Acknowledgments

Above all, I would like to thank the contributors to this volume, especially Laura Snyder, Miriam Chirico, and Sharon Friedman, who have supported this project with advice and encouragement since its conception. I would like to thank also my friends and colleagues at the Comparative Drama Conference for stimulating conversations and presentations, many of them on the topic of dramatic adaptation. In fact, several of the papers in this volume began life at the CDC. The English Department of Loyola University, Chicago has provided me with the time and the Loyola library staff with the resources to edit this collection. I am grateful to Julia Daniel, graduate student in English at Loyola, for assisting me with the final technical details in putting the book together. Finally, I thank my husband, Stephen Foster, for all manner of support, both academic and personal, and for his forbearance.

Table of Contents

Introduction

Verna A. Foster

In *The Haunted Stage* Marvin Carlson comments that drama, more than other literary forms, "has always been centrally concerned" with "the retelling of stories already known to its public" (17). The numerous revisions of myth, fairy tale, and legend in contemporary drama no less than the retellings of Greek myth in classical tragedy or Shakespeare's retellings of English history bear out Carlson's observation, and they constitute one major strand of the current vogue for literary and specifically dramatic adaptation or revision. All plays, as Timberlake Wertenbaker has observed, arise "from something" (39), but many plays arise from something, some story, that their audiences can recognize. Critics typically designate such plays "adaptations." Sources commonly adapted by contemporary playwrights include earlier literary and dramatic works, especially Greek drama and the plays of Shakespeare, historical events and figures, and myth and legend. The essays in this book explore plays that variously revise myth, fairy tale, and legend and thus raise somewhat different theoretical issues than do works based on specific literary sources that are more commonly the subject of adaptation studies.

Many earlier studies of myth and literature focus on non-dramatic literature, while those that treat dramatic revisions of myth tend to deal exclusively with Greek myth, which has indeed been one of the richest sources of modern drama. This collection, however, demonstrates and explores the extensive range of mythical, folkloric, and legendary sources (including Greek, West African, North American, Native American, Québécois, British, Japanese, Western European, Eastern European/Jewish) that have been used by contemporary dramatists writing, for the most part, in English; and by focusing on specifically dramatic revisions, the collection fills a lacuna in the critical literature.[1] Discussing plays that draw on mythic or legendary sources from a variety of cultures, the essays in this volume offer readers interested in drama and mythic revision a broader as well as a more precise appreciation of both authorial purpose and the consequences for reception in dramatizing mythic stories. The volume includes essays on plays based on familiar myths

1

(Antigone, Euridice, Helen), popular political myth (the myth of the Wild West), as well as historical figures who have become legends (Ono no Komachi, Lizzie Borden, La Corriveau, Marguerite de Nontron), and fairy tale ("The White Cat"). While offering studies of a broad range of plays and the myths, fairy tales, and legends on which they are based, the collection also focuses on three important current theoretical issues: the dramatic use of "mythic" sources, dramatic revision or adaptation, and, in many of the essays, the changing representation of gender.

The dramatists discussed here range from well-established playwrights such as Caryl Churchill, Timberlake Wertenbaker, and Tony Kushner to new theatrical stars like Sarah Ruhl and Tarell Alvin McCraney. By "dramatic" I am referring to both text and performance. While some theorists regard drama as inherently an adaptive art as a play moves from page to stage (Fischlin and Fortier 4, Sanders 48), Margaret Jane Kidnie in *Shakespeare and the Problem of Adaptation* more accurately insists that production per se is not adaptation (though some productions might be adaptations of specific texts) but rather one of the two "media"— text and performance — in which drama uniquely exists (6). The word "dramatic" in my title refers, then, to the play texts addressed by the essays in this volume and concomitantly to their stage productions. As both scripts and performances, the works discussed constitute adaptations or revisions of stories that are already known.

Adaptation is currently a leading area of inquiry that is only just beginning to be theorized, notably by Daniel Fischlin and Mark Fortier in the introduction to their book *Adaptations of Shakespeare: A Critical Anthology of Plays From the Seventeenth Century to the Present* (2000) and in two broader studies published in 2006, Linda Hutcheon's *A Theory of Adaptation* and Julie Sanders's *Adaptation and Appropriation*.[2] Fischlin and Fortier tackle the dizzying proliferation of terms associated with adaptation, distinguishing among the nuances of "alteration," "spinoff," "tradaptation," "offshoot," "appropriation," and "adaptation," but finding all of these terms, even the "adaptation" of their title, deficient in some way (2–3). Timberlake Wertenbaker also makes helpful distinctions among the various terms commonly used for indicating the relation between a text and its "source": "translation," "adaptation," "based on," "version." Both Wertenbaker and Hutcheon note the Darwinian implications of the term "adaptation" in the sense of making "fit"— for a new cultural environment, or a new audience (Wertenbaker 36; Hutcheon 31). Hutcheon more precisely defines adaptation as "an extended, deliberate, announced revisitation of a particular work of art" (170). This definition works for the intercultural and intertemporal dialogue between specific texts of various kinds with which Hutcheon is chiefly concerned.[3] But in the case of sources in mythology there is often no specific source text to be adapted.

Wertenbaker makes this point in taking issue with those who referred to her play *The Love of the Nightingale* (a retelling of the story of Philomele) as an "adaptation." The term is inappropriate, she says, because there was no "original" work to adapt (39). For this collection, then, I have chosen the term "revision" (not listed by either Fischlin and Fortier or Wertenbaker) to refer to the various kinds of retellings of myth, fairy tale, and legend discussed in the following essays. "Revision" is in any case a happier term than "adaptation" (or any other cognate) not only because of its greater flexibility but because, as Sharon Friedman notes in the introduction to her edited collection *Feminist Theatrical Revisions of Classic Works*, "revision," in the sense of looking again, places more emphasis on interpretation, both the contemporary dramatist's interpretation of the story he or she is retelling and also the interpretative possibilities opened up for audiences (8).

Many acts of revision — or "re-vision" (Adrienne Rich's term) — are politically motivated and proceed by a process of "defamiliarization" (Rich 35; Sanders 7, 97, 99). This process is illustrated in *Mythic Women/Real Women: Plays and Performance Pieces by Women* (2000), selected and introduced by Lizbeth Goodman. Goodman's collection, germane to my own project, focuses on contemporary feminist representations of "mythic" women such as Philomele and Medusa and women who have become "mythic" or legendary such as Joan of Arc or Shakespearean heroines, and their connections to women of the late-twentieth century. The volume attests to the importance of mythic revisions for women's self-understanding, but since it is primarily an anthology for feminist performance, it offers only limited, though provocative, commentary. Especially germane to my own collection is Friedman's volume, *Feminist Theatrical Revisions of Classic Works* (2009). Like Friedman's collection, mine also includes essays on plays that revise a range of cultural sources. My collection differs from hers in that for the most part the plays discussed revise myth, fairy tale, and legend rather than other literary texts, while in scope it includes but ranges beyond explicitly feminist concerns to address the process and uses of myth-making itself. I realize that sources in myth and sources in literature are not entirely separable since in some instances the best-known version of a particular myth is an earlier literary work. This is especially true in the case of Greek myth, dramatic revisions of which are discussed in several essays in the collection: for example, Karelisa Hartigan addresses plays by A. R. Gurney and Charles Mee that revise Greek dramatic revisions of myths, while Miriam Chirico writes on plays by Karen Hartman and Caridad Svich that similarly revise Greek plays but also on Sarah Ruhl's *Eurydice*, for which there is no single source; Tony Kushner's *A Dybbuk*, discussed in Sharon Friedman's essay, is an adaptation of S. Ansky's early-twentieth-century Yiddish play, *The Dybbuk*, again the best-known version of this particular folk tale. And, indeed, fairy tales are typically the already revised written forms of oral folk tales, just as Greek tragedies are the already revised written forms of existing myths. But in general most of the plays discussed in my volume do not have single specific literary sources, as most of those addressed in Friedman's collection do. This means that one major strand of adaptation theory, that which deals with specific intercultural and intertemporal dialogue between texts, is not relevant to many of the plays discussed in my collection. It is necessary, therefore, to refine our understanding of how literary revision works. Gregory J. Reid's essay in this volume in particular addresses this question.

Mythical literature, Julie Sanders observes, "depends upon, incites even, perpetual acts of reinterpretation in new contexts" (63). Each generation rewrites its national myths, and often the myths of other nations, especially ancient Greece, to address its own concerns. For, as Marina Warner puts it, "Myths convey values and expectations which are always evolving"; myths are thus retold to be made more useful, more fit, for new times and circumstances (14). Unlike works based on earlier texts, retellings of myth do not talk back to an "Ur-version" because none exists; instead, "Every telling of a myth is a part of that myth" (Warner 8). In fact, there have always been multiple versions of myths (Von Hendy 265–66). But modern literary revisions offer especially deliberate retellings that depend in some way on one or more earlier versions. It would seem obvious, then, that the audience's knowledge of an earlier version or of a popular conception of a myth is important both to the dramatist's purpose in retelling it and, as Ellen McLaughlin stresses in the preface to her collection *The Greek Plays*, to the audience's appreciation of the new version (xv).

Indeed most of the plays discussed in this volume are based on well-known myths, fairy tales, or legends. But a few use mythic sources that may not be familiar to the majority of audience members so that we must inquire also into the authorial purpose and the effect on audiences of using possibly unfamiliar mythic sources. It is uncertain, for example, how many members of Tarell Alvin McCraney's American audience are likely to be familiar with the West African mythology that underpins *The Brother/Sister Plays*, discussed here by Kevin J. Wetmore, Jr., or how many members of even a British audience are likely to be familiar with all of the creatures in Caryl Churchill's *The Skriker*, discussed by Amelia Howe Kritzer. Julie Sanders asserts that knowledge of the source material is "fundamental to the reading and spectating experience of adaptation" (120). Linda Hutcheon, however, while describing reading or spectating an adaptation with whose source we are familiar as "a kind of oscillating experience," allows that if we do not know that a work is an adaptation or if we know but are unfamiliar with the source, then "we simply experience it the way we would any other work of art" (2). In the case of mythic revisions especially, we must then ask what is the point for dramatist and audience in revising an unfamiliar story in the first place. Theatre companies, however, often do their best to mitigate this difficulty by making audiences aware of the story being retold; typically they adopt paratextual means (program notes, lobby displays, reviews) to inform audiences' reception of plays based on otherwise possibly unfamiliar source material (McKinnon 55).[4]

While all of the plays discussed in this volume have their "sources" in "myth" (broadly conceived), the nature and degree of exactness of the relationship between play and "source" varies widely. Indeed, "source" is almost as vexed a term as "adaptation." Noting the numerous words with different shades of meaning available for "source" (for example, "influence," "tradition," "heritage," "precursor," "intertext," among others), Robert Miola concludes, "The word 'source' can now signify a multitude of possible relations with a text, ranging from direct contact to indirect absorption" (Miola 7; qtd. in Fischlin and Fortier 10). The plays addressed in this volume illustrate such a range of appropriation. Some derive from myth and legend as they have already been dramatized (for example, A. R. Gurney's *Another Antigone*, Ellen McLaughlin's *Helen*, discussed by Elizabeth W. Scharffenberger, Tony Kushner's *A Dybbuk*, based, respectively, on the plays of Sophocles, Euripides, and S. Ansky). Others retell generally familiar myths and legends without purporting to be based on any particular literary or historical source (Sarah Ruhl's *Eurydice*, Sharon Pollock's version of Lizzie Borden in *Blood Relations*, discussed by Laura Snyder). In yet other plays dramatic revision is more a matter of allusive references (such as those to the myth of Demeter in the plays of Tina Howe, discussed by Jeffrey B. Loomis, and to the Pied Piper and other tales in Martin McDonagh's *The Pillowman*, discussed by Anthony Ellis). Beth Henley's *Abundance*, which I discuss in my own essay, exemplifies the process of "absorption" (from the movies) of the American myth of the Wild West. The principles on which the revisions are made vary also. Chirico, for example, in her essay "Hellenic Women Revisited: The Aesthetics of Mythic Revision in the Plays of Karen Hartman, Sarah Ruhl, and Caridad Svich" distinguishes among several approaches to mythic revision based on Gérard Genette's structuralist schema of adaptation.

The final terms of my title are the most complex of all. What is myth? Or how is myth popularly understood? And how is it related to and distinguishable from cognate forms such as legend and fairy tale?

I will begin with a couple of definitions from *The New Shorter Oxford English Dictionary*. "Myth" is: (1) "A traditional story, either wholly or partially fictitious, either providing an explanation for or embodying a popular idea concerning some natural or social phenomenon or some religious belief or ritual; *spec.* one involving supernatural persons, actions, or events; a similar newly created story"; (2) "A widely-held (esp. untrue or discredited popular) story or belief; a misconception; a misrepresentation of the truth." The word *myth*, then, can convey opposing resonances or values. "Myth" can be used to mean an old respected story conveying some kind of wisdom or truth about the human condition or human relations or a "widely disseminated falsehood" (Von Hendy 278). Greek myths obviously are examples of the former. A quick search of Amazon Books readily provides examples of the latter enshrined in titles such as *The Myth of Political Correctness, The Myth of the Rational Market,* and *50 Great Myths of Popular Psychology,* where "myth" clearly connotes at best a mistaken assumption and at worst a lie. I would suggest that there is an element of both resonances in our understanding of mythic revisions. The myth selected for revision is perceived to be sufficiently revered, significant, and usually well-known to be worth retelling, but the retelling, while it may demonstrate the relevance of the story for our own times, often offers an implicit critique of earlier versions, especially, in many of the plays addressed in this volume, in regard to gender.

The word "myth" first appeared in European vernaculars in the eighteenth century (in the 1760s), displacing the earlier somewhat discredited "fable" and giving greater dignity to the stories it denotes (Von Hendy 2–3). In his comprehensive study *The Modern Construction of Myth* Andrew Von Hendy traces the history of our modern ambivalent understanding of myth from the romantics to the present day. The romantics valorized myth as providing transcendental insights into human experience (25). Subsequent understandings of myth during the course of the nineteenth and twentieth centuries competed with but never entirely superseded the romantic view. These include the opposing negative view of myth as ideology; anthropological or folkloristic conceptions of myth (such as those of the Brothers Grimm), which viewed myths as narratives once regarded as sacred (77); and the psychoanalytic perceptions of Freud and Jung in their work on the unconscious, which, Von Hendy argues, actually feed into the romantic view of myth (113). In his concluding chapters Von Hendy examines the contributions to the construction of myth of important twentieth-century anthropologists, notably the structural theory of Claude Lévi-Strauss, and then goes on to examine the intellectual background, deriving primarily from Marx and Nietzsche, of the pejorative sense of myth as ideology (that is, a set of unexamined assumptions comprising a fusion of values and emotions largely left implicit) that prevails in common parlance today. Roland Barthes's *Mythologies* (1957), essays examining the underlying assumptions or mystifications of various aspects of French mass culture, in particular, conflates myth and ideology in this way (290–91). In his final chapter Von Hendy discusses what he calls the "constitutive" conception of myth, that is that myths are human-made "necessary cultural fictions" (316). Von Hendy concludes his study by noting that several different historical conceptions of myth — romantic, folkloristic, ideological, constitutive — remain current today (338).

It is not my intention to examine or adjudicate among these different conceptions of myth. Dramatists who retell myths are not in any case generally concerned with this kind of theoretical question. However, Von Hendy's explanatory conceptions of myth may be helpful heuristically in evaluating the kinds of work done by the dramatists examined in this book.

Von Hendy includes a chapter on the use of myth in the work of modernist writers Yeats (who was important in reviving Irish mythology), Lawrence, Eliot, and Joyce, but like other scholars of myth and literature, he spends relatively little time on dramatic retellings of myth. In fact, numerous dramatists in the first half of the twentieth century as well as novelists and poets retold myths. In her 1969 study, *Ancient Greek Myths and Modern Drama*, Angela Belli shows how dramatists such as O'Neill, Williams, Eliot, Cocteau, Anouilh, and Giraudoux variously reinvented Greek myths for their own purposes, exploring the stories they retold from psychoanalytic, political, and other contemporary perspectives, and offering modern takes on the characters, either by placing them in modern settings or by incorporating anachronisms into Greek settings. (And, of course, there have been numerous more recent studies of modern versions of Greek plays.)[5] The essays in my volume take up the discussion for plays of the late-twentieth and the beginning of the twenty-first century and extend Belli's range to national myths and legends other than Greek.

One less traditional kind of myth that has aroused increasing interest in the last few decades is political myth. Christopher G. Flood in *Political Myth: A Theoretical Introduction* (1996) distinguishes between "sacred" myth and political myth, arguing that political myth exists at the intersection of sacred myth and ideology (5). Political myth, he asserts, is an account of political events that is "true for the social group which believes it," shaping their political perceptions (8, 82). Both Flood and Henry Tudor in *Political Myth* (1972) note that myth and history are easily confused or conflated (Flood 82, Tudor 123). The functions of political myths, according to Tudor, range from explaining the present circumstances of their audiences to inspiring them "with confidence in their destiny and glorify[ing] their achievements" (139). One such political myth that fits these parameters (cited by Flood, 68) is that of the American Frontier. This is the myth underlying Beth Henley's *Abundance*, which I discuss in this volume.

Myth has been seen as both conservative and subversive. Roland Barthes in *Mythologies* argues that myth "transforms history into nature" (129) or, as

Marina Warner explains, that myth "works to conceal political motives and secretly circulate ideology through society" (Warner xiii–xiv). Against this view Warner herself expresses the more optimistic opinion that retelling mythic stories can improve the way we understand society (xiv). Ellen McLaughlin, too, writing on Greek myth, believes that our "common mythology" helps us to find a way to make bearable "the unbearable truth of our times" (xviii), and Caridad Svich asserts: "We seek myth because it is our inheritance" (11). Even though the dramatists discussed in this book usually feel the need to revise the ideology of the myths they retell to make them "fit" for contemporary audiences, implicitly, by invoking such stories they validate these sources as lenses for viewing our own world.

Myths, legends, and fairy tales "blend easily" into one another (Sale 23), are often discussed together (by Marina Warner, for example), and in many respects function in similar ways, by providing, as Julie Sanders puts it, "archetypal stories available for re-use and recycling by different ages and cultures" (82). There are, however, distinctions among them. In the first half of the nineteenth century the Brothers Grimm, while solidifying myth as "a distinct narrative genre," also distinguished among myth, legend, and fairy tale, establishing some of the parameters, especially for legend and fairy tale, still accepted today (Von Hendy 62). Fairy tale can be distinguished from legend in that the former is not restricted to any particular place and is poetically or fictively more creative, while legend is tied to a specific context and often takes on the authority of history. *The New Shorter Oxford English Dictionary* definition of "Legend" as "A traditional tale popularly regarded as historical"; "A person about whom such stories are told" confirms the continuing conflation of history and legend in popular consciousness. The popular predilection for historicizing legend may be why history itself can so easily turn into legend, as is the case in several of the legends (such as those of Lizzie Borden or "la Corrivau") that underlie plays discussed in this volume. Myth, according to Jacob Grimm, shares in the characteristics of both fairy tale and legend: like fairy tale, it is "untramelled in its flight," and like legend, it "can yet settle down in a local home" (Grimm xv; qtd. in Von Hendy 63). That is, myth possesses the creative freedom of fairy tale but also the geographical and historical specificity and credibility of legend.

The New Shorter Oxford English Dictionary definition of "Fairy tale" as "a tale about fairies, or about a strange incident, coincidence, marvellous progress, etc." particularizes Jacob Grimm's definition but is clearly inadequate since, as Roger Sale notes, "few stories we call by that name contain fairies" or such-like creatures (23). Fairy tales are the written versions of oral folk tales (Bacchilega 3, Zipes 11). In the late-seventeenth century salons of French writers such as Charles Perrault, Mme. D'Aulnoy, and other, especially women, writers established the literary fairy tale as a more cultured, private, and aristocratic genre than the communal oral folk tale and imbued the tales they wrote with values of civility and propriety for their aristocratic and bourgeois readers (Zipes 11). Jack Zipes reminds us in *Fairy Tale as Myth/Myth as Fairy Tale* that fairy tales have always been ideological and have always been revised. In her essay in this volume Sheila Rabillard discusses Wallace Shawn's revisionary use of the tale of the White Cat in *Grasses of a Thousand Colors*.

Since myth, fairy tale, and legend, blend into one another and since creative writers, including the contemporary dramatists whose plays are discussed in this volume, have been putting myth, legend, and fairy (or folk) tale to similar revisionist uses, it seems reasonable to incorporate studies of plays based on all three in this volume rather than try to make unprofitable distinctions. I do, however, attempt what I hope may be a suggestive taxonomy in the order in which I have placed the essays. They range from essays on plays that use sources that are indubitably mythic, beginning with Greek myth, through studies of plays that draw on folklore and fairy tale to conclude with three essays on plays that dramatize legends based on historical figures and one on a play that revises political myth.

More important, however, than any classificatory distinctions among the broadly "mythical" sources of the plays discussed in this volume are the common concerns and themes with which the contributors engage. Their essays variously address theoretical issues pertaining to the dramatic revision of mythic or legendary material, the contemporary social and political significance of dramatizing myth in particular cultures, and especially representations of women and/or the politics of gender relations. Some essays address plays that revise their mythic sources by giving voice to otherwise unheard or misinterpreted women (Euridice, Helen, Lizzie Borden, American women who went West). Other essays demonstrate how contemporary dramatists have incorporated myth to explore women's lives today (plays by Howe). Yet others focus on plays that examine legends associated with central female characters (Ono no Komachi in Timberlake Wertenbaker's play *Inside Out*, discussed by Maya E. Roth, "La Corriveau" in *La Cage* and Marguerite de Nontron in *L'Île de la demoiselle* by Anne Hébert, discussed by Reid). And others explore plays that use female mythic or folkloric figures or fairy tale to address contemporary political and social issues: Caridad Svich's *Iphigenia Crash Land Falls on the Neon Shell That Was Once Her Heart (A Rave Fable)*, discussed by Chirico, deals with the violation of human rights in a fictive Latin American country; Kritzer and Rabillard show how Churchill's *The Skriker* and Shawn's *Grasses of a Thousand Colors*, respectively, address environmental destruction; Christy Stanlake shows how Tomson Highway's *Dry Lips Oughta Move to Kapuskasing*, which features the female trickster figure Nanabush, explores the social healing afforded Native Americans by Native mythology. Other important issues attended to in this collection include the complex relationship between mythology and theology (in Wetmore's essay on McCraney's *The Brother/Sister Plays* and Stanlake's on *Dry Lips Oughta Move to Kapuskasing*); between myth or legend and history (in the essays by Roth, Reid, Snyder, and Foster), and between myth or legend and its dissemination through popular culture (in the essays by Sharffenberger, Snyder, and Foster). Many of the essays and the plays they discuss, of course, fit into overlapping categories.

Miriam Chirico, Karelisa Hartigan, Elizabeth W. Scharffenberger and Jeffrey B. Loomis examine the use of Greek myth in contemporary drama from a variety of theoretical perspectives. Chirico's "Hellenic Women Revisited: The Aesthetics of Mythic Revision in the Plays of Karen Hartman, Sarah Ruhl and Caridad Svich" theorizes the purposes of and various approaches to the dramatic (especially feminist) revision of myth by examining the different strategies adopted by Karen Hartman in *Troy Women*, Sarah Ruhl in *Euridice*, and Caridad Svich in *Iphigenia Crash Land Falls on the Neon Shell That Was Once Her Heart (A Rave Fable)*. In "Greek Tragedy Transformed: A. R. Gurney and Charles Mee Rewrite Greek Drama," Hartigan compares Greek and modern dramatic versions of myths to draw conclusions about the nature of modern tragedy. Scharffenberger in "'That story is not true': Unmaking Myth in Ellen McLaughlin's *Helen* and Saviana Stanescu and Richard Schechner's *YokastaS*" explores two plays that challenge familiar patriarchal myths by retelling them from the perspectives of their traditionally silenced female protagonists and thereby caution their audiences against the uncritical reception of commonly accepted stories in their own lives. Loomis in "Tina Howe and Demetrian Seriocomedy" looks at more allusive ways in which myth can be incorporated in drama, arguing for the presence of both the life-affirming myth of Demeter and Demetrian ritual in Howe's presentation of relations among contemporary women in her plays.

Kevin J. Wetmore, Jr., in "Children of Yemayá and the American Eshu: West African Myth in African-American Theatre" and Christy Stanlake in "Punctured by Patriarchy: Theatricalizing the Christian Assault upon Native Mythology in Tomson Highway's *Dry Lips Oughta Move to Kapuskasing*" focus on plays that draw on West African and Native American myth, respectively. Wetmore explores the use of Yoruban myth in African-American drama, specifically the way in which it illuminates African-American experience in Tarell Alvin McCraney's *The Brother/Sister Plays*, while Stanlake examines the collision between two belief systems and the power of Native myth in recuperating the role of women in Native American culture.

Amelia Howe Kritzer, Sharon Friedman, Anthony Ellis and Sheila Rabillard explore dramatic revisions of folklore and fairy tale. In "Damaged Myth in Caryl Churchill's *The Skriker*," Kritzer examines how Churchill uses the Skriker, a menacing female earth spirit from British folklore, to dramatize how we have degraded the ability of our environment to nurture us. In "Between Desire and Authority: The 'Dybbuk' in Modernist and Postmodern Theatrical Adaptations from S. Ansky to Tony Kushner," Friedman investigates the history of theatrical interpretations of the East European Jewish folkloric figure of the dybbuk, in particular Tony Kushner's in his play *A Dybbuk*. Friedman focuses on the representation of gendered issues, especially homoeroticism and the regulation of the female body and sexuality, in a homosocial community. In "Martin McDonagh's Fractured Fairy Tales: Representational Horrors in *The Pillowman*," Ellis argues that McDonagh uses his central writer-character Katurian's distortions of well-known tales, which are reflected in real-life happenings in the play, to explore the role of myth-making in our lives. In "Food, Sex and Fairy Tales: Wallace Shawn's *Grasses of a Thousand Colors*," Rabillard shows how Shawn employs elements from the fairy tale "The White Cat" to structure his play and to explore both ecological damage and gender conflict and the connections between them.

Maya E. Roth, Gregory J. Reid and Laura Snyder examine plays that revise historical women who have become legends. In "Turning Komachi Legends, Gender and Noh *Inside Out*: Remaking Desire in Timberlake Wertenbaker's Early Play," Roth shows how Wertenbaker dramatizes legends about Ono no Komachi, ninth-century Japanese poet and courtesan, from a feminist and cross-cultural perspective in her early unpublished play *Inside Out*. In "Romancing 'La Corriveau' and Marguerite de Nontron: Anne Hébert's *La Cage* and *L'Île de la demoiselle*," Reid draws on Northrop Frye's account of the relation between myth and romance in *Anatomy of Criticism* to argue that Hébert romanticizes in order to celebrate her two heroines, creating for them a position between demonizing legend and prosaic historical reality. In "Bloody Relations of Exchange: Sharon Pollock's Revision of Legend and Feminine Myth in *Blood Relations*," Snyder argues that Pollock's feminist and metatheatrical revision of the legend of Lizzie Borden critiques a social system that is at once patriarchal and capitalist. Finally my own essay, "Beth Henley's *Abundance*: The Cinematic Myth of the Wild West Revised," shows how Henley, drawing on tropes from popular Westerns, rewrites the masculine political myth of the American Frontier from the perspective of women who also went West.

The essays in this collection demonstrate the vitality and versatility of both well-known myths, fairy tales, and legends and some that may be less familiar to general audiences in serving as the inspiration or groundwork for contemporary drama no less than for fiction or poetry. Contemporary playwrights have engaged with their mythic sources in a similar variety of ways, using the old stories for new cultural purposes, often critiquing their sources' assumptions about gender and political relations, but equally often using the stories they retell to criticize aspects of their own society, always providing for audiences the double pleasure of reading or spectating "alongside" (Sanders 160). Contemporary dramatic revisions of myth, fairy tale, and legend delight us with their retellings of old stories and at the same time provoke us to reconsider how we think about these stories and their meanings in our own lives.

NOTES

1. John B. Vickery, *Myths and Texts: Strategies of Incorporation and Displacement* (Baton Rouge: Louisiana State University Press, 1983) and Laurence Coupe, *Myth* (London and New York: Routledge, 1997) do not include much drama in their respective discussions (except for Shakespeare in Coupe's book). Nor do Cristina Bacchilega, *Postmodern Fairy Tales* (Philadelphia: University of Pennsylvania Press, 1997) and Donald Haase, ed. *Fairy Tales and Feminism: New Approaches* (Detroit: Wayne State University Press, 2004). Many monographs, collections of essays, or anthologies of plays that deal with specifically dramatic revision or adaptation focus more narrowly than mine on a particular national culture: adaptations of Greek myth and drama, for example, or adaptations of Shakespeare. Notable examples of the former are John Dillon and S. E. Wilmer, *Rebel Women: Staging Ancient Greek Drama Today* (London: Methuen, 2005) and Caridad Svich, ed, *Divine Fire: Eight Contemporary Plays Inspired by the Greeks* (New York: Back Stage Books, 2005); examples of the latter are Daniel Fischlin and Mark Fortier, *Adaptations of Shakespeare: A Critical Anthology of Plays from the Seventeenth Century to the Present* (London and New York: Routledge, 2000) and Margaret Jane Kidnie, *Shakespeare and the Problem of Adaptation* (London and New York: Routledge, 2009). A recent collection of essays on the plays of Timberlake Wertenbaker, Maya E. Roth and Sara Freeman, eds. *International Dramaturgy: Translation and Transformation in the Theatre of Timberlake Wertenbaker* (Brussels: Peter Lang, 2008), as its title suggests, also emphasizes adaptation of various kinds, though it is limited to the work of one dramatist. To make the scope of this book manageable the essays for the most part address only plays by dramatists writing in English. Gregory J. Reid's essay on French Canadian dramatist Anne Hébert's *La Cage* and *L'Île de la demoiselle*, written in French, is an exception. Hébert's plays were translated into English in 2009 (see Reid's essay in this volume).

2. Sanders helpfully articulates different ways of looking at adaptation; Hutcheon usefully gets away from "fidelity" criticism, but her study takes too broad a view of adaptation to be especially useful to dramatic theory. A more recent study, *Performing Adaptations: Essays and Conversations on the Theory and Practice of Adaptation* (Newcastle-upon-Tyne: Cambridge Scholars Publishing, 2009), edited by Michelle MacArthur, Lydia Wilkinson, and Keren Zaiontz, does focus on various kinds of adaptations in performance (theatrical, filmic, and digital). But, except for some brief discussion in Sanders's book, none of these works has much to say about dramatic revisions of myth.

3. Hutcheon draws on Susan Bassnett's work in translation studies (Hutcheon 16, Bassnett 9).

4. For example, for a recent production of McCraney's *The Brother/Sister Plays* at Steppenwolf in Chicago (21 Jan.–23 May, 2010) descriptions of the Yoruban deities underlying the contemporary characters were displayed in the lobby for the audience to view before seeing the plays. See also Marvin Carlson's discussion of theatrical strategies for informing the audience's reception of plays in *Theatre Semiotics*, 21–24.

5. See, for example, John Dillon and S.E. Wilmer, eds. *Rebel Women: Staging Ancient Greek Drama Today* (London: Methuen, 2005); Edith Hall, Fiona Macintosh, and Amanda Wrigley, eds. *Dionysus Since 69: Greek Tragedy at the Dawn of the Third Millennium* (Oxford: Oxford University Press, 2004); Marianne McDonald and J. Michael Walton, eds. *Amid Our Troubles: Irish Versions of Greek Tragedy* (London: A&C Black, 2002); Kevin J. Wetmore, Jr., *The Athenian Sun in an African Sky* (Jefferson, NC: McFarland, 2002).

WORKS CITED

Bacchilega, Cristina. *Postmodern Fairy Tales: Gender and Narrative Strategies*. Philadelphia: University of Pennsylvania Press, 1997.

Barthes, Roland. *Mythologies* (1957). Selected and trans. Annette Lavers. New Yotk: Hill and Wang, 1972.

Bassnett, Susan. *Translation Studies*, 3rd ed. London and New York: Routledge, 2002.

Belli, Angela. *Ancient Greek Myths and Modern Drama*. New York: New York University Press, 1969.

Carlson, Marvin. *The Haunted Stage*. Ann Arbor: University of Michigan Press, 2001.

_____. *Theatre Semiotics*. Bloomington: Indiana University Press, 1990.

Fischlin, Daniel, and Mark Fortier. Eds. *Adaptations of Shakespeare: A Critical Anthology of Plays from the Seventeenth Century to the Present*. London and New York: Routledge, 2000.

Flood, Christopher G. *Political Myth: A Theoretical Introduction*. New York: Garland Publishing, 1996.

Friedman, Sharon. Ed. *Feminist Theatrical Revisions of Classic Works*. Jefferson, NC: McFarland, 2009.

Goodman, Lizbeth. Ed. *Mythic Women/Real Women: Plays and Performance Pieces by Women* London: Faber and Faber, 2000.

Grimm, Jacob. *Teutonic Mythology* 3. 1883. Trans. James Steven Stallybrass. New York: Dover Publications, 1966.

Hutcheon, Linda. *A Theory of Adaptation*. London and New York: Routledge, 2006.

Kidnie, Margaret Jane. *Shakespeare and the Problem of Adaptation*. London and New York: Routledge, 2009.

McKinnon, James. "'Look into Fengo's Hole ... and Win!!': Paratextuality as a Strategy for Evading Anti-Adaptation Prejudices in Michael O'Brien's *Mad Boy Chronicles*." *Performing Adaptations: Essays and Conversations on the Theory and Practice of Adaptation*. Ed. Michelle MacArthur, Lydia Wilkinson, and Keren Zaiontz. Newcastle-upon-Tyne: Cambridge Scholars Publishing, 2009. 43–58.

McLaughlin, Ellen. *The Greek Plays*. New York: Theatre Communications Group, 2005.

Miola, Robert S. *Shakespeare and Classical Tragedy: The Influence of Seneca*. Oxford: Clarendon Press, 1992.

Rich, Adrienne. "When We Dead Awaken: Writing as Re-Vision" (1971). *On Lies, Secrets, and Silence: Selected Prose 1966–1978*. New York: W.W. Norton, 1979.

Sale, Roger. *Fairy Tales and After: From Snow White to E.B. White*. Cambridge, MA: Harvard University Press, 1978.

Sanders, Julie. *Adaptation and Appropriation*. London and New York: Routledge, 2006.

Svich, Caridad. Ed. *Divine Fire: Eight Contemporary Plays Inspired by the Greeks*. New York: Back Stage Books, 2005.

Tudor, Henry. *Political Myth*. New York: Praeger Publishers, 1972.

Von Hendy, Andrew. *The Modern Construction of Myth*. Bloomington: Indiana University Press, 2002.

Warner, Marina. *Managing Monsters: Six Myths of Our Time*. London: Vintage, 1994.

Wertenbaker, Timberlake. "First Thoughts on Transforming a Text." *International Dramaturgy: Translation and Transformations in the Theatre of Timberlake Wertenbaker.* Eds. Maya E. Roth and Sara Freeman. Brussels, Belgium: P.I.E. Peter Lang, 2008.

Zipes, Jack. *Fairy Tale as Myth/Myth as Fairy Tale.* Lexington: University Press of Kentucky, 1994.

Hellenic Women Revisited

The Aesthetics of Mythic Revision in the Plays of Karen Hartman, Sarah Ruhl and Caridad Svich

MIRIAM CHIRICO

Some years ago in a conference paper, I coined the term "mythic revisionary drama" as a way of encapsulating both a genre and a practice: the category of plays that take classical myths for their theme and content, as well as the particular creative act of responding to or re-envisioning these Greek and Roman stories for the stage. While playwrights throughout history have invoked classical legend as content for their tales, the modernist twist — and now post-modernist inflection — to the classical heritage is worth considering as a category of its own. In "Twentieth-Century Plays Using Classical Mythic Themes: A Checklist" (1986), Susan Harris Smith compiled over 740 plays that drew upon mythology and classified each play by its mythic character (Antigone) or by its collective topic (Troy). Even while recognizing that these twentieth-century plays differed from their nineteenth-century forbears that were merely "stiff adaptations uninformed by the modern spirit" (111), Smith makes no mention of the unique approach to playwriting behind re-envisioning a myth nor the specific audience response prompted by such a play and instead identifies this group simply by the shared connection of the plays' classical themes. Yet the endless permutations of approaches to revision, as well as the plurality of myths, fairy-tales, and legends that have been rewritten for the stage, have rendered classification of such plays problematic. While it is easy to recognize a play that involves "mythic revision," the wide range of plays falling within this category of "dramatic mythic revision" is so diverse as to defy a "one-size-fits-all" theoretical framework and thus precludes any unifying methodological framework for analyzing such plays. In fact, the impetus behind this collection of essays came from the editor's recognition that developing a methodology for studying mythic revision in a comprehensive and systematic way proved difficult; thus the essays in the first part of this book, taken collectively, offer a plurality of approaches to analyzing plays that revise Greek and Roman mythology in particular.

As a basic description, mythic revision is the act of creatively re-writing a myth in order to move closer to the myth's essential meaning. For the purposes of this discussion, a myth is understood as a sacred story of unknown authorship, often linked to a ritual, recounting the deeds of gods, supernatural beings, or heroes, chiefly drawn from Homer's *Iliad* and *Odyssey*, the plays of Aeschylus, Sophocles, and Euripides, Apuleius' *Golden Ass*, or Ovid's *Metamorphoses*. Myth's inherent identity as an oral genre necessitates the act of revision or transformation each time the myth is told; it is as if the narrator tries to present a more accurate or complete view of the story to his or her listeners. As Roland Barthes asserts in *Mythologies*, "the fundamental character of the mythic concept is to be appropriated" (119), and Northrop Frye includes this quality of mythic literature as part of its very definition:

> In secular literature ... a standard relating to completeness in telling traditional stories seems often to be implied. Others have told this story before, the author gives us to understand, but I'm going to tell it better and more fully, so you won't have to refer to anyone else for missing features [Frye 12].

Thus, revising the events of a myth is intrinsic to its form. Part of the process of transmitting a myth from one generation to the next is to offer corrections or make adjustments to the story, and in this way mythic revision acts as a critical as well as creative apparatus opening up new meanings behind each myth. In "The Structural Study of Myth" (1955), Claude Lévi-Strauss explained the structuralist approach to reading myths by identifying the gross constituent units of a myth or its *mythemes*. The structural analysis should take into account all the variants of the myth in order to present as accurate a reading as possible; in order to explain this point, Lévi-Strauss proposed an analogy comparing myth to a large room into which we receive partial glimpses through the multiple windows that access the room and from the mirrors that reflect the interior contents of the room. The mirrors, positioned at different angles, give us an ampler depiction of the room and therefore of the myth; the more variants we have of the myth, including even latter-day Freudian renderings, the more secure we can be in our structural analysis. Each re-telling of the myths in Western culture represents another opportunity to peer inside the room and fill out our interpretation.

The history of mythic revisionary criticism begins with T. S. Eliot's concept of the "mythical method," devised while discussing James Joyce's reworking of Homer's *Odyssey* into his novel *Ulysses*. Evolving from a modernist literary aesthetic that valued classical allusions as a means of imposing an order upon "the immense panorama of futility and anarchy which is contemporary history," T. S. Eliot's "mythical method" urges that all writers "manipulat[e] a continuous parallel between contemporaneity and antiquity" (177). Eliot's conception that myth can impose order upon the current fragmentation of existence corresponds to the aesthetic of his own allusive poem *The Waste Land*, wherein references to classical texts and mythology endow the present with meaning. Adrienne Rich, writing sixty years later, advises a similar revisionary gesture, to enter "an old text from a new critical direction," but for reasons in direct contradistinction to Eliot's conservative gesture: "not to pass on a tradition but to break its hold over us" (35). Critical interest in mythic revision for the stage peaked in 1969 with the publication of three scholarly works: Angela Belli's *Ancient Greek Myths and Modern Drama: A Study in Continuity*, Hugh Dickinson's *Myth on the Modern Stage*, and Thomas E. Porter's *Myth and Modern American Drama*. But since this flurry of interest, little has been published regarding mythic revisionary drama, perhaps due to the difficulty in creating a satisfactory methodology for a sustained, comparative focus.[1]

Historically, the means adopted by most scholars to analyze mythic revision involved either thematic, comparative, or structuralist approaches. The thematic treatment of myth examines the accretion of its variant retellings, such as George Steiner's detailed account of the Antigone/Creon conflict in *Antigones* (1996). In tracing its iterations within the various historical or cultural indices of a given period, this approach provides a layered understanding of the myth. Certain scholars drew attention to the surprising number of mythic revisions evolving from Northern Ireland's political tension; three versions of *Antigone* were published in 1984 alone.[2] Marianne McDonald, for example, who charted eleven Greek revisions in her article "When Despair and History Rhyme," explained this pattern as the desire of a colonized people to reappropriate classical texts from Western civilization to represent their own plight. Revising a myth within a particular historical or political context provides more than a barometric reading of the times; it reveals the human struggle within a larger context of religious tension, divided loyalties, or the State versus the individual.

Second, the comparativist approach to mythic revision considers the revised version in relation to the earliest known rendering of the myth, usually the dramatic version written by Aeschylus, Sophocles, or Euripides, and questions whether the revised version captures the same theme, tension, or belief system as the original. Often, a comparativist approach, such as that of Karelisa Hartigan in this volume, yields fruitful discoveries about the original classical story as well as the contemporary revision, emphasizing features of the myth that may go undetected until such a transformation appears. Taking her theoretical cue from Adrienne Rich's concept of "re-vision" as the act of engaging with a text from a new direction, Allison Hersh compares two contemporary British "re-conceptualizations" of *The Bacchae* by Euripides, where each feminist writer offers a radical critique of Euripides' depiction of orgiastic female violence. By first criticizing Euripides' premise of female power as temporary because of its origination in madness, Hersh demonstrates how Caryl Churchill (*A Mouthful of Birds*) and Maureen Duffy (*Rites*) re-write the myth to offer a contested and revised image of female violence that undercuts such patriarchal representation. Only by returning to and holding up Euripides' version as a model of misogynistic representation can Hersh demonstrate how both contemporary playwrights revise the play with the women in control of the sacrifice, their aggressions, and their violent actions.

The third approach to mythic revision, the structuralist approach, looks for specific mythic elements or narrative building blocks rather than themes. These mythemes, that is, transferable units of story-telling, can be considered in relation to the dramatic structure of a play, and include how a writer might alter the characters, setting, dialogue, and plot, or theatrical devices such as *deus ex machina*. As early as Eva Kushner's essay "Greek Myths in Modern Drama: Paths of Transformation" (1980), scholars have advocated structuralist readings of mythic revision, tracing the specific changes writers have made to the elemental features of the myth and examining how myths may acquire new elements or symbolic formulations (e.g., how characters interact with one another) through the process of revision.[3] Taking this third approach, I propose engaging in a structuralist analysis of three recent, mythic revisionary plays, drawing upon Gérard Genette's approach to adaptation and revision. Genette's work *Palimpsestes: La littérature au second degré* (1982), whose title recalls the medieval practice of writing on a parchment where the original script has been erased, details systematically the hundreds of ways writers respond creatively to other texts, a process he terms *transtextuality*. The first five categorical approaches[4] identified below constitute the different patterns by which, according to Genette, playwrights engage with mythic material; the sixth is one I have devised based on the performative nature of drama.

(A) **Diegetical transposition**: Since the diegesis of a myth is the historical moment and geographical location of the story, transposing its diegesis involves moving the story to another time or place, or both, potentially altering the region, class, or ethnicity within the process. The most familiar example of a diegetical transposition is James Joyce's novel *Ulysses* with the obvious one-to-one correspondences between Homer's text and Joyce's modern-day Dublin. A diegetical transposition reveals specific analogies between the earlier depiction of the myth and the latter-day revision; even as anachronisms appear, they underscore both the dissonance *and* similarity between classical antiquity and the contemporary moment and ignite a spark of recognition that is the hallmark of this genre. The appeal of diegetical transposition explains the numerous productions of Aeschylus' *The Persians* since the United States invaded Iraq after September 11.

(B) **Pragmatic transformation**: This type of revision alters the mythic material so much that the one-to-one correspondences between the original and the revision are no longer visible or important. Usually, the playwright has significantly lengthened or enlarged a specific event in the plot, while shortening or eliminating other aspects of the myth, as in the case of *La Machine infernale* (1932), Jean Cocteau's revision of *Oedipus Rex*, that reconstructs the death of Laius and Oedipus' conversations with the Sphinx. On the other hand, the writer might shorten or eliminate other aspects of the myth, a process Genette describes as "élaguer," a horticultural term meaning to remove the superfluous branches from a tree, so that the second author appears to be "pruning" the text to allow its fundamental meaning to emerge. Frequently, the myth serves as a germ of an idea, a basic jumping-off point, from which the playwright takes full license to create.

(C) **Transfocalization**: Often, the playwright does not bother with the myth as a narrative, but instead focuses on an individual character's story. Thus Shaw's revision of the myth of Pygmalion borrows only the initial device (bringing a sculpture of a woman to life) and the characters (Pygmalion, the sculptor, and Galatea). Genette considers this narrative shift from Pygmalion's point of view to Galatea's as *transfocalization*; even though the term "point of view" is not an appropriate descriptor for dramatic literature, the intentional focus on a different character renders a distinctive reading of the play. A writer might transfocalize a myth to examine a character's motivations more fully, as O'Neill did when he asked: "Why should the Furies have let Electra escape unpunished?" ("Working Notes" for *Mourning Becomes Electra*).

(D) **Transvalorization**: Greek audiences were drawn to the transgression of ethical lines in their plays, with characters testing the boundaries of incest, abandonment, and patricide. The revision of a myth can alter these ethical values — the axiology — as well as where the characters position themselves *vis-à-vis* this axiology. In Sophocles' *Antigone*, for example, Antigone buries her brother in defiance of Creon's edict to observe the proper rituals owed a family member; in Anouilh's revision she attempts to bury him as an act of moral integrity, even while aware that such rites are empty gestures. Genette considers this shift from Antigone's duty to family to her act of adolescent idealism a slight *devalorization* of her position with respect to the myth's original axiology of honoring the dead. The contemporary playwright either adopts the myth's axis of values or transvalorizes it during the course of revising the play.

(E) **Transmotivation:** Alongside the process of heightening a character's worth or presence, the playwright must consequently provide additional motivation behind the character's actions. *Transmotivation* is the creative process of revising the character's reasoning to correspond to his or her new actions. Thus, when Albert Camus re-reads Sisyphus within an existential frame of self-conscious awareness, he provides Sisyphus with an internal monologue that provides plausible motivation for rolling the stone up the hill; Sisyphus concludes that his freedom depends on his ability to see his task as meaningful, resulting in his feeling "content" rather than persecuted. Often transmotivation provides an opening for exploring the psychological motivation of a character previously misunderstood.

(F) **Dramaturgical adoption:** Because we inherit much of our knowledge about classical mythology from Greek drama and its attendant religious origins, our cultural understanding of mythology often corresponds to certain performance elements that also evoke ritualistic behavior: choral speaking, masking, ceremonial gestures, antiphonal debates, and even stage properties such as the *ekkyklema* or *machina*. These devices, which constitute for us the stylized quality of ancient drama, can be used by contemporary dramatists to highlight this mystical quality of myth, lifting the stage action outside of the profane space of the everyday world and placing it back *in illo tempore* ("in that time"). A playwright adopts or "quotes" dramaturgical devices from classical Greek theatre in order to convey the transcendental aspect of the myth. O'Neill's initial choice, for example, to incorporate the Greek dramatic use of masks in *Mourning Becomes Electra* resulted in the frozen "mask-like" expressions of each family member, signifying not only their familial resemblance but their mutual entrapment in the family curse. Thus any structural analysis of dramatic mythic revision must consider the performative mode, with particular attention to how the playwright consciously incorporates classical dramatic devices.

These categorical approaches to revision — transposition, transformation, transfocalisation, transvalorisation, transmotivation, and dramaturgical adaptation — are not mutually exclusive; any play will demonstrate more than one of these means of handling mythic material. In order to demonstrate the value of these approaches in analyzing revisionary texts, I have chosen three plays from a recent anthology of mythic revisionary plays entitled *Divine Fire: Eight Contemporary Plays Inspired by the Greeks*, written within the same ten-year period, yet strikingly different in the ways the writers have handled and approached the mythic material. While I am not able to explore these plays to the extent they fully deserve, my goal is to demonstrate how the various structuralist approaches outlined above can be instrumental in investigating how writers revise myths beyond simply comparing artistic styles. Karen Hartman's adaptation of Euripides' masterpiece *The Trojan Women* infuses the speeches with contemporary idioms, enabling an audience to appreciate the original play through her pragmatic adjustments. The surrealistic *Eurydice*, by Sarah Ruhl, transfocalizes the myth by placing the responsibility for Orpheus' backward glance on Eurydice herself. Caridad Svich's *Iphigenia Crash Land Falls on the Neon Shell That Was Once Her Heart (A Rave Fable)* transposes the diegesis of Iphigenia's story to a present-day Latin America to retain the societal devaluation of women's lives that persists across time and culture.

Troy Women *(1997): Adapted from* The Trojan Women *by Euripides, by Karen Hartman*

Karen Hartman offers an adaptation that is faithful to Euripides' *The Trojan Women*. Her chief revisionary maneuver is linguistic *transposition*, adopting a contemporary idiom in order to modernize the Trojan women's pain and perspective for a current audience. In preparing her adaptation, she stayed close to the language of Euripides' script, describing her writing process in vaguely apostolic terms: "Line by line, image, by image, I stepped into the shoes of a great play, and Euripides became my teacher. This tale of war, aging, complicity, love and defeat begins on the worst day of a mythic queen's life, then descends. *The Trojan Women* touches bottom, the floor of human possibility, the low note of survival. Working my way through it taught me how to dive for that bottom" (21). Unlike the other writers in the collection, Hartman aimed not to alter the myth, but rather to make the expansive quality of fifth-century Greek tragedy viable for a contemporary audience. Hartman's anachronistic language and choice of words provide the audience with a conduit to understand the women's experience of losing a husband, a lover, a child, and a city. As a play, *The Trojan Women* is plotless; each woman — the Queen Hecuba, her daughters Cassandra and Andromache, and Helen — comes forward after the invasion of Troy to document the massacre she has seen and provide testimony for the slain. Even as they detail their grief, further atrocities mount; the Herald arrives to take away and murder Astyanax, Adromache's and Hector's son, by tossing him off a cliff, and later, each woman learns she is to become the concubine of a Greek soldier. Finally, the city of Troy herself is burned. Gilbert Murray describes the movement of the play as "a gradual extinguishing of all the familiar lights of human life" (5). Hartman closely traces this feature, replacing Euripides' chorus of "women" with a chorus of five distinct personalities: an Attendant to Hecuba, the Attendant's daughter, a spirited girl, a romantic one, and a Mother of Sons.

Hartman retains Euripides' axiology of grief and victimization. The women offer their visceral responses to the slaughter they have witnessed: "Child's bones strong and yielding. The Greek discovers he has not struck a man. Begins to stomp and to hack. Cuts the boys apart, hand from wrist, leg from thigh. Covers himself and our ground with blood. When I got there he had placed his shield on my last son's skull and was grinding it with his boot" (31). Not only does the women's perspective include their painful memories of beholding their husbands and sons murdered, but they recount the fear of being treated as a war prize. They wonder aloud about their new lives in Greece and what purpose they will serve as a nursemaid, a slave, or a wife. The physical repulsion of sexual violation is made evident: the choral figures ask, "Mommy, will marriage be like what they did last night?" (29) In Hartman's hands, this play stands as testament to the emotional and physical wounds women experience after a war; they are the ones left to mourn and bury their men, to see a city destroyed, and to be carried away, powerless, as war booty.

Furthermore, Hartman tones down the oratorical distancing inherent in Greek tragedy by individualizing the details of the women's speeches, rendering them more recognizable to contemporary audiences. Andromache contemplates how carefully she regulated her personality in order to be the model wife for Hector: "They say a woman who walks will stray," she states, and concludes, "So I kept home." "They say wit in a wife is a wayward sign/ So I spoke to myself." And finally, "They say talk in a woman is brass, so I was gold" (45). Thus, by following the decrees and behaving correctly, she earned the approbation of a "model wife," but now is painfully aware that her good behavior has brought her to the attention of Neoptolemus, the son of Achilles. By having Andromache repeat the phrase "They say," Hartman signals that Andromache's sense of self, like that of so many women, is cultivated in response to the external judgment of the patriarchal order. Hartman also eliminates Andromache's 40-line declamatory exhortation to Astyanax before he is murdered and softens her speech into a mother's intimate address: "I touch. I think you will offer your palm to a girl who wants something smooth and say, here. The arch of your foot. The dent of your hipbone, or just above" (48). Gone is the description of Andromache's marriage to Hector, her cursing of the Greeks' barbarity, and her recognition of the gods' implacable will in favor of a more naturalistic farewell.

In addition to transforming the language, Hartman occasionally shifts the focal point outside the frame. The chorus perceive themselves both as characters within the play's diegesis and as outside of time. At one point, the chorus pause to acknowledge Troy's relationship to history; Chorus Woman 1 states: "The tropical paradise of Troy is uniquely glorious, harmonious, and wronged. We must ask ourselves why this particular strip of coast has attracted attention. We must be willing to get historical" (48). More than mourning the loss of their city, the choral women question how the city of Troy will be seen by outsiders, imagining that one day anthropologists will return to this ancient, destroyed city, and try to piece together its nature and functions: "What were we called?" "What were the crops?" "Which linguistic system did this civilization use?" and "Why are the unearthed bodies disproportionately male?" The women comprehend that history belongs to the victors, and had Troy not lost the battle to Greece, their city and their culture would have played a central role in the development of Western Civilization: "Troy: A Multi-Millennial Perspective. We ask our pointed question — what would be the West with a second cradle?" (66–7). Thus from this transdiegetical perspective of an imaginary projected time in the future, the chorus perceive their current loss as fixing Troy's identity forever in history. By drawing attention to the story in this self-conscious fashion, Hartman can emphasize the aesthetic function behind tragedy as a genre. Taking Euripides' choral commentary about the relief women receive from sharing pain ("They who are sad find somehow sweetness in tears, the song/ of lamentation and the melancholy Muse" [l. 607–08]), she shifts the language to a more clinical register:

> In times of bottomless distress, women are known to heal one another through speech. The physical act of facing another person and letting forth a stream of sentences can create a sense of order. The language of disaster never matches reality. Therefore listing one's losses serves to de-escalate and to soothe [44].

With this interjection, Hartman's chorus of women act like sociologists studying female interdependency and how women use conversation for support. Consequently, Hartman's revision becomes a literary critique, attesting to tragedy's worth as an artistic genre that can therapeutically reshape disaster.

Finally, Hartman recasts Cassandra's speech and in so doing transforms her from a hysterical visionary to sardonic virago. In Euripides' version, Cassandra is signified as mad by her bizarre directives (she beckons her mother to dance and laugh), by the chorus's description of her (they refer to her "bacchanal" speech), and by her own actions (she threatens to set everything on fire with the torches she carries from the temple). Her final words equate her marriage with Agamemnon to his demise: "it is by marriage that I bring/ to destruction those whom you and I have hated most" (l. 404–405). Or as Hartman's Cassandra puts it succinctly: "This marriage means revenge" (36). For in Hartman's hands, the character develops a feminist personality, no longer hysterical but in control of the situation. Cassandra's delirium is tinged with sarcasm and obscenity: "Fire Song!/ Fuck song!/ Take torches everyone because this is going to be good" (33). Rather than act shocked and afraid, she mocks the false superiority of men who make women into their sexual toys. She pretends to be an innocent young bride, inquiring about sexual relations, when in actuality, she only parodies the role of the ingénue:

> Maybe have a little talk with me Mother about whisper?
> Because I'm kind of starting to blush
> Just thinking
> About loving
> Such a big, big, hero.
> I'm kind of starting to shiver.
> ...
> What if I gag
> Or scream in a way he finds unappealing?
> What if I bleed too much
> Or not enough?
> What if I fart? [34].

Historically, the depiction of Cassandra as a hysterical visionary has evoked pity as she is powerless to communicate the horrific images of harm she foresees. But in Hartman's hands, her role of *histrione* grants her license to be naughty, to speak offensively to authority because she takes no responsibility for what comes out of her mouth. When Cassandra encounters the messenger, Talthybius, she defies appropriate submissive norms for women by her tart verbal assaults: "I'm looking at you in that suit and thinking about your dick," she states, and later crudely remarks, "I wonder if I could eat you without using my throat" (38). Hartman's Cassandra is bold, powerful, and raunchy — a bad "grrrl" with attitude. No longer does her madness elicit fascinated revulsion, but admiration for her free use of language and her brazen nature. Thus, by contemporizing the language of Euripides' version of *The Trojan Woman* and interjecting into the text a self-reflective awareness, Hartman does not so much revise as extend a historical perspective on women as prisoners of war.

Eurydice *(2002), by Sarah Ruhl*

Transfocalization best describes Sarah Ruhl's revisionary approach to the myth of Orpheus, the grief-stricken musician whose passion for his deceased wife promotes his descent into the Underworld. Rather than consider the myth from Orpheus' point of view, Ruhl focuses on Eurydice and dramatizes her time in the underworld, where she becomes reacquainted with her deceased father. Ruhl believes that the all-encompassing structure of myth enables it to signify a variety of stories and experiences, such as her own longing to reconnect with her father, who passed away when she was twenty and he was fifty-five (Ruhl 279). As she explains in an interview, "A myth exploring the underworld and the connection between the dead and the living was a way to negotiate that [personal] terrain" (Weckwerth 30). Thus, in addition to transfocalization, Ruhl opens up the myth *pragmatically*, stretching the narrative to include the space of the Underworld where Eurydice and her father meet and converse. The shift in focus involves *transmotivation* as well: Eurydice, torn between loving her father and returning to her new husband, instigates her own forced return to the Underworld as she calls out to Orpheus and prompts him to turn back to her.

Ruhl's particular dramatic style is reminiscent of Jean Cocteau's enchanted, surrealistic *Orphée*, thus situating her work within a tradition of mythic retellings. Eurydice arrives in Hades transported by a "raining elevator" in which a torrential downpour envelops her; as the doors open and Eurdyice steps out, a flood of water rushes out across the stage, symbolizing her passage across the "River Lethe" that eradicates human memories. This anachronistic symbol of the River Lethe adds a dimension of *ostranenie*, the familiar made strange, which correlates to the genre of mythic revision where oft-told tales are depicted in a new way. Furthermore, Ruhl devises a chorus of three Stones, a *dramaturgical adoption*, based on the familiar epithet that Orpheus' vocal abilities could even charm stones.[5] Their "language of stones" dominates Hades; it is the language of silence, "like potatoes sleeping in dirt" (296), and prohibits any form of emotional connection. The chorus of Stones comment cynically on Eurydice's actions and insist, "That's not allowed!" any time the father tries to teach Eurydice to read, to sing, or introduce her to words that signify relationships: "Father is not a word that dead people understand. He is what we call subversive" (298). The insensate Stones stand in marked counterpoint to Eurydice and her father who connect to one another through the use of language.

The dynamic connection among language, memory, and relationships lies at the heart of Ruhl's play. No longer a story emblematizing Orpheus' grief and desired restoration of his beloved, Ruhl's *Eurydice* depicts how humans use language to construct and narrate their memories, rooting them in place and binding them to one another. As a manifestation of his desire to communicate with this still-living daughter, the Father has been writing letters to her every day and fills the stage with them; they appear as a protective shield surrounding her, even if she cannot see them. When Eurydice meets her father in the Underworld, she does not recognize him, but her Father, who managed to retain his memories, slowly re-establishes a relationship with her, using the language of family and home. When she does not comprehend the word "father," he finds a substitute image, asking her to envision a strong and protective tree in the backyard under whose shade she would sit all day.

He tells her stories from his childhood and they sing songs and read passages from Shakespeare aloud. The easy rapport of these scenes differs markedly from earlier, awkward moments between Orpheus and Eurydice when he chides her for not remembering the melody he has composed for her. One particular speech correlates language and memory of home: when the Father relays the driving directions to his house. The matter-of-fact diction and the concrete reality of the markers indicating the route reinforce the power language possesses to designate a space as "home":

> I remember.
> Take Tri-State South — 294 —
> To Route 88 West.
> Take Route 88 West to Route 80.
> You'll go over a bridge.
> Go three miles and you'll come
> To the exit for Middle Road.
> Proceed three to four miles.
> Duck Creek Park will be on the right.
> ...
> Pass the first entrance to the alley on the right.
> Take the second entrance.
> You'll go about one hundred yards.
> A red brick house will
> Be on the right [323].

Having held his breath across the River Lethe, the father was able to retain his memories, but to his own detriment; his emotional tug to return to the land of the living remains strong. In this speech, he reinforces his identity by the individualized marker of home, whereas in the Underworld, where the dead are defined by the absence of memories of people and places, home does not exist. When Eurydice asks for her own room, he creates a cubicle-space outlined by string where they sit together, the stringed space reinforcing their relationship and defying the admonition of the Stones.

This pragmatic transformation that enables Ruhl to create hypothetical conversations between Eurydice and her father relates directly to the character's *motivational* shifts. While Ovid squarely casts the responsibility of the backward glance upon Orpheus, in Ruhl's hands Eurydice is to blame. The relationship she has re-established with her father while in the Underworld is more compelling than the one with her new spouse, and, like other wayward heroines, Eurydice rebels against convention. She is depicted as intelligent, albeit indecisive; bright, but unsure of herself and of love. When asked if she's enjoying a book, she replies, "I think it's interesting," and when Orpheus asks her to marry him, she responds, "Yes, I think so" (286). The re-envisioning of Eurydice no longer as the object of Orpheus' romantic love but as an autonomous woman implies that she is unable to meld her life with Orpheus.' Eurydice confides that Orpheus, absorbed with his own artistry, is always mentally absent: "Inside his head there is always something more beautiful" (306). He is enamored of Eurydice as his inspiration, but does not speak to her in the relational language that her father uses in Hades. Thus, when she finds herself searching for intellectual stimulation on the day of her wedding, she is led away by the Nasty Interesting Man with the promise of a letter from her dead father, as well as an invitation to a more appealing party. Hades in disguise, the "Man" lures Eurydice to his high-rise apartment where she falls down a flight of stairs and dies. In Ruhl's version, she becomes the victim of her own inquisitive, dissatisfied nature.

By the play's end, Ruhl has recast the myth to show a woman divided between two strong loyalties: her love of her husband versus her love for her father. Once reacquainted with her father in Hades, Eurydice is indecisive about whether to follow her husband when he descends into Hades to fetch her. The backwards glance that defines the myth is re-imagined as Eurydice's fault: her romantic passion for Orpheus is of equal weight to the love she bears her father — and this ambivalence can only be measured by placing it against the dividing line of death. The moment when she must follow Orpheus out of Hades, she bewails to the Stones that she does not recognize her husband, and yells, "I want to go home! I want my father" (318). When she calls out Orpheus' name, she causes him to turn around, startled, thus disallowing her return to life. It is not that she does not love Orpheus, but the language her father has used to connect with her has resonated more strongly than Orpheus' poetry due to its familiarity. Like Rainer Marie Rilke before her, Ruhl gives voice to a female character whose worth was heretofore only determined by the strength of Orpheus' love. Ruhl's revision advocates the ability of language to forge interpersonal bonds, reinforced in the high-stakes arena of a myth, where a woman stands between the living and the dead, between a lover's adulatory praise and a father's protective love.

Iphigenia Crash Land Falls on the Neon Shell That Was Once Her Heart (A Rave Fable) *(2004), by Caridad Svich*

While Ruhl rewrites the mythic storyline to create an autonomous identity for Eurydice, Caridad Svich embraces the customary characterization of Iphigenia as a martyred woman in her revision of Euripides' *Iphigenia at Aulis*. As an emblem for women murdered in the name of state-sanctioned violence,

Iphigenia becomes an ideal representative for mistreated women, particularly in countries that violate human rights. In *Iphigenia Crash Land Falls on the Neon Shell That Was Once Her Heart* (hereafter, *Iphigenia*), Svich *transposes the diegesis* of the myth to an autocratic regime somewhere in Latin America. Rather than Agamemnon deliberating over whether to sacrifice his daughter for trade winds to sail his troops to Troy, an out-of-favor dictator attempts to subdue a country terrorized by guerrilla soldiers, drug wars, and natural disasters. In constructing this performance piece, Svich engages in a dual maneuver regarding the myth's *axiology*: first, she maintains the myth's value system by deploring the brutalization of women both past and present; secondly, she introduces the practice of glamorizing celebrities as the contemporary approximation of mythologizing a character.

Svich recasts the characters of the myth by assigning them radically dysfunctional traits: Iphigenia, a sheltered girl "of privileged means"; Achilles, "an androgynous rock star, beautiful and damaged"; Adolfo (i.e. Agamemnon, the dictator); Camila (Clytemnestra, "a narcotized prop wife"), and Orestes (a crack-addicted baby carried around in a Gucci shoe box) (334). Escaping from her family home, Iphigenia wanders around the city at night; she enters a church where she meets Violeta Imperial, a spiritual guide who was tortured by the police; she goes to a rave where she encounters and makes love with Achilles; finally, at dawn, she meets a guard who leads her to her execution, a fate she has accepted. Because the country suffers from great unrest, it is widely understood that if her father, the general, endured a personal tragedy like the death of his child, the country would approve of him once more and his public office would be secured. As the News Anchor predicts, "One senseless death, of a rich girl, and we will be united in grief, sorrow, and peace. Do you hear me, Iphigenia?" (338). Even while transposed to the current day, the trajectory of Svich's play follows the myth: Iphigenia's gradual acceptance of her destined role as a sacrificial object for the state's well-being. Svich transfocalizes the story to Iphigenia's point of view rather than her father's and brings to the fore the self-referential awareness Iphigenia possesses, "knowing too well what awaits her in the unchanging pattern of fate" ("From the Writer" 331).

Harkening back to the pure powerlessness Iphigenia feels in obeying Agamemnon's request, Svich provides a political overlay to the myth. In addition to meeting Violeta Imperial, Iphigenia encounters the chorus of "*fresa* girls" whose back-breaking labor in sweat shops and factories transforms them into residual by-products of a capitalist system. The city is filled with abused women who work for slave wages; poor, "strawberry" girls, fresh from rural areas who came for better work in the city and who were murdered for no reason except they are expendable. Svich sums up their categorical pain: "the fresa girls work for 40 U.S. dollars a week in *maquilas* [factories that produce inexpensive clothing, mainly for U.S. consumption] all over Latin and South America" ("Notes" 29). Not only does the state fail to protect them from physical harm, but the view of their violated bodies, "Killed by anonymous hands.... Outside the clubs, ... on the dirt-gravel fields" (347), compels the lower classes to live in subservient fear. The director for the Arizona State University production (2007), Lance Gharavi, associates these fresa girls with the women of Juarez, Mexico, a city across the border from El Paso, where 400 of them have been murdered since 1993 and more than 600 are missing.[6] The fresa girls are first represented as pink crosses and glowing names that emanate from the factory walls to symbolize their deaths; next, the women themselves appear with metallic crescents painted on their foreheads, "anime" eyes, and shiny, red lips. They are the chorus of phantoms that hover about the factory, voicing lives of damaged innocence ("Who spend twelve hours a day at a sewing machine" [346]), as well as horrific mutilation and pain. Iphigenia's initial ignorance of these women suggests her privileged life, and the fresa girls circle her angrily, jealously ripping off her Gucci clothes. But Iphigenia willingly takes on the pain of these women, asking to be sacrificed to redeem their deaths, thus providing new *motivation* behind Iphigenia's sacrifice. Violeta agrees, clothing her like a sacrificial animal with a dress made from the remnants of the dead girls' dresses: "Your death will help us make some sense of it all. Our grief will finally have a place" (368). Svich shows us that such primitive rites of sacrificing women still exist today, but by having Iphigenia choose to stand in as the sacrificial victim for the other women's pain, she transforms her death into a feminist gesture of solidarity.

As the famous daughter of a political leader, Iphigenia has grown up with a double-consciousness about her, seeing herself as an object of the public gaze. Furthermore, she is aware of herself as a mythic figure, caught in a larger destiny she is unable to change. She remarks:

> I have let myself be adored by the faraway gaze of a crowd who wants to get a look at the girl, a good look at the girl, whom fortune has blessed.
> And now on this day of saints, all I want is to be free of Iphigenia, to be free of her certain fate [338].

In order to capture Iphigenia's sense of double-consciousness as herself and as a mythic figure, Svich creates a digitally-mediated environment to represent celebrity culture and to accentuate Iphigenia's public identity. The actors play both live people and images; surrounded by television monitors, the characters onstage interact with the characters projected on the large on-stage screen, while their own "live" actions are simultaneously captured on televisions.

Meanwhile, news reporters manipulate and distort the events that unfold. On screen and in the newspapers, Iphigenia is "owned" in the same way the personhood of various movie stars and celebrities is owned; their lives are constructed fabrications, driven by the imagination and desires of the consuming public. At some point in the recent past, Iphigenia had been kidnapped and photographed in order to extort money from her father; the photograph of her circulated in the newspapers has been transformed into a fetishized object for public fantasy. After making love to her, Achilles admits to having fallen in love with the "tabloid photo" of Iphigenia, sadistically relishing the image of her bound and gagged. In so admitting, he speaks of a world that glamorizes the violence done to women, rendering the harm insubstantial through the endless reproduction of the image. In marked contrast, the theatre of classical Greece kept violent actions off-stage and away from the prurient interest of the populace.

Thus, in this revision, Iphigenia's acceptance of her sacrificial fate occurs when she re-claims her identity from the media and integrates her public image with her true self. Svich censures the way "Iphigenia is trapped by a notion of heroism that is not even hers, but which over time she has been made to believe is noble" ("From the Writer" 331). Her revision underscores the character's self-identity as the constant object of the public gaze and not a subject in and for herself. Furthermore, as the daughter of a significant man, she is aware of herself as destined to be sacrificed for affairs of state; the soldier leading Iphigenia to her death informs her as much: "Give us back your body, girl. It's never been yours to keep" (368). Through the dramaturgical device of dance, Svich depicts her Iphigenia reintegrating and reclaiming her divided self before she dies. According to the Greeks, Bacchic revelry allowed for an integration of the self by dissolving the boundaries between reason and the irrational, between control and excessive behavior. Svich transposes the play's diegesis to the wild "rave" club scene, popular in the 1980s and 1990s, where dancers used Ecstasy to induce stamina to dance all night long, bopping mindlessly to techno, punk, or house music, and wearing stylistic accessories evoking themes of "infantilism, kitsch, S&M, and retro hippie-ness" all with the goal to "spur feelings of departure" (332). The "god" of this club, Achilles, is a "glam messiah" wearing a woman's slip, fishnet stockings, boots, glitter lipstick and black nails, like Ziggy Stardust. As Achilles side-steps categorical definitions of gender through transvestism and claims the body for himself, dancing permits Iphigenia to be freed from the weight of fame, privilege, and public opinion. As she "spins" in ecstasy-enhanced movements (*ex-stasis*, meaning "out of state"), she moves outside of herself and becomes a person on whom the state cannot lay claim. The dramaturgical device of dance, adopted from Greek classical theatre with its roots in Dionysian ecstasy, enables Iphigenia in Svich's version to achieve "a state of exaltation in which the self is transcended" (331). In the repressive police state where these characters cannot be themselves, the dance rave represents the sole recourse left to people for hedonistic escape and subsequent re-integration of the body. Lost in the sensual experience of dance and feeling the rhythms of her own core, Iphigenia moves into her body as the subject of her own story, willingly taking on the role of sacrificial victim. This version of Iphigenia is no longer the object of the public's gaze or of Euripides' interpretive depiction.

From the brief survey of the three plays above, Hartman's *Troy Women*, Ruhl's *Eurydice*, and Svich's *Iphigenia*, one witnesses how mythic revision is not consistent as a genre nor are stylistic approaches readily comparable. One cannot assume, for example, that women playwrights always wish to break with the traditional stories of the past. While thematic and comparative approaches to mythic revision are still instrumental in analyzing the texts, I have demonstrated that a structuralist approach to mythic revision can work in tandem with the other two. Genette's terminology, while lexically dense, provides a categorical approach to mythic revision by tightening our gaze upon particular structures of the myth. These structuralist categories invite us to identify the divergent means of handling mythic material; one writer may honor the playwright's message while modernizing the language; another opens up spaces in the myth to add new events, simultaneously shifting the focus to a different character and her motivation; while a third might alter the diegesis of the myth but maintain the story's axiology. Above all, it is important to realize how mythic revision acts as a critical lens as well as a creative apparatus that can open up new meanings behind each myth while reminding us of how our present values, ideas, and practices are indebted to our past.

NOTES

1. Scholarly studies of individual myths continue, as Julie Sanders demonstrates in her work *Adaptation and Appropriation*, dedicating individual chapters to adaptations of Shakespeare and Ovid.

2. They are: *The Riot Act* (Antigone), by Tom Paulin; *Antigone* by Aidan Carl Mathews; and *Antigone* by Brendan Kennelly (1985).

3. John Vickery's *Myths and Texts: Strategies of Incorporation and Displacement* (1983) argued the need for a structuralist approach to mythic revision; however, he detailed these structural devices as literary traits intrinsic to fiction and poetry, such as structure, theme, character, and point of view, emphasizing the *literary* nature of mythic revision more than its *mythic* nature, not to mention excluding drama from his discussion.

4. As a point of comparison, Deborah Cartmell categorizes how films are adapted from novels by considering the work as a whole and determining whether it is a transposition, a commentary, or an analogue. The categories I offer discuss instead methods by which

playwrights rework mythic material by focusing on the constituent building blocks of the myth.

5. There seems to be some confusion about the source of this epithet. Ruhl's Stones remark that after his wife died, Orpheus "played the saddest music. Even we — the stones — cried when we heard it" (295). However, in Ovid's *Metamorphoses*, the only mention of the rocks is made in Book 11 just before Orpheus's death: "with his songs, Orpheus, the bard of Thrace, allured the trees, the savage animals, and even the insensate rocks, to follow him" (947). Similarly, in Euripides' last play, *Iphigenia in Aulis*, Iphigenia draws a contrast between herself and Orpheus as she pleads with her father for her life: "If I had the tongue of Orpheus, father, an eloquence that could move stones and make them trail behind me..." (52).

6. Lance Gharavi writes, "The bodies of these women and girls turn up in deserted lots that surround the industrial centers of the border city — frequently, the bodies have been mutilated, showing signs of repeated rape and brutal torture. Mexican authorities have yet to produce a single credible prosecution for any of these murders" (239).

WORKS CITED

Barthes, Roland. *Mythologies.* Trans. Annette Lavers. London: Vintage. 1993 [orig. 1972].

Cartmell, Deborah. "Introduction." *Adaptations: From Text to Screen, Screen to Text.* Eds. Deborah Cartmell and Imelda Whelehan. London: Routledge, 1999.

Eliot, T. S. "Ulysses, Order, and Myth." *The Dial* (Nov. 1923). Rpt. in *Selected Prose of T.S. Eliot.* Ed. Frank Kermode. New York: Harcourt Brace Jovanovich, 1975.

Euripides. *Iphigenia in Aulis.* Trans. Nicholas Rudall. Chicago: Ivan R. Dee, 1997.

Frye, Northrop. *The Secular Scripture: A Study of the Structure of Romance.* Cambridge, MA: Harvard University Press, 1976.

Genette, Gérard. *Palimpsests: Literature in the Second Degree.* Trans. Channa Newman and Claude Doubinsky. Lincoln: University of Nebraska Press, 1997. Trans. of *Palimpsestes: La littérature au second degré.* Paris: Seuil, 1982.

Gharavi, Lance. "Of Both Worlds: Exploiting Rave Technologies in Caridad Svich's *Iphigenia.*" *Theatre Topics.* 18:2 (September 2008): 223–242.

Hartman, Karen. *Troy Women.* In *Divine Fire: Eight Contemporary Plays Inspired by the Greeks.* Ed. Caridad Svich. New York: Backstage Books, 2005.

Hersh, Allison. "'How Sweet the Kill': Orgiastic Female Violence in Contemporary Revisions of Euripides' *The Bacchae.*" *Modern Drama.* 35:3 (Sept. 1992): 409–23.

Kushner, Eva. "Greek Myths in Modern Drama: Paths of Transformation." *Literary Criticism and Myth: Yearbook of Comparative Criticism.* Vol. 9. Ed. Joseph P. Strelka. University Park: Pennsylvania State University Press, 1980.

Levi-Strauss, Claude. "The Structural Study of Myth." *The Journal of American Folklore.* 68: 270. (Oct.— Dec., 1955): 428–444.

McDonald, Marianne. "When Despair and History Rhyme," *New Hibernia Review,* 1:2 (1997): 57–70.

Murray, Gilbert. "Introductory Note." *The Trojan Women of Euripides.* Trans. Gilbert Murray. New York: Oxford University Press, 1905.

O'Neill, Eugene. "Working Notes and Extracts from a Fragmentary Diary." Ts. ZA O'Neill 38. Photostatic copies from original in the American Academy of Arts and Letters. 8 leaves. Beinecke Rare Book and Manuscript Library, the Collection of American Literature, Yale University, New Haven.

Ovid. *Ovid's Metamorphoses (Translation in Blank Verse).* Trans. Brookes More. Francestown, NH: Marshall Jones Company, 1978.

Ruhl, Sarah. *Eurydice.* In *Divine Fire: Eight Contemporary Plays Inspired by the Greeks.* Ed. Caridad Svich. New York: Backstage Books, 2005.

Smith, Susan Harris. "Twentieth-Century Plays Using Classical Mythic Themes: A Checklist." *Modern Drama* 29 (March 1986): 110–34.

Steiner, George. *Antigones: How the Antigone Legend Has Endured in Western Literature, Art, and Thought.* New Haven, CT: Yale University Press, 1996.

Svich, Caridad. "Divine Fire: The Myth of Origin." *Divine Fire: Eight Contemporary Plays Inspired by the Greeks.* Ed. Caridad Svich. New York: Backstage Books, 2005.

_____. *Iphigenia Crash Land Falls on the Neon Shell That Was Once Her Heart (A Rave Fable).* In *Divine Fire: Eight Contemporary Plays Inspired by the Greeks.* Ed. Caridad Svich. New York: Backstage Books, 2005.

Vickery, John B. *Myth and Literature: Contemporary Theory and Practice.* Lincoln: University of Nebraska Press, 1966.

_____. *Myths and Texts: Strategies of Incorporation and Displacement.* Baton Rouge: Louisiana State University Press, 1983.

Weckwerth, Wendy. "More Invisible Terrains: Sarah Ruhl, Interviewed by Wendy Weckwerth." *Theater* 34: 2 (Summer 2004): 28–35.

Greek Tragedy Transformed

A. R. Gurney and Charles Mee
Rewrite Greek Drama

KARELISA HARTIGAN

Greek myths have been retold by new writers since the days of the Athenian dramatists themselves. Sophocles and Euripides revised the familiar myths to express their new ideas; both wrote their own versions of various parts of the House of Atreus myth; Euripides, indeed, deliberately put a different spin on Aeschylus's telling of the story. The Romans followed suit, and the custom of turning to these early legends as inspiration for new dramas has continued into the twentieth century. In the following pages I discuss a script by A. R. Gurney, *Another Antigone,* and two plays of Charles Mee's Greek "(re)making" project: *Agamemnon 2.0* and *Iphigeneia 2.0.* My quest is to show how the ancient plays, which everyone would agree fit most standard definitions of a tragedy, have changed in their contemporary guise to something so different that it may be necessary to redefine "tragedy" for the modern stage.

First, however, it seems appropriate to consider some of the issues that come into play when a contemporary playwright chooses to write a new play based on the ancient Greek originals. One can argue, of course, that the archetypes developed by the Greeks are the basis of much modern literature, that the old themes are forever new. When modern playwrights turn to the ancient dramas for inspiration, they either write versions that are a direct updating of the plays by the Athenian dramatists or set up conflicts similar to those staged by the Greeks but taking place in a modern setting. Nevertheless, in both the form and the subject matter the Greek plays are different from shows seen in theatres today. In form the plays differ in the shape of the theatre and the shape of the text. The action of a Greek drama is bound by that round space and rectangular building which define the movement of the tragic actor,[1] while the ancient text is written in meter, the modern in prose. And the contemporary playwrights face a further issue if they wish to keep a certain likeness to the ancient form: they must find a way to make the chorus, that ever present group of witnesses, an integral part of the script. As the Greek plays took place entirely out of doors, the attendant chorus was not intrusive.[2] Charles Mee has found a way to transpose the ancient text in form and with its chorus to the modern stage. A. R. Gurney, on the other hand, has not attempted to recreate either setting or text, for he is interested in the conflict presented in *Antigone*: it is the ancient theme that attracts his attention, not the ancient play itself. The modern audience, furthermore, expects more action than words, while the idea of a hero standing forth as an example is almost bizarre. We can like the main character and perhaps identify with him (or her), but few figures in contemporary plays offer a vision of something terrible and beautiful as they face their ultimate destiny.

Finally, there are two further problems that contemporary playwrights who turn to the Greeks for inspiration face: their audience's unfamiliarity with the myth enacted in the plays and their disbelief in the gods who so frequently directed the events portrayed. The ancient audience knew the myths upon which the plays were based, but the modern playwrights, wanting to cut directly to the action, must offer program notes to explain the retold myth. And the playwrights who wish to include the deities must assume the audience will recognize that they are part of the story and are to be accepted on its terms. When the deities are included, often they do not appear on stage but are represented only as a voiceover; at other times the playwrights integrate them into the modern world by dressing the divinities in a business suit or a cocktail dress.

Despite the differences, the ancient plays still speak to an audience far removed from ancient Athens, either in a direct reproduction or in a modern version, because the issues faced by men and women on the Greek stage are the same in any time and any place and seldom change. As Helene Foley wrote, "Contemporary playwrights also turn to Greek tragic plots to reflect on the relation between twentieth-century reality and an irrecoverable past, on a failed aspiration to civilization" (3). The situations played out by the characters in a Greek tragedy, although based on myth, remain archetypes for behavior. Wrongs done still need to be in some way avenged, life and death choices must be faced, passions do run out of control, personalities warp when put in difficult circumstances. The plays which address these issues last and have continual appeal.

A. R. Gurney

A. R. Gurney's many plays are among the most frequently produced pieces in America today on both professional and community stages. Born in

Buffalo on November 1, 1930, Gurney grew up in the middle-class society of upstate New York and New England. After college and a stint in the Navy, Gurney returned to the Yale School of Drama to earn his master's degree in playwriting. He taught at MIT until 1987, at which time his plays had become so successful that he could retire from regular teaching and turn full time to playwriting. His best known works include *The Middle Ages, Love Letters, The Dining Room*, his first big hit, and more recently, *Silvia*.

Although Gurney sets all his plays in middle-class contemporary society, his theory and philosophy of playwriting are based on traditional ideas of drama. He has said that he often seeks a classical allusion and that even his major themes of family feelings and conflicts come from the ancients; he writes, "Family feelings have been an important part of my own life, and I think they are central to most people's concerns. After all, what is Greek tragedy all about? The Oedipal conflict originated in a Greek play, after all, as Freud is quick to tell us" (qtd. in DiGaetani 117). Throughout his work Gurney has tried to cling to one idea he has taken from the Greeks: his plays must have a sense of shape and form. "I'm just unhappy," he says, "unless the plays I write have a beginning, middle, and an end, and a kind of shape to them. I enjoy making artistic shapes" (qtd. in Sponberg 193).

While he often seeks an underpinning of a familiar work of literature from which he can develop the ironies and contrasts he wishes to present, *Another Antigone* is his only play based so directly on an ancient text. Here both title and script are taken from Sophocles' play, but as my discussion will show, these serve more as foundation than theme. Gurney's play is not a retelling of Sophocles' drama or in any way an updated translation. The script offers a play-within-a play: the conflict arises from the writing of another *Antigone*.

ANOTHER ANTIGONE

> Tragedy has nothing to do with choice... Tragedy occurs when you cannot choose, when you have no choice at all... What [Greek] tragic heroes do after the net has closed in on them, even in the teeth of disaster, is accept responsibility and assert their own destiny and mete out proudly their own punishments.

Professor Henry Harper speaks these words in his final monologue in Gurney's drama. He says them as one who is familiar with Greek tragedy and with Sophocles' play. As Harper's creator, Gurney knows well how the Greek playwright staged the great clash of values between Antigone and her uncle Creon. His 1987 play is intended to be a modern version of this conflict, how individuals cling to their own ideas of what is important and are willing to lose everything to be vindicated in their decision.

To begin, let me review the issues that form the basis of the conflict between Creon and his niece Antigone, and that between Professor Harper and his student Judy Miller. When Creon ascends to the throne of Thebes after the sons of Oedipus have killed each other fighting to have that throne, he declares that Eteocles, who died fighting from within Thebes, will receive an honorable burial. But he denies burial for Polyneices, who died attacking Thebes to regain the city's throne. Antigone, sister of the two combatants, believes every man deserves a burial and determines to bury Polyneices. She knows she is going against Creon's royal edict, but counters that the gods demand burial rites for all the dead, that gods' law is stronger than that of man. Creon refuses to back down from his command and determines that Antigone must die for her arrogant insistence; he will not listen to her words of defense, those of his son, or those of the Theban citizens. Only when Tiresias points out the political danger of his stance does Creon relent, but he is too late. Antigone has hung herself in the cave, his son has turned his sword on himself when he finds her, and his wife commits suicide when she hears of her son's death. Creon is left broken and alone: too late he has learned that family and traditional values are more important than a throne. Both Antigone and Creon faced a challenge and they challenged each other, and each made a choice based on their beliefs. Sophocles's play is a tragedy that reaches across the ages as audiences recognize what Creon did not: man cannot go against the rules of society and the laws of gods.

In Gurney's play, Professor Henry Harper has asked the students in his Greek drama class to write a term paper based on the plays they read during the term. Judy Miller decides to write her own play instead. She rewrites Sophocles's *Antigone* as a protest against the ills of modern American society, in particular the political debate on the nuclear arms race. Harper will not accept it, for a new play was not one of the assigned topics nor is it well written; he sees it as "a juvenile polemic on current events" (7). Nor will he grade her play, and unless Miller writes an appropriate paper, he will not pass her, thus jeopardizing her graduation. As she has been accepted to work at a prestigious financial institution — only the second Jewish woman ever so hired — her graduation is crucial. Harper suggests she spend her time in fulfilling his assignment, not in staging her play. She refuses. The battle lines are drawn.

As Gurney's play unfolds, Judy Miller goes forward with her plan to produce her play on campus, her boyfriend writes a paper for her, submitting it under her name, the dean suggests that Harper's class has become less popular each year (his all important enrollment figures are way down) and there have been rumors that he is anti–Semitic (a charge without substance but still commonly held). In the end, Harper is virtually forced out from teaching and thus loses his profession. Judy turns down a prize based on her academic record because she no longer believes in the values it represents. The audience of Gurney's play can recognize that both professor and student have lost what they cherished through their refusal to back down from their chosen positions.

In this review of the two plots it is evident that all four characters made a choice: a choice to rule on his own terms, a choice to honor the dead and defy the ruler, a choice to insist that his directions be followed, and a choice to interpret those directions on her own terms. But there is little grandeur in the choices made by the characters in the modern play. As Frank Rich wrote in his review of the play, "The Creon-Antigone–like clash between Harper and Judy is more a juvenile war of stubborn wills than a battle royal over communal obligation and private conscience."[3] Thus in looking back at Professor Harper's monologue (quoted above), one is compelled to ask what he means, "Tragedy has nothing to do with choice" (58).

There are, I argue, two types of choice in ancient tragedy. The first is the one Sophocles presents in the *Antigone*, where people make deliberate choices and cling to them at all costs. Pentheus in Euripides' *Bacchae* makes a similar choice: he will stamp out the new religion Dionysus offers and will not heed the words of any who try and persuade him. The second type of choice we see in Greek tragedy is what I usually call "tragic choice." In these situations, a character must choose between two options, either one of which will lead to disaster. This is the type of choice Agamemnon faces at Aulis: sacrifice his daughter and take the war to Troy, spare Iphigeneia, disband the army, break oaths sworn to the gods, and ignore Paris's violation of hospitality when he abducted Helen. Aeschylus's play clearly presents the tragedy that arises from the inescapable choice.

From the examples of choice presented in the *Antigone* or *Bacchae*, an audience can learn to make decisions more wisely and to admit when one's choice is wrong. Antigone did make the proper choice, of course, but at the cost of her own life. Agamemnon's position is the one that arouses the Aristotelian "pity and fear" in an audience: the king cannot choose to opt out from a decision; he must step forth on a path of ruin. Thus does Aeschylus say that Agamemnon "put on the yoke of necessity" when he led Iphigeneia to the altar.

Clearly Gurney's modern *Antigone* presents a choice that, despite Professor Harper's summation, falls into the first category. In that way his play seems to echo the Sophoclean original. But the echo, I argue, does not recur exactly, for Gurney's characters face choices far different from those of Sophocles. While both teacher and student consider their points of view valid and worth fighting for, we can doubt their convictions. Why cannot Professor Harper bend his assignment and why cannot Judy fulfill the course requirements since her future job depends on her graduation? Furthermore, at the end of the modern play, an audience might well sympathize with Harper, while Creon can arouse pity, perhaps, but not sympathy. For the ancient king stood up against the dictates of both gods and men and through his arrogance he earned his fall. Harper was stiff, perhaps, but he fell to trumped-up charges of anti–Semitism and administrative counting of enrollment figures. Harper loses his job and while he believes that without it he has nothing, he has not lost his family or the opportunity to teach elsewhere. Gurney's play would not seem to be a tragedy according to the traditional idea of the genre.

But perhaps he was not seeking to write such a script. In reference to *The Cocktail Hour* he has written: "[T]he play is tragic — or at least not comic — in the sense that the relationship between father and son has not really been resolved. Communication on really significant issues has remained impossible between them" (qtd. in DiGaetani 116). In the ancient world, tragedy arose when mortals and gods came into conflict, when mortals failed to understand the will of the gods. In the secular world in which we live today, difficulty and unhappiness seem to arise when communication between family members or those persons who make up one's social circle fails. Professor Harper could not communicate his understanding of what was academically acceptable to Judy Miller; Judy could not understand that there are times when a person must consider — and obey — the rules of the society in which she lives. *Another Antigone* is not a tragedy in the way of Sophocles' play, for the issues upon which each character takes a stand are small, not grand. In Gurney's play one sees a drama in which a failure to communicate has brought unhappiness, displacement, and temporary sorrow, but not tragedy. There is, however, a message to take from the theatre. As the ancients could learn from shows which taught them to honor the gods and be aware of a mortal's position in the world, so a contemporary audience can see Gurney's play and learn that communication, understanding, and a lack of prejudice are important. Mortals work out their own lives and must know how to do this well.

Charles Mee[4]

Charles Mee, born on September 15, 1938, was raised in Barrington, Illinois. Polio attacked him violently when he was fourteen, and the fight through this illness influenced his future writing as well as his worldview. Even after he left the hospital he realized that he had to undergo recovery again and again. In his autobiographical account of his battle with polio, he tells how the experience influenced his writing style. His life had been shattered like a crystal goblet and even the collected pieces cannot be remade into a whole glass.[5] Thus he prefers to write sentence fragments rather than flowing paragraphs, and leave intact people to write intact books:

> My body of work, to feel true to me must feel fragmented. And then, too, if you find it hard to walk down the sidewalk, you like, in the freedom of your mind, to make a sentence that leaps and dances now and then before it comes to a sudden stop [Mee, *Nearly* 40–41].

After graduating from Harvard in 1960, Mee settled in New York, and embarked upon a career in writing and editing. While serving as editor of American Heritage's bi-monthly *Horizon: A Magazine of the Arts*, he published many history books. Soon he turned to playwriting and developed a particular collage-like style based on radical reconstructions of found texts. He considers his plays as "re-making" of existing texts, ancient and modern; the (re)making is often radical, at other times more subtle. He claims to use the classic text as "scaffolding" on which to hang his own construction; he then smashes the new piece into fragments and presents it held together in a different way.[6] In re-making his plays drawn from the Greeks, he sometimes offers an almost direct translation or transposition interspersed with several passages of contemporary comments; at other times he changes the theme as well as the form and the ancient text remains in shadow. Here I discuss *Agamemnon 2.0*, created in 1994 and *Iphigeneia 2.0*, written in 2007. The two are part of a trilogy Mee later titled "Imperial Dreams."[7]

AGAMEMNON 2.0[8]

The first play of Aeschylus's *Oresteia* trilogy and Charles Mee's remade version tell the story of Agamemnon's triumphant return from the war at Troy to meet a grim death at the hands of his wife, Clytemnestra. Before discussing Mee's play, a brief review Aeschylus's *Agamemnon* is in order. Set at Mycenae ten years after Agamemnon has set sail for Troy, the play opens on the day Troy has fallen, and during the course of the action the king arrives back at his palace. In his absence Clytemnestra has plotted to take revenge on the man who sacrificed his daughter to lead the troops to war and has taken up with his cousin Aegisthus. The latter has his own reasons for seducing Clytemnestra: it was Agamemnon's father, Atreus, who killed his two brothers and served them en casserole to his father, Thyestes.

The play opens when a watchman sees the signal fire that reports the fall of Troy. As he announces the victory, the chorus of Argive Elders enters; in their opening song and during the course of further verses they sing the background of the story: the cause of the conflict with the Trojans, how Agamemnon chose to sacrifice his daughter to pursue the war the gods and his brother

Menelaus compelled him to wage. They also set out the greater import of Aeschylus' play: what is justice and how can it be worked out by mortals in a way that will bring a lasting harmony between those on earth and those on Mount Olympus?

Soon Agamemnon returns vainglorious, but he does not come alone. He has brought his spear-won bride, Cassandra, with him and asks Clytemnestra to treat her well. Gleeful at this new addition to the king's insensitive and hubristic behavior, Clytemnestra announces that she has prepared a welcome appropriate for the man who has laid waste Troy. In the central scene she strews his path with crimson tapestries and compels him to enter his palace on the sacred cloths. After his exit Cassandra envisions what will happen within the house and then enters it to meet her doom. Soon Clytemnestra comes out and reports that she has taken her axe to Agamemnon and Cassandra, delighting in the blood she has shed. As she closes her boast, Aegisthus enters, proclaiming that the long-awaited day of justice has come and the play ends. This is the story and script that Charles Mee (re)made into the first play of his trilogy, *Agamemnon 2.0*.

In Mee's version a mini-chorus of the best-known Greek historians retell history, often in violent juxtapositions with modern events. Like the Argive Elders, Homer, Hesiod, Herodotus and Thucydides serve to make the past present. Mee's stage directions ask that these men be in some way mutilated, suggesting that history itself has been deeply injured. The historian-chorus set the stage, but the events of Mee's play unfold as do those of Aeschylus's drama. Here too Clytemnestra responds to the news of Troy's capture by describing the mixing of victors and conquered in the manner of a salad dressing: oil and vinegar are in the same jar but stand apart (*Ag* 322–325; *Ag* 2.0: 11).[9]

A messenger from the armies arrives reporting the horrors of war; his descriptions are fuller than those of Aeschylus' messenger but true to the actions of soldiers past and present, acts of cruelty which Mee includes in all of his anti-war plays. The story is set in a mythic past, but the violent and ugly military actions the characters describe are those of current wars.[10] Mee's Messenger has a new prop: he draws behind him a heavy bag, which he opens to reveal various mementos he has collected from the battlefield, bringing out "battered, dirt-encrusted gold cups/ and/or rusted 19th century wagon wheels/ a broken glass of indeterminate age/ and other ruined precious or not-so-precious items/ from various epochs" (*Ag. 2.0*: 21).

Mee's Agamemnon enters with the same words he spoke in Aeschylus' drama. He draws behind him a collection of trophies in which Cassandra is not yet visible. Although the modern king assures the Chorus of Historians that the horrors of war they have heard about are not really true, his denials ring hollow.

The Carpet Scene, the powerful central scene of Aeschylus's play, unrolls in almost exactly the same way as it did on the ancient stage. While the words of Mee's Clytemnestra are more sexually explicit than those of the Greek queen, when the king removes his boots to tread the red tapestries, the same terrible sense of doom fills the stage.

After his exit Cassandra bursts forth from one of the trunks, returning the play to Aeschylus's text but with Mee's graphic and lurid additions. As Laura Hitchcock wrote in her review of the 2006 City Garage production, "With her gifts of prophecy and intuition, she is the character Mee uses to bewail the senselessness of repetitive butchery and the deceit leaders use to impel men to kill and be killed for greed and glory."[11] When, through Cassandra's vision, Clytemnestra lifts her axe to slay the king, the words describing the murder of Agamemnon are very close to those of Aeschylus; the lines may be juxtaposed:

Mee writes:

> The altar is prepared
> a hunting net made ready
> the treacherous water's poured, the bath is full
> she holds him in a trap made like a gown
> despairing hands reach out[Cassandra screams]
> She strikes!
> He crashes down!
> She has murdered him!
> Agamemnon is dead! [*Ag 2.0*: 44].

Aeschylus' lines:

> Ah, look! look! Hold back the bull from the cow.
> Taking him in tangling devising robes
> With the black horn she strikes!
> He falls face down in the water.
> I say to you it is a treacherous murdering bath!
> I say you will see Agamemnon dead! [*Ag.* 1125–1129 & 1246].

Clytemnestra's speech over the bodies of Agamemnon and Cassandra also has direct echoes of the original. Mee knows that the terror and awe aroused when viewing Aeschylus' play need no changing for modern understanding. The violent cruelty of the ancient queen needs no updating, no contemporary additions. Here, too, Clytemnestra asserts that she knows her deed was both wrong and unforgivable — but that she would do it again. When Aegisthus enters, his words almost directly repeat the ancient script. Mee "updates" the role with costume and stage directions: the opportunist seducer wears only a sheet and a helmet, and speaks lines that Mee in his stage directions says are "history as vitriol, history as vengefulness" (48). After venting his anger Aegisthus invites Clytemnestra into the palace and into his bed, and they exit to his explicit sexual invitation. Mee's change here is important: it is the usurping lover who has the last word, not the queen who wielded the axe in what she explained as proper justice, and that change alters the play from one in which the larger theme is justice to one in which the sexuality and brutality are the key ideas.

But Mee realized these are not the major issues one should take from the (re)made ancient text and has given Hesiod a final monologue. The ancient poet/epileptic soldier comments on what has transpired and tries to connect the modern play to its ancient original, to the ideas that have made Aeschylus' play forever moving and meaningful:

> This is the riddle of time:
> the human capacity to achieve remembrance
> is the capacity to transform time
> into eternity.
> Nothing human is forever;
> everything perishes;
> except the human heart
> that has the capacity to remember
> and the capacity to say:
> never again
> or forever. [*Ag 2.0*: 52].

That final statement lies at the heart of Mee's (re)making project. The events from the ancient stories should teach us that such deeds as war and its horror, infidelity and its pain, vengeance and its cruelty, should never be repeated. But the very fact that these three themes can be told over and over again, updated with bits of modernity but still the ancient story, shows that the deeds go on forever. Mee understands the world cannot, will not change, but he hopes that through his work he can urge people to consider the option of a better world.

Iphigeneia 2.0

Standing first in a chronological order of the mythic story, *Iphigeneia 2.0*, Mee's last addition to the Greek (re)making project, has been popular since its first staging. The reasons for this are easy to find. When a theatre group wishes to speak out against the violence and suffering of war, it will choose to stage either Euripides's *Trojan Women* or his *Iphigeneia at Aulis*. The first is a play that has been offered to protest war since it was first staged in the American commercial theatre in 1915.[12] During the 1960s and the years of the Vietnam War, *Iphigeneia at Aulis* was added to the anti-war repertory. In the early years of the twenty-first century, as the wars in Iraq and Afghanistan dragged on, directors, producers, and actors chose to speak out through dramas that hold up the suffering of war. Mee, always a pacifist and always intent to show his audience the madness of war, saw in Iphigeneia's story a way to make the point yet once again.

Mee's *Iphigeneia 2.0* is almost a direct echo of Euripides' play. First, then, I review the action of the Greek drama. According to the myth, when the fleet has gathered at Aulis to sail to Troy to punish Paris for his abduction of Helen, Agamemnon in some way offended Artemis. In her anger the goddess refused to allow the fleet to leave for Troy until he offered her an appropriate sacrifice, and she considered the only suitable offering the king's first-born daughter, Iphigeneia. Agamemnon lured the girl to Aulis on the pretext of marriage to Achilles, but used the hero's name without telling him the plan.

When Iphigeneia arrives with her mother, the king attempts to keep secret his real intent, pretending all preparations are for the wedding. But an old servant reveals the true situation and both Clytemnestra and Iphigeneia rage against Agamemnon. But suddenly, at the crucial moment and after seeing Achilles, Iphigeneia accepts her destiny, arguing that her life is worth little when so many men are willing to die in battle to keep Greece free. Although Clytemnestra does not accept her daughter's words, Iphigeneia decks herself in her wedding attire and goes bravely to the altar. Thus ends Euripides' play. The fleet sails, leaving Agamemnon in the belief that his knife had fallen and Clytemnestra in the belief that her husband had killed her daughter.

An alternate ending, possibly added in later times, says that Artemis, arriving *ex machina*, saved Iphigeneia by substituting a deer for the daughter. That is the version Euripides had developed in his earlier play, *Iphigeneia at Tauris,* and it was a common variant in a society which did not want to admit to a virgin sacrifice. Whether or not the girl was spared the knife, neither Agamemnon nor Clytemnestra saw the substitution. Thus the king went forth to war with a bitter wind and the queen awaited his return with bitter vengeance.

Mee takes this story and uses many of Euripides' lines: if the two scripts are juxtaposed, there are numerous parallels. But the differences are what make Mee's play entirely new. He has added to the text his usual collection of bits of modern culture, here stuck on in the lines of the soldiers who form a chorus more closely tied to the ideas of the play than Euripides' chorus of bridesmaids. Mee's soldier Chorus is closer to that of Michael Cacoyannis' 1977 film version of the play, where the clamoring men compel Agamemnon to choose for war. Mee's soldiers also update the carnage of war from that of Troy to that of Iraq or Afghanistan. While Clytemnestra has some updated lines, she is basically the same as her Greek original. And Iphigeneia is a direct echo, from the moment she enters, expressing her love for her father and her joy at seeing him, to her shock on realizing that her marriage is to be a sacrifice, to her culminating acceptance of her destiny and her reasons for accepting it.

In his directions for the opening music of his *Iphigeneia* Mee offers choices ranging from traditional Macedonian folk songs to any of several solos by contemporary Greek singers. Leaving the choice of the music in the director's hands underscores the fluidity of Mee's interpretation of these ancient texts. His plays have a message and the way in which that message is given is not as important as its intent. Unlike Gurney, who likes to give full shape to his scripts, Mee prefers to sketch out the major details and leave it to his director and cast to blend them into the play. He would be the last to insist upon an "authoritative" text, for he believes "there is no such thing as an original play." He writes of his project, "And so, whether we mean to or not, the work we do is both received and created, both an adaptation and an original, at the same time. We re-make things as we go."[13]

The action of *Iphigeneia 2.0* begins as does that in Euripides' play, just after Agamemnon has sent the false letter to his wife and now has second thoughts about his decision to slay his daughter to enable the fleet to sail for Troy. In his opening lines, the king talks to the Old Man about the choices a man faces and must make. Euripides' king is troubled by what he has done and wants to recall the letter, but the reasons for his changed attitude are not fully developed. In Mee's text, they are.

Agamemnon's lines echo Mee's own words written in *Playing God. Seven Fateful Moments When Great Men Met to Change the World*. In this study of seven significant moments in history, Mee considers such details as the difficulty of knowing all the facts, the role of chance in human affairs, failing to recognize that any decision produces both intended and unintended results, and finally, the recognition that all these factors combined still do not give an accurate picture of the world as it is or is becoming. The Greek king appears to be considering these concepts as he spells out his fears about war and its consequences, how empires rise and fall because their leaders cannot see the full picture.

Mee's Agamemnon debates his altered decision with a mini-chorus of three soldiers. They variously spell out the real issue they and the king face: can he ask others to die when he is not willing to put his own child to death? First Soldier sums it up, saying that "you can't ask [your ministers] to send their sons to war knowing, without fail, some of them will die, unless you prove your equal commitment to your goal and sacrifice one of your own children first" (*Iph 2.0*:4). The soldier voices a sentiment familiar to families throughout time: why can a leader ask others' sons to die when he is not sending his own offspring to battle?

Mee also develops further the exchange between Agamemnon and his brother, Menelaus. In the ancient play the second (and lesser) Atreid offers a foil for Agamemnon's debate while his own motivations are not fully developed. This gave Mee space to give Menelaus up-to-date lines about the true horror of war. He is the one to introduce the extreme and almost mindless violence that exists in war, any war; through his words Mee brings the ancient story to the modern world, jarring the audience into understanding that this is not an old play in a new setting with new music, but a strong statement against all wars. Whereas Euripides' play might be seen as a play of tragic choice, playing out Agamemnon's dilemma and decision at Aulis, the productions of the play from the 1960s to the present focus on the vanity of war and the sacrifices it demands, and how the rhetoric of the death for one's country can overwhelm any rational thought. Mee's *Iphigeneia 2.0* plays into this view by making the horrors of war explicit.

A final change in the modern play lies in the final scene. Mee stages a celebration between the soldiers and the bridesmaids underscored with joyous music. But as the party continues, the cast turns the scene into one of chaotic destruction, hurling wine and cake against the terrible action they have just witnessed. At the height of the melée Agamemnon returns, bearing his dead daughter in his arms, and his entrance stills the chaos. The sudden quiet brings home the lie which Iphigeneia claimed to believe, that it was her noble destiny to die for the war. It also returns the story to the opening lines, wherein Agamemnon debated the reasons empires come to ruin.

Greek Tragedy Transformed

Aristotle's definition of tragedy, given in his *Poetics* (VI.2) is familiar to all:

> A tragedy, then, is the imitation of an action that is serious and complete in itself. [It] is a form of drama ... presenting a reversal of fortune involving persons of superior attainments ... with incidents arousing pity and fear, with which to accomplish its catharsis of such emotions.

Aristotle wrote the *Poetics* many years after the Athenian dramatists entered their plays into the annual competition for Dionysus and few of their plays fit into the philosopher's definition. On the modern stage as well only a few texts meet Aristotle's requirements. A list of plays which are serious, show a reversal of fortune, and leave their audience moved to tears of sympathy might include any play by Eugene O'Neill, Arthur Miller's *Death of a Salesman*, and more recently, David Henry Hwang's *M. Butterfly*. But the characters who experience any reversals on the modern stage are usually ordinary people whose lives sink to ruin through their own actions, their own attempts to achieve one goal and accidentally hit another.[14]

How, then, do the plays discussed here fit into this definition? *Another Antigone* is a serious play and both Professor Harper and Judy Miller fail to attain their goals. But, as I noted above, their situations are not fatal; no real ruin, no true doom, falls on either of them. The play describes the unhappiness that results from a breakdown of communication and a misunderstanding of values. A. R. Gurney's play offers its audience something to think about, but it arouses no pity, no fear, and maybe only little sympathy.

Charles Mee's (re)made Greek plays are more complex. While Aeschylus's *Agamemnon* and Euripides' *Iphigeneia at Aulis* are among those considered "true" tragedies, Mee's modern plays with their jarring juxtapositions might seem to force his creations to crash away from the tragedies of the ancient dramatists. I argue, however, that despite the explicit and often ugly language, despite the boisterous action and often cacophonous diction, Mee has written tragedies for the modern world. When Agamemnon returns to the stage with the body of his daughter in the closing scene of *Iphigeneia 2.0*, his entrance halts the action on stage and compels the audience to understand the full sense of the tragedy which the choice for war has initiated. Hesiod's final words in *Agamemnon 2.0* also confirm for the audience what makes a true tragedy.

Mee's (re)making project recreates the ancient plays in a way that is relevant to the contemporary world. The issues presented by the Athenian dramatists reflected the world in which they lived and we still face these issues today. But we meet them in a world that is not clean, clear-cut, or directed by gods. We live in a world shattered by such realities and distractions as Mee describes. Charles Mee has transformed Greek tragedy into something that, while it may not always be attractive, speaks to and defines a world in which harsh reality is very much present.

In the three dramas I have discussed here, Gurney and Mee developed the themes of the ancient plays in a way appropriate for our times. Their tragic vision is not that of the Greek originals, but their scripts suggest that for the current world (that of the last years of the twentieth and first years of the twenty-first centuries) the ancient themes can help define a new form of tragedy. Tragedy transformed today is not tied to the universal but to the individual. The jagged pieces of the modern world have cut away the great overarching ideals and allow the contemporary dramatist to present on stage plays that show the pain, agony, and suffering of the individual in a world he or she has created.

NOTES

1. See Holland, "Space: the final frontier," 47.

2. The origin of Greek drama lies in the chorus. While a group of citizens gathered in the town square would be normal, such a group is out of place in the living- or bedroom.

3. Rich, Review of A. R. Gurney, "Another Antigone."

4. Mee signed his works as Charles L. Mee, Jr., Charles L. Mee or just Charles Mee depending on the work; his use of his name is as fluid as is his use of texts, as he does not believe any form of text or name is so fixed it cannot be changed.

5. Mee tells the story of his polio in *A Nearly Normal Life.*

6. Cummings, *Remaking American Theatre*, 60. Mee's description of his work is cited by all who write about him.

7. Mee's plays were not written as a trilogy any more than were Sophocles' "Theban Trilogy," whose *Antigone, Oedipus the King*, and *Oedipus at Colonus* were written over a forty-year period and only later grouped in thematic order. Here I focus on the last two plays of the triad as written; some ten years separate their composition.

8. Mee added a number to his scripts in the manner of the constantly updated computer program versions.

9. Mee does not use line numbers in his plays. Citations here are given by page number of Mee's on-line texts.

10. Mee used soldiers' blogs to make accurate reports from the front. Such blogging is no longer allowed.

11. Hitchcock, Review of *Agamemnon* for *A CurtainUp Los Angeles Review* (July 7, 2006), posted on The Internet Theater Magazine of Reviews: www.curtainup.com.

12. See Hartigan, *Greek Tragedy on the American Stage: 1882–1994*, 15–19 *et passim.*

13. For Mee's full description of the (re)making project, see his website where his texts are published: http://www.charlesmee.org/html/about.html.

14. Closely associated with Aristotle's definition is *hamartia,* from the Greek *(h)amartano*, "to aim and miss the mark," i.e., to fail in one's attempt.

WORKS CITED

Cummings, Scott. *Remaking American Theater. Charles Mee, Anne Bogart, and the SITI Company*. Cambridge: Cambridge University Press, 2006.

DiGaetani, John L. *A Search for a Postmodern Theater. Interviews with Contemporary Playwrights*. Westport, CT: Greenwood, 1991.

Foley, Helene. "Modern Performance and Adaptation of Greek Tragedy," Presidential Address/American Philological Association (*TAPA* 129: 1999): 1–12.

Gurney, A. R. *Another Antigone*. Dramatists Play Service, 1988.

_____. *The Cocktail Hour* and *Love Letters*, In *A. R. Gurney, Collected Plays* Vol. III. Lyme, NH: Smith & Kraus, 2000.

_____. *The Dining Room* in *A. R. Gurney, Collected Plays* Vol. II (1974–1983). Lyme, NH: Smith & Kraus, 1997.

Hartigan, Karelisa. *Greek Tragedy on the American Stage*. Westport, CT: Greenwood, 1995.

Hitchcock, Laura. "Charles Mee's Take on Iphigenia," *A CurtainUp Review* (January 14, 2007/Los Angeles) posted in The Internet Theater Magazine of Reviews: www.curtainup.com.

_____. Review of *Agamemnon* for *A CurtainUp Los Angeles Review* (July 7, 2006), posted on The Internet Theater Magazine of Reviews: www.curtainup.com.

Holland, P. "Space: The Final Frontier." In Scolnicov and Holland. 45–62.

Mee, Charles. *A Nearly Normal Life*. Boston: Little, Brown: 1999.

_____. *Playing God. Seven Fateful Moments When Great Men Met to Change the World*. New York: Simon and Schuster, 1993.

_____. the (re)making project at http://www.charlesmee.org/html/about.html.

Rich, Frank. Review of A. R. Gurney, "Another Antigone." New York Times, January 15, 1988.

Scolnicov, Hanna and Peter Holland, eds. *The Play Out of Context. Transferring Plays from Culture to Culture*. Cambridge: Cambridge University Press, 1989.

Sponberg, Arvid F. *Broadway Talks. What Professionals Think about Commercial Theater in America*. Westport, CT: Greenwood, 1991.

"That story is not true"
Unmaking Myth In Ellen Mclaughlin's Helen *and Saviana Stanescu and* Richard Schechner's *YokastaS*

ELIZABETH W. SCHARFFENBERGER

A pair of the best-known myths from ancient Greece return to the stage in two recent dramas: Ellen McLaughlin's *Helen,* which was first performed in March 2002 at the Joseph Papp Public Theater in New York City, and Saviana Stanescu and Richard Schechner's *YokastaS,* which opened at New York City's LaMama ETC in March 2003.[1] McLaughlin's play updates the story of the Spartan queen Helen, the wife of Menelaus, whose notorious abduction by the Trojan prince Paris precipitated the war at Troy, and the collaborative venture of Stanescu and Schechner reconceives the tale of Oedipus king of Thebes, the infamous murderer of his father Laius, who was also husband to his mother and father to his brothers and sisters.

Variant versions of both myths circulated in ancient times, and the discrepant details even within a single genre, such as Athenian tragedy, are sometimes noteworthy. For example, Sophocles' *Oedipus the King* (c.428 BCE) and Euripides' *Phoenician Women* (c. 409 BCE) differ considerably in their presentations of the timing of the suicide of Oedipus' mother, called Iokaste in most sources dating to the classical period and more commonly known as Jocasta in English-language translations.[2] In the many tales about the Trojan War, little agreement emerges concerning Helen's complicity in her abduction. What is more, a fragment from a poem by Stesichorus, which dates to the early fifth century BCE, preserves a completely different account of what happened to Helen when she left Sparta: "That story is not true;/ you did not go on the well-benched ships,/ nor did you reach the citadel of Troy..." (fr. 192 *PMG*).[3] The premise that Helen herself did not go to Troy, but was kept "safe" (i.e., chaste) in Egypt by its king, Proteus, while a deceptive phantom image, fabricated by the gods, was sent to Troy in her stead is the basis for the plot of the tragedy by Euripides titled *Helen* (412 BCE). It seems likely that Euripides' conception of Helen is indebted to Stesichorus' poem,[4] as may be Herodotus' rationalized account of the Egyptians' confiscation of Helen from Paris (*Histories* 2. 112–20).

Despite the apparent freedom with which ancient texts of all types handled the details of these and other myths, alterations to their fundamental features are rare.[5] No ancient poet or playwright permitted Jocasta to avoid her incestuous marriage and her eventual suicide, and, if Helen herself was allowed to sit out the Trojan War in far-off Egypt, the war was still fought over someone, or something, that looked just like her, and the reputation for adultery still dogged her. The biases inculcated in male poets, playwrights, and mythographers by the patriarchal cultures of the ancient world imposed additional limitations on the ways in which these stories were presented, especially when they dealt with aspects of female sexuality and sexual behavior that were perceived as transgressive.[6] A willingly adulterous Helen who was nonetheless a sympathetic figure, or a Helen who failed to return to Sparta with her lawful husband, was as inconceivable as a Jocasta who felt no regret nor suffered any consequences for her incestuous relationship with Oedipus. The gender-based biases in the transmission of myths and legends were acknowledged even in ancient times. Euripides has the chorus of Corinthian women in his *Medea* (431 BCE) sing in its first stasimon:

> Flow backward to your sources, sacred rivers,
> And let the world's great order be reversed.
> It is the thoughts of *men* that are deceitful,
> *Their* pledges that are loose.
> Story shall now turn my condition to a fair one,
> Women are paid their due.
> No more shall evil-sounding fame be theirs.
>
> Cease now, you muses of the ancient singers,
> To tell the tale of my unfaithfulness;
> For not to us did Phoebus, lord of music,
> Bestow the lyre's divine
> Power, for otherwise I should have sung an answer
> To the other sex. Long time
> Has much to tell of us, and much of them
> [Euripides' *Medea* 409–30, trans. Warner 73].

Yet, for all of its self-consciousness about the limited perspective of traditional story-telling and song, Euripides' drama represents Medea's murder of her children and vengeance on her husband, Jason, as the monstrous disruption of proper social order, and the tragedy as a whole seems to affirm the conventional view that the woman who dares to appropriate the prerogatives reserved for men poses grave danger to the very fabric of society.[7]

The fact that myth-making and story-telling have been, until very recently, the exclusive privilege of men is something to which several contemporary feminist "revisions" of ancient myths and texts have drawn attention.[8] Novels such as Christa Wolf's *Cassandra* (1980) and Ursula K. LeGuin's *Lavinia* (2008) give voices to marginalized female figures by permitting them to relate, in their own first-person narratives, their experiences in the wars at Troy and in Italy. They emphasize that the female figures we encounter in canonical mythological texts, such as the *Iliad*, Aeschylus' *Agamemnon*, and Virgil's *Aeneid*, are but fabrications of male imaginations, and Wolf's *Cassandra* takes the additional step of challenging the accuracy of the accepted "facts" in the well-known story about Troy.[9] So, too, a host of contemporary theatrical productions, such as Ellen McLaughlin's *Iphigenia and Other Daughters* (1995), have retold familiar myths in ways that bring out the prejudiced, mistrustful, and even misogynistic aspects of their traditional presentations, and they expose the fixation with "bad women" in the myth and art of ancient Greece as a means for maintaining the status quo of patriarchal authority.[10]

Nonetheless, as they contest the biases of the mythological tradition inherited from the Greeks, these recent works also arguably participate in the open-ended process of reinvention that characterized this very same tradition from the earliest days of the archaic period, and we might appropriately think of them as intensifying the challenge to the dominant versions of popular myths that was launched long ago in Stesichorus' "palinode" about Helen and the Euripidean tragedy it inspired. Indeed, Stesichorus' insistence, "*that* story is not true," resonates loudly in both McLaughlin's *Helen* and *YokastaS* by Stanescu and Schechner.

This essay explores the different ways in which *Helen* and *YokastaS* "unmake" myth as they bring their titular figures into direct confrontation with widely disseminated narratives that get the "facts" of their experiences wrong. Like her Euripidean and Stesichorean forebears, McLaughlin's Helen never went to Troy and, instead, waits patiently in Egypt for Menelaus to retrieve her. Stanescu and Schechner's Yokasta announces in the first scene that she is "here to set the record straight," correcting "what those rats Sophocles and Seneca wrote" about her unhappy suicide (scene 1: 3–4). Exploiting the conceptual slippage between the modern English usages of the term "myth" to denote both "traditional story" and "untruth," the two plays expose how myths created by male storytellers have taken on lives of their own, independent of the actual experiences of their female subjects, and they debunk not only the traditional images of Helen and Yokasta as individuals, but more generally the conceptions of appropriate female conduct that have been sanctioned by canonical treatments of their stories.

As part of their playfully irreverent unmaking of the familiar myths concerning Helen and Yokasta, both dramas incorporate pointed anachronisms. With remote in hand, Helen fruitlessly surfs television channels as she searches for news about the Trojan War in the luxurious hotel room equipped with all kinds of modern amenities, including concierge service. Yokasta, now separated from Oedipus, grants an interview to a figure named "Media" and even appears on a tell-all television talk show, during which she, Phaedra, and Medea wrangle over the title of "History's Baddest Mama" (scene 7: 23–28). Helen and Yokasta are thus recast as modern-day celebrities — in particular, as glamorous women who once stood behind powerful men and are now the objects of scandal — whereas contemporary media, especially news reports, TV talk shows, and gossip magazines, are posited as the vehicles responsible for circulating the myths that have been handed down to us from antiquity. These anachronisms, I propose, further "unmake" myth by associating it with quotidian forms of discourse — particularly gossip and rumors — that court distrust. At the same time, these anachronisms also invite spectators to reflect on their own participation in, and vulnerability to, the phenomenon of mythopoesis, as it manifests itself in the twenty-first century. Like contemporary feminist revisions of "classic" dramas, both *Helen* and *YokastaS* are concerned with our reception of canonical texts (Friedman, 6–7). Yet their "metamythopoetic" aspects have broader implications, insofar as both dramas encourage spectators to embrace active, responsible roles in every act and process of communication, and to see a direct connection between the myth-making of ancient times, with all its biases and limitations, and the discursive practices that still hold sway today.

Ellen McLaughlin's Helen

McLaughlin's *Helen* dramatizes the last day that its protagonist will spend in Suite 29-B of a posh Egyptian hotel. She has resided in this room, we quickly learn, for the past seventeen years, living in a kind of suspended animation (she neither eats nor drinks, and she uses the toilet only to flush away the flies she has killed) and not daring to leave even for a minute lest she miss Menelaus' arrival. All this time, she has stayed in complete isolation except for the regular visits of a figure called "The Servant," who helps her in a daily ritual of dressing and grooming. The play is structured around the arrival of three visitors, and each of them moves Helen closer to ending her lonely vigil: Io, one of Zeus' many sexual conquests among mortal women, who aroused the jealous anger of Zeus' wife, Hera, and, transformed into a cow, was consequently hounded around the entire Eastern Mediterranean by a stinging gadfly; the goddess Athena, the erstwhile patron of the Greek army at Troy;

and finally Menelaus himself, who has wandered the seas for seven years on his homeward journey after the fall of Troy and has just checked in to the same hotel (in Suite 28-B) with the "copy" Helen — the phantom who was at Troy — in tow. After each of these visits, the Servant enters to help Helen dress, arrange her hair, manicure her nails, massage her feet, and finally undress for bed. Each time the Servant arrives after one of the visitors has left, Helen bids her, "Tell me a story." Each of these three requests is met with a narrative that opens with phrases familiar from modern-day fairytales ("Once upon a time...") and features a nameless woman or girl as its central figure. Unlike all ancient versions of Helen's story, this play does not end with Helen's return to Sparta in Menelaus' company. Despite stumbling into the wrong room and eventually recognizing the woman there — the Helen on stage — as his real wife, and despite his abiding love for her, this exhausted and war-weary Menelaus decides to abandon her and go back to Sparta with the copy won at Troy because, as he puts it, "It's not you they want. They want her" (McLaughlin 185).

Comparison with Euripides' *Helen*, an important inspiration for this dramatization (McLaughlin 121–5), illuminates the significance of McLaughlin's choices in plotting and characterization. Euripides' strategy for re-contouring Helen's myth centers on assimilating his protagonist to Penelope, the archetypically faithful wife in the *Odyssey*, whose sexual loyalty to her husband was traditionally posited as the opposite of Helen's unchastity.[11] To this end, Euripides has his Helen valiantly resist the unwanted advances of a suitor, Theoclymenus, the current king of Egypt and the now deceased Proteus' son; once reunited, she and Menelaus collaborate in a clever ruse that thwarts the love-struck Theoclymenus' designs, thus effecting their escape from his clutches and their return to Sparta. McLaughlin, however, eliminates the sub-plot involving Theoclymenus and his sister, the seer Theonoë, and she also forgoes having the phantom Helen vanish — an event that is described in detail by one of Menelaus' crew in Euripides' play (lines 605–210).[12] Denied the chance to act out her fidelity *à la* Penelope, McLaughlin's Helen is further distanced from stereotypically "good" women by her early displays of petulance and self-absorption. She complains about the service in the hotel, imperiously bosses around the Servant, and thoughtlessly interrupts the beleaguered Io (McLaughlin 133–4, 144, 153, 157). She even admits to Io that, but for Hera's intervention, she was all set to elope with Paris (McLaughlin 139–40). Nonetheless, she is not devoid of feeling or concern, and in this she resembles her Euripidean counterpart. The war in Troy, fought (she knows) in her name, deeply troubles her, and her desperation for news of it and of Menelaus' whereabouts lies behind her impatience. She is also capable of adjusting her expectations and behavior. By the time Menelaus leaves her in favor of the "copy" Helen, depriving her of the long-awaited reunion that Penelope enjoyed with Odysseus, she has learned enough about her insignificance to let him depart with grace (McLaughlin 188).

McLaughlin's Helen is thus not the selfish, adulterous Helen made famous by myth, nor is she Euripides' "new Helen" modeled on the faithful and resourceful Penelope.[13] The sense of her complexity is deepened every time we are reminded of the many other "copies" of Helen — i.e., the stories about her — abroad in the world, each of which corresponds in some regard to the figure we see on stage, but none of which does real justice to her. As Io relates her own story, in which her experience of being ravished by Zeus is elided with the awkward physical alienation experienced by adolescent girls, she bluntly confesses that the images of Helen she had seen in "magazines and movies" while growing up "were some of the first ways I learned to feel bad about myself." But, now that the real woman stands in front of her, Helen has become "just someone else ... not this impossible, perfect ... *thing* to me" (McLaughlin 139–41). After Io leaves, the imprecision of all accounts that purport to represent the true character of Helen (or anyone else) is underscored by the Servant's first story, which concerns an "incident" (or abduction, or elopement) centered on the sudden disappearance of an unnamed "lady of the house," whom we — and Helen — are invited to associate with Helen herself. According to the Servant's story, members of the lady's household staff, her secretaries, the security personnel all have a story to tell about what happened, but their accounts are at complete odds. As for the sketches made by the police artists, "there was no consensus on any single detail, from the color of the eyes to the length, even the color, of the hair" (McLaughlin 154). The story about the nameless lady prompts the following exchange, which suggests that Helen has an inchoate grasp of the tale's relevance to her own situation:

> HELEN (*quietly disturbed*): I do worry about the world. This splitting of image from body never bodes well. The first knockoff only begs for another. Copy spews forth copy, an infinite proliferation, like a nuclear reaction. Each replication spawning yet another generation of duplicates until she moves like a virus through the city, facing you at every turn. Her name spelled out on the night sky. Her pictures blown like debris to be trod underfoot and washed into gutters. She is everywhere.
>
> SERVANT: Hard to believe there was ever an actual Helen. Just some woman. With breasts that swell or sag, hair that grows, menstrual cycles.
>
> HELEN: THOUGHTS! THOUGHTS! SHE HAS AN INTERIOR LIFE! SHE'S NOT JUST A BODY! [McLaughlin 155].

Indeed, Helen's existence in McLaughlin's play is hedged by stories: stories about her that elude her control, even when she has voluntarily performed the roles (e.g., perfect wife, glamour queen, *femme fatale*) they prescribe for her; stories told to her, which she struggles to comprehend; stories that she would like to hear (about the war and Menelaus) but has not. The logic-defying encounter with Io who, as Helen notes after her departure, lived "*way before my time*," underscores the ubiquity of stories, myths, and tales of all sorts; not only did Io grow up with tales about Helen ringing in her ears, but Helen claims to have heard Io's story since she "was a kid" (McLaughlin 154). When she finally learns from the jaded Athena about the long-ago dénouement of the war at Troy ("It was a nightmare, really... *Ten years* ... I mean, really, who can stay interested?" [McLaughlin 160]), she also confronts the fact that her importance has been eclipsed by what people say about her, whether accurately or not. As Athena callously puts it, the war was fought to its bitter, destructive end not for Helen herself, but for "some idea of you ... a concept ... not even a good concept ... a rumor of a chick pretty much everyone despised" (McLaughlin 160–1). This fact is painfully affirmed by Menelaus' rejection. The "copy" Helen — who is nothing more (nor less) than the embod-iment of the myths that have been circulating about Helen — is the one for whom "a generation of men threw down their lives in that hellhole" (McLaughlin 185), and she is the one whom Menelaus will take home.

When Io presses Helen about her reasons for never leaving her suite, Helen dismisses the suggestion that she "just get in the elevator" with the assertion, "...I'm supposed to wait here, in this room, until [Menelaus] comes. And he's supposed to take me home. That's the way it works" (McLaughlin 143). Other details corroborate the impression that Helen is accustomed to being acted for (and acted on), rather than taking initiatives. Every aspect of her grooming, including the choice of dress and the doing and undoing of her elaborate coiffure, is performed for her by the Servant; without compre-hending their origins, she recites snippets of verse from the *Iliad* that "go through her head" as if her "unconscious mind is tuned into some frequency — WGR-EEK or something, who knows?" (McLaughlin 134; *cf.* 128). The Ser-vant's second story, about a stunningly beautiful Sleeping Beauty or Rapunzel-like girl who "sleeps in a coffin made of ice in the center of a forest of thorns," puts Helen on the defensive when it is suggested that the deathlike suspended animation holding the girl in its grip is in fact "all her idea," and that the girl "climbed into the coffin all by herself ... without help from anyone ... and she pulled the lid down after her ... and that's where she's been for a long time now, pretending to be asleep" (McLaughlin 169–72). The story plainly hints, much to Helen's discomfort, that her own passivity and isolation have been self-imposed pretenses — something from which she could rescue herself. She cannot control the proliferation of the myths, stories, and "copies" of her that move around the world "like a virus" (McLaughlin 155). But she does not have to live in the isolation she has chosen; that she hears no news of the Trojan War until Athena's arrival is at least partly her fault. And, as the Servant's final tale suggests, it may be possible for her, like the once beautiful woman who is the story's subject, to choose to "lift the lid of her own casket and climb out, then slip through the thicket of thorns in the dead of night into utter invisibility," leaving the work of being a sex goddess to the "other girls" that are her "immortal copies" (McLaughlin 189–90).

According to McLaughlin's "unmaking" of Helen's myth, it is not the "copy" Helen that disappears — indeed, its self-proliferation and consequent immortality guarantee that it cannot. Helen herself, though, has the option of accepting the anonymity brought about by the process of aging and the loss of that notorious beauty, much-feared phenomena that nonetheless bring great freedom and the prospect of genuine creativity to the woman in the Servant's story. At the story's end, which is also the end of the play, the woman, now very old, is envisioned encountering a blind old man, himself a storyteller, at the counter of a diner "in the high desert":

> She's smiling now, this ancient woman, crumbling crackers in the old man's soup for him. He can't see her, of course, but he can tell she was probably beautiful once; it's like a scent that comes off her. But they're so old, these two, that they look like twins. It's hard to say who's the woman and who's the man — that's how ancient they are... And then as she hands him a spoon, he catches her hand, the blind poet, and he says the thing she's been waiting all her life to hear. He says, "Tell me a story." And she opens her mouth at last. And she does [McLaughlin 190–1].

With this final image derived from the "old notion" that Helen, not Homer, composed the *Odyssey* (McLaughlin 129),[14] McLaughlin holds forth the possibility that Helen has finally learned enough about herself — and about the nature of myth — to speak for herself, and to resist the easy temptation of being imprisoned by the expectations imposed by other people's stories. As the Servant utters the concluding words, the door of the elevator to Helen's suite opens, and we are left to imagine what she will do next, and perhaps to hope that, like the woman in the story, she might walk through the door and climb out of her "casket."

By making Menelaus' departure the necessary condition for Helen's potential liberation, McLaughlin challenges age-old assumptions concerning the significance of marriage and men in women's lives, at the same time drawing attention to the role that myths, such as those concerning Helen, have played throughout the ages in cultivating normative ideas about the centrality of marriage and the "natural" dependence of women on men. Few of us will be as overwhelmed by stories and myths as are Helen and the celebrities who are her modern counterparts. Yet, by insinuating that ancient myths are cut from the same story-telling cloth that supplies the material for the latest gossip about the breast implants of some Hollywood starlet, McLaughlin supplies her spectators with grounds for thinking about how powerfully affective myths are made today, and how stories, or "copies," shape our ideals, values, and aspirations, as they sculpt our notions of (to quote Helen) "how it works." McLaughlin's "unmaking" of myth also encourages us to consider the ways in which absorbing tales focused on the rich and famous can distract us from news that is difficult to hear — for example, about masses of refugees such as those described by Io, who are still "swirling in a twisting wash across the face of the earth ... unwelcome everywhere ... stumbling from nightmare to nightmare" (McLaughlin, 144). If Helen's passivity holds up a mirror to habits to which we too might fall prey, the possibility held forth by the final tableau speaks to the hope not just for Helen, but also for us, that we will claim for ourselves the power to "unmake" myth.

Saviana Stanescu and Richard Schechner's YokastaS

The power to unmake myth is exactly what the Yokasta brought to the stage by Saviana Stanescu and Richard Schechner has seized. When her interviewer in the opening scene, the male character named "Media," reads quotations from Sigmund Freud's *Interpretation of Dreams* concerning the Oedipus complex that are (in his words) "about you," she exclaims, "That's not about me. That's about Oedipus and Laius." Disinclined to discuss her "private life in public," she nonetheless does not "like the fact that [Oedipus] gets all the attention," and her pique at the neglect of what happened to her has caused her to break her "long silence" in a bid to "set the record straight" (scene 1: 2–4).

What Yokasta reveals about herself in this first scene is astounding. Not only is she alive and well, contrary to the ubiquitous tales of her suicide, but she also knew all along, thanks to a very explicit letter sent to her by Zeus when she was still a young girl, that the young man whom she would "fuck for fourteen years" after the disappearance of her first husband would be her son. Fully aware of his identity, Yokasta married Oedipus and bore the four children that were infamously his siblings as well as his offspring; as Zeus' note puts it, Oedipus and the fantastic sex life she had with him were a "gift" to her after years of unhappy, sexually unsatisfying marriage to Laius "the gimp." The subsequent scenes unfold Yokasta's experiences and decisions, as she relives the key moments of her life: the night that Laius took baby Oedipus away from her; Laius' subsequent effort to win back her affections by playing a game called "Blind Date"; the day that Laius left for Delphi to consult the oracle about having another child; the next evening, when Yokasta bathes the swollen foot of the newly arrived Oedipus and begins to seduce him; her tutoring of her new husband, so as to prepare him for the responsibilities of kingship; her happiness as a perpetually pregnant mother; the coming of the plague, Oedipus' discovery of his true identity, and the dissolution of their marriage. At the center of the play is the talk-show scene, moderated by Media, in which Yokasta, Medea, and Phaedra contend for the title of "History's Baddest Mama," with each of the three contestants quoting "what my author(s) wrote for me"—i.e., passages from ancient tragedies by Euripides and Seneca—in support of her claim.

Schechner is well known for his revolutionary approaches to theatre that eschew conventional techniques of "realistic" representation, and, in particular, for his groundbreaking experiments with casting, improvisation, and adaptation of source texts, all of which were in evidence in *Dionysus in 69*, his famously controversial version of Euripides' *Bacchae*.[15] This more recent collaboration with his former student Stanescu finds an innovative way to capture the many facets of its titular character; as the title's plural *YokastaS* with its emphatically capitalized final "S" hints, there is not just one Yokasta on stage in this production. After the introductory scene, in which the mature, post–Oedipus Yokasta is interviewed, she is joined onstage by three other Yokastas, who are her selves at different times in her life: "Yoyo" the teenaged Yokasta, tomboyish and bratty, but energetic and bursting with a vivid, irreverent imagination that spurs her to imagine herself as Avenger Yokasta, a comicbook heroine with an array of super-powers enabling her to rule the universe; tough, funny, but also bitter "Yoko," the Yokasta married to Laius; and "Yono," radiantly happy and always pregnant, who is Yokasta married to Oedipus.[16]

From the second scene on, all four Yokastas are always present on stage, although Yono is smilingly silent until the antepenultimate scene 12 (titled "The Good Years"), in which she grants Media an extensive interview in the manner of a contemporary First Lady or royal consort. Otherwise, the Yokastas interact with Laius, Oedipus, and Media (who are all meant to be played by the same male actor) at times singly, at times in pairs or as a trio. In the final scene, which depicts Oedipus' discovery of his true identity, the four Yokastas act in consort as they first attempt to dissuade Oedipus from reacting violently to the revelations familiar from Sophocles and Seneca, and then shoo him away in disgust at his self-mutilation, with Yoyo literally waltzing him offstage (Caldazilla 711). The Yokastas also interact with one another as if they were distinct individuals, occasionally quarreling and criticizing each other ("we're a little like sisters," the mature Yokasta explains [scene 2: 7]), but more typically working together to relive the most important moments of their shared existence and so unmake the story of Oedipus as it is typically known. The Yokastas' collaborative effort of revision begins with Yoko's request at the end of scene 2 that her sister-selves "help me with this" in recreating "the scene that matters to me most"—a request that sets the stage for scene 3's reenactment of Laius' confiscation of her newborn son. The reenactment relies on the two different personae of the protagonist to highlight both the mother's revulsion (evinced by Yoko) and tenderness (manifested by Yokasta) for the baby. There is even more fluidity in the presentation of character in the "Baddest Mamas" scene, in which the actors playing Yoko and Yoyo temporarily take on the identities of Medea and Phaedra. At the end of this showdown among the infamous mothers of classical myth, the actor playing the heretofore silent Yono finally comes forward to speak, not in the voice of Yono, but as their modern analogue—a woman chillingly reminiscent of Texas mother Andrea Yates, who dispassionately describes her systematic drowning of her four small children in a bathtub because (she alleges) "they weren't developing correctly" (scene 7: 28–9).

Comparably to McLaughlin's vision of Helen, Stanescu and Schechner's characterization of Yokasta as a celebrity wife, who grants a long-awaited interview after dropping out of sight following a messy scandal and marital estrangement, elides ancient myths with the gossip swirling about today's rich and famous—a form of discourse that exerts great influence but is notorious for its half-truths and unreliability. Moreover, *YokastaS* repeatedly emphasizes the reverence accorded to canonical texts that are our sources for classical mythology, namely the tragedies by Sophocles, Seneca, and Euripides. The Yokastas, also Medea and Phaedra, and eventually Oedipus cite these texts liberally, with the female characters typically flagging their quotations with the words "quote" and "unquote" and calling attention to the fact that the text in question was written for them by an "author" (e.g., scene 7: 27–8; scene 14: 73). From the opening scene, in which Yokasta dismisses as irrelevant the passages from Freud's *Interpretation of Dreams* quoted by Media, the play establishes a tension between the vantage points of authoritative texts of all sorts — not just tragedies, but also expository texts by Freud, Machiavelli, and Plato, and even the sacred utterances of the Delphic oracle — and the alternative possibilities of action and interpretation that these "authorities" seek to crowd out. Accordingly, myth in *YokastaS* is associated not just with less creditable forms of communication (gossip and self-promotional talk on TV chat shows), but also with authoritative texts that are highly respected, even revered, for their truthfulness. The play thus imputes a kind of mythopoesis to expository works purporting to offer objective truths about (for example) female sexuality. Yokasta's battle against mythology's misinterpretation and oversimplification of her experiences is, then, nothing short of a challenge to the credibility of texts of all sorts, on which we might rely for basic guidance about how to live (and assess) our lives. To be sure, spectators may not want to follow Yokasta's lead in assenting to the propriety of mother-son incest. But her refusal to sacrifice her sexual satisfaction and to feel regret over her relationship with Oedipus demand that we interrogate how our perceptions concerning "normal" and "abnormal" sexual behavior derive from the judgments of "expert" authorities, whether scientific, philosophical, or religious. The long, difficult path that she travels toward incest with her son also calls attention to the ways in which positive interest in female sexual satisfaction has been completely absent from the cultural tradition represented by the texts that constitute the western canon. Juxtaposed against Yono's impersonation of the murderous mother who methodically drowned her children in the tub, Yokasta's loving seduction of her son in his bath is made to seem less than sinister, raising questions about the "badness" of her illicit desire.

This is not to say that the Yokastas cite texts only to challenge their truthfulness and relevance. At times, they appropriate words written by others as aids in their own undertakings. For example, when teaching the tender-hearted young Oedipus how to be a king, Yokasta and Yoko pepper their lesson with quotations from Plato's *Republic* and Machiavelli's *Prince* in support of their assertions that Oedipus must make his people fear him, and that he must "banish poetry" from his city (scene 11: especially 46, 52). The two songs that the Yokastas sing as choral numbers strengthen the impression of their dexterity in taking over and assuming "ownership" of pre-existing texts. Anticipating the arrival of Oedipus in scene 9, Yokasta, Yoko, and Yoyo perform a witty adaptation of *West Side Story*'s "I Feel Pretty," which coyly captures the awakening of hope, confidence, and desire in the queen after the disappearance of the despised Laius (scene 8: 29–31). Immediately before the play's denouement, all four Yokastas perform the second number, "I Know Him So Well" from *Chess* (scene 13: 69–70). With its original lyrics intact ("Nothing is so good it lasts eternally/ Perfect situations must go wrong..."), the song nonetheless sounds like something that the Yokastas composed for themselves, so aptly does it capture their wistful resignation in the face of the imminent break-up of their once happy marriage.[17]

The judicious, self-conscious use of texts by the Yokastas stands in contrast with Laius' and Oedipus' slavish devotion to the utterances emanating from the Delphic oracle. Just like his father, who insists that the oracle "is always right" (scene 3: 11), Oedipus exclaims when confronted by the horrors of the plague, "The Oracle tells us what to do. The Oracle will save us!" (scene 14: 71). The ensuing action calls into question the inevitability of the events that, in Sophocles' and Seneca's tragedies, follow Oedipus' consultation of the oracle: his realization of his true identity, his self-blinding, his despair at his monstrous crimes. After Yoko and Yono fail to talk Oedipus out of harming himself, Yoko explodes, "You over-tragic weasel! Why did you do that? Because Sophocles told you? Or Jesus Christ? Or Buddha? Or Mohammed? Or George fucking Bush?" (scene 14: 73). The dialogue continues:

> YONO: Look at you: blood spattered on your beard, your eye sockets like red hail, your face contorted.
> OEDIPUS: I've punished the murderer. [*Quoting from Seneca's* Oedipus] "I've forced him to pay his debt,/ And his marriage, I've found darkness for it/ I've found the night it deserves."
> YONO: You're a mess.
> YOKO: You're bleeding all over my stage.
> OEDIPUS: Where shall I go — mother?!
> YOKO: Do what Sophocles told you to do. Go to Colonus. Or think up something for yourself.

With this brusque rejection, the Yokastas complete the unmaking of their myth, severing their story from the tale of humiliation and suffering that Sophocles and every author since him has scripted for Oedipus (and incidentally for Yokasta), which the irreverent Yoyo scoffs at as a "funny hilarious ridiculous story" (scene 14: 73). As he prepares to blind himself, Oedipus delivers a speech amalgamating the final words delivered by the chorus in Sophocles' *Oedipus the King* with a quotation from Seneca's *Oedipus*, holding himself up as lesson in human misfortune to the "people of Thebes"; in unison the Yokastas frame his speech with an emphatic "Quote!" and "Unquote!" (scene 14: 73). But, after he is berated as "an overtragic weasel" and waltzed offstage by Yoyo, Yoyo returns and adopts her Avenger Yokasta persona to deliver her own corresponding version of the speech, beginning with the same invocation to the "people of Thebes." Instead of the negative lesson concerning human limitations that Oedipus draws from his experience, Yoyo idealistically envisions every citizen, under the leadership of "brave queen Yoyo," capable of making anything (s)he want out of her/his life and able to become everything and everyone, from "hockey player" and "pope" to "freak," "waiter," "Nobel prize winner," and "porn star" (scene 14: 75). With this breathless, enthusiastic enumeration of careers and callings, the play's scripted dialogue gives way to improvisation, and the boundaries between actors and audience, and between what is staged and what is "real," are completely overrun.[18] The Yokastas create a party space on stage, while Media announces to the audience, "It seems we've run out of script." In the spirit of Yoyo's open-ended vision of infinite possibilities for the people of Thebes, he invites spectators to "come down to the stage if you like, get something to eat, talk to the actors, or just go home."

Like Ellen McLaughlin's *Helen*, Saviana Stanescu and Richard Schechner's *YokastaS* does not deliver the myth it retells to its traditional destination.

Helen does not return to Sparta with Menelaus, and Yokasta does not commit suicide in shame and disgust. A major difference in the two plays lies in the attitudes of the protagonists concerning what is supposed to happen to them. Helen wants to go home with Menelaus and is forced by his rejection to accept a new vision of her life; Yokasta, in contrast, actively seeks — and has sought all along — to live with regard for her happiness and satisfaction, in defiance of what her authors "wrote for her." What the plays share is an interest in encouraging us to consider how ancient myths and their modern equivalents, which have proliferated like the "copies" in *Helen* and have consequently taken a variety of unprecedentedly powerful forms, can influence our perceptions of the proper destinations of our own stories. This is not to say that these plays are hostile to the myths they retell — far from it. Both *Helen* and *YokastaS* pay homage to the abiding relevance of the stories of their protagonists, as they reshape them into "metamythopoetic" tales that address the phenomena in today's world that can blinker our view of what we need and what we want. As Fernando Calzadilla puts it in the final sentence of his performance review of *YokastaS*, "Yoyo's open invitation to the audience [at the play's conclusion] put responsibility about many things back into our hands: women's oppression, the war, democracy, peace, and defending our truth" (713). Indeed, like the people of Thebes in brave queen Yoyo's speech, and like the woman in the Servant's last story, we ourselves are invited by both *Helen* and *YokastaS* to become responsible for what happens next, and to unmake myths so as to remake them on our own terms.

NOTES

1. Ellen McLaughlin, *Helen, The Greek Plays*, 119–91; Saviana Stanescu and Richard Schechner, *YokastaS*, unpublished script. I am very grateful to the authors for sharing the script of *YokastaS* with me; all references to the text will follow the format of scene number, followed by page number(s).

2. In *Odyssey* 11. 271, the mother of Oedipus is called Epikaste. In having his Jocasta kill herself immediately after discovering her incestuous relationship with her son, Sophocles appears to follow the Homeric account of Epikaste's suicide (*Od.* 11. 277–80). Euripides postpones the suicide of Jocasta until after the deaths of her sons by Oedipus, Eteocles and Polyneices, perhaps in accordance with a variant version popularized by the West Greek lyric poet Stesichorus. On Euripides' possible debt to Stesichorus, see Gostoli, 23–27.

3. Text and translation are from Campbell, ed., *Greek Lyric* III, 92–93. The standard abbreviation *PMG* refers to Denis Page, ed., *Poetae Melici Graeci*.

4. Allan, ed., *Euripides: Helen*, 20–22.

5. In *Poetics* 13.1453a36–8, Aristotle asserts, "[in comedy] those who are the greatest enemies in myth, like Orestes and Aegisthus, become friends and go off at the end [of the play], with no one being killed" (my translation). The remark holds forth the possibility that, during the classical period, there may have been a comedy performed in Athens that represented Orestes making friends with Aegisthus, the murderer of Orestes' father, Agamemnon, and the lover of his mother, Clytemnestra, rather than killing him, as Orestes

is said to have done in all extant sources, beginning with *Odyssey* 1. 35–43. But it may also be that Aristotle merely uses this example to illustrate the freedom with plot developments enjoyed by ancient comedy, and not that he knew of a comedy that featured the reconciliation of Orestes and Aegisthus.

6. Case, "Classic Drag: The Greek Creation of Female Parts."

7. Segal, "Euripides' *Medea*: Vengeance, Reversal, and Closure."

8. I borrow the term "revision" from Sharon Friedman, Introduction, *Feminist Theatrical Revisions of Classic Works*, 8–9. In my view, the term as Friedman uses it (to describe the processes whereby "[feminist] theater artists observing, reflecting on their observations, and interrogating the underpinnings of their responses to works that have historical currency produce new texts that are layered and open-ended, inviting audiences to engage the process of interpretation") also aptly describes non-dramatic texts such a Wolf's and LeGuin's novels.

9. See Case, 318–9, on the representation of "Woman," not actual women, in Athenian dramas of the fifth-century BCE. Linda Hutcheon, *The Politics of Postmodernism*, 78–81, discusses "the discrepancies between the *res gestae* and the *historia rerum gestarum*" in Wolf's *Cassandra*.

10. See Case; also Foley, "Bad Women: Gender Politics in Late Twentieth-Century Performance and Revision of Greek Tragedy"; Malnig, "All Is Not Right in the House of Atreus: Feminist Theatrical Renderings of the *Oresteia*"; Ekaterini Douka-Kabitglou, "Mistresses of Mimesis: Ancient (Meta)Drama and (Post)Modern Feminism."

11. See Eisner, "Echoes of the *Odyssey* in Euripides' *Helen*."

12. McLaughlin's other important alterations to Euripides' treatment include the substitution of Io for the veteran warrior Teucer, who appears in Euripides' prologue and fills Helen in on the Greek victory at Troy, the introduction of Athena as *deus ex machina* (taking the place of Helen's apotheosized brothers, Castor and Polydeuces), and the transposition of the divine epiphany (which takes place at the end of Euripides' play) and Menelaus' arrival (which occurs in Euripides' first episode). For further discussion of McLaughlin's alterations, see Scharffenberger, performance review of Ellen McLaughlin's *Helen*.

13. Within a year of the tragedy's first performance, the "new Helen" of Euripides' *Helen* was acknowledged as such in Aristophanes, *Thesmophoriazusae* 850.

14. Samuel Butler, *The Authoress of the* Odyssey (1897), advanced the theory that the *Odyssey* was composed by a woman. See Mary Ebbott, "Butler's *Authoress* and gendered readings of the *Odyssey*," available at: http://chs.harvard.edu/wa/pageR?tn=ArticleWrapper&bdc=12&mn=1822.

15. See Zeitlin, "Dionyus in 69," especially 58–65.

16. Calzadilla, performance review of Saviana Stanescu and Richard Schechner's *YokastaS*, supplies an excellent and thorough account of the different personalities of the Yokastas and their interactions.

17. *Cf.* Caldazilla: "The lyrics are sung verbatim as in the original Broadway show although it sounded as if written for *YokastaS*" (712).

18. See Zeitlin, especially 53–66 and 64–65, on the use of improvisation and the experimental breaking of boundaries between audience and actors in *Dionysus in 69*.

WORKS CITED

Allan, William. Ed. *Euripides: Helen*. Cambridge: Cambridge University Press, 2008.

Butler, Samuel. *The Authoress of the* Odyssey. London: Longmans and Green, 1897.

Calzadilla, Fernando. Performance review of Saviana Stanescu and Richard Schechner's *YokastaS*. *Theatre Journal* 55 (2003): 710–13.

Campbell, David. Ed. *Greek Lyric* III. Cambridge, Mass.: Harvard University Press, 1991.

Case, Sue-Ellen. "Classic Drag: The Greek Creation of Female Parts." *Theatre Journal* 37.3 (1985): 317–27.

Douka-Kabitglou, Ekaterini. "Mistresses of Mimesis: Ancient (Meta)Drama and (Post)Modern Feminism." *(Dis)placing the Classical Greek Theatre*. Eds Savas Patsalidis and Elizabeth Sakellaridiou. Thessaloniki: University Studio Press, 1999. 404–18.

Ebbott, Mary. "Butler's *Authoress* and gendered readings of the *Odyssey*." Available at: http://chs.harvard.edu/wa/pageR?tn=ArticleWrapper&bdc=12&mn=1822.

Eisner, Robert. "Echoes of the *Odyssey* in Euripides' *Helen*." *Maia* 32 (1980): 31–37.

Foley, Helene. "Bad Women: Gender Politics in Late Twentieth-Century Performance and Revision of Greek Tragedy." *Dionysus Since 69: Greek Tragedy at the Dawn of the Third Millennium*." Eds. Edith Hall *et al*. Oxford: Oxford University Press, 2004. 77–111.

Friedman, Sharon. Ed. *Feminist Theatrical Revisions of Classic Works*. Jefferson, NC: McFarland, 2009.

Gostoli, Antoinette. "Some Aspects of the Theban Myth in the Lille Stesichorus." *Greek, Roman, and Byzantine Studies* 19 (1978): 23–7.

Hutcheon, Linda. *The Politics of Postmodernism*. London and New York: Routledge, 1989.

Malnig, Julie. "All Is Not Right in the House of Atreus: Feminist Theatrical Renderings of the *Oresteia*." In Friedman, 21–41.

McLaughlin, Ellen. *The Greek Plays*. New York: Theater Communications Group, 2005.

Page, Denis. Ed. *Poetae Melici Graeci*. Oxford: Oxford University Press, 1962.

Scharffenberger, Elizabeth. Performance review of Ellen McLaughlin's *Helen*. *Theatre Journal* 55 (2003): 146–8.

Segal, Charles. "Euripides' *Medea*: Vengeance, Reversal, and Closure." *Pallas* 45 (1996): 15–46.

Stanescu, Saviana, and Richard Schechner. *YokastaS*. Unpublished script, 2003.

Warner, Rex, trans. *The Medea*. In Euripides I. Eds. David Grene and Richmond Lattimore. Chicago and London: University of Chicago Press, 1955. 65–108.

Zeitlin, Froma. "Dionysus in 69." *Dionysus Since 69: Greek Tragedy at the Dawn of the Third Millennium*." Eds. Edith Hall *et al*. Oxford: Oxford University Press, 2004. 49–75.

Tina Howe and
Demetrian Seriocomedy

JEFFREY B. LOOMIS

In a pivotal scene of Tina Howe's play *Museum*, when gallery visitors furiously destroy part of an art exhibit, the playwright appears to postulate a world overwhelmed by Dionysian chaos. And, indeed, Tina Howe fully acknowledges the force of such chaos in much of our lives. Yet the particular noted scene is still not *Museum*'s absolute culmination. The actual final episode of the play leaves alone onstage Mr. and Mrs. Moe, the parents of the artist character Zachery Moe (whose works did not happen to be attacked during the afternoon's slaughtering of art). The parents tenderly express (in sign language, since they are deaf mutes) their lifelong loving commitment to their son, a boy whose all-white paintings they define, with much paradox, as ever "NOISY WITH LIFE" (*CD:4Ps* 53–54).

"NOISY ... LIFE" is a term that amasses within its connotative compass all sorts of fiery passion, and it therefore acknowledges as undeniably real such very reckless, passionate self-centeredness as had, on this play's dramatized afternoon, even toppled and ransacked expensive artifacts. Yet, in Tina Howe's full canon of work, Demetrian nurturing, suffused within other-centered *com*passion, often takes its own striking place on the stage, as in the above-described scene with Mr. and Mrs. Moe. Such compassionate caring, in Howe's work, does not curb the destructive Dionysian passions — and she, indeed, seems to recognize that the most primal maternal myths fully would own both life's pain and its balm (Sjöo and Mor 167). Still, she does sense that Demetrian solace can vitally assuage life's traumas. Demeter herself (as the mother of a woman who, however reluctantly, becomes the bride of Death) can surely, like many cosmic mother figures, confirm the human need to accept and deal with mortality (Sjöo and Mor 48–49, 180–182). Yet she emerges as a much more cheer-inspiring being in her actions that valorize nurture.

The Homeric "Hymn to Demeter," indeed, at one point describes its older goddess heroine as "like a [Dionysian] Maenad" ("HH" 237). She becomes so, and vengefully causes earth's crops to cease growing, after her daughter Persephone is abducted (and perhaps immediately raped) by her underworld-dwelling uncle, Hades, who has even had his act of girl-napping approved by the girl's father (and her mother's incestuous brother), Zeus ("HH" 229). Yet the Homeric Demeter myth also and ultimately (like Howe's plays) includes, and seemingly emphasizes (Foley 116), "bonds of intimacy" in Demeter's resolute caregiving impulses toward her offspring. The major motif in Demeter's myth is, after all, her love for her daughter — love which is eventually rewarded when her daughter is allowed to return to be with her mother for most (but not all) of the year ("HH" 240).

The Homeric "Hymn to Demeter" (probably written between 650 and 550 B.C.E. [Mylonas 3, 41; Foley 29]) is meaningfully labeled as hymnic, for its very much focused literary genre is that of a functioning liturgical narrative (or "sung prayers" [Foley 28]). Its chief goal is to announce the Eleusinian ritual Mysteries, held in the town where Demeter was supposed to have come when looking for (or simply mourning) her lost daughter. The Eleusinian Mysteries, says Helene Foley (118), allowed human beings to "be adopted by the goddess": to feel "fear" from having confronted her tale of loss and frustration, but also to experience, here and now and additionally in an afterlife, the nourishing "bliss" that she tried to pass on, both to her daughter and to the earthly boy Demophoon — for whom, during a brief season in Eleusis, she served as nurse (Foley 114–118). An advantage of the Demetrian Mysteries, Foley claims, is that people, while alive on earth, could nourish their souls through these rites not just once but often. In the afterlife they might also experience "maternal plenitude," restored "unity" with the goddess (133).

Tina Howe's plays, to a considerable degree, reveal a very similar sort of focused complexity as that for which the Homeric "Hymn to Demeter" strives. These plays, through their broad range of episodes, grant (and to both men and women) not only an awareness of life's Dionysian destructiveness, but also (and usually somewhat dominantly) an intuition of Demetrian tender "access" to the spiritualizing "relational" life (Foley 116). At times it appears that Howe even alludes, more than obliquely, to Demeter's specific chronicled mythic experiences and to her cult's specific rituals. For example, at the climax of Howe's *Approaching Zanzibar* an entire cast seems to utter a communal Eleusinian Mysteries incantation of the word "Paradise" around the deathbed of a noble and beloved family matriarch (*AZ&OPs* 76–77). A few minutes before, the old woman herself had actually launched the ritual by picking as her partner in a word game called "Geography" a young girl who resembled Persephone in her great fear of death. The jubilant old Olivia and the adolescent Pony, as they exult over *mystical* geography by hurrahing a possible realm called "Paradise," seem to acknowledge two Demetrian ritual elements. First comes the joy specifically known to women sharing communal experiences together (as ancient Greece's women importantly could do at religious ceremonies, even though they were "excluded ... from the rest of public life" [Foley 75, 140; see also Zeitlin 129]). Secondly, the shouts of "Paradise" may prophesy aged and sick Olivia's imminent passing on toward paradisal Elysium.

In a second telling dramatic motif, Howe's *The Art of Dining* shows three women characters indulging in what looks like a modern version of ancient Demetrian ritual *aischrologia* (Foley 45, 67). That term by denotative definition means "that which cannot be said" (Zeitlin 144). The term refers to the interchange of "jokes" (and especially also the lighthearted mocking of fellow cult-members' anatomical features) that were a norm of Demetrian worship. By such relatively friendly teasing, the Eleusinians affirmed, as a space in which spirituality could gradually develop, a lively, "fertility"-rich, mostly female community (Foley 73). In other words, these jests, Froma Zeitlin implies, reminded participants in the Mysteries that *unspeakable words* could be associated with their cult's deepest "religious secrets" — but that, meanwhile, even generally unspeakable "obscenity" could enshrine a sacral earthiness belonging to the rite's human participants (Zeitlin 144).[1]

Even though their tone may or may not be a joking one, the three restaurant-going women in Howe's *The Art of Dining* are comparing a vast variety of female breasts (many of them reportedly not quite perfect); they have been inspired to do so by a report that a woman was proudly "flashing" her bosom while strolling down a public thoroughfare (*CD:4Ps* 118). If they are, as a community of women, specifically mocking both social disrespect and personal shame, treating both attitudes as wrong ways to greet either female anatomy or female being, this trio of modern ladies follows the tradition of one specific character in the Homeric "Hymn to Demeter." That is the mortal maid Iambe, who tried to quell, with guffaw-inducing ribaldries, the self-centered and morose defeatism that had characterized Demeter just after her daughter had been stolen from her (Foley 79). The abject bitterness of Demeter especially had allied her story, during her early defeatist period, with the myths expressing Dionysian tragic fury. But Iambe's jocoseness quite likely helped to heal Demeter and thus prepared the way for the eventual, relatively serio*comic*, resolution of Demeter's conflict.

For four decades, while revealing a complexity of tone reminiscent of the Homeric "Hymn to Demeter," Tina Howe's plays have themselves highlighted, in part, a Dionysian sort of acquaintance with the unhappy predicaments of life that culminate in the threat of death. Howe's first published play from the 1970s, *Birth and After Birth*, might make us at first expect a jubilant

Demetrian celebration of Nicky Apple's fourth birthday party. Instead, even if he is far from equal to the cagy and somewhat cruel Dionysus who, in Euripides's *Bacchae*, threatens and then seizes the life of King Pentheus, Nicky is still played by a sizeable adult male, and his massiveness vividly illustrates how huge is the burden a child can impose on fretting and tormented parents. Meanwhile, this *Birth* play also includes some rather freakish, hardly comforting, Dionysian-toned human rituals. One is a seemingly sadistic attempt, by the Apples, to make their professional anthropologist friend Mia, a nonparent in her daily life, simulate giving birth (*AZ&OPs* 130–135). And Mia herself earlier had testified to shocking human birth practices, when she spoke of the supposed Whan See tribal women, whose ferocious version of mothering made them repeatedly re-insert their newborns back into the womb, until the children died (*AZ&OPs* 125–130).

Dramatic details such as these demonstrate that Howe senses horrifyingly maenadic responses capable of invading even traditionally sweet maternal rites — due to the stresses placed on parents', and especially on mothers', lives. On multiple other occasions, Howe depicts women engaging in behavior starkly echoing the harsher maenadic aspects of the Homeric Demeter. For instance, in *The Art of Dining*, the female chef Ellen at one point almost appears directly to mimic the angriest manifestation of Demeter, when that deity responded to her loss of Persephone by refusing to let earth's crops grow ("HH" 235–236).[2] Ellen, in mid-play, totally halts her own acts of nurture (cooking gourmet meals) and — while *"hurling pots and pans," "pick[ing] up whatever is big and throwing it across the room"* (*CD:4Ps* 100) — becomes enraged at the often-patriarchalist troublemaker who is her version of abusive Zeus and Hades: her husband, Cal.

While serving as her restaurant's official waitperson, Cal is also its business manager, and he generally cares more for the establishment's profit margin than for its food quality. He even actually diminishes quite a few of the food supplies, for he devours (casually and inattentively, while simply talking with Ellen in the kitchen) large amounts of "HOLLANDAISE SAUCE" and poached pears. Thus he forces Ellen to adjust downwards the quality of her culinary ingredients (*CD:4Ps* 100).

In Howe's play *Women in Flames*, the middle-aged playwright Isobel Graves, much like Ellen in the *Dining* play, establishes rapport with us in the audience — as we encounter, first, her worries over her current play's tryout performances, as well as her inner perplexity over her sexual attraction to the production's boyish leading man. When she is forced to take over the leading role because an actress becomes ill, we may rejoice as she wins great plaudits for her supposed histrionics. Actually, though, she seems not very much to be acting a role at all — for she has burst forth, with the wild abandon of a woman who has already lusted after him for weeks, and has passionately seized in her grasp onstage the dazzlingly handsome young male co-star. Later, however, she rebuffs this behavior, judging that her lust is of limited value in defining her total self—or even in matching well with the largely *maternal* responses that she has come to feel toward this boy. Additionally, menopausal hot flashes help coax her psychic ego to sublimate almost all sexual urges and to "give [her] body," instead, "to the flames" of newly emerging dramatic scripts (*W in F* 17, 82, 91, 105–106,117).

Howe's play *One Shoe Off* reveals another intriguing conflict between harsh Dionysian stances and a more tender Demetrian sort of behavior. The drama concludes with its primary couple shouting about their dire financial debts — and also about the frightening literal invasion of their house by almost monstrously fertile carrots, potatoes, and cabbages. This situation at first looks quite different from the Homeric Demeter story — for the goddess in that opus angrily *reduced* (and to nothing) the fertility level of natural vegetable crops. But, if we think more about the matter, we sense that Leonard and Dinah are likewise striving to quell nature's overly wild energies.[3] And, indeed, through their launching of very noisy protests, they do apparently cause at least the fierce outside winds to abate (*AZ&OPs* 211).

Such a concluding scene, set in an obviously threatened house, fittingly enough had already been prefigured earlier, when Parker, one of Dinah's and Leonard's dinner guests, arrived at their home only after having first encountered a highway accident caused by a runaway house trailer (*AZ&OPs* 164). This play, as such details indicate, may depict Tina Howe's absolutely starkest vision of malevolent forces besieging the homes (and, indeed, the entire world) of human beings. Yet Dinah also pronounces, just before her husband's and her tirade against hefty winds and other plagues of life, how she had, for years, essentially held a fortress against such harsh energies. She confesses, to be sure, a long-troubling and still-lingering adulterous desire for that evening's guest Parker. Yet she adds that she has also never dared to yield to that desire. Her husband, Leonard, then tells her (perhaps, one will admit, out of his own self-interest) that he himself perceives her to be very courageous: just as "tenacious" as the "cauliflowers" that are burgeoning underneath their house (*AZ&OPs* 210). To some degree, then, *One Shoe Off* seems to end not fully as a Dionysian outcry of sensed tragedy, but rather as a text that utters, albeit *sotto voce* and with some potential irony, more serio*comic* Demetrian moods. Even if fairly obliquely, the central couple do appear to affirm at the play's curtain the nourishing strength, the lasting bonds, of their relationship.

Dinah and Leonard thus may in spirit resemble the mother and daughter, in Howe's play *such small hands*, who found a kind of crazy unity with each other in the very final hours of the mother's dying process (*ssh* 27).[4] They also resemble *Museum*'s Mr. and Mrs. Moe, when that couple rejoices lovingly over their son's exhibited art even while they are standing near a less fortunate, almost-completely-vandalized, gallery exhibit (*CD:4Ps* 53–54). The Homeric Demeter, who appears vitally to discover that vengeful rage may actually have less real power than does resilient tenderness, would for that reason probably admire the lovingly parental Moes. Like my friend the Rev. Michael Kyle, when he saw Howe's play performed, Demeter might deem *Museum* to prove that "love alone survives apocalypse."

*   *   *

At an earlier stage in its character development, however, The Homeric "Hymn to Demeter" powerfully proclaims, as do also most Tina Howe plays, some rather dark observations about how life cannot ever fully escape catastrophe and its inevitable price of loss. Right away in the "Hymn," Demeter's beloved Persephone learns, alas, that "picking flowers along a soft meadow" is not merely a frolic, but also a "snare."[5] A lustrous "narcissus" so entrances her love of beauty as to make her inattentive to her surroundings, and it thus also makes her vulnerable to be "snatched," unawares, by the fleetly-riding, malevolently-motivated Hades, god of the underworld. He suddenly takes her away from those flowers, and from all other earthly bounties besides ("HH" 228–229).

In Howe's *Approaching Zanzibar*, little Pony Blossom seems to be surnamed for the very posies that in her life, too, symbolize both alluring and dangerous beauties. Pony had longed to avoid her family's cross-country trip to visit her dying great-aunt, the ironically surnamed (but, as a result, Pony's rather closely allied binary) Olivia *Childs* (emphasis mine). Like many a youngster, Pony dreadfully fears the notion of encountering, in someone like Olivia's obviously mortal presence, the force of death. And yet we note very early that Pony is herself an analogue to Death's prematurely abducted myth-figure Persephone — for we see her spontaneously picking, and even *eating*, flowers (*AZ&OPs* 18–20). She will again eat them, as also will the bedridden Olivia, at play's end (70.)[6] Thus there are marked patterns linking both the plots and themes of the Homeric "Hymn to Demeter" and Howe's *Zanzibar*—even if Howe has made the child, rather than the old lady, her protagonist. Howe's play is not so centrally Demeter's story as the Homeric "Hymn to Demeter" is. Yet the playwright does manage to show, more directly and exuberantly perhaps than the "Hymn" does, the vital ultimate, seriocomic, communal celebration of life together by a Demetrian crone and her ingénue descendant.

The Homeric "Hymn to Demeter," when depicting the reunion of Demeter and Persephone, shows us a much-enhanced calm in Demeter's mind after many story pages in which she has behaved mostly like a stormy harridan. She also now integrates herself with the human community of Eleusis by initiating the Eleusinian Mysteries. Yet, of course, even at the close of her tale, Demeter has to admit that she has not regained her daughter, Persephone, completely. The girl will be hers only for "two-thirds" of the year, with the "third part" of Persephone's "revolving year" to be spent "in the gloomy depths below" ("HH" 240).

Likewise, in Howe's dramas, before the final curtain scenes, and even during them, in spite of their (usually) quasi-positive closure, dark moods remain. Howe has a truly exceptional gift for comical farce, but she is, nonetheless, a *serio*-comic scribe. As with Olivia Childs at the end of *Approaching Zanzibar*, disease and the approach of death do frequently hamper other Howe characters' approaches to climactic jubilation. Rennie in *Chasing Manet* and Gardner in *Painting Churches* both appear victims of Alzheimer's disease; Walter in *Rembrandt's Gift* suffers from obsessive-compulsive disorder; Mabel Tidings Bigelow in *Pride's Crossing* has multiple dire physical ailments (*CM* 92–93; *CD:4Ps* 172; "R's G" 125; *P's C* 46–47, 106, 110–111). *The Art of Dining* portrays eating disorders that resemble bulimia, in Tony Stassio, and anorexia, in Elizabeth Barrow Colt — while combined anorexic and bulimic tendencies seem to have characterized the youthful Mags from *Painting Churches* (*CD:4Ps* 92–94, 101, 158–163; Backes 41–60). Playwright Isobel Graves in *Women in Flames* has experienced during her life multiple mental sanatorium "time outs" — while Holly Dancer and her friends in *Coastal Disturbances* also often seem trammeled by either neurasthenia or full-scale mental breakdowns (*W in F* 9; *CD:4Ps* 197, 204).

Yet, despite an array of somber circumstances, Holly and her companions remain friends — and, as a women's community, give lasting solace to each other. Indeed, women's need for communal relationships is, as a key Demetrian theme, amply present throughout Howe's work. The theme appears in Howe's presentation of groups of young women in *Coastal Disturbances*, middle-aged women in *The Art of Dining*, geriatric women in *Chasing Manet* and *Pride's Crossing*, and mixed groups of relatively or very young and much older women in *Approaching Zanzibar*, *Painting Churches*, and *such small hands*. It is clear that Howe firmly believes in women's community fellowship as a means for blessing even highly constrained female lives.

Sometimes, like the Homeric "Hymn to Demeter," Howe's dramas closely focus on specific mother-daughter struggles — as in *such small hands*, *Painting Churches*, some early scenes in *Pride's Crossing*, and the Elizabeth Barrow Colt segments of *The Art of Dining*.[7] Writing of the Demeter myth, Carl Jung, Nancy Chodorow, and Helene Foley all note that it corresponds well with the ways in which mothers and daughters, in all sorts of societies, consistently rely very closely on each other (Chodorow 243–265; Foley 119, 128). Howe would certainly seem to share this view — even though her mother and daughter characters, most definitely women of our troubled contemporary era, together experience quite frequent dysfunctional tensions, bickerings, and even calcified spite. By contrast, however much suffering of separation the Homeric Demeter and Persephone endured, they seem more idealized personages, always apparently knowing that they felt immense love and need for each other.

Howe's characters most often actually find their major women's communities in other realms than the immediate family: at a beach (*Coastal Disturbances*); at restaurant mealtimes (*The Art of Dining*); in nursing homes (*Chasing Manet*). When Mabel Tidings Bigelow in *Pride's Crossing* cannot solicit adequate support for her English Channel swimming ventures from her own mother, she turns, instead, to the family's servant women — in order to obtain from them the bolstering of spirit that her ambition so much needs (*P's C* 99).

As Helene Foley points out (131), there do exist for Demeter, too, extended female communities beyond her immediate family: Hecate and Rhea among Demeter's associate goddesses; Metaneira's daughters among mortals. But the focus on the central two mother-daughter goddesses Demeter and Persephone remains dominant in the Homeric "Hymn to Demeter" — whereas only in *Painting Churches* (the Mags-Fanny portions of that script) and in *such small hands* do mother-daughter relations monopolize Howe's stage.

Howe actually is often very intrigued, besides, by mother-*son* interactions. Take, for example, Ariel Took's occasional encomiums of praise for her son Winston, even though that boy is frequently quite the frisky brat. Winston does provide, or so Ariel testifies, enormous amounts of aid to her in such projects as crocheting a gigantic afghan (*CD:4Ps* 241). Consider, also, Charlotte Blossom's mimicking of her son Turner (and not, as one would have expected, miming of her daughter Pony). She does this as the Blossoms engage in an odd family activity (somewhat *aischrologic* in nature?) where all participants choose to imitate, generally with abundant low-key mocking, the style and language of others in their hearthside group (*CD:4Ps* 52–57).

Howe's representation of mother-son relations actually, of course, does have a parallel in the Demeter myth. When she disguises herself as the nursemaid Doso and cares for the human Metaneira's infant son Demophoon ("HH" 231–235), Demeter demonstrates in that one key instance her interest both in human children and specifically in a male child.

Demeter appears to be quite sincere in her caregiving for Metaneira's little boy ("HH" 232–234). Yet Metaneira balks at seeing Demeter/Doso heating Demophoon at night in the fireplace in order to immortalize him — making him, indeed, a lad who "grew and flourished before his time." In her tempestuous consternation over seeing her son "in the fire, like a brand," Metaneira shouts out and causes Demeter to become equally, or probably even more, exasperated than Metaneira, so that the goddess deliberately drops Demophoon onto the floor. Contending that "Mortals are ignorant and stupid who cannot foresee the fate both good and bad that is in store," Demeter then asserts that she "would have granted him imperishable honor, but now as it is he will not be able to escape death and the Fates" ("HH" 234). She seems here to be providing a potential etiology for all tragic visions of existence: i.e., "the Fates," she proclaims, just cannot be evaded. One supposes that she could even be interpreted as turning highly maenadic and justifying as inevitable large amounts of both earthly and cosmic violence. Yet this last and rather dire exegesis ultimately seems a bit overextended. The Demophoon episode is definitely dialogical: its narrator seems to affirm nurturing whole-heartedly, but still also observes the human and perhaps cosmic imperfection that limits the success of many a would-be nurturer. Still, in terms of the entire Homeric "Hymn," the parallels are very, very strong between the nurturing of Persephone, the divine child, and Demeter's nurturing of the little earthly boy Demophoon. Hence, one might justifiably subordinate the "Hymn"'s undeniable motifs of some Dionysian violence to its contrasting, but eventually its ultimate, affirmations of Demetrian care.

In general, after all, goddess Demeter has only found her way to earthly queen Metaneira's home because she is anxious to rebuff the violent male gods and their patriarchal realm. Irked that both Zeus, by approving Persephone's abduction, and Hades, by performing that abduction, had proved to be disgustingly unsupportive as brothers ("HH" 229), when posing as Doso, not surprisingly, she represented herself as having been "carried away" by patriarchal "pirates" from her proclaimed original home of Crete. She went with them, she claimed, "not willingly but against [her] wishes," letting them become her "overbearing masters" ("HH" 231).

Although she has received some criticism for not being a militant enough feminist (Farfan 33–50), Tina Howe's plays do really abound in basic, and deeply sincere, feminist concern. In opposing patriarchs' crude manipulation of, and frequent disdain for, females, Howe resembles any other modern feminist — and even somewhat the mythic Demeter herself, in that goddess's wrathful opposition to patriarchs' abduction of her daughter. We sense the oppression of twentieth-century patriarchy when Mabel Tidings Bigelow in *Pride's Crossing* gives up a continued relationship with the man she truly loves, Jewish athlete David Bloom, because her anti-semitic male relatives would likely never fully approve of him (*P's C* 78–80, 102). In *Coastal Disturbances* Ariel Took has divorced Fisher, a man who, she laments, "gave [her] enough 'male companionship' to last a lifetime" (*CD:4Ps* 203). The main character of *Women in Flames*, Isobel, has to admit that her ex-husband was "the love of [her] life," but that she would still *"rather crawl through a field of white maggots!"* than reunite with him (*W in F* 111).

Even a male character who apparently loves his wife fairly ardently, Cal in *The Art of Dining*, would willingly tear down the couple's own bedroom walls in order to expand their home-located restaurant's available dining space (*CD:4Ps* 107). When, in the same play, the trio of women restaurant customers together discuss the varied appearance of breasts, they may be, as according to my earlier interpretation of the text, contented *aischrologia*-shouting Demetrians: gals who admit that flaws just exist and must be acknowledged, in mammaries and elsewhere. Yet, in a variant interpretation, their outcry, "WHAT CAN WE DO ABOUT IT?" (*CD:4Ps* 119), also sounds potentially like the frequent lament of women against patriarchal men's demeaning scorn of female anatomies.

One feminist by whom Howe was especially influenced (Barlow 171) is Virginia Woolf.[8] From Woolf she adopts considerable emphasis on the concept of human androgyny — something we can see operating in such motifs as Cal's and David Osslow's highly surprising familiarity with the nature of clothing fabrics in *The Art of Dining*, or in the tender nursing of wounds that is displayed both by highly masculine lifeguard Leo Hart in *Coastal Disturbances* and by the young heartthrob actor Billy in *Women in Flames* (*CD:4Ps* 90, 216–218; *W in F* 14–16). *Women in Flames* protagonist Isobel also comments on young Billy's "tender, yet manly" "trajectory" as he "lifted [an accident victim] up in his arms" (*W in F* 17). Meanwhile, part of the punning in the title of *Pride's Crossing* refers to cross-dressing, and across-gender-casting, among the actors in its roster of roles (*P's C* x–xii).

This exposure of male psychological androgyny is just one measure that Howe has employed in order actively to battle against patriarchal sexism. A declared goal at the time when she wrote *Coastal Disturbances* in 1987 was actually "to redress the way men are perceived onstage these days in American theater" — as "raging, lost souls" (qtd. in Bennetts H-3). Howe longed, instead, as often as possible "to write about men who love women" (qtd. in Bennetts H-3). I have, indeed, heard her claim (and evidently sincerely so) considerable degrees of respect for all the male characters in *Coastal Disturbances*—and this even though Dr. Hamilton Adams evidently has a history of adulterous womanizing; even though lifeguard Leo Hart may be too impulsive and sexually demonstrative, and even though art gallery owner André Sor often sounds smarmily "manipulative" in dealing with his supposed and yet reluctant girlfriend Holly (Bennetts H-3; *CD:4Ps* 208–209, 235–241, 245).

Given such abilities to appreciate even moderately flawed men, Tina Howe has fairly often proved able also to portray a potential beneficence in marital relations. To be sure, she does have her character Isobel Graves praise Dickens's Miss Havisham in *Great Expectations* as an unmarried, independent, "[f]laming older woman," someone who was, because of her independence, wrongly despised by society as fully "unsavory" and "freak[ish]" (*W in F* 69). Yet, while the couples in *Painting Churches* and *Rembrandt's Gift* suffer from traumatizing disease, and while in *Approaching Zanzibar* the wife confronts menopause and the musician husband a paucity of creative inspiration (*AZ&OPs* 15, 23), all these characters do obviously still have viable and helpful marital partnerships. Even if Hamilton Adams may have sometimes been a womanizer, his wedding anniversary celebration picnic with his wife causes young Leo Hart, when he observes the old couple together, to leap up and run off, several states away, in order to hunt out his own potential bride, Holly (*CD:4Ps* 248–250).

Hence, if she were to travel back in time, Tina Howe might well be expected to tell the author of the Homeric "Hymn to Demeter" that marriage may indeed be imperfect, but that it is still often abundantly worthwhile. And that ancient "Hymn"'s author, it appears, would have probably concurred with her. After all, interpreting the Homeric "Hymn to Demeter," Helene Foley does judge that the work's portrayal of the mother-daughter goddesses "hints strongly," from its launching point, "at Persephone's readiness for marriage": a marriage that she eventually cannot, in any case, "escape," and which she accepts more readily for the "Hymn"'s having very largely set itself "within the context of a human world where marriage with all its variations is a fundamental aspect of the cultural system" (Foley 89, 107, 109).[9] Marriage is not, in the "Homeric Hymn to Demeter," rejected — although it nearly is so in some divergent versions of this Demeter-Persephone myth. In those texts the virgin goddesses Artemis and Athena, for instance, strive hard to keep Persephone from giving in to what looks like her evidently certain marital fate with Hades (Foley 33).

Ultimately, though, the expression of attitudes concerning marriage does not seem to constitute the final purpose behind the Homeric "Hymn to Demeter." Supremely, this manifestation of the myth focuses, most of all, on the very same core concern most central in Tina Howe's plays: the affirmation of a vital, dynamic, life-heralding spirituality.

As a drama scholar, I cannot but feel very satisfied to learn that a pageant recalling the long struggles of Demeter and Persephone to achieve even a partial reunion with each other probably was featured as part of the Eleusinian Demetrian rituals. As George Mylonas analyzes the phenomenon, the "passion play" pageant's goal was "to unfold the myth of the Goddesses to the initiates [in the Mysteries] but also to make these initiates partakers of the experiences of the Goddesses, to share with them the distress, the travail, the exultation, and the joy which attended the loss of Persephone and her reunion with the mother" (Mylonas 282). Not surprisingly, Aristotle, so renowned to us for defining the affective experiences of dramatic audiences (Golden 287), once declared that the Eleusinian Mysteries initiates would "not" so much "learn" from their experience as they would, through that experience, like theatergoers, most saliently simply "suffer, ... feel, ... experience certain impressions and psychic moods" (qtd. in Mylonas 262). Perhaps quite in keeping with a cult whose practitioners were sworn to much secrecy, Foley only somewhat vaguely defines the cult's ultimate purpose as being to help one "acquire" a "better lot" in both "life" and "afterlife" (80). And Mylonas cannot seemingly be much more precise than Foley about what Demetrian religion promised to its followers, although he does aver that Elysian fields *might* have been proclaimed to them as their possible, but not their certain, destination. Still, "[this religion] holds," Mylonas says, "no punishment for the uninitiated and only the promise of good things for the mystai" (Mylonas 282). It mostly appears (as Howe's modern spirituality seems to me)[10] anxious to develop human compassion and hope.

Tina Howe has regularly evoked compassion and hope, viewing them as like constantly necessary calisthenics for the human spirit. For example, she has Pony and Turner Blossom, in one scene of *Approaching Zanzibar*, awake at night in a campground far from civilization to realize that their parents have walked away from the family compound. After only a slight panicky and petulant delay, Pony and Turner begin, for the most part, to try to cheer each other up, and thus they make the imaginary threat of invading beasts seem less terrifying. Then, upon stepping outside of the tent themselves, the two siblings suddenly encounter in the sky, with epiphanic tremblings of awe, a paradisal "*starlit night*" (*AZ&OPs* 40–41). Compassion and hope have led to spiritual vision. And Howe makes her recent nursing home play, *Chasing Manet*, sound as if it offers a similar potential experience when she speaks, most tellingly, of its "far-flung journeys of the departing soul" (qtd. in Cohen C2).

At their final curtains Howe's plays do not conclude with ecstasies of absolute happiness. And yet compassion and hope always still feature in them. Cal and Ellen, for example, reconcile their differences and celebrate a communal party with their restaurant customers (*The Art of Dining: CD:4Ps* 122–126). Sandy Apple appears, eventually, to rejoice once again in her life as mother despite the patent tensions likely still to be involved in that life (*Birth and After Birth: AZ&OPs* 140–141). Olivia Childs, Catherine Sargent, and Mabel Tidings Bigelow come to look upon death as a mere vestibule space: a liminal region, stretching out toward realms of fuller spiritual transcendence (*AZ&OPs* 76–77; *CM* 92–93; *P's C* 106). And not one of Howe's plays ends without either expressing dreams about a future swathed in love (*Pride's Crossing, Chasing Manet, Rembrandt's Gift*); or wistful memories of past love (*Birth*

and After Birth, Museum, Painting Churches, such small hands); or joyful out-
cries at grand new discoveries of love (*Coastal Disturbances, Approaching Zanzibar*); or ritual affirmation of communities endowed with love (*The Art of
Dining, One Shoe Off*). Ultimately, too, the community of love that Howe
affirms perhaps most of all is that of humane artists: those who can move past
mere throes of Dionysian frenzy to affirm, with the *Women in Flames* character
Aida Montenegro, "the work that reminds us what it is to be human. To
wound and forgive, to suffer and laugh" (*W in F* 36).

Tina Howe created Aida Montenegro, it would seem, as a *raisonneur:* a
spokesperson for Howe's own artistic philosophy. Aida's credos, after all, surely
remind one of those that seem to define Howe herself. Due to Howe's resolute
honesty about life's rather tough and constant battles, she does often reveal
expressive tonalities much like the darkest ones featured in the mythic Demeter
story — so that we encounter in her plays a "wound[ed]" and "wound[ing],"
indeed often a fairly grim, Dionysian-maenadic voice. Still, Howe does generally prove, at the last, a jocose Iambe, or even a rather fully solacing disciple
of Demeter. Her work can thus help us, even as we "suffer," both to "forgive"
and (at least *serio*comically) to know joy in our commonly experienced gift
of human "laugh[ter]."

NOTES

1. At the same time, however, George Mylonas (256) speaks of a different variety of
aischrologia —when males, instead of females, stood on the bridge approaching Eleusis and
mocked *male* initiates into the Mysteries, evidently with the goal of keeping those gentlemen
humble before they entered the divine ceremonies in which they would engage.

2. Although such does not seem to be the case with the tale's treatment in the "Homeric
Hymn to Demeter," Demeter's reputed etiological link to the agricultural cycles of planting,
growth, and harvest is often deemed, as it is by myth historians Morford and Lenardon
(241), the central application of the ancient story. See Allaire Chandor Brumfield's full-
length book on Demeter's agricultural festivals.

3. In this example nature's energies may, admittedly, have become more identified with
Dionysus than with Demeter. Impulsive, overly zesty plant life appears to convey, especially
as a symbol of dilemma for Leonard's and Dinah's marriage, the barrier-busting vigor
(sometimes quite amoral) of *Eros* as life-force (Lamont 20).

4. Since the daughter in *such small hands* is caring for the expiring mother, however,
Demeter and Persephone analogues are a bit reversed from the norm.

5. Foley informs us that ancient Greeks considered "meadows" to be "liminal sites,"
places associated with both the boundary experience of sexual awakening and the boundary
experience of dying. She adds that the "narcissus," in ancient Greek culture, was deemed
a "soporific" flower, associated with "torpor and death" (33).

6. It seems that the actual *eating* of the flowers hints at the little girl's innate (but probably unaware) acceptance of death (and also aged Olivia's similar acceptance of mortal
limits). The devoured flowers thus function somewhat like the pomegranate seed that
Hades makes Persephone swallow in order to guarantee, in the original myth, that she will
remain with him as his mate ("HH" 239; Foley 120).

7. The impression is given, in *The Art of Dining*, where nerve-wracked authoress Eliz-

abeth talks in loudly voiced jitteriness about her parents, that Mr. Colt, the businessman father, may have insisted upon conversation at the dinner table, but that he probably led the conversations as a pontificator — "talk[ing] a blue streak" (*CD:4Ps* 115), but doing so while quite detached emotionally from the women in his life (one of whom, young Elizabeth, could not comfortably eat and thus gave numerous reasons to be excused from the dinner table [*CD:4Ps* 93]). Meanwhile, Elizabeth's mother, when forced to cook, was liable to injure herself with knives, whether deliberately or accidentally (*CD:4Ps* 115–116).

8. Knowing that I have focused in other essays on her clear links with Woolf (Loomis, "Moments," 46–55; Loomis, "Howe, Tina," 221–222; Loomis, *"Pride's Crossing,"* 385–386), Howe has personally told me that she reads Woolf's novel *Between the Acts* at least once annually.

9. When Demeter, disguised as Doso, first meets the women of Eleusis, she comments to them that "all those who dwell in homes of Olympus [should] grant that you have husbands and bear children just as parents desire" ("HH" 231).

10. To me, that spirituality looks to be a non-sectarian, syncretist, openness. It acknowledges many variants of the mystical — like that splendor which arrives in *Museum* when Tink Solheim serendipitously discovers the spot on Agnes Vaag's mini-sculptures from which Bach organ music can stream forth into the art gallery, so that the mixed media plentitude of the aesthetic experience can lead some characters to quote from the Christian gospels, others to recite Japanese haiku, and all to feel how "beautiful" and life-culminating their moment together feels (*CD:4Ps* 45–46).

WORKS CITED

Backes, Nancy. "Body Art: Hunger and Satiation in the Plays of Tina Howe." *Making a Spectacle: Feminist Essays on Contemporary Women's Theatre.* Ed. Lynda Hart. Ann Arbor: University of Michigan Press, 1989. 41–60.

Barlow, Judith. "An Interview with Tina Howe." *Studies in American Drama, 1945–Present* 4 (1989): 159–175.

Bowlby, Rachel. *Feminist Destinations and Further Essays on Virginia Woolf.* Edinburgh: Edinburgh University Press, 1997.

Brumfield, Allaire Chandor. *The Attic Festivals of Demeter and Their Relation to the Agricultural Year.* Salem, N.H.: Ayer, 1981.

Chodorow, Nancy. "Family Structure and Feminine Personality." In Foley, 243–265.

Cohen, Patricia. "A Friend-and-Family Network of Inspirations." *New York Times* 9 April 2009: C2.

Euripides. "The Bacchae." Trans. William Arrowsmith. *Euripides V.* Chicago: University of Chicago Press, 1959. 141–222.

Farfan, Penny. "From *Birth and After Birth* to *One Shoe Off.* Tina Howe and the Uses of Feminism." *American Drama* 9.1 (Fall 1999): 33–50.

Foley, Helene, ed. *The Homeric "Hymn to Demeter": Translation, Commentary, and Interpretive Essays.* Princeton, N. J.: Princeton University Press, 1994.

Golden, Leon. "Aristotle on Comedy." *Journal of Aesthetics and Art Criticism* 42 (1984): 283–290.

"Homeric Hymn to Demeter." In Morford and Lenardon, 228–241. ("HH")

Howe, Tina. *Approaching Zanzibar and Other Plays.* New York: Theatre Communications Group, 1995. (*AZ&OPs*)

_____. *Chasing Manet.* Manuscript, May–October 2007. Used by permission of Tina Howe. (*CM*)

_____. *Coastal Disturbances: Four Plays.* New York: Theatre Communications Group, 1989. (*CD:4Ps*)

_____. *Pride's Crossing.* New York: Theatre Communications Group, 1998. (*P's C*)

_____. "Rembrandt's Gift." *Humana Festival 2002: The Complete Plays,* ed. Tanya Palmer and Amy Wegener. Hanover, N. H.: Smith and Kraus, 2002. 80–125. ("R's G")

_____. *such small hands.* Final draft, July 2003. Used by permission of Tina Howe. (*ssh*)

_____. *Women in Flames.* November 14, 2004 Draft. Used by permission of Tina Howe. (*W in F*)

Lamont, Rosette C. "After Ionesco: The Surrealist Comedy of Tina Howe." *Theater Week* 3 May 1993: 19–20.

Loomis, Jeffrey B. "Howe, Tina." *The Facts on File Companion to American Drama.* Ed. Jackson R. Bryer and Mary C. Hartig. New York: Facts on File, 2004. 221–222.

_____. "Moments That Fade, Love That Abides in Tina Howe's *Painting Churches.*" *American Drama* 16.2 (Summer 2007): 46–55.

_____. "*Pride's Crossing.*" *The Facts on File Companion to American Drama.* Ed. Jackson R. Bryer and Mary C. Hartig. New York: Facts on File, 2004. 385–386.

Morford, Mark P. O. and Robert J. Lenardon. *Classical Mythology.* New York and London: Longman, 1985.

Mylonas, George E. *Eleusis and the Eleusinian Mysteries.* Princeton, NJ: Princeton University Press, 1961.

Sjöö, Monica and Barbara Mor. *The Great Cosmic Mother: Rediscovering the Religion of the Earth.* San Francisco: Harper, 1991.

Zeitlin, Froma I. "Cultic Models of the Female: Rites of Dionysus and Demeter." *Arethusa: American Classical Studies in Honor of J.-P. Vernant* 15:1&2 (Spring and Fall 1982): 129–157.

Children of Yemayá and the American Eshu

West African Myth in African-American Theatre

KEVIN J. WETMORE, JR.

> The true purpose of the theater is to create Myths, to express life in its immense, universal aspect, and from that life to extract images in which we find pleasure in discovering ourselves... May it free *us*, in a Myth in which we have sacrificed our little human individuality, like Personages out of the Past, with powers rediscovered in the Past.
> — Antonin Artaud, *The Theater and Its Double*[1]

West African myth is prevalent in modern West African drama, such as Obotunde Ijimere's *The Imprisonment of Obatala* (Nigeria) and Efua Sutherland's *The Marriage of Anansewa* (Ghana), and, of course, the plays of Nobel Laureate Wole Soyinka, who states that African tragedy arises out of "the mysteries of Ogun," even as Greek tragedy arises out of the worship of Dionysus, to name but a few.[2] It informs such new-world drama as Abdias do Nascimento's *Sortilege (Black Mystery)* and *Sortilege II: Zumbi Returns* (Brazil) and Derek Walcott's *Dream on Monkey Mountain* (St. Lucia).

Richard Priebe reminds us that the two dominant modes in West African literature are the "realist" and the "mythical" (xii). The mythical mode is "metaphorical and paradoxical" but also "the dominant one in West African elite literature," yet the two modes are "complementary rather than exclusive" and are not always separated even within a single text (Priebe xii–xiii). This description could also apply to many new-world texts that employ African-based myths; the mythical and the realistic modes blend.[3]

Similarly, Martin Owusu identifies four categories of the use of myth in African drama: straightforward dramatization "with little or no reinterpretation by the dramatist," dramatization as metaphor for contemporary social or cultural issues, as plot device, and the transformation of Western myth into African experience (16–18). In the Americas, the use of African myth in drama is a reversal of Owusu's final category: the transformation of African myth into African-American experience or, alternately, the transformation of African-American experience into African myth. When African Americans employ African myth, they are engaging in very different cultural work than when Americans of any ethnicity adapt ancient Greek myth, or Native American stories, or Norse mythology. African-American use of African myth is often an attempt to link to a Motherland severed by the Middle Passage, which means that it is a form of identity creation and historical connection.

These transformations between African and American are made more complex and complicated, however, by the syncretic religions of the New World, which developed when Yoruba *orisha* worship was combined with national variations of Roman Catholicism to make new faiths such as Voudun, Santeriá, Candomblé, and Macumba.[4] The centuries-old presence of African religious belief and practice in the New World means that African-American playwrights adapting African myth to the American stage might not be adapting strictly "African" myths, but part of the lived experience of African Americans as well. This aspect also demonstrates the complexity and difficulty of engaging with "myth" as a concept. One person's "myth" is another person's belief system. African-American writers employing African myth attempt to link to a culture from which they have been disconnected. Yet practitioners of Voudun, Santeriá, and Candomblé believe, and the stories of the orisha are not myths in the Western sense. Witness the reaction of even mainstream American Christians when atheists refer to Christ or the Nativity as a "myth"—the word itself is seen as offensive when applied to a genuinely held living belief system. No one still worships Dionysus, Zeus, or Apollo, but there is a very large global population that worships Ogun, Shango, Oya, and Yemayá.

We face even more of a challenge when looking at Yoruba cosmology in African-American theatre. African-American culture is both inside and outside Western modernity and culture as a result of forced enculturation. African-American culture is also both inside and outside traditional African culture. Just as Voudon and Santeriá are syncretic faiths, African-American use of African "myth" might just be a form of syncretic theatre.

All of these suppositions are borne out in the plays of African-American playwright Tarell Alvin McCraney, whose "Brother/Sister Trilogy" (the three plays *In the Red and Brown Water*, *The Brothers Size*, and *Marcus, or the Secret of Sweet*), which has had multiple productions since 2006, both individually and as a full trilogy, draws upon both Yoruba myth and New World variations on those myths.[5] A statement at the front of the published script of *The*

Brother/Sister Plays reads, " *The Brother/Sister Plays* draws on elements, icons and stories from the Yoruba cosmology."[6] Yet in a 2009 interview in *American Theatre*, McCraney contradicts this by stating, "You can trace the myths to Africa, but that's not how I learned them. The *orisha* stories I learned are American myths, not West African stories" (qtd. in Gener, 26). In other words, in different texts McCraney has posited different origins for these plays — African and African American. It seems fair and accurate to state that the *Brother/Sister Plays* are both African and American in their use of myth, or, more accurately, African transculturated into American. The stories of the *orisha* are the stories of New World Africans, to steal a phrase from Marta Moreno Vega (154).

The Yoruban mythological origin of the stories is not abundantly apparent from the plays. If one did not know the stories, or recognize that many characters are named after *orisha*, or did not see either the program note or the published script notation that the plays are based on Yoruban myth, one might not know that one was encountering African culture or Americanized Yoruban culture because it is not stated overtly in the text. New World African use of Yoruba cosmology is both local and transnational. In this essay, after a brief overview of Yoruban cosmology, I propose to examine McCraney's different uses of New World African myth in *The Brother/Sister Plays* and their effect, and then use Henry Louis Gates's theory of the Signifying Monkey to consider McCraney as an American Eshu, a trickster figure who also links the worlds of the profane and the divine.

More than thirteen million West Africans were brought to the Americas between the sixteenth and nineteenth centuries (Vega 154).[7] As LaVinia Delois Jennings writes, "Those who arrived on the shores of the American South as human cargo during the transatlantic slave trade brought with them many individual and collective beliefs" (86). The predominant belief system of the New World Africans (bearing in mind, as Jennings notes, that there is no "monolithic African worldview") is rooted in Yoruban cosmology (Jennings 1). In this belief system, humans interact with the *orisha*: anthropomorphized spirits and deities who mediate between the Supreme Being/Ultimate Reality (Olorun) and humanity. The *orisha* have different powers and different domains over which they rule, which continue to develop in the modern world. Ogun, for example, is the *orisha* of iron and those who work with metal. As a result, he is also the *orisha* of taxi-drivers, pilots, and others who work with and inside things made of metal. Shango is the *orisha* of lightning, which means that computers, televisions, and other things that run on electricity also fall within his purview. Yemayá is a mother goddess who is also the *orisha* of water and water journeys, which makes her the protector of those who endured the Middle Passage. Many of these *orisha* have variant names in New World African versions of the *orisha* faith. Yemayá is also known as Yemoja. Eshu-Elegba, a trickster deity, among other attributes, is also known as Eshu-Eleggua or Papa Legba.[8]

There are many stories of the *orisha*, their origins, their history, and how they function in the world. The *orisha* are present and active in the world, and one might visit a diviner to learn their wishes. *Orisha* worship is votive: one may influence their behavior by offering gifts and sacrifices in exchange for protection, favor, or a change of destiny. This aspect of *orisha* worship is a constant in both Africa and the New World.[9]

The *orisha* themselves frequently undergo experiences which then serve as the basis for stories not only to explain how and why the world is the way it is, but to give insight into the experiences of the people who worship them. Wole Soyinka refers to the *orisha* as "the tolerant gods" and "the very embodiment of Tolerance" ("The Tolerant Gods" 40). He sees them as models for an intolerant world. The *orisha* are "bridges between the living and the ancestor world," which also makes them bridges between the New World and the Motherland ("The Tolerant Gods" 44). Lastly, "Orisa is community" (49). The role of the *orisha* is to repair tears in the fabric of the world. Soyinka also sees the origins of drama and theatre in the *orisha* themselves. In "The Fourth Stage: Through the Mysteries of Ogun to the Origin of Yoruba Tragedy," Soyinka posits the origins of African theatre in the *orisha* Ogun, whom he calls "the first actor" (55). It is from the *orisha* that drama comes, and it is through the *orisha* that the world might be healed. I will not here outline the specific *orisha* present in McCraney's plays, but will do so below. I would posit here, however, that McCraney uses *orisha*, as Soyinka does, to bring about tolerance within the African-American community, bridge the Motherland and the New World, mythologize the African-American community and the lives of rural Blacks, and theatricalize the lived experiences of people of color in the New World through stories of the *orisha*.

McCraney "has devoted a good portion of his playwriting life to re-envisioning African-American theatre by reconnecting with, recuperating and creatively modifying the visual and verbal fragments of those *orisha* retentions" (26), writes Randy Gener, although this particular phrasing is problematic. *Orisha* retentions are not "fragments," but a complete syncretic faith, westernized yet linked to Yoruban religious practice. McCraney himself notes their multicultural and global nature in the New World, citing a painting of the Virgin Mary in Miami that is simultaneously a painting of Yemayá, the mother goddess of water of the Yoruba and the protector of those who were taken on the Middle Passage in New World variants of *orisha* worship: "They are actually one and the same.... The merging created something new that is neither West African nor European" (Gener 26). McCraney's plays similarly merge

West African myth with Euro-American dramaturgy, although he also maintains some African dramaturgical practices as well.

McCraney does not so much present "Yoruba myth" on stage (as noted above, there is nothing inherent in the plays to suggest that they are about gods or mythic heroes), as mythologize the lives of rural African Americans and link them to a much larger global culture. He uses various dramaturgical devices to give a mythic quality to the plays while simultaneously locating them in the realistic lived experiences of rural African Americans. He employs *orisha* names and qualities ascribed to the *orisha* for his characters. Lastly, underlying the narratives, McCraney uses stories from the *orisha* tradition, but transforms them into "something new that is neither West African nor European."

The trilogy is set in the "distant present" in Louisiana (McCraney 10). Similarly, in most cultures, myth is set in the "distant present" as well as the prehistoric past. The moment of myth is always present, but the events of myth are ahistoric. Myths happened in the historic now. The trilogy itself is also not linked linearly, with one play directly following another. The three plays use several of the same characters and track their experiences over the course of a generation, but the entire narrative does not tell the story of a single individual or group. Instead, it is a collection of events that together create a world, not unlike myth, while tracking the effects of the events through generations. (The plays of the *Oresteia* similarly track events and characters through decades and generations — Orestes is an infant in *Agamemnon* and the central character of *Eumenides*.) Lastly, McCraney writes in a griotesque, presentational style in which characters narrate their actions in the third person: "Oshoosi Size wakes from a nightmare/ Realizing, ah hell, he late for work" or Oba's "Marcus! Marcus ... Enter Oba calling for her son," to give but two random examples (177, 259). This style makes the drama less naturalistic, more like storytelling, more like a narrated myth in which the storyteller assumes both an omniscient perspective and speaks for the characters as well, much as in the storytelling style of West African griots.

McCraney also uses specific *orisha*, their histories, and their qualities as characters and events in the three plays, which I will now consider individually for their mythic content. *In the Red and Brown Water*, the first play, is an adaptation of Lorca's *Yerma* with an overlay of *orisha* culture. Oya is a teenaged girl and a runner with a dream of leaving her depressed and oppressed home town of San Pere. The Man from State offers her a track scholarship, but she stays with her dying mother, Mama Moja, to help her, sacrificing her own education and future. Mama Moja, we might note, is short for Yemoja, another name for Yemayá, the *orisha* of water. Here is one place where

McCraney transforms Yoruba myth, as Yemayá is not the mother of Oya but the mother of Ogun and Oshoosi, about whom more will be said below.

Oya has aspirations that link African-American success and athletics but must care for her mother, which also links her to the importance of community and family in African-American culture. After Mama Moja dies, Oya must choose between two lovers: Shango, who is flashy, but destined to leave (in fact, in the play, he joins the military and upon his return takes up with another woman), and Ogun, who is boring but reliable and owns his own auto repair business. Oya then discovers that she is infertile, and the play concludes with her metaphoric end.

Many of the characters in the play are *orisha*-inspired, in name if not in action, and the story itself, while based on *Yerma*, is also *orisha*-derived. The title of the play refers (in part) to Elegba's dream. Elegba, who will be analyzed in greater detail below, is a young boy in the neighborhood who is also a trickster figure who just might bring messages from the gods. He steals candy from the local store and seems like he is headed for a life as a thief and gangster, but he also has a deep connection to the ancestors. He dreams of water, walks on the floor of the ocean, and meets "the bone people," who, when asked why they don't go home, tell him, "When we walk there, it/ Wasn't there no more" (23). This dream might be interpreted as Elegba walking under the ocean back towards Africa, meeting those who died in the Middle Passage. He links the New World and the Motherland in his dreams, yet he also dreams of Oya. Oya floats on top of the water, naked with menstrual blood flowing: "Brown skin in the red water ... red and brown water" (23–24). Water is a symbol of the womb and fertility in Yoruba culture, yet Oya's water is red — it is bloody and incapable of giving birth. She is infertile in a culture that values fertility.

Her plight in the play is also *orisha*-inspired. Oya is the goddess of the River Niger, Shango's "first and favorite wife" who "decided to end her life when she felt disillusioned in consequence of the ignominious end of her husband's career" (Awolalu 46). Oya is "a patron of feminine leadership" (Gleason 1). Oya literally means "she tore" in Yoruba, a reference to her violent potential (Gleason 11). She manifests sometimes as a strong wind, which also makes McCraney's representation of her as a swift runner (who runs like she's "flying through the air") appropriate (Gleason 11; McCraney 28). According to Yoruba belief, Oya was the first wife of Ogun, but she fell for Shango while Ogun worked at his forge (Gleason 278–279, Adepegba 119).

While following the plot of *Yerma*, the first of the *Brother/Sister Plays* offers an Oya who is linked romantically with both Ogun and Shango, who is fast as the wind, who is an embodiment of female leadership, and who passes away into another world when her romances end poorly. Oya is the protagonist of the first play, but the first play does not demonstrate a one-to-one correspondence between Oya the myth and Oya the character. Instead, McCraney employs the *orisha* and the myth as a source through which he might more directly engage the challenges to young African-American women.

The *orisha* Eshu manifests in the *Brother/Sister Plays* as two characters. Eshu is frequently presented in the West as a trickster deity who is also a messenger, the opener of the way between the human and the divine, and the one who must be placated in order to have positive relations with *orisha*. Eshu is "the sole messenger of the gods; he who carries the desires of man to the gods. Eshu is the guardian of the crossroads ... master of that elusive, mystical barrier that separates the divine world from the profane" (Gates 6). McCraney splits this *orisha* into two characters. Eshu-Elegba is the West African name of the *orisha*. In McCraney's play, "Elegba" is a boy at the beginning of *In the Red and Brown Water* and a young man by the end of it. In that play, Little Elegba "dream[s] with messages I can't read yet ... know they messages, just don't know who they to,/ Where they from, how to get them there" (22). Elegba is a trickster who steals from O Li Roon's store and jokes about it when caught. He is a trickster who does not yet understand the messages the divine world gives him. By *The Brothers Size*, one of three characters, he is an ex-convict, Oshoosi's best friend, and possibly his seducer in more ways than one. While absent as a character in *Marcus*, his presence is acutely felt in that play as it begins with his funeral and burial, and the characters discuss his role as Marcus's father and how Marcus inherited his being on "the down low" (closeted gay) (257).

Sexuality and trickster qualities, however, are absent from the other Eshu-based figure in the plays. Eshu-Eleggua is the Cuban (Santeriá) name of Elegba, represented in McCraney's play as Aunt Elegua. This name would also indicate more of an African-American understanding of Eshu than the African conception inherent in Elegba. Whereas Elegba primarily represents the trickster aspect of Eshu, Aunt Elegua represents the messenger, the divine opener, and the one who bridges the worlds of the human and divine. She is present in the first and last plays and frequently serves to tell the characters about their dead relatives and ancestors and to offer advice. She is the voice of history and community in the plays, not unlike August Wilson's use of Aunt Ester, whose name is almost echoed in McCraney's Aunt Elegua.

Ogun Size, who "was good to" Oya and who just wants "to take care of" her after Shango breaks her heart, "leaves his own heart behind" (115–116). He is also based on the above-mentioned deity Ogun, who is both "primordial divinity" and "deified ancestor" (Awolalu 31). Ogun "is associated with clearing the way or removing barriers," the divinity of iron and war, taxi drivers and blacksmiths, mechanics and anyone who works with iron or steel (Awolalu 31–32). In the *Brother/Sister Plays*, Ogun Size owns his own auto repair business and is a mechanic. Ogun Size is based on the *orisha* Ogun, but, like Oya, he does not follow his namesake's mythic narrative nor share his exact qualities. The myth serves as metaphor for African-American experience.

Other *orisha* appear as characters in the plays. Ogun's brother, not seen until the second play in the trilogy, is Oshoosi, who is a hunter *orisha* and a wanderer. Ogun's rival is Shango, a deified ancestor, divinity of lightning whose family and palace (including his wives Oya, Oshun, and Oba) were destroyed by lightning the first time he called it down from heaven (Awolalu 33–34). The character Shun, "a girl from around the way," is a variation of Oshun, divinity of the River Oshun, goddess of sweet water, and a fertility goddess—"giving the joy of childbirth to barren women" (McCraney 9; Awolalu 47). In the second act of *In the Red and Brown Water*, Shun is now Shango's girlfriend and pregnant with his child. She walks past Oya's house to mock her infertility, telling her, "I'm having his baby/ So I'm his woman now!/ You ain't shit to him" (120). Just as Oya was Shango's first wife and he then married Oshun in Yoruba belief, the same triangle plays out in McCraney's play. While mythic in origin, however, the scenes also reflect a lived reality in rural African America.

Interestingly, there is also a character named Egungun in *In the Red and Brown Water*. Egungun is "an embodiment of the spirit of a deceased person who is believed to have returned from *òrun* (the spirit world) to visit his children" (Awolalu 65). The term also refers to a masquerade in honor of the spirits. Egungun in McCraney's play is a DJ who appears when a block party begins. He sets up his speakers and "The music comes tumbling down the street/ calling you out by name" (107). Egungun, however, is less an embodiment of the ancestral spirits than a manifestation of fertility and libido. His music summons everyone who "Needs to get to know that freak within" (110), encouraging the women to display their most erotic dance moves. Paradoxically, the play also implies that he might be gay. Egungun might be named to remind us of the ancestors, but the character is more interested in the descendents and in making the next generation while simultaneously hiding his own romantic relationship with Elegba, a theme that will come to fruition in *Marcus, or the Secret of Sweet*.

In the second play, *The Brothers Size*, only three characters appear: Ogun and Elegba, who were characters in the first play, and Ogun's brother, Oshoosi, who has just returned from prison. Oshoosi, like his *orisha* namesake, is a wanderer who cannot remain in one place too long. As part of his parole, however, he must live with his brother and work in his auto repair shop. There is a Yoruba proverb, "We do not give the child of Oba to Oshun."

Likewise, we do not expect a hunter to work with iron. Oshoosi does not fit in well with his brother's lifestyle or business.

Elegba in this play is also an ex-convict, as well as a seducer and tempter of sorts, both sexual and criminal. He wants to have physical intimacy with Oshoosi but also bring him back into a life of crime. Oshoosi begins to be tempted by both. He needs to wander and dreams constantly of escape. At one point, Oshoosi tells of a book about Madagascar in the prison library (201). He read the book repeatedly, and would stare at the pictures; he now wants to go to Madagascar, but is also disturbed because there is a picture in the book of a man who looks exactly like him: "Him and me could've been twins man!" (203). The book, Africa, and the man represent a form of imaginative escape, but they also represent a link back to the Motherland. Lost in a judicial system that sees him only as a black criminal and likely repeat offender, Oshoosi sees Africa as a place to which he might escape. He wants to find his African doppelganger because:

> He got something to tell me man.
> Something about me that I don't know 'cause I am living
> here and all I see are faces telling me what's wrong with me. (203)

Oshoosi is incomplete and broken in this play. He needs to wander and find his true self. Eventually, Elegba gets Oshoosi in trouble and Oshoosi wants to run. Ogun, despite his best efforts to help his brother avoid temptation, realizes he cannot stay, and so fixes a truck and lets Oshoosi take it and run away to Mexico. What is important is not only the *orisha* origins of the characters and their conflicts, but the inherent brokenness of Oshoosi, which Ogun cannot fix; only Africa can.

The final play, *Marcus, or The Secret of Sweet,* is the least Yoruban in one sense, but also the key as to how and why McCraney uses New World African myth. It is a coming-of-age story and coming-out story with fewer *orisha*-derived characters and concerns and instead themes that are more pertinent to twenty-first century America than historic or mythic Africa. Three characters in *Marcus* do not have *orisha* names: Terrell (which would seem to suggest the character is autobiographical), Marcus (the protagonist, who is also, according to McCraney, not so much autobiographical as "personal"), and Shua, a nickname for Joshua that makes him sound more Yoruban, but he is actually from the Bronx (qtd. in Gener 81).

Most directly, the "secret of sweet" is that Marcus, like his father, Elegba, is "sweet," or gay. McCraney thus introduces sexual orientation, a contemporary American concern, far more than a Yoruban one, into his mythic structuring of black masculinity. But the "secret of sweet" functions on multiple levels and carries multiple meanings. Marcus is "sweet," meaning gay, but tries to keep it a secret, first and foremost from himself. He is "on the down low," hiding his homosexuality in a culture that suffers from "Black-MoPhobia," as one character puts it, homophobia as applied to black men (257). The other "secret of sweet" is the origin of the term. After being accused of being "sweet," Marcus wonders why that nomenclature is used. Shaunta Iyun explains that both the term "sweet" and the practice of keeping one's orientation on the down low are legacies of slavery. Male slaves caught having a secret sexual relationship with one another were punished in a unique way:

> Master tie and tether the lovers in front of e'rybody,
> Talking bout "sending a message." Placing weights
> On their private portions. Lashing into the skin that they just held
> To tight moments ago. Skin that was just kissed now
> Split ope' from th' slash of dis white man's hands.
> When the wounds right he run down get some sugar
> Prolly pour it on so it sting not as bad as salt but it get sticky
> Melt in the singing Southern sun. Sweetness draw all the
> Bugs and infection to the sores... Sweetness harder to wash. It
> Become molasses in all that heat and blood and... [258].

This monologue underscores some of the major themes of the play and also serves to link Marcus himself to the history of gay black men in the New World and to the Motherland. Gay slaves were punished primarily for their lack of reproduction ("slave owners get pissed if they find/ Out they slaves got gay love./ That means less children, less slaves" [257]). So black homophobia is a negative legacy of the transatlantic slave trade, learned from slave owners who saw homosexuality as unprofitable. If this is the case, then black homophobia, as a legacy of slavery, is something to be overcome not only on moral grounds but because it runs counter to the *orisha*. Homophobia is, instead, a Western behavior forced upon Africans. Marcus even claims, "They ain't even have gay folks in Africa" (295). To which Aunt Elegua responds, "Don't let 'em fool you all your life" (295). One manifestation of Eshu teaches the child of another manifestation of Eshu not to believe what he has learned from a homophobic society.

The second theme to be derived from this monologue is that something ordinarily seen as positive (sugar/sweet) is used to make a punishment worse and to last — infection, insect infestation, etc. ensures that the gay slave suffers long after the flogging is over. The European legacy is to transform positive things into negative ones. The role of the *orisha* is to overcome that negative legacy and transform it back into a positive one. As noted above, Soyinka states that the *orisha* are the "tolerant gods," which would imply that homophobia is unacceptable in Yoruba religion. Lastly, there is the linguistic legacy—a "sweet man" is a gay slave. The term has remained in the African-American community as a euphemism for homosexuality, but the term is derived from slavery. Even the language of homophobia is a European legacy that the African *orisha* reject.

Elegba is a young trickster in the first play, a playful but dangerous tempter in the second play, and an absent father whose legacy of both homosexuality and dreams and messages from the gods lives on in his son, Marcus. If Elegba is a manifestation of Eshu, who, as Gates reminds us, is "he who carries the desires of man to the gods" (6), then there is something of the divine in the sweet father and son's orientation. Elegba is the one who "carries the desire of man"—he represents homosexual desire as well as other desires. His carrying of the desires of men "to the gods" also implies a divine approval of same-sex love. If Eshu himself is gay, then black homosexuality is divinely ordained.

We might further note that, according to Gates, quoting Melville J. Herskovits, the *orisha* Elegba is "hugely oversexed and therefore not to be trusted with women" (27). Eshu's "sexuality is a sign of liminality, but also the penetration of thresholds" (Gates 27). Gates, therefore, sees Eshu-Elgeba's sexuality as a metaphor for "the exchange between discursive universes" (27). In his version of the *orisha*-inspired character, McCraney, however, expands on Elegba's mythic sexual prowess to demonstrate that he cannot be trusted with men either, so to speak. This variation on the myth is new. McCraney demonstrates Eshu's liminal sexuality as a counter to historic and contemporary New World homophobic oppression. What McCraney does is link the African-American experience into an archetypal and divine past from the Motherland and then use the *orisha* to create room in black masculinity for black homosexuality.

McCraney does this because he himself is a trickster in Gates's sense. According to Gates, "Black texts Signify upon other black texts," and the dominant trope of African-American literature is the Signifying Monkey (xxvii). The Signifying Monkey, like Eshu, Spider, and Rabbit, is a trickster who destabilizes meaning and interpretation. Eshu is a fluid figure, a uniter of worlds and of words. The Signifying Monkey allows for multiple meanings present in the moment and hidden meanings rooted in African-American history. *The Brother/Sister Plays* signify on Yoruba myth, structuring African-American experience on the *orisha* stories. The result is a "double-voiced text," in Gates's terminology, a narrative that relies upon "repetition and difference" in order to make its point and tell its story, recognizing that multiple audiences will receive the text in different ways (Gates 88). Eshu, as the messenger of the gods who is also a trickster, delivers instructions on interpretation, even as he himself remains open to many interpretations. Eshu represents the open-ended possibility of multiple interpretations, in which no one meaning is fixed. This attribute also holds true for *The Brother/Sister Plays*, which can be read on multiple levels and which, along with multiple forebears, resist interpretation as well.

Part of the challenge of these plays, which furthers my contention that McCraney also functions as an American Eshu, is that though the plays draw on elements of Yoruba cosmology or New World variations and transformations of it, the vast majority of the readers and audience members likely will not recognize any of those elements without dramaturg's notes in the program or the script. Major productions of the trilogy and individual plays have been mounted in New York, New Haven, Pittsburgh, Chicago, London, Washington D.C., and Atlanta. In many of these locations, no major Santeriá, Candomblé, Macumba or Voudun audiences attended the production, even if they exist in the municipality (as in New York City, which has a substantial Yoruban and Caribbean population; even here the production at the Public Theatre was neither aimed at nor marketed to these groups). The average theatre-goer encountering these plays is not in the Yoruban tradition. McCraney has thus written plays whose source material will be recognized only by a very small number of people who encounter the plays. Others will simply understand them as "draw[ing] on ... Yoruba cosmology" with no idea what that actually means or refers to.

All of which raises the question: what is the purpose of adapting myth if the audience will neither recognize the stories and characters nor find meaning in the difference between the established version and the artist's variation? As I noted in my introduction, West African dramatists use identifiable myths that their audiences will readily recognize. The meaning of the play will frequently reside in the difference between the original myth and its dramatized version. African-American playwrights will frequently employ African myths to connect to the Motherland in a manner that argues that the Middle Passage was not a complete break and that African spirituality survived in the New World in an unbroken tradition of *orisha* worship. McCraney, however, adapts African and African-American myths for audiences most likely not familiar with them and who cannot identify differences between his own and traditional versions. While American audiences get a sense of the mythic from the plays and productions of them, the use of myth in this case functions very differently than previous uses of West African myths by dramatists. In previous cases, the playwright uses the familiar (the myth) to address the unfamiliar (the author's cultural or social concern). McCraney uses the most likely unfamiliar (the myth) to address the familiar (concerns about relationships and homosexuality in the African-American community, African-American identity, and the challenges of rural poverty).

The plays propose a complex and fluid identity, therefore, in terms of African diasporan identity, in terms of sexual orientation, and in terms of dramaturgy. All of which makes McCraney an American Eshu who allows mere mortals to dialogue with the divine and who is a creative force, but who also is a trickster. The stories of *orisha* are told to link African America to the Motherland, but they are also repurposed to allow for the tolerant gods to expand their milieu to include gay African Americans. By setting the stories of Oya, Ogun, Shango, Oshoosi, Elegba, and Yamayá in rural Louisiana and intertwining them with the invented tale of Marcus, the young African-American man who is both discovering and developing his own identity as a gay black man, McCraney mythologizes experience but also links African-American history with African culture. If one of the roles of the *orisha* is to make community, McCraney's plays expand the idea of community from small American town to the African diaspora and indeed the entire cosmos. Only a trickster could link the smallest of worlds with the entire universe and do so while simultaneously advocating for a reevaluation of homosexuality in black history, all through the use of African and African-American myth interpreted through western-style drama. As McCraney says of the Miami Madonna, *The Brother/Sister Plays* show that African myth and African-American life "are actually one and the same ... something new that is neither West African nor European."

NOTES

1. Artaud, *The Theatre and Its Double*. 116.
2. See Soyinka's essay "The Fourth Stage: Through the Mysteries of Ogun to the Origins of Yoruba Tragedy" in his volume *Myth, Literature and the African World*. Soyinka argues that African drama emerges out of Yoruba myth and metaphysics (as represented by Ogun, "the first actor") and the lived African world (142; 155).
3. See, for example, much of the work of Derek Walcott, whose *Omeros*, to cite but one example, uses the Greek epic of the *Odyssey* (with all of its mythic content) to create a realistic yet mythic poem about a Caribbean cab driver's return to Africa, or his *Odyssey*, to cite a dramatic example, in which the events of that epic are played out in a much more realistic fashion than the original, yet still links to the mythic quality of the original.
4. *Orisha* worship combined with French Catholicism to form Voudon (frequently represented in the west as "voodoo"); Spanish Catholicism combined with *orisha* worship to form *Santeriá*, and in Brazil, Portuguese Catholicism combined with *orisha* worship to form Candomblé and Macumba. For more information on the globalization of West African religion in the New World, see Olupona and Rey, eds., *Òrìṣà Devotion as World Religion*.
5. *In the Red and Brown Water* and *Marcus, or the Secret of Sweet* were workshopped at Yale in 2006. *The Brothers Size* was workshopped at Yale in 2006 with subsequent productions at the Public Theatre in New York in October 2007, the Young Vic in London in November of that year, and Pittsburgh's City Theatre Company in November 2008. The full trilogy was presented at the McCarter Theatre Center in Princeton in April 2009, then again at New York's Public Theatre in October of that year, and in January 2010 at the Steppenwolf Theatre in Chicago. Additionally, the plays have received multiple per-

formances, both individually and as the full trilogy, in the United States and abroad, including Ireland and New Zealand.

6. Tarell Alvin McCraney, *The Brother/Sister Plays* (New York: Theatre Communications Group, 2010), vii. Subsequent citations are in the text.

7. Note, the actual total number of Africans in the Middle Passage is debated. Estimates range from twenty to one hundred million. Vega's number seems accurate for the purposes of this essay, representing a significant number of *West* Africans, who would be *orisha*-worshippers. By the nineteenth century, most Africans in the Middle Passage were taken from Southwest Africa, and brought with them different beliefs.

8. For in-depth explorations of *orisha* worship and Yoruban beliefs, see Awolalu, *Yoruba Beliefs and Sacrificial Rites*; Gleason, *Oya: In Praise of the Goddess*; Karade, *The Handbook of Yoruba Religious Concepts*; and Olupona and Rey, eds., *Òrìṣà Devotion as World Religion*.

9. See Karade, Awolalu, and Olupona and Rey's edited collection for information on *orisha* belief in the Yoruban diaspora and in syncretic religions of the New World.

WORKS CITED

Adepegba, Cornelius O. "Associated Place-Names and Sacred Icons of Seven Yoruba Deities." In Olupona and Rey, 106–127.

Artaud, Antonin. *The Theater and Its Double*. Trans. Mary Caroline Richards. New York: Grove Press, 1958.

Awolalu, J. Omosade. *Yoruba Beliefs and Sacrificial Rites*. London: Longman, 1979.

do Nascimento, Abdias. *Sortilege (Black Mystery)*. Alexandria, VA: Alexander Street Press, 2003.

Gates, Jr., Henry Louis. *The Signifying Monkey: A Theory of Afro-American Literary Criticism*. New York: Oxford University Press, 1988.

Gener, Randy. "Dreaming in Yorubaland." *American Theatre* (September 2009): 24–27, 81–82.

Gleason, Judith. *Oya: In Praise of the Goddess*. Boston: Shambhala, 1987.

Ijimere, Obotunde. *The Imprisonment of Obatala and Other Plays*. English adaptation by Ulli Beier. London: Heinemann, 1966.

Jennings, LaVinia Delois. *Toni Morrison and the Idea of Africa*. Cambridge: Cambridge University Press, 2008.

Karade, Baba Ifa. *The Handbook of Yoruba Religious Concepts*. York Beach, ME: Samuel Weiser, 1994.

McCraney, Tarell Alvin. *The Brother/Sister Plays*. New York: Theatre Communications Group, 2010.

_____. *Sortilege II: Zumbi Returns*. In *Crosswinds: An Anthology of Black Dramatists in the Diaspora*. Ed. William Branch. Bloomington: Indiana University Press, 1993.

Olupona, Jacob K. and Terry Rey, eds. *Òrìṣà Devotion as World Religion*. Madison: University of Wisconsin Press, 2008.

Owusu, Martin. *Drama of the Gods: A Study of Seven African Plays*. Roxbury: Omenana, 1983.

Priebe, Richard K. *Myth, Realism and the West African Writer*. Trenton, NJ: Africa World Press, 1988.

Soyinka, Wole. *Myth, Literature and the African World*. Cambridge: Cambridge University Press, 1976.

_____. "The Tolerant Gods." In Olupona and Rey, 31–50.

Sutherland, Efua. *The Marriage of Anansewa*. London: Longman, 1975.

Vega, Marta Moreno. "The Candomblé and Eshu-Eleggua in Brazilian and Cuban Yoruba-Based Ritual." *Black Theatre: Ritual Performance in the African Diaspora*. Eds. Paul

Carter Harrison, Victor Leo Walker II, and Gus Edwards. Philadelphia: Temple University Press, 2002. 153–166.

Walcott, Derek. *Dream on Monkey Mountain and Other Plays.* New York: Farrar, Straus and Giroux, 1970.

_____. *The Odyssey: A Stage Version.* New York: Farrar Straus Giroux, 1993.

_____. *Omeros.* New York: Farrar Straus Giroux, 1993.

Punctured by Patriarchy

Theatricalizing the Christian Assault Upon Native Mythology in Tomson Highway's Dry Lips Oughta Move to Kapuskasing

CHRISTY STANLAKE

Tomson Highway's *Dry Lips Oughta Move to Kapuskasing* has earned the Cree playwright high praise and intense criticism from both Native American and non–Native theatre communities. *Dry Lips* premiered at Toronto's Theatre Passe Muraille in 1989, but when producers remounted the production in a 1991 revival at Toronto's most celebrated commercial venue, the historic Royal Alexandra Theatre, Highway gained prominence not only as a lauded Canadian playwright (the first produced at the Royal Alexandra),[1] but also as the leading figure of the contemporary Native American theatre movement. Subsequently, *Dry Lips* was canonized when major anthologies of dramatic literature began to include the play, further establishing Tomson Highway's reputation and introducing Native dramaturgy into mainstream theatre studies. Yet, despite the milestones *Dry Lips* has achieved for Native American theatre, many Native and non–Native viewers have lambasted the play for dramatizing the violent treatment of Native women, particularly in one scene in which a female trickster character is raped with a crucifix wielded by a mentally ill boy. Certainly, the play is disturbing and unflinchingly portrays extreme misogynist views held by a couple of its characters. At the same time, *Dry Lips Oughta Move to Kapuskasing* is a complex work of theatre, one that functions as a kind of ceremony that draws upon ancient Greek, Christian, and Native mythologies to dramatize the assault that occurred upon Native people and their beliefs, while simultaneously offering healing through the resilience that Native American mythology offers its communities.

Tomson Highway's own story is one that mirrors Native beliefs that storytelling and imagination possess powerful transformative possibilities for individuals. Highway was born in 1951 in a tent on "his father's trap-line on a remote island [...] up in northern Manitoba" (Highway, *Rez Sisters* vi). The eleventh of twelve children, Highway was raised traditionally, "trapping in the winter, fishing in the summer," listening to the stories of his family, and speaking only Cree (vii). When he was six, Highway was removed from his family, as was tragically customary for many Native American children, and sent to a Roman Catholic boarding school, where western education, Catholicism, and English language were enforced. Despite this separation from his family and culture, Highway continued to thrive, studying as a concert pianist, earning a BFA in music in 1975 and a BA in English in 1976 (vii). Upon his graduation, Highway returned to the Native community, serving as a social worker for First Nations' people for seven years.[2] Then, Highway began to weave his experiences as a social worker together with his love of storytelling and his understanding of musical compositions: the plays he crafted became richly layered; lyrical by nature; intermingled with Cree, Ojibway, and English voices; and always centered upon Native concerns.

Similar to that of other Native playwrights, Tomson Highway's dramaturgy is informed by Native epistemologies. This quality of Native American dramaturgy is something that Native plays share with other forms of Native literature, which many theorists have argued must be viewed as a "separate discourse" emanating from Native worldviews (Weaver 23). Jace Weaver's *That the People Might Live* argues for a criticism that considers Native American works from a Native critical context based on experiential theology that "fails to recognize any split between sacred and secular spheres[;] this worldview remains essentially religious, involving the Native's deepest sense of self and undergirding tribal life, existence, and identity, just as the Creator undergirds all the created order" (28). The term Weaver coins for this theological/critical perspective is *communitism*, "formed by a combination of the words 'community' and 'activism.' Literature is communitist to the extent that it has a proactive commitment to Native community, including ... the 'wider community' of Creation itself" (xiii). This wider community is one that includes not only the people within a community, but the animals, natural world, and spirits that also exist simultaneously within a community's interconnected sacred/secular sphere. The impulse for Native writers to craft literature from Native worldviews is one that ultimately offers Native communities a sense of wholeness; as Weaver argues, "In communities that have too often been fractured and rendered dysfunctional by the effect of more than 500 years of colonialism, to promote communitist values means to participate in the healing of the grief and sense of exile felt by Native communities and the pained individuals in them (xiii).

At their core, Highway's plays are communitist works, theatre that employs Native epistemologies to present worlds where there are no boundaries between the sacred and secular worlds, yet there are often debilitating obstacles — residue from colonization — that the characters must work through in order to heal their communities and return to a sense of wholeness. While Jace Weaver uses the term "theology" to describe the nature of Native American worldviews, Highway uses the term "mythology," which he believes is more accurate. He explains that the etymology of mythology is "the Greek word 'myth,' whose meaning is 'narrative,' or 'story,' and 'logos,' whose meaning is 'word' or 'discourse,' while theology comes, in the same language, from 'theos,' meaning 'god' or 'divinity,' and, of course, the aforementioned 'logos'" (Highway, *Comparing* 21). For Highway, the distinction between the words 'mythology' and 'theology' is vital: "the former ends up being a discourse on narrative, or the art of story-telling, including, most notably, a narrative on all three of humankind, animalkind, *and* god, the latter a discourse on god (or gods), and god only" (21). The narrative and communal aspects of the definition are essential to Native American playwrights, like Highway, who relate theatre to the oral and communal nature of traditional Native story-telling.

In 2002, Highway delivered a lecture entitled *Comparing Mythologies* to the University of Ottawa. He began by providing an extended definition of mythology. In addition to being a source of a person's and culture's language and expressions, mythology helps individuals answer existential questions and "delineates the *spiritual* nervous system [...] of that person, that tangle of electrical cords and wiring in all its wondrous, mystical, magical complexity" (Highway, *Comparing* 20). In terms of an entire community, mythology "tells the story of the *spiritual* movements of [a] people across the landscape"; additionally, "mythology defines, mythology maps out, the collective subconscious, the collective dream world of races of people, the collective spirit of races of people, the collective spiritual nervous system" (19, 26). In an attempt to provide a common ground for his Native and non–Native audience, Highway explains that all cultures have mythologies that exist halfway between truth and lie, because mythology is "the region of our collective dream world, our collective subconscious, where men sprout wings, horses sprout wings, [...] where people exist who are half-man and half-goat, half-woman and half-fish, half-man and half-coyote, half-woman and half-spider, [...] women give birth without having had sex, men — and women, too — are half-human and half-divine" (25). As he simultaneously draws upon examples from ancient Greek, Christian, and Native mythologies, Highway places those cultures on equal ground and provides both a sense of familiarity with those mythologies that are foreign and a sense of distance from those mythologies that the audience might consider "natural": Spiderwoman, the Virgin Mary, and Pan emerge together from their respective dream worlds. Highway then explains that mythology is more than a system of understanding the world; it also produces human actions: "it is the principle, or driving force, that decides whether nature or our bodies [...] are friends or foes, enemies to be conquered or lovers to be loved, gardens to be killed or gardens to be tended" (27). In the remainder of the lecture, Highway compares the mythologies that he claims have had the most influence over North America: ancient Greek, Christian, and Native American — specifically for his discussion, Cree — mythology. Though he does not speak directly about his plays, Highway's discussion of the three mythologies offers an effective way to view *Dry Lips*, a play in which these three mythologies intermingle and often battle until Native mythology is re-embraced by the characters living in the play's fictitious setting of the Wasaychigan Hill Indian Reserve in Manitoulin Island, Ontario.[3]

Dry Lips is a companion play to Highway's 1988 *The Rez Sisters*; in their respective premieres, each play won the Toronto Alliance for Performing Arts's Dora Mavor Moore Award for outstanding new play and was nominated for Canada's Governor General's Award. *The Rez Sisters* features seven women from Wasaychigan Hill who join together, despite their differences, to travel to the world's largest bingo game. During the play, audiences learn about the women's struggles and dreams, while Nanabush, a mythical trickster spirit played by a male dancer in the guise of a seagull, nighthawk, and bingo master, visits the women. *Dry Lips* features seven of the reservation's men, some of whom are married to the women previously introduced in *Rez Sisters*. Again, Highway balances gender by introducing a trickster character, this time a female dancer who plays the spirits of Gazelle Nataways, Patsy Pegahmagahbow, and Black Lady Halked, reservation women who figure largely in the imaginations of the men. Unlike *Rez Sisters, Dry Lips* is a particularly violent play, as Highway focuses on how the men, abandoned by their more proactive wives and lovers who have banded together to create an all-women's hockey team, languish at home in alcohol, weakness, and rage, while wrestling with western societal expectations of masculinity.

Some of the men appear somewhat effeminate. Zachary Jeremiah Keechigeesik, the husband of Hera Keechigeesik, wants to open a bakery to provide for his family; when he is stressed, he spends his time baking. Creature Nataways, the husband of Gazelle Nataways, who is living with Big Joey, is happy to provide Gazelle and anything else to Big Joey, whom he adores. Spooky Lacroix, an evangelical Catholic, and his wife are expecting a baby: Spooky endlessly knits blue baby booties and blue outfits, as he ruthlessly quotes scriptures to his neighbors. These more effeminate characters are joined by others. Big Joey is the group's alpha male. Angry, hulking, loud, and a heavy drinker, he dominates conversations and other men on the reservation. He is the father of Dickie Bird Halked, the son of Black Lady Halked, who is the sister of Spooky. Dickie, a seventeen-year-old suffering from fetal alcohol syndrome, muteness, and anger, is cared for by his uncle, Spooky. Until the play, Dickie has no idea that Big Joey is his father. Pierre St. Pierre is a bootlegger who has found a new calling as a referee for the women's hockey team, news of which he proclaims through town. Finally, Simon Starblanket, at twenty the youngest of the men, dreams of returning Nanabush and Native ceremony back to the reservation.

In a foreword to *Dry Lips*, Highway explains the significance of Nanabush, the Ojibway name for the trickster figure that populates the mythology of almost all Native nations. Highway states that the trickster is "as pivotal and important a figure in our world as Christ is in the realm of Christian mythology" (Highway, *Dry* 12).[4] Tricksters are shape-shifters that can assume numerous identities, including different sexes and species. In terms of mythic significance, Highway explains that the trickster is "Essentially a comic, clownish sort of character, his role is to teach us about the nature and the meaning of existence on the planet Earth; he straddles the consciousness of man and that of God, the Great Spirit" (12).

To dramatize these qualities of Nanabush, Highway divides *Dry Lips*'s set into two levels. The lower level depicts the more mundane locations of the reservation: Big Joey's living room, Spooky's kitchen, the hockey rink, and the forest. The upper level is Nanabush's realm, where the actor playing her perches upon the top of a spectacular, lighted jukebox that is only partially visible. Each time the audience sees Nanabush, she wears a costume piece that symbolizes one of the several "guises," or personas, that the trickster enacts within the play (Highway, *Dry* 13). This character-shifting reflects the trickster's shape-shifting potential that Highway mentions above. In addition to Nanabush's transformative magic, Highway calls for the jukebox to sometimes rise fully into the audience's view, an effect the playwright hopes will convey "a haunting and persistent memory, high up over the village of Wasaychigan Hill" (10). Behind the perch is a large, full moon that appears only at night. From this perch, Nanabush watches the men's actions, changes her different guises, and often interacts with the other characters, summoning their memories, setting their actions in motion, and even receiving their abuse.

It is important to note that, although tricksters are deities functioning in intermediary roles between the human and divine, often bringing about healing, as Christ does in Christianity, that is about where the similarities end. As Native American theorists Clara Sue Kidwell and Alan Velie explain, Native theologies do not operate according to universal laws of good and evil, as Christianity and many other world religions do; rather, individuals can acquire a personal "relationship with spiritual forces," which are seen as pure power (Kidwell and Velie 21). In Native philosophies, power is ambiguous, full of chance, similar to the elements of the natural world: storms, seasons, water, and wind. Kidwell and Velie argue that tricksters embody this ambiguity of power by displaying a vast range of behavior, from creative to destructive, and so "teach that moderation and self-control are the important values in society, that greed is destructive, and that individuals have different qualities and abilities that must be respected" (33). Similarly, Highway's three visages of Nanabush are powerfully creative and destructive. Gazelle Nataways possesses a voracious sexual appetite that often distracts the men of Wasaychigan Hill. Black Lady Halked haunts the men's memory of how the community let her drink herself almost to death prior to Dickie's catastrophic birth. Patsy Pegahmagahbow playfully dances with a man's fancy dance powwow bustle, encouraging Simon to bring back the communal ceremonies. Each guise is differentiated from the others by an oversized prosthetic costume piece: Gazelle's breasts, Black Lady Halked's pregnant belly, and Patsy's bum.

It is these prosthetics which presented "exaggerated representation of male images of women [that became] one of the major sources of the controversy that attended the play in 1991" (Filewod 41). While one could certainly read the body parts through a sexualized male gaze, as several of the Wasaychigan men do, the costume pieces simultaneously expressed what makes women uniquely powerful: the ability to create and sustain life, a power that women share with the Great Creator, also a female. In *Comparing Mythologies*, Highway argues that one of the major differences between Cree mythology and Greek and Christian mythologies is that the Cree universe was female-generated, "the result of the efforts of a female force of energy known as O-ma-ma, a miraculous entity eventually to be known, in the English language as Mother Earth" (Highway, *Comparing* 39). Moreover, this female deity did not have a puritanical relationship with human bodies and sex; rather, "this girl was endlessly sexual, endlessly sensual, endlessly fertile, a creature of pleasure, a creature of the flesh who gave birth, in no particular order, with no great fixation on the concept of time, to many, many most wondrous and most, most beautiful things" (39). Notably, one of her children was the part human, part divine mythic trickster (40). The clownish prosthetics Highway's trickster wears in *Dry Lips* are representations of this divine sexual, creative power, neither wholly good nor evil. In adherence to Native mythology, the prosthetics are intentionally comic, drawing upon trickster humor.

Tricksters and sacred clowns populate Native cultures. Often, one sees the terms used interchangeably, for sacred clowns are the embodiment of tricksters during ceremony. As Kidwell and Velie explain, Native spiritual traditions incorporate a great deal of humor into their most sacred ceremonies because "the association of humor and sacredness comes in the break between the expected and the unexpected that inspires a person to stop and consider the nature of reality, and to come to new understandings of the world" (Kidwell and Velie 34). Humor loosens people's inhibitions and defenses, allowing them to hear and see things differently. Humor also allows people to laugh and survive through the worst of times. For example, Gerald Vizenor's body of theoretical work examines the role of trickster action and humor as the essential attribute of Native American *survivance*, survival and resistance to societal forces that seek to eradicate Native American cultures.[5]

Dry Lips functions as a ceremony with the intention of healing Native communities. Highway opens the play with a quote from Lyle Longclaws, a man who has dedicated his life to Native social welfare: "'...before the healing can take place, the poison must first be exposed...'" (qtd. in Highway, *Dry* 6). The notion of a play functioning as a communal healing ceremony is common throughout Native American theatre. Playwright Monique Mojica and Ric Knowles open *Staging Coyote's Dream: An Anthology of First Nations Drama in English* with a statement that pulls together the elements of ceremony, playmaking, tricksters, and healing. They claim Native theatre artists draw "on a known and lived sense of what is essentially ritualistic. They know that in all theatre there's a healing that takes place on stage, in the audience, and between the stage and the audience, a healing that is part of the mutability of Coyote, part of the humour, and part of the ritual" (Mojica and Knowles v). Although a play may not be a tribal-specific, private, religious ceremony, it creates a kind of secular ceremony with Native mythic, or theological, implications, as a community gathers for a shared ritual of storytelling. Kidwell and Velie describe ceremony as "a way of physically renewing the world," and explain that such events are "necessary to establish appropriate senses of relationship with the non-human beings of the world, and the maintenance of social harmony among the members of the group and beneficial relations with the forces of the physical environment — that is, the non-human world — required knowledge of appropriate and respectful behavior" (21). In *Dry Lips*, Highway draws his audience's attention to the violent intrusion of patriarchal world views, expressed through Christian mythology and enforced upon a once matriarchal, Native community. The renewal of Wasaychigan's world occurs once the men recognize the futility of patriarchal perspectives, honor the power and role of women in the community, and return to communitist values. The path to achieve this renewal is harsh, full of gendered differences, religious battles, and sexual assault; yet, in the end, the community achieves healing.

From the first scene, Highway deftly interweaves the three mythologies. Zachary sleeps naked on Big Joey's couch, as Nanabush in the guise of Gazelle

Nataways, Big Joey's lover, dresses in an oversized hockey shirt, and *"plants a kiss on Zachary's bum, leaving behind a gorgeous, luminescent lip-stick mark"* before leaving for her higher-level perch (Highway, *Dry* 16). A hockey game blares on the television, while Big Joey returns home with booze and Creature Nataways to find Zachary talking in his sleep, telling Hera that she cannot play on a women's hockey team after having just had a baby. The plot is set in motion: Big Joey kicks the befuddled Zachary out of his house for having had sex with Gazelle, though Zachary only remembers having followed Gazelle home to get her bannock apple pie recipe for the bakery he and Hera plan to open. Big Joey, who wants the chief to grant him tribal money to begin a radio station (instead of giving the money to Zachary to start a bakery), tries blackmailing Zachary, telling him to withdraw his request for tribal funding "or else I get my Gazelle Nataways to wash these skivvies of yours, put them in a box all nice and gussied up, your picture [of Zachary's lip-smacked bum] on top, show up at your door-stop and hand them over to your wife" (24). From their scuffle, Zachary leaves with a torn pants' crotch and no underwear. He cannot return home to his jealous wife, Hera, until he has figured out an entire business plan for the bakery. Meanwhile, Pierre arrives at Big Joey's requesting his skates and spreading the word about the newly formed women's hockey team, the Wasy Wailerettes. Pierre, the team's referee, zealously heralds the team's arrival, until he learns that he must go to Spooky Lacroix's home to retrieve one of his skates and then laments, "Spooky Lacroix's gonna preach at me" (34). Gazelle Nataways, who has placed these events in motion by setting up Zachary and becoming the Wasy Wailerettes's captain, watches and laughs at the men's antics.

Obviously, Gazelle Nataways's trickster behavior introduces Native mythology to the plot. Greek mythology and Christian mythology appear in a more subtle manner, through the names of Highway's characters. Specifically, Zachary Jeremiah and Hera Keechigeesik's names combine the three mythologies. Zachary means "the Lord calls," and Jeremiah, "the Lord exalts," names from the Judeo-Christian tradition. Hera, comes from Greek mythology's goddess of marriage and birth, the jealous sister and wife of Zeus. Together, their last name is Cree for "heaven" or "great sky," allowing Zachary and Hera to represent a leading, spiritual couple in the reservation community (Highway, *Dry* 14). Highway also gives Judeo-Christian names to Pierre/Peter, "the rock," or foundation of the church; and Simon, "he who hears the word of God," Starblanket.

Throughout Act One, Nanabush continues to shape the play's action. Simon, enchanted by the dancing bustle of Patsy Pegahmagahbow, has decided that he and Patsy will get married, have a child, and spread the knowledge of Patsy's stepmother, Rosie Kakapetum, the reservation's only living medicine woman. In a surreal moment in the forest, where sounds of wolves' howling, women's wailing, and rocks hitting boards are heard, Simon tells Zachary of his vision. He has heard a baby's voice crying for him, but trapped within a large rock. Simon explains, "I am somehow responsible for it being caught inside that rock. [...] Then this ... eagle ... lands beside me, right over there. But this bird has three faces, three women. And the eagle says to me: 'the baby is crying, my grand-child is crying to hear the drum again'" (Highway, *Dry* 44–45). Nanabush as Patsy appears and, "*her face surrounded by the brilliant feathers of her bustle, so that she looks like some fantastic, mysterious bird, begins to wail, her voice weaving in and out of the other wailing voices*" (45). Simon wails, too, before continuing his vision: "Then the eagle is gone and the rock cracks and this mass of flesh, covered with veins and blood, comes oozing out and a woman's voice somewhere is singing something about angels and god and angels and god" (45). Simon interprets the vision as, "I'm the one who has to bring the drum back. And it's Patsy's medicine power, that stuff she's learning from her step-mother Rosie Kakapetum that ... helps ... me" (45). Simon's vision of god as a woman with three faces displays his understanding of the immediate spiritual world that intersects his own. He also sees the balance of the sexes, a world in which men and women partner to teach and nurture the following generations.

The version of Nanabush that watches over the scenes in Spooky Lacroix's home is that of Black Lady Halked. Highway's stage directions describe her as "*nine months pregnant (i.e., wearing a huge, out-sized prosthetic belly). Over this, she wears a maternity gown and, pacing the floor slowly, holds a huge string of rosary beads. She recites the rosary quietly to herself. She is also drinking a beer and, obviously, is a little unsteady on her feet because of this*" (Highway, *Dry* 52). Dickie is the only character who can see this image of his mother, which he prays to, as Spooky knits blue baby booties and rattles on about his plans to use Dickie in his mission to "prepare this reserve for the Lord" (53).[6] Nanabush's image foreshadows the drunken invasion of Creature Nataways and Big Joey, who follow Pierre to Spooky Lacroix's home in search of his other ice skate; her image also serves to haunt the men's memories, as the men end up fighting about how Dickie's birth ended Big Joey's and Spooky's friendship. Spooky attacks Big Joey's masculinity because Big Joey "can't take the sight of blood least of all a woman's blood, this MAN who, when he sees a woman's blood, chokes up, pukes and faints" (61). The reference, we learn later, comes from the moment Big Joey saw Black Lady Halked go into labor with Dickie. Spooky tells Big Joey, "after what you went and done to my sister, this here boy's own mother, you're no buddy of mine" (62). Meanwhile, Big Joey accuses Spooky of turning his back on the community, his family, and culture: "You never let a friend for life go, William Hector Lacroix, not even if you turn your back on your own father, Nicotine Lacroix's spiritual teachings and pretend like hell to be this born-again Christian" (64). In a fit of anger, Spooky shoves Dickie toward Big Joey, the man Dickie has just learned is his biological father. Spooky screams, "For what you did to this boy at the bar seventeen years ago, Joseph Jeremiah McLeod, you are going to hell. To hell! [...] Look at him. He can't even talk. He hasn't talked in seventeen years!" (64). Confused and angry, Dickie grabs the crucifix off Spooky's wall and runs out, leaving the grown men crying and physically fighting one another.

Representative of the next generation, which the Wasaychigan community should be teaching and protecting, Dickie symbolizes the violent confusion experienced in Native cultures where individuals are forced to deny their own mythologies in favor of an outside Christian mythology. At the women's hockey game that ends Act One, Simon Starblanket, who carries the bustle, tells Dickie, who's holding the crucifix, "Your grandpa, Nicotine Lacroix, was a medicine man. Hell of a name, but he was a medicine man. Old priest here, Father Boucher, years ago — oh, he was a terrible man — he went and convinced the people old Nicotine Lacroix talked to the devil. That's not true. Nicotine Lacroix was a good man" (Highway, *Dry* 65). The division that wracks the men in the community stems from this moment, when a priest convinced a number of the reservation's people to see their spiritual leader as evil. Not only did this action divide the community into two spiritual camps, it also divided familial relationships, fracturing the very core of communitist life. Individuals like Spooky and Black Lady Halked chose to deny their own father, a Native spiritual leader, and viewed themselves as spiritually depraved, tainted. For Black Lady Halked, this self-hatred turned into self-abuse through alcoholism, and abuse of her own fetus through her heavy drinking during pregnancy. Highway distills this communal conflict, essentially a conflict of mythologies, within a surreal moment that ends Act One. During the hockey game that only the male characters can see, Black Lady Halked shoots the puck directly at Gazelle Nataways. That puck becomes lost in Gazelle's cavernous cleavage. A fight erupts on the ice. Meanwhile, Nanabush, still in the guise of the nine-month pregnant Black Lady Halked, appears in profile baptizing her belly with beer and silhouetted by the blood red moon. She stands on the rising, flashing, colored jukebox that plays "It Wasn't God Who Made Honky Tonk Angels," a song about how men's actions have often "caused many a good girl to go wrong" (77). Dickie runs to the ice, looks up at this image of his mother, and attempts a "grotesque, fractured version of a Cree chant" to save his mother from falling from the sky (75). The final images that complete the act's tableaux are Simon, holding up his bustle, and Spooky, holding up his crucifix, above Dickie, now prostrate before his mother's haunting image.

In Act Two, *Dry Lips*'s actions stage a very clear battle between Christian and Native mythologies and the ways each shapes the mundane choices of the people who adhere to them. Zachary, who is afraid to return home, and Pierre, who has lost his job as a referee until the Wasy Wailerettes can locate the lost puck, help Spooky with his knitting. Dickie has run away, and memories taunt the men in the form of Nanabush playing first the role of Gazelle Nataways, who was stripping at the bar the night Black Lady Halked gave birth, and then Black Lady Halked, who gave birth alone in a corner of the bar as the men's attention was drawn to Gazelle's dance. In the midst of their memories and debate about which bar Dickie was born in, Simon arrives to tell Spooky that Rosie Kakapetum wishes to deliver Spooky and Lalala Lacroix's baby. At first, the two men argue over the proper way to bring children into the world. Spooky believes that the medicine woman is a "witch," and that it would be wrong to have her deliver his son: "My son will be born at Sudbury General Hospital [...] like any good Christian boy" (Highway, *Dry* 88–89). Spooky associates western medicine with Christianity and "civilized" behavior; conversely, Simon views hospital births as barbaric, precisely because they separate women from their children and children from the sacred earth. Simon laments that hospital babies are pulled "right from their own mother's breast the minute they come into this world and they put them behind these glass cages together with another two hundred babies like they were some kind of scientific specimens... [...] ...and they'll hang Lalala up in metal stirrups and your baby's gonna be born going up instead of dropping down which is the natural way" (89). Zachary agrees, "...to the earth, Spooky Lacroix, to the earth" (90).

Spooky takes offense and moves the debate from birthing practices to the religious belief systems that undergird the cultures that create them. He asks, "If Rosie Kakapetum is a medicine woman, Simon Starblanket, then how come she can't drive the madness from my nephew's brain, how come she can't make him talk, huh?" (Highway, *Dry* 90). Simon blames the church, institutionalized medicine, and members of the Native community who have turned against Native mythology for diminishing the power of Native cultural traditions. He returns Spooky's attention to the Native community asking whether he or Black Lady Halked even care that "your nephew hasn't been home in two days, since that incident at the hockey game" (90). Finally, Simon challenges Spooky: Why can't the bible "and all it stands for cure your nephew's madness, as you call it, Spooky Lacroix? What has this thing [Spooky's bible] done to cure the madness of this community and communities like it clean across this country, Spooky Lacroix? Why didn't 'the Lord' as you call him, come to your sister's rescue at that bar seventeen years ago, huh, Spooky Lacroix?" (90–91). Spooky's only answer is to attack Rosie with the same accusation that others once made about his own father: "Rosie Kakape-tum works for the devil" (91).

Although Spooky has not won the theological debate with Simon, he does win the debate with Zachary and Pierre over which bar Dickie was born in. Spooky's assurance maddens Simon, who lunges at him screaming, "It doesn't matter what the fuck the name of that fucking bar was! [...] The fact of the matter is, it never should have happened, that kind of thing should never be allowed to happen, not to us Indians, not to anyone living and breathing on the face of God's green earth" (Highway, *Dry* 94). Simon accuses the older men of being a generation that has given up, claiming, "You'd rather turn your back on the whole thing and pretend to laugh, wouldn't you?" (94). In contrast, Simon appropriates language from Christianity's Beatitudes to proclaim: "This is not the kind of Earth we want to inherit" before telling the men that he is going to fetch the female spiritual leaders of the community, Patsy and Rosie, and bring them to the men (94). Being reminded by a young person of their ineffectuality as men in the community, Zachary, Pierre, and Spooky are speechless and embarrassed before returning to a conversation that ignores Simon's accusation. Spooky mutters that it was the "devil that stole the baby's tongue," so that he and the men do not have to face that everyone in the community had chosen to abdicate responsibility for caring for Black Lady Halked as her life spiraled out of control in a world where bingo money, alcoholism, and men's ogling at dancing girls had replaced their Native culture (95).

In *Comparing Mythologies* Highway argues that an imbalance between men and women occurred in Native America when Christian mythology, a system characterized by a linear sense of time, and single, omnipotent, male god, invaded a world that functioned according to cyclical time, pantheism, and a reverence for female power. He writes:

> Christian mythology arrived here on the shores of North America in October of the year 1492. At which point God as a man met God as a woman [...] and thereby hangs a tale of what are probably the worst cases of rape, wife battery, and attempted wife murder in the history of the world as we know it. At that point in time, [...] the circle of matriarchy was punctured by the straight line of patriarchy, the circle of the womb, was punctured, most brutally, by the straight line of the phallus. And the bleeding was profuse [47].

Theatrically, Highway stages this violent encounter in *Dry Lips*, when Nanabush, in the guise of Patsy Pegahmagahbow, comes down to earth to comfort Dickie, who wanders naked through the forest under the full moon after having been haunted by memories of his mother's telling him to not ask about his grandfather, Nicotine Lacroix — a man who spoke with the devil; Dickie is to say his Hail Marys, instead. As Creature and Big Joey smoke a

joint and watch the encounter from the trees, Patsy bounds on stage, helps
Dickie dress, and invites him to Rosie's house for fry bread and deer meat.
Patsy coaxes Dickie to leave the crucifix to which he clings in the forest
"because Rosie can't stand the Pope" (Highway, *Dry* 99). Dickie responds by
playfully poking Patsy with the crucifix, an action that turns from tickling to
an attack, as Creature pleads with Big Joey to stop his son. Soon, "*Dickie Bird
grabs Nanabush/Patsy and throws her violently to the ground, he lifts her skirt
and shoves the crucifix up against her*" (99). He rapes her with the crucifix as
Big Joey turns against Creature, his only friend, "Get out. Get the fuck out
of here. You're nothin' but a fuckin' fruit. Fuck off" (100). Big Joey watches
the rape and does nothing.

Nanabush/Patsy's rape is the play's most disturbing scene. Symbolically,
it represents that violent moment of contact in which a patriarchal mythology
invaded the Native American world of matriarchal mythology. To move the
audience's focus from the realism of rape toward the scene's larger, mythic
meanings, Highway's stage directions call for the scene to split, literally. Dickie
remains on the lower level, "*holding the crucifix and making violent jabbing
motions with it, downward [...] in slow motion. The crucifix starts to bleed*"
(Highway, *Dry* 100). Meanwhile, on the upper, mythic level, Patsy/Nanabush
stands "*gather[ing] her skirt, in agony, until she is holding it up above her waist.
A blood stain slowly spreads across her panties and flows down her leg*" (100).
Dickie becomes covered in blood, as he represents a Native American son
who has used an instrument of a patriarchal mythology to abuse and potentially kill his female Native deity. Meanwhile, Nanabush/Patsy falls to the
floor in the world above (100). Highway draws a vivid correlation between
the Christian attack on Native mythology and the cultural degradation of
women in societies that are shaped by patriarchal mythologies. Accordingly,
the moment takes the form of abuse that violent men seeking power over
women have used historically: rape. Indeed, later in the play, when the men
ask him why he allowed the rape to occur, Big Joey — a veteran of Wounded
Knee II[7] — claims, "Because I hate them! I hate them fuckin' bitches. Because
they — our own women — took the fuckin' power away from us faster than
the FBI ever did," to which even Spooky must respond, "They always had it"
(120).

Although Big Joey lets the rape occur, the moment is somewhat ambiguous. Once Nanabush/Pastsy collapses, Highway's stage directions state that
Big Joey "*staggers almost faints and vomits violently. Then he reels over to Dickie
Bird and, not knowing what else to do, begins collecting his clothes and calming
him down*" (Highway, *Dry* 101). Big Joey's actions parallel the events during
Black Lady Halked's delivery in the bar, when Big Joey almost fainted, vom-
ited, and then ran away from the sight of her blood and his infant son. This

time, Big Joey runs toward his son, gathers him in his arms, and speaks to him in Cree saying, "It's okay," and "You are my son. [...] I'm ... your father" (101). This moment of Big Joey's accepting responsibility for Dickie is the beginning of a string of actions that are tragic, comic, and ultimately healing as they unravel.

Building upon the trickster triad of tragedy, humor, and healing, Simon drunkenly searches the woods looking to kill Dickie for raping Patsy, but accidentally shoots himself instead when he is distracted by a vision of her dancing bustle. Mourning Simon, Zachary cries out a challenge to god: "I dare you to come down from your high-falutin' fuckin' shit-throne up there, come down and show us you got the guts to stop this stupid, stupid, stupid way of living" (Highway, *Dry* 116). Nanabush's answer is for Zachary, and the others too, to first look after his own community. Highway plays with the ambiguity of trickster power and shape shifting, as well as the Cree language's omission of gendered words, when Nanabush appears above dressed in a gray, "father God" wig and beard combination, sitting on a heavenly toilet, wearing high heels, and "*nonchalantly filing his/her fingernails*" (117). Other moments of trickster humor occur when Dickie takes a gun from Big Joey and tries to commit suicide, though Nanabush replaces the gun's firing with a celestial fart, and Rosie delivers Spooky and Lalala's baby *girl* (a surprise to Spooky) because the ambulance has rushed Patsy to Sudbury General hospital.

By the play's end, the men have gathered to watch and cheer their wives, the Wasy Wailerettes, who have reconvened under a new captain, Hera Keechigeesik, and are playing for an even larger gathering of women: the *World's* Aboriginal Women's Hockey League. There is also more unity within the community. Spooky has given up his evangelical mission to care for his daughter and knit *pink* baby booties with Creature, who is now openly gay. Meanwhile, Pierre tells Dickie, now working at his father's radio station covering the women's games, that he will give background testimony at Dickie's court hearing. In *Comparing Mythologies*, Highway writes, "Circles, however, and fortunately, can be repaired" (48). We see this healing in *Dry Lips*; however, we also see Highway's prediction for the future. In *Comparing Mythologies*, Highway continues, "And perhaps, just perhaps what we're looking at today [...] is the death of the male god and the rebirth of the female" (48). As proof, the playwright looks toward the greater societal acceptance of gays, lesbians, and transgendered people and wonders if this shift has occurred because the fear "of the one very alone, and very lonely male god" can no longer prohibit individuals from "taking their lives and the lives of their communities into their own hands, into their own *healing* hands" (48). Significantly, the image of the Wasaychigan Hill Reservation community that Highway presents at the end of *Dry Lips* enacts the same sense of hope he offers in *Comparing Mythologies*. There is an awe and reverence for the women's ability to empower themselves through a world-wide network playing, what is typically thought of as, a male game. Moreover, there is an acceptance of the members of the community, regardless of sexual orientation or horrific past actions, that allows everyone to feel protected by all their relations.

In the final scene, Highway turns to the home of Zachary Jeremiah and Hera Keechigeesik, the couple that bridges the three mythologies. Zachary is naked, lying on the couch, as he is in the play's opening; however, the home is not Big Joey's but his own. Hera, the first human female character in the play, appears carrying their daughter. She wakes Zachary from his dreaming and hands him his missing shorts, which were stuck under a couch cushion. It has all been a dream, a mythic experience of the Wasaychigan collective spirit. The couple speaks mainly in Cree, as Hera teases Zachary about talking in his sleep and Zachary asks Hera if she would ever consider starting a women's hockey team. As they laugh, Hera gives Zachary their daughter. Highway's stage directions call for a striking final tableaux: "*this beautiful naked Indian man lifting this naked baby Indian girl up in the air, his wife sitting beside them watching and laughing*" (Highway, *Dry* 130). As the father honors his baby girl, Highway reinforces Native mythological perspectives through a final sound effect, Hera's laugh morphing into a "*magical, silvery Nanabush laugh*" that then reverberates with the sounds of the family: Zachary's harmonica, and the baby's laughter "*magnified* [...] *to fill the entire theater*"(130). *Dry Lips* leaves its audience with a visual and aural image that reveals man as both protective and vulnerable, woman as part divine, and the new generation as one that will grow happy and healthy in a Cree community. The family is complete. There is balance, healing, and a sense of communitism.

Drawing upon three compared mythologies, ancient Greek, Christian, and Native American, Highway's *Dry Lips* articulates not only the moment of historic violence that occurred when Christian mythology entered Native America, but also how the systems of thought associated with Christian mythology still reverberate within and can damage Native American communities. At the same time, through the mythic trickster figure, Highway offers his viewers new ways of understanding the conflict of mythologies, what is at stake in Native communities, and how to move toward healing by rekindling communitist values that honor all the relations. When viewed from such a framework, *Dry Lips* becomes anything but a misogynist play. Rather, it is a bravely wrought ceremonial action intended to present viewers with a clear "window"[8] into the challenges facing Native American communities; it is also a transformational example of how communities can take their lives "into their own *healing* hands" with the aid of the Native mythology (Highway, *Comparing* 48).

NOTES

1. For more on the controversy surrounding the 1991 revival, see: Filewod, "Receiving Aboriginality: Tomson Highway and the Crisis of Cultural Authenticity."

2. First Nations is the general term that most Indigenous people of Canada use to refer to themselves. In the United States, Native American is most often used. While both terms are problematic, I will most frequently use the general term "Native American," to refer to Indigenous people from North America, unless I am referring only to Indigenous people of Canada, in which case I will use the term "First Nations."

3. Highway notes that Wasaychigan is Cree for "window" (*Dry* 14).

4. For this analysis, I am using the first edition of *Dry Lips Oughta Move to Kapuskasing*, published by Fifth House 1989. Please see Works Cited.

5. For an overview of Vizenor's theories see: Vizenor and Lee's *Postindian Conversations*.

6. What people refer to as reservations in the United States are referred to as reserves in Canada.

7. Wounded Knee II began at the Pine Ridge Reservation in 1973 and grew into a standoff between the American Indian Movement (AIM), who were invited guests of the Oglala Lakota community, and the FBI, who supported the community's tribal president, Richard Wilson. Many in the Oglala Lakota community believed that Wilson was engaged in corrupt practices that threatened tribal sovereignty and the lives of the reservation's community. The political tensions climaxed in a 1975 shoot out between the protestors and the FBI. Although AIM was composed of male and female activists, many women accused AIM's leadership of being resentful of and hostile toward female leaders in the movement. One female leader, Anna Mae Pictou Aquash, was believed to have been brutally murdered in 1975. Her death ignited suspicion that she may have been a victim of the FBI or of men within AIM who resented her power.

8. Here, I am referring directly to Highway's choice to use the Cree word, Wasaychigan, or "window," as the name of his play's setting.

WORKS CITED

Filewod, Alan. "Receiving Aboriginality: Tomson Highway and the Crisis of Cultural Authenticity."1994. *Aboriginal Drama and Theatre*. Vol. 1. Critical Perspectives on Canadian Theatre in English. Ed. Rob Appleford. Toronto: Playwrights Canada Press, 2005. 37–48.

Highway, Tomson. *Comparing Mythologies*. Charles R. Bronfman Lecture in Canadian Studies. University of Ottawa. 23 Sep. 2002. Ottawa: University of Ottawa Press, 2005.

_____. *Dry Lips Oughta Move to Kapuskasing*. Saskatoon, Saskatchewan: Fifth House Publishers, 1989.

_____. *The Rez Sisters*. Saskatoon, Saskatchewan: Fifth House Publishers, 1988.

Kidwell, Clara Sue and Alan Velie. *Native American Studies*. Lincoln: University of Nebraska Press, 2005.

Mojica, Monique and Ric Knowles. Ed. *Staging Coyote's Dream: An Anthology of First Nations Drama in English*. Vol. 1. Toronto: Playwrights Canada Press, 2003.

Vizenor, Gerald and A. Robert Lee. *Postindian Conversations*. Lincoln: University of Nebraska Press, 1999.

Weaver, Jace. *That the People Might Live*. New York: Oxford University Press, 1997.

Damaged Myth in
Caryl Churchill's *The Skriker*

AMELIA HOWE KRITZER

In *The Skriker* (1994) Caryl Churchill explores change as a negative force. In contrast to earlier plays that celebrated the creative and generative potential of change, *The Skriker* considers change as a process of destruction and decay. Mental illness provides an opening into which change enters, similarly to *A Mouthful of Birds*, the 1986 play co-written with David Lan. In *The Skriker*, however, none of the characters who experiences madness, with its release from the constraints of normality, finds it to be a source of personal reinvention. Instead, all suffer deterioration and loss. Rather than affirming personal choice and change, Churchill issues a sharp warning about changes already in process that endanger the future. To heighten the intensity of the warning and communicate the omnipresent nature of the dangers that occasion it, she draws from universal themes within folklore and mythology. The play's title character, the Skriker, derives from Irish and northern English myth, in which the Skriker is a banshee spirit who wails loudly to announce an imminent death. As created by Churchill, this character also presents broader mythical overtones connected with the Greek myths of Persephone and the Furies, as well as the West African trickster figure Anansi. Other characters from British folklore who appear in the play include Johnny Squarefoot, the Kelpie, Yallery-brown, Rawheadandbloodybones, Nellie Longarms, and Jenny Greenteeth — all of which have been employed to frighten small children. These folkloric figures, with their distinctive appearance and forms of communication, emphasize the disturbing threats inhabiting the familiar, everyday world, while the broader mythic resonances of these figures suggest universal and irreversible damage in the natural world.

The play took form as a collaboration between Churchill and the Second Stride dance company, with which she had also created *Lives of the Great Poisoners* (1991) and would go on to create *Hotel* (1997). It stands as one of Churchill's experiments in communication, with dance and movement, as well as the music composed for the work by Judith Weir, conveying much of the play's meaning. Of the twenty-six characters (played by sixteen performers), only three — the Skriker, Josie, and Lily — speak. In her introduction to *Plays: 3*, the volume of her works from 1986 to 1994, Churchill emphasizes that the play uses multiple levels of communication, most of which are nonverbal: "a number of stories are told but only one in words" (viii). Dialogue in itself forces a relationship among the three speaking characters — a relationship that each seeks at some point to escape — as they move through an incomprehensible world of sound and movement that does not recognize or defer to them. The play begins with a blast of inarticulate sounds, including a baby crying, which place the audience in the position of infants who cannot comprehend the sounds they hear. The Skriker's monologues, with their way of confounding meaning by stringing together unrelated phrases, suggest the difficulty young children may have in interpreting language at the point when they understand words but do not yet grasp syntax. In exploring forms of signification and power that are prior to and outside of language, Churchill imbues her characters with primal desires and fears connected to a natural environment continually engaged in the dual processes of creation and destruction.

The Skriker's position in the chronology of Churchill's work suggests that mythology was on her mind during its development. It opened at the Royal National Theatre in January, 1994, while her translation of Seneca's *Thyestes* opened in June of that year at the Royal Court Theatre Upstairs. In her introduction to *Plays: 3*, furthermore, Churchill mentions that her writing of *The Skriker*, which occurred over a period of several years, encompassed the development and production of *A Mouthful of Birds*, which focuses on the Greek myth of the Bacchae. Both the Bacchae and Thyestes myths reverberate with the violence of elders toward the young: in the former, Agave kills her son Pentheus while in the throes of ecstatic possession, and in the latter Thyestes unknowingly eats the flesh of two of his children after they are killed, cooked, and served to him by his brother Atreus. In one scene Churchill's play echoes a theme of Thyestes, as a dead child sings: "My mother she killed me and put me in pies/ My father he ate me and said I was nice/ My brothers and sisters, they picked my bones/ And they buried me under the marley stones" (19).[1] With these stories of child murder informing the mood, a sense of dire threat pervades *The Skriker*. Without explicit statement, the play makes it clear that the Skriker will somehow harm Josie and Lily, the two teenage girls with whom she interacts.

The Skriker, an "ancient and damaged" spirit, embodies change as mutation. She continually changes her physical form, appearing variously as a spider-like monster, an old homeless woman, a little girl, a man, an inebriated

American woman, a theatrical fairy dressed in pink frills, and even a sofa. Her speaking enacts the uncertainty and instability of language, as each word in a series alters the meaning of what went before, in a continually twisting chain of joined phrases impossible to understand in the usual manner of deciphering speech, but nevertheless understandable in terms of emotional states and general patterns of thought. The Skriker's opening monologue, for example, begins with the following: "Heard her boast beast a roast beef eater, daughter could spin span spick and spun the lowest form of wheat straw into gold, raw into roar, golden lion and lyonesse under the sea, dungeonesse under the castle for bad mad sad adders and takers away" (1). Neither in appearance nor in speech does the Skriker provide the reference point for reality or truth that the young Josie and Lily seek throughout the action. Though her name comes from British folklore, the Skriker, as an ancient figure, connects with several mythical currents that extend back into the earliest of human societies. The Skriker at different times manifests as Persephone of classical and much earlier myths, who personified the fertility of nature and the yearly changes of the seasons, but who also reigns as queen of the underworld and is associated with the retreat of the sun and the loss of vegetation in the winter months. First appearing in the form of a large spider, the Skriker also presents the image and some of the behavior of the West African trickster figure Anansi, who is associated both with nourishing humans and exploiting them. The Skriker's magic is like that of the English folklore character Yallery Brown: the wishes she grants turn to curses. Finally, the play positions the Skriker as a Fury, a spirit of revenge brought into being by an act of violence, especially against a blood relative. In Greek mythology, the Furies relentlessly pursue and torment the wrong-doer, driving him or her to insanity and death. The Skriker hints at her wounding and mission in the first monologue: "they poison me in my rivers of blood... Revengeance is gold mine, sweet" (4, 5). The Skriker's name, an archaic form of the word *screamer*, thus joins an emblem of fatality to the concept of terrifying and unavoidable consequences of previous action.

The simple motive of revenge, however, does not fully explain the Skriker's single-minded obsession with stalking and exploiting the young. Her speech, in all its voluminous expressiveness and brilliantly prismatic phrasings, reveals an abundance of imagination. Imagination, as well as change, has been associated with positive transformation in earlier Churchill work; but the Skriker shows a singular and warped imagination that drives relentlessly toward control and destruction. Declaring "an open grave must be fed" (5), she employs her magical powers to enlist the teenage Josie and Lily as collaborators and finally ensnare them in her campaign of death. Posing alternately as a victim or perpetrator of the destruction she fosters, the Skriker manipulates the young women she has targeted by means of frenetic movement and anxious pleadings. As a damaged and deranged Persephone figure who long ago had been dragged off to the underworld and raped by its ruler, the Skriker now exerts the power amassed in the course of long survival to subject others to a similar fate. Her actions show an unconscious repetition of destructive and violent patterns more than a consciously held desire for revenge. Habitual exploitation and destruction have caused that which formerly had been nurturing and abundant to shift into patterns of exploitation and annihilation.

The Skriker uses her shape-changing magic to appear to her intended victims as the fulfillment of their desires. When Josie, confined and isolated in the hospital, recognizes her own powerlessness, the Skriker offers to enhance her personal power by granting her wishes. To the independent and empathetic Lily, she offers the chance to feel the warmth of helping others, appearing to her first as a beggar woman and later as an emotionally needy child. Lily, who wants to buy things for her soon-to-be born baby, undergoes a magical transformation into a kind of human slot machine spilling out winnings. Though the Skriker takes on frightening forms at times, she never assumes the guise of an authority figure; instead she makes a show of ceding power to the teenage girls. Even when she appears as an American businesswoman, she plies Lily with questions about how television works, as though Lily has all the answers, and when she seems to be a man with the capacity to care for and protect Lily, she presents this self as someone who desperately needs to be loved.

The strange and malevolent Skriker is not the only presence in the play from the spirit or natural world, but the other folkloric figures have no dialogue or direct contact with Josie and Lily. While the Skriker frequently vents emotion in protracted eruptions of incoherent speaking, the others inhabit the stage wordlessly, crouching like animals, engaging in repetitive actions, or dancing to music that serves to heighten their mystery. Dominating the stage, but unacknowledged by the speaking characters, they represent the everyday tumult of creatures and processes in the natural world. Particular characters bring associations with the inherent dangers of nature lurking below its surface — in a rippling river with hidden depths and currents that can sweep a human away and drown them in an instant, or an enticing forest with the potential to bewilder and trap the inexperienced explorer. Folkloric characters have long been used by parents and caretakers to warn against the temptations held out by the natural world. Jenny Greenteeth, a river spirit, is said to pull children into the water and drown them. Kelpie, who also haunts rivers, is said to appear as a horse, but to take any rider who mounts it into swift currents and certain death. Black Annis, according to folk legend, hides in a forest oak and snatches children, carrying them to her cave, where she skins and eats them. Spriggans are said to guard ruins, steal treasure, and sometimes steal children, leaving hideous changelings in their places. In other stories, Rawheadandbloodybones dwells near ponds or in dark places, waiting to catch and eat children who lie or steal, while Yallery Brown promises to grant a wish to the person who helps free it from a stone, but ultimately places a curse on his rescuer.[2] The warnings implicit in these stories intensify the play's dark mood, presenting the natural world as a threatening place rather than a welcoming and sustaining one.

Non-speaking human characters also inhabit the landscape of the play, sometimes interacting with the folkloric figures. They include a man who creates an artistic cake and grows ill and weak after he allows a spirit to consume it, a girl who continually peers through a telescope, but fails to see things that are directly in front of her and subsequently becomes depressed, a group of businessmen with Thrumpins — evil spirits that weaken and kill those on whom they light — on their backs, a woman who mounts a Kelpie and is then killed and dismembered by it, and a family that picnics in the midst of a crowd of blue men, which Scottish folklore calls sea spirits that swim alongside ships and lead them to destruction. Throughout it all, a character identified only as the passerby dances alone. Combined with the weird denizens of the spirit world, these human characters create a constantly shifting environment that dwarfs and overwhelms the two girls at the center of the play's action, emphasizing their smallness and fragility, their slowness in reacting and adapting to the dramatic changes that they encounter, and their inability to see or understand important aspects of the world that surrounds them.

Josie and Lily, the two speaking human characters in the play, epitomize youth, innocence, and generative potential. They represent the life-giving force of humanity, but their vulnerability exposes humankind's endangered state. The two teenage girls, one having recently given birth and the other pregnant, confront the responsibilities of adulthood without sufficient preparation or development. They lack the guidance of parents or the support of lovers and have only each other for companionship. The friendship they do offer each other is subject to the fickle tides of adolescence; at one moment fearing separation, and at the next insisting on it. The Skriker at times appears to hold out the possibility of serving as a substitute for the absent parent or lover, seducing the girls in those guises, but she always reverts to coercive and exploitative behavior. The two girls are closer to nature than to culture. They show little thought or imagination outside their struggle to survive and desire to nurture. In contrast to the turgid but poetic monologues of the Skriker, the speeches of Josie and Lily are simple and direct, full of questions, grounded in immediate experience, and aimed at separating truth from illusion. For example, when trying to respond to the insistent queries of the Skriker regarding how television works, Lily explains, "It has to be plugged in so it's got power, right, electricity, so it's on so you can turn it on when you press the button... " (13). The girls try to interpret the changing images and slippery language of the Skriker, but, though they grow more suspicious of her as the action progresses, they remain ignorant of the full extent of the danger she represents. They prove unable, at crucial moments, to articulate what they are experiencing. Both girls show concern for others, but their immaturity, lack of discipline, and especially their inability to conceptualize the outcomes of actions prevent them from supporting others, or even pursuing their own best interests, in a consistent manner. Lacking the ability to influence their world, they resort to wishing, but their lack of power does not exempt them from responsibility or consequences. Their vulnerability is what has attracted the Skriker; as she says, "I knew you were desperate, that's how I found you" (28). The two are most desperate to find certainty and stability in their shifting world, but their efforts do not result in finding or establishing anything of permanence.

A fatal action and its consequences separate the two girls. Josie has killed her ten-day-old infant, and is therefore a patient in a mental hospital at the beginning of the play. Josie's mental illness provides the opening into a world that oscillates between nightmare and reality. At first Josie inhabits that world alone, but soon her friend Lily visits her in the hospital, curious to know what impelled Josie to kill her own child. While expressing pain and guilt, Josie wants to leave the hospital and go home with Lily. Josie wants to escape from the Skriker, who has begun to haunt her, but her talk of the Skriker convinces Lily that she is truly mad. Telling Josie of her plans to run away from home and go to London, Lily departs. The Skriker appears, complaining angrily about the way Josie has described her, pleading with Josie to "please keep" (10) her, and offering her a wish if she will continue their relationship. Josie wishes that the Skriker will leave her alone and instead pursue Lily, who is "stronger ... more fun" (9) and due to have her baby soon. Though Josie immediately regrets this wish, the Skriker starts following Lily. Taking the form of an old woman, the Skriker attracts Lily's attention by falling down in front of her, begs for money and then for a "hug and a kiss" (11) — both of which Lily impulsively gives her. Lily suddenly finds that pound coins issue from her mouth whenever she speaks.

Josie and Lily, throughout the play, show an indecisiveness that proves fatal. Though Josie warns her about the Skriker, Lily cannot decide whether or not the Skriker is a genuine threat, because to her the Skriker appears in seemingly harmless forms such as a homeless woman, a child, and an inebriated woman asking child-like questions about the workings of television. After wishing the Skriker on Lily, Josie feels she has made a mistake and attempts to get the Skriker to return to her. The Skriker's magical power to produce pound coins out of Lily's mouth serves Lily's immediate desires, but as with the folkloric character Yallery Brown, the Skriker's granting of a wish also confers a curse. Josie, when she gets out of the hospital and catches up with Lily and the Skriker, discovers that when she speaks, toads come out of her mouth. To prevent this, she has to avoid speaking, and thus cannot adequately warn Lily of the price she will have to pay for accepting the Skriker's money. Lily, who consistently shows kindness toward others, cannot believe in the evil of the Skriker. Torn between conflicting emotions and tempted by the Skriker's power to grant wishes, Josie allows the Skriker to take her away.

Heralded by a deafening shriek, Josie and the Skriker enter the underworld, a place of amplified strangeness. The dialogue, employing the twisting phrases of the Skriker, is sung rather than spoken. A large banquet table displays a feast, but the display is, as the stage directions state, "*all glamour*" (29); the food includes twigs and beetles. The Skriker reigns as a queen over the other spirits. All appear at first sight to be dressed in lavish finery, but a second look reveals "*rags ... a claw hand or a hideous face*" (29) unseen at first because of the overall impression of grandeur. A hag, who dashes in demanding, "Give me my bones" (29), re-introduces the theme of human cannibalism: "They cut me up. They boiled me for dinner. Where's my head? is that my shoulder?" (29). In this vision of hell the play signals the principal danger of contemporary life: humans sell themselves and harm others in order to possess, display, and consume things that have no intrinsic value, but only seem desirable because of their aura of glamour. The sense of power gained through association with the aura of glamour constitutes a form of madness that prevents these humans from understanding or resisting their enslavement.

Following the concept of the underworld introduced in the Perspehone myth, a "lost girl" (30) warns Josie against eating anything, because to do so would bind her to the underworld forever. In spite of the warning, Josie drinks with the Skriker, who toasts her: "Your wealth, Josie, happy and gory" (30). The Skriker and the spirits celebrate, dancing wildly. Josie joins in the celebration, but almost immediately finds that it has evaporated while she is left in an enslaved state, scrubbing floors on her hands and knees. Josie begs to be returned to the upper world, if only momentarily, to see her friends, but the Skriker scorns her, because she has nothing to offer. Josie's blood, memories, and even her dreams have all been drained dry by the voracious Skriker. With nothing to lose, Josie plunges her hands into the water of a forbidden fountain and finds herself instantly back with Lily.

Josie's experience of the underworld only serves to further widen the gap between the two friends. While Josie states that she has been away for many years and anxiously asks for reassurance that she and Lily are not dead, Lily has observed nothing out of the ordinary and cannot comprehend the urgency of Josie's inquiries or the reason for her distress. The two girls move in together, but find that they have less in common than before. Lily has given birth and now becomes focused on the baby, while Josie resents losing Lily's attention. Josie remains obsessed with her experience in the underworld, which Lily interprets as a dream or an episode of madness. The pressure increases when Josie suggests that Lily's baby is a changeling, telling her she should lay it on a shovel and put it in a fire to get her own child back again. Exasperated, Lily wishes that Josie were sane. Josie then breaks down and tells Lily that she killed her own baby in an attempt to rid herself of overwhelming pain and fear — repeating, "It should have been me" (39).

With her friend in agony and with no power to help other than wishing, Lily does not even know what to wish. Nothing she can wish for could restore Josie to wholeness; nevertheless she wishes for Josie to be just as she was before the previous wish, even though Josie in that state was making her uncomfortable. As Josie has warned, however, this spate of wishing brings the Skriker back into their lives — this time in the form of a thirty-year-old man who admits to stalking Lily but tries to make it seem romantic. The man urges Lily to trust him, speaking in a normal way and promising to take care of her and the baby. The man, however, betrays the Skriker's association with death when he speaks of climate change, predicts a time soon when "spring will return and nothing will grow" (44), and expresses a sense of satisfaction in being there to "witness unprecedented catastrophe" (44). When Lily hesitantly asks him to slow down in his courtship of her, he begins to play victim and demand assurance of her love. Josie, who has been chopping vegetables nearby, attacks him with her knife and exposes him as the Skriker. In the next scene the Skriker reappears in the guise of a young woman who had been one of Lily's schoolmates and begs for help, but Lily refuses to get involved this time.

In the final phase of the play, both Josie and Lily resist the Skriker's power as each tries to save the other from the Skriker, but the Skriker uses their concern for each other to accomplish her goal. In an attempt to distract the Skriker, Josie kills a homeless woman, reports it to the Skriker, and promises to do more. Finally left alone by the Skriker, Lily worries about what might be happening to her and to Josie. She finds the Skriker and volunteers to go with her, expecting a nightmarish but transitory experience as described by Josie that would not interrupt her life for more than a few seconds. In trying to help others, Lily does not intend to abandon her baby, but her choice has that consequence. She enters a dizzying rush of energy amid black darkness and then finds herself looking at a very old woman and a child. The Skriker informs Lily that she has been transported not to the underworld, but to the future. Her baby is long dead. The old woman she sees before her is her grand-daughter, and the child is that woman's granddaughter. The great-great-granddaughter "*bellows wordless rage at LILY*" (52), though the old woman, using the Skriker's damaged language, makes excuses: "they couldn't helpless... they were stupid, stupefied ... not evil weevil devil take the hindmost of them anyway" (52). The play ends with Lily accepting the food held out to her, while the Skriker exults, announcing Lily's destruction: "And she was dustbin" (52).

With this final statement, the passerby stops dancing, putting an end to human activity. The play implies that humans annihilate themselves through their inability to resist evil; when they try to cast it off, they find their lives unbearably empty. Personified by the Skriker, evil comes in many guises, but continually plays into human desires and weaknesses, much as commercial appeals play into the basic desires and weaknesses of consumers. The ancient and damaged spirit of the Skriker makes a quick and unimpeded entry into an imperiled human world, where babies — the tenuous link to the future — must depend on ill, weak, unprepared, and conflicted caretakers. Lily and Josie, despite their inability to perceive, interpret, and understand the world around them, struggle bravely throughout the play, reaching out to each other in friendship and need. The girls, however, are like two non-swimmers thrown into deep water: their struggles only hasten their drowning, and their embrace of each other only insures that both will perish. These fragile and ordinary girls enact the drama of human survival. Their end, which brings the lone dancer's activity to a halt, even though the passerby seems to belong to a different world, warns of a dark fate for humans — a time when, as the Skriker warns, "Spring will return and nothing will grow" (44).

The play thus takes the form of a classical tragedy in that Lily, an individual who attempts to make good choices while supernatural forces combine with human relationships to place her under extraordinary pressure, loses her life as a result of her action, provoking the Aristotelian response of pity and fear. Lily, of course, does not fit the Aristotelian pattern of a male ruler or person of high position who falls from power, but Churchill positions her as a character with whom the audience should empathize and in whom they should recognize elements of themselves. The assumptions inherent in this positioning accord with Churchill's feminist assertion of the freedom to place women and girls at the center of dramatic action and present them making choices of their own. Lily makes these choices explicitly as a woman and as a mother, and as a person with the capacity to nurture others around her. The Skriker remarks on her kindness, describing her as "the only good person I've ever met" (45). Interestingly, the Skriker too is written as basically feminine, though the character sometimes appears in the guise of a man. While feminists have sometimes celebrated mythical female monster figures like Medusa as positive symbols of female power, Churchill, as in previous plays, finds nothing positive in female power based on exploitation and cruelty. The Skriker gives mythic form to a character pattern found in Marion, the rapacious real estate dealer of *Owners* (1972) and Marlene, the self-obsessed career woman of *Top Girls* (1982).

The Skriker, as a female figure with extraordinary power and destructiveness, strikes a political note in the immediate post–Thatcher environment of the play's inception. During the years 1979–1990, when she served as England's prime minister, Margaret Thatcher, who developed mythic status as the Iron Lady, initiated a radical transformation of the British economic and social system. Insisting, like the Skriker, "I am here to do good. I am good" (17), she cut funding for education, the National Health Service, and social services while breaking the power of trade unions and privatizing government-owned companies and property. Thatcher's policies drained the modest means of the working class to further enrich those who were already well off, and drained the northern and western areas of England to concentrate wealth in London. In spite of the harm she did to them as a group, working-class people played an important part in Thatcher's three successive electoral victories. The Skriker's magnetism, ability to play to the needs of those she intends to exploit, slippery speech, single-minded persistence, and use of divide-and-conquer tactics connect with the view of Thatcher held by Britain's socialists, with whom Churchill has consistently allied herself.

From a similar political standpoint, Josie and Lily can be seen as ordinary teenagers struggling to come of age in the wake of the Thatcher years, when public institutions designed to provide support for vulnerable individuals and groups were in serious decline. Young people of the early 1990s had grown up amid the economic crises of the 1970s, the cuts to education and social services, the increase in unemployment, and a general decline in traditional family life — all this time being told by their government's leader that they should take responsibility for themselves. The public began to ask questions about the deleterious effects of this environment on young people when a shocking act of violence occurred in 1993: in Liverpool, two-year-old James Bulger was tortured and murdered by a pair of ten-year-old boys who had enticed him away from his mother in a crowded shopping area. In the mid-1990s an outpouring of plays by young people, dubbed "in-yer-face" plays by the media, focused attention on their generation. Young playwrights like Sarah Kane portrayed their generation as crippled, ineffective, isolated, and either spurred to violence by anger or paralyzed by drug-induced indifference. When placed in political context, the isolation of Josie and Lily, their weakness, their ambivalent anger and indifference mark them as members of the generation known as Thatcher's children.[3] The Skriker makes visible the psychological, social, and economic burden carried by young people of the mid–1990s, as they confronted moral choices in a society that had embraced a creed of selfishness, callousness, and ruthless competition.

The use of mythic figures and themes, however, expands the scope of the play beyond its immediate historical moment. It warns of both social breakdown and natural catastrophe as a result of neglecting those in need of nurture and care and continuously assaulting the natural environment — sacrificing the future in order to meet demands for excess in the present. The Skriker's relentless pursuit of the young reveals her need to annihilate the future. Lily's loss of her baby, her friend, and her own life foretells the fate of humankind. The play's final line, "And she was dustbin" (52), expresses not just death but total erasure. Unlike the classical treatment of the Furies in which they ultimately become the Eumenides and create the concept of justice, this play does not end with acceptance, reconciliation, or restoration of balance. It briefly reveals a future in which the only forms of human life are the hag and the horrible, raging changeling child. Both humanity and nature have been drained of vitality. As the Skriker warns, "Spring will return and nothing will grow" (44).

NOTES

1. This rhyme, as the program for the Royal National Theatre production explained, comes from an English folk story about a little girl named Rosy whose stepmother killed her by beheading her with the heavy lid of a trunk. Page numbers here and throughout the essay refer to *The Skriker* by Caryl Churchill published in 1994 by Nick Hern Books.

2. For further information on the figures from British folklore referred to in the play, see Briggs, *The Fairies in English Tradition and Literature*.

3. The phrase "Thatcher's children" was suggested by drama critic Benedict Nightingale's characterization of the "in yer face" playwrights as "Mrs Thatcher's disorientated children," as quoted in Saunders, *"Love Me or Kill Me": Sarah Kane and the Theatre of Extremes*, 6.

WORKS CITED

Briggs, Katherine Mary. *The Fairies in English Tradition and Literature*. Chicago: University of Chicago Press, 1967.

Churchill, Caryl. *Plays: 3*. London: Nick Hern Books, 1998.

_____. *The Skriker*. London: Nick Hern Books, 1994.

Saunders, Graham. *"Love Me or Kill Me": Sarah Kane and the Theatre of Extremes*. Manchester: Manchester University Press, 2002.

Between Desire and Authority

The "Dybbuk" in Modernist and Postmodern Theatrical Adaptations from S. Ansky to Tony Kushner

SHARON FRIEDMAN

A dybbuk, a deceased's spirit that enters the body of the living and manifests itself through the utterance and action of its host, has its origins in Jewish folklore and popular belief as well as in conceptions of the human soul and reincarnation envisioned in the Jewish mystical tradition of Kabbalah in early modern Europe, particularly Spain. It becomes more prominent in Jewish literature featuring accounts of possession and exorcism in sixteenth century Safed (Palestine) after the Spanish expulsion of the Jews in 1492[1]; however, dybbuk narratives appear throughout the Jewish Diaspora for over four centuries, and were popularized in rituals and folk tales among Eastern European Jewry, especially Hasidim, in the eighteenth and nineteenth centuries.[2] Indeed, in Hasidism, a pietistic and ecstatic form of Judaism, storytelling was an integral part of religious worship (Ben-Amos xxvi). Dybbuk possession is most famously the subject of S. Ansky's play *The Dybbuk, or Between Two Worlds* (1914–1919), written in Yiddish and based on ethnographic research conducted by its author in Russia and the Ukraine, where he gathered songs, stories, rituals, and superstitions. Translator Joachim Neugroschel observes that Ansky "splices Hasidic tales and parables into the action [of the drama] almost as if they were arias" (xiii).

Ansky's play was first produced by the Vilna Theatre troupe in Warsaw in 1920 as a tribute to him following his death, and then in Moscow in 1922 by the Habimah Theatre, whose mission was to "introduce the sacred to the secular world" (Alekson 150). Constantin Stanislavsky, an admirer of the play in its earliest incarnation, recommended it to the Habimah Theatre, and his student Evgeny Vakhtangov directed it from a Hebrew translation of the Yiddish in a highly theatricalized and expressionist production.[3] Since that time

The Dybbuk and dybbuk-inspired folklore have spawned a plethora of trans-lations and adaptations in a range of genres — theatre, opera, novels, film, musical compositions, and dance by such noted artists as Aaron Copland, George Balanchine, Jerome Robbins, Leonard Bernstein, Anna Sokolow, Pearl Lang, and Eliot Feld. Theatrical adaptations include productions by Paddy Chayefsky, Joseph Chaikin, Katie Mitchell, and Tony Kushner.

Several scholars point out that in historical, cultural, and literary contexts surrounding the dybbuk (accounts, reports, and folklore) most of the possessed have been women and the possessors men, and that many of these accounts and scenarios are integrally related to a patriarchal system that regulates the body and sexuality through religious law, cultural norms, and communal prac-tices.[4] Furthermore, the dybbuk narrative in its variant forms was traditionally mediated by men — participants, witnesses, and storytellers. Ansky's dramatic scenario, as well as subsequent adaptations, involves the penetration of a female body by the spirit of her (un)dead beloved on the eve of her arranged marriage to another, and the exorcism of this spirit is undertaken by a community of pious men through the authority and metaphysical knowledge of its religious leader.

This paper will bring a gendered reading to a legendary tale as it has been interpreted theatrically by Ansky in his foundational twentieth-century play and by contemporary theatre artists who have adapted its scenario. I will give special attention to Tony Kushner's *A Dybbuk,* staged at New York City's Joseph Papp Public Theater in 1997, and published the following year.[5] Clearly the continuing appeal of *The Dybbuk* for theatrical performance speaks to the drama inherent in a possession narrative that is sexually charged (Chajes 2). Indeed, in all these productions, the entry of a male spirit into a receptive female body surrounded by a homosocial community of men intent on ousting that spirit and reclaiming the woman's body to perpetuate their line both eroticizes and politicizes the possession and the exorcism. The performance of the *The Dybbuk* in any of its incarnations stages and often subverts gender norms and power relations in both spiritual and bodily manifestations. In reading for gender in dramatic adaptations, however, it is also important to call attention to historical moment, cultural ideology, dramaturgical practice, and theatrical venue for shaping an interpretation of a story that has achieved mythic stature.

Dybbuk Mythology and Folk Tales

According to Rachel Elior, the dybbuk was inspired by a "collective myth" within traditional Jewish society grounded in a set of beliefs shared by various communities (64), although, as Neugroschel points out, the doctrine of reincarnation was generally unknown in the Torah and Talmud and condemned by Jewish theologians (ii). In a particularly lucid description of the universe imagined in mystical kabbalistic doctrine, which gives rise to dybbuk accounts and narratives, Elior explains that "concealed and revealed realities were interwoven in a complex network of invisible forces and mythic beings" that linked the human world to "representations of the sacred world and eternal life" as well as to the world of "impurity and death" (46). Beliefs included the transmigration of souls, a "permeable boundary" between the realms of the dead and of the living, and a system of "reward and punishment that transcended the borders of life and death" (64). Practitioners of Kabbalah perceived human action and the life of the soul within a cosmic polarity of holiness and impurity, and sins and transgressions were seen to strengthen the forces of evil. Thus, an individual could be caught "against his or her will" by negative forces aligned with the realm of impurity. The dybbuk is "a spirit of impurity," a soul of a deceased person who cannot even enter Gehenna (a hell-like realm) because of sins committed when among the living. This soul attempts to escape the pursuing forces by "penetrating" a living body — possibly a body of one who has committed transgressions — "seizing" it, "adhering" to it, and speaking from the mouth of the person possessed in the persona of the departed (46–48; 59–60).

The presence of a dybbuk induces in the possessed a disturbed state of mind, an altered consciousness, a distorted physical demeanor, deviant conduct that resembles an affliction, and in women a lowered voice. The disturbance that erupts when a body is inhabited by a dybbuk requires a ritual exorcism conducted by rabbis, revered kabbalists, or, in Eastern Europe, *tzaddikim* ("righteous ones") — Hasidic leaders and wonder-workers. These mystical ideas and ritual orders were encoded in kabbalistic morality literature, and popularized and disseminated through conduct literature, hagiographies of revered rabbis, pietistic literature, and folk tales (Elior 48).

The dybbuk, therefore, constitutes an element in the kabbalistic mythic cosmology as well as a motif in folk tales about possessions and legendary figures who have performed exorcisms among other miraculous feats. Tamar Alexander notes that written folk tales coexist with oral narration, thus widening the audience privy to the narrative. She sees oral narrative as a "communicative performance event that mutually relates the narrator and audience, as well as a cultural communicative event that relates the individual to the surrounding society" (308). Eli Yassif argues that the folk legend is close to historical narrative, but "demands that its hearers believe what is being told and seeks to strengthen society's faith in the events related" (362). Thus, legendary dybbuk tales became exemplary, testifying to the existence of God, to his dominion over the world, and to the religious system of reward and punishment. Yassif argues that "edification" is one function of this tale that emerges from the self-awareness of the sinner (364). And the community who either witnesses or learns about the exorcism participates in a public moral lesson that is reinforced by the narrative form as well as the exorcism ceremony (Alexander 317). The legendary rabbi or tzaddik becomes the central figure of hagiographies and biographical legends, and makes this edification possible, thus further reinforcing the community's religious norms and its cohesiveness. In his study of spirit possession in Judaism, Matt Goldish speculates that possessions might be symptomatic of an era of uncertainty and "identity displacement" (25–26) such as the expulsion of Jews from Spain and the brutal assaults on Jews of Eastern Europe. However, the context and purpose of the narration transforms each account, depending upon time and place, historical circumstances, and purpose of the narrator.

Gender and the Dybbuk

Several scholars from a range of disciplines have focused on the predominance of women inhabited by dybbuks in possession narratives, and offer various interpretations of this phenomenon. In her book-length analysis of dybbuks and Jewish women, Elior examines the interrelationships between mysticism, folklore, and social history. Drawing on the scholarship of Gedaliah Nigal, Yorum Bilu, and J.H. Chajes, she notes that many of the possessed women came from lower social classes, and the majority of the girls above the age of puberty, in the liminal stage between virginal maidenhood and arranged marriage, were brides about to be married or recently married. In accounts and stories, men constituted ninety percent of the possessing spirits. Inferring from Nigal's more than eighty stories about dybbuks and exorcisms from the sixteenth through the twentieth centuries, Elior suggests that the possessed body is controlled not only by representations of the "chaotic world of the dead," but also by the social expectations and conduct associated with matchmaking, marriage, enforced sexual relations, and family that supported religious, sexual, and social norms, particularly of early and arranged marriages. Elior sees in the victim's implicit story "anxiety over undesired matches, compelled marriages, rape, incest, or bodily or psychological compulsion of the weak by the strong." She also suggests the possibility that women who did not have the vocabulary or the means for speaking out about their needs and fears, and were not to be heard in public, could, through dybbuk possession, express themselves through physical and mental ailments and the madness associated with these symptoms (52–57; 60–62). This behavior would disrupt ordinary life and provide a reprieve at a critical moment only to be followed by the often grueling ritual exorcism.

Both Elior and Alexander observe that the language of dybbuk possession (the Yiddish word *dybbuk* stems from the Hebrew root meaning "adhere") resonates with the notion of clinging, adhering to, breaching bodily boundaries that are permitted only in intercourse within marriage. Indeed, the dybbuk is often described as an "ibbur," an earlier term for the spirit's entry into a person's body. In males this might indicate possession by a deity and thus be highly valued, but in women it is more likely to be seen as "impregnation" or even "rape" by an evil spirit (Elior 65–67; Alexander 311–313, Keller 200). However, as Alexander maintains, the victim performs a "double function, both passive and active." Although she is envisioned as the "vessel" for the spirit and the "conduit" for the spirit's story, she is simultaneously an "instigating force who manifests her personality through those powers" (313).

Mary Keller, a feminist philosopher and historian of religion, rejects "dualistic notions" such as "active-passive" or "agent-victim" and gives credence to what witnesses to the possession articulate as a "power" that overcomes the possessed from an ancestor, deity, or spirit. Indeed, she argues against interpretations that theorize the possessed as "repressed psychological bodies, oppressed sociological bodies, or oppressed women's bodies" (vii–viii). In her study of women, power, and spirit possession, she reformulates agency and subjectivity, and revalues "receptivity and permeability" beyond the negative connotations of fragility or passivity of the "less than rational agent" that she perceives in Western scholarly paradigms of the possessed. Within this framework she proposes the concept of "instrumental agency" to suggest the power of receptivity, which she compares metaphorically to a "hammer, flute or horse that is wielded, played, or mounted" (9, 73–101). This instrumentality points to the "practical work, war, and play" that is achieved by possessed bodies. More specifically, she sees in the predominance of women's bodies in Hasidic dybbuk stories a "gendered parallel sacred space," and counters the gendered differentiation between positive and negative possession. Instead, she argues that "'evil' possessions are not evil because they save the soul of both the *dybbuk* and its host" and thus provide evidence of women's participation in the religious dimensions of a community as instrumental agencies (205–206).

Even within these divergent feminist interpretations of dybbuk narratives, it is important to note that Elior, Alexander, and Keller all give attention to Ansky's play *The Dybbuk* as an important source with which to investigate the subject of women's relationship to power and authority in accounts and tales of dybbuk possession. However, these theorists also acknowledge that the play is a highly mediated form and must also be interpreted in the context of the playwright's historical moment. Ansky brings a modernist perspective to his work that recognizes the fragmentation and gradual disappearance of village communities at the turn of the twentieth century, including the absolute patriarchal authority of its elders, impacted by modernity. Discourses of gender pervade Ansky's depiction of the brotherhood of Hasidim in their schools, their prayers, in marriage contracts, and in their ceremonial efforts to preserve their traditions. However, it is worth noting from the outset that the dybbuk in Ansky's tale emerges not from an impure spirit (that threatens the community) but a fated love between a man and a woman thwarted by the community of elders. The authority of this brotherhood, and even its esteemed rabbi, is subject to scrutiny when the exorcism, rather than ousting the spirit from the woman's body, gives rise to a fusion of their souls.

Each subsequent production and adaptation of this mythical dybbuk narrative is informed by the discourses of its historical and cultural moment. What seems most consistent in artistic re-workings of the scenario is attention to, and in some cases amplification of, the performative as well as erotic aspects of the possession and exorcism. A man's spirit welcomed into a young woman's body, a male voice emanating from that body, and the community of men that authorizes itself to exorcise both spirit and voice have prompted artists and scholars to ponder the ways in which power relations in this legendary story are gendered, eroticized, and performed.

S. Ansky's The Dybbuk[6]

S. Ansky's drama has become almost synonymous with the mythic folklore surrounding dybbuk possession, and deserves as much attention as a primary source of the modernist and postmodern adaptations that it has produced. Almost all interpretations of Ansky's text point to the romance in his version of the story, in which two young lovers eventually possess each other to resist the claims of their elders and transform possession into a kind of holy fusion. As David Roskies asserts: "No story before Ansky's had ever told of a dybbuk who was a lover in disguise" (xxvii). The scenario unfolds through a series of obstacles that thwart a young couple's desires for an earthly union.

Leah, the daughter of Sender, a wealthy merchant, has been betrothed to a prosperous member of the community in the shtetl (small village) of Brinnitz in Poland. However, her father's arrangement of her marriage betrays the love of her former suitor Khonen, a poor Yeshiva scholar. Ironically, the arranged marriage also betrays an earlier pact that Leah's father (Sender) had made with Khonen's father (Nissin) in their idealistic and impassioned youth — that if one had a son and the other a daughter, their children would someday marry. All of these circumstances are at first unknown or unacknowledged between the characters. Khonen's father had moved away and died long before the events depicted in the play. And Sender claims not to have known that the quiet young Yeshiva scholar (Khonen) who visited his home so often for dinner was the son of his old friend Nissin, and therefore Leah's original betrothed, when he arranged a new and profitable marriage for his daughter. Khonen never discloses his feelings for Leah to Sender, and the chaste couple never acknowledges their feelings to each other, beyond shy glances, until the exorcism. Despite his private attempts to win Leah's hand through fasts, ritual ablutions, spells, mortification of the flesh, and kabbalistic meditations, Khonen fails. When her engagement is announced in the temple, he whispers forbidden words ("the two-fold utterance of the Holy Name" [Ansky, act 1, 20]) and dies of grief. As the wedding ceremony begins, he possesses Leah's body as a dybbuk that can only be exorcised by the incantations of the tzaddik, Rabbi Azriel.

Leah's betrothal to the wealthy prospective bridegroom sets off a series of events (including her visit to the cemetery) that disrupts not only the wedding, but also the cohesive community centered on the synagogue, the religious sanctuary of men in their prayers, and the harmonious relationship between the community and the spiritual world. The negotiations undertaken to re-establish order begin with a rabbinical court that reviews the sins of Sender, accused by the deceased spirit Nissin of breaking their youthful vow. The exorcism ceremony that follows involves worship and communion with the dead in the presence of fourteen men summoned as witnesses. The tzaddik issues threats of excommunication to the dybbuk Khonen, and then promises of divine forgiveness if he leaves Leah's body. However, the moment is tense and the outcome uncertain. Just prior to these ceremonial incantations, we hear the anguished plaint of the tzaddik, plagued by doubts that he might not be the emissary of God. Furthermore, a mysterious messenger is present throughout the play, interceding at key turns in the plot to utter kabbalistic pronouncements that remind audiences of a higher power at work overseeing bonds as well as rifts in cosmic realms.

In the final moment of Ansky's play and in subsequent adaptations, the traditional exorcism fails and the conflict resolves in an unexpected turn. Although Rabbi Azriel has succeeded in "ripp[ing] apart all the threads that tie ... [Khonen] to the world of the living and to the body and soul of Leah," Leah awakens to Khonen's soul (act 4, 48). She steps out of the circle drawn around her by the tzaddik and "fuses" with Khonen as they ascend together in what she sees as a "giant light" pouring all around them, no longer, as the title suggests, "between two worlds." Whereas Roskies interprets the romance in Ansky's adaptation as a secularization of the tale, Keller critiques the notion of secularization in this context as placing an "artificial barrier" between "religious bodies and sexual bodies." She perceives Leah as both a "desiring subject" and an "instrumental agency" for the sacred vow between the fathers and a cultural memory to be brought before the community (210, 220). Paradoxically the original betrothal arranged between the fathers when they were young and passionate Yeshiva scholars uninterested in financial gain becomes not only fated between the lovers but also desired by them. Both affective bonds — between the fathers and between their children — have given rise to varied interpretations, including homoeroticism between the men, in subsequent adaptations of the play.

"Between Two Worlds," the alternate title of Ansky's *The Dybbuk* has often been invoked to describe the playwright himself as he oscillated between assimilation into other cultures and a return to his roots. As a young man, Ansky (born Shloyme-Zanvl Rappoport) brought an enlightenment perspective to his critique of the religious ideology of Jews living in the Pale of Settlement between Europe and Russia. Through his travels, however, he also became interested in socialism and nationalism. Influenced by Revolutionary thought, he became active in the General Jewish Labor Bund (General Union of Jewish Workers) in Lithuania, Poland, and Russia, that incorporated traditional elements into their socialist activities. Given the dire threats of anti–Semitism and pogroms, Ansky was eventually drawn to Zionism and a developing Jewish nationalism. His ethnographic project sought to record his people's history and at the same time to advance their rights. As Neugroschel points out, during the period in which Ansky wrote his play, Jewish life in Eastern Europe experienced major transformations: modernism, industrialism, technology, economic hardship, pogroms, mass emigration, World War I, the Russian Revolution, and the collapse of the tsarist and the Austro-Hungarian empires. Clearly, this is a period of great uncertainty and displacement, and the world that Ansky depicts was already vanishing by the time that his play was produced in 1920 (Neugroschel 115–116). Not surprisingly Ansky's vision combines modernity and tradition, transforming folklore into modern theatre and critiquing the materialist underpinnings of arranged marriage against the background of the romantic ideals he saw in folklore about marriages "decreed in heaven." He characterizes his play as a "realistic drama about mystics" that adds a Messenger from a "higher world" to suggest that Khonen's yearnings might be as much "celestial" as earthly ("*From* A Letter to Khaim Zhitlovsky" 1–2).

Naomi Seidman articulates the paradox of this unusual combination of modernity and tradition as "Ansky's superimposition of a Haskalah [Jewish Enlightenment] narrative of sexual rebellion over a layer of folkloric beliefs in the predestination of love" (232–233). This combination speaks to both the older generation confronting cultural displacement and the new generation struggling to assert itself through different movements and discourses. Seidman argues that Ansky's play shapes a new conception of the relationship between modernity and tradition that rejects an exclusive reliance on European modernism to include folk wisdom. The play becomes "the very insignia of his literary generation of Yiddish post–Haskalah (Enlightenment) modernists." Khonen and Leah's attraction might be seen to emerge from two derivations at once: "one instinctual and preconscious, the other historical and traditional," and they are "one and the same" (233).

The question, however, remains: do traditional gender norms remain in place insofar as Ansky's modernist scenario envisions a heterosexual love between two desiring subjects who not only reject the authority of their immediate elders in a romantic tale of love beyond death, but also achieve their union through a spiritual concept of transmigrating souls? Does Leah claim a kind of agency in Ansky's version of a dybbuk story by reaching out to her possessor and to the celestial bonds that they both pursue? Scholars ponder a range of interpretations. Neugroschel asserts that "metaphysically Leah is passive, but psychologically, by admitting or imagining the dybbuk, she is active" (xii). Keller, as we have already noted, sees her as metaphysically active in her assertion that the possessed Leah comprises instrumental agency in a metaphysical struggle. Elior suggests that Leah is active, both psychologically and metaphysically, as she defies both the wedding and the exorcism. She observes a central element of the staging of *The Dybbuk* that is carried over in every adaptation: "the wedding ceremony [arranged by Sender in act 2] and the dybbuk exorcism ceremony [arranged by Rabbi Azriel in act 4] are like "photographic images of each other" in the play's depiction of Jewish life in eastern European communities during the eighteenth and nineteenth centuries (111–112). Both scenes exert the power of authority. For Elior the wedding ceremony serves as the "epicenter" for the conflict between the social norm of arranged marriage and the emergence of individual desire that disrupts the normative order of the community intent on exorcizing this intruding spirit. Elior interprets Leah's possession as a pathway to resist the marriage imposed upon her. (Indeed, the wealthy bridegroom and his family stand waiting to seal the marriage just moments after the exorcism.) The failed exorcism might be seen as symbolic of Leah's and Khonen's power to recover their bond beyond "social domination and regulation, relationships between strong and weak, rulers and ruled, men and women" (118) and to enter a kind of "paradise" where both are engaged in the ecstatic life of *devekut* (bonding) with the divine (123).

Although Ansky's play has been interpreted as a critique of the politics and economics of arranged marriage (Bienstock Anolik 47), Ansky, in a letter to his friend Khaim Zhitlovsky, suggests an ambivalent attitude toward Khonen and Leah's plight: the "battle between the individual and the collective — more precisely, between the individual's striving for happiness and the survival of the nation," symbolized by the tzaddik's worry that that if Leah joins Khonen, "'a living branch [Leah] will wither on the eternal tree of the people of Israel.'" The second conflict occurs between the higher power that impels Khonen to pursue his claim and the tzaddik who will not deviate from the exorcism no matter the cost. In both conflicts the playwright asks, "Which side is right? ... Ultimately Khonen and Leah are the victors. But is the tsaddik [*sic*] wrong? ... For the Messenger, both sides are right — right and even more righteous in their battle." However, as Khonen loses his strength, "his spark," he blends with Leah's flame, and "[t]he Messenger holds with the tsaddik — that is, he holds him back" ("*From* A Letter to Khaim Zhitlovsky" 1–2). Although Leah regrets her unborn children with Khonen, she does not acquiesce in the community's wishes to produce heirs. Instead, she finds her own spiritual redemption, her own voice, in adhering to Khonen and ascending with him into the flame. The ambiguities in both the conflicts and the resolution have generated numerous interpretations by leading artists and scholars.

Modernist and Postmodern Adaptations *of* The Dybbuk

Twentieth-century adaptations of *The Dybbuk* abound. Even before it was translated into Hebrew by H.N. Bialik and staged in Moscow by the Habimah Theatre in 1922, it was produced by Maurice Schwartz at New York City's Yiddish Art Theatre in 1920, followed by a successful production in English at the Neighborhood Playhouse in New York City (1925–1926). The play became the hallmark production for the Habimah Theater, which traveled extensively before settling into its permanent home in Israel in 1928, and it has been translated and produced worldwide. In 1959, Paddy Chayefsky's Tony-nominated Broadway production of *The Tenth Man*, directed by Tyrone Guthrie, transposed the play, with significant alterations, to Mineola, Long Island, where the protagonist is a depressed and dissolute young Manhattan lawyer who in becoming the tenth man of the minyan (as suggested by the title) discovers his own dybbuk as do the other men in the community. The focus is clearly on the men in this play as they try to exorcise an imagined demon from the granddaughter of one of the synagogue members — a young woman about to be institutionalized for schizophrenia. As the protagonist exorcizes his dybbuk, the young girl becomes his salvation. Most of the subsequent adaptations of *The Dybbuk* stay closer to Ansky's scenario, focused on the intense possession scene and/or the exorcism that only brings the couple closer together as they ascend to a celestial realm.

Several modernist stage productions invite audiences to consider the performative aspects of dybbuk possession and exorcism to "make things happen," and theatre artists use the body, voice, language, and stage space to effectively represent the "performance within the performance" (Keller 220) and the erotics of this mythic and legendary tale. The original Habimah Theatre production in Moscow, directed by Evgeny Vakhtangov (1922), one of the most renowned expressionist directors in Russia, used elements of fantasy and distortion in an intensely theatricalized production. According to Pearl Fishman, he "employed theatrical freezes, silences, chanting, singing, ghostly makeup and grotesque formalized movement" — a "fantastic-grotesque" performance style. When the company moved to Israel, its aesthetic became the Israeli National Theatre's signature style, and the play was mounted at least 1,100 times between 1922 and 1980 (Fishman qtd. in Alekson 150–151). It is not surprising, then, that *The Dybbuk* has inspired several choreographers of note (Anna Sokolow, Pearl Lang, Nora Kaye and Herbert Ross, Eliot Feld, and Jerome Robbins with music by Leonard Bernstein) to create dance adaptations that use the body in inventive spatial configurations to express the emotional intensity involved not only in thwarted love but also in possession, exorcism, and ecstatic worship.[7]

Perhaps the most cited rendering of this mythic drama is the celebrated 1937 expressionist Polish-Yiddish film *Der Dibek*, directed by Michal Waszynski, the wunderkind of Polish cinema, who claimed to have studied with Stanislavky in Moscow. The film also employs the aesthetic of the fantastic-grotesque in its *danse macabre* that suggests alterity and the nightmarish quality of transgression. A death-masked figure, shrouded in a prayer shawl, embraces the "entranced" bride who not only hallucinates the dybbuk but also warms to the specter's embrace (Hoberman 280). Furthermore, the film envisions the earlier relationship between the fathers that critic Noami Seidman reads as homoerotic even in Ansky's version. (233). In a striking departure from other dramatizations of the scenario, *Der Dibek* inserts a lengthy prologue in which Sender and Nissin, depicted as passionate young students, enact their pledge to unite their children in marriage and thus form a lifelong biological bond. Thus, the film not only privileges the earlier arrangement born out of religious study and deep feeling, but also foregrounds the profound love between the men.

The Dybbuk has continued to attract new translators and avant-garde directors who have found innovative strategies to stage the struggle between tradition and modernity and the constraints and desires rooted in spiritual and earthly concerns. In a 1977–1978 production, Joseph Chaikin, founder of the Open Theatre, directed an adaptation of *The Dybbuk* with a new translation by Mira Rafalowicz, for the New York Public Theater. Reviewer Oscar Giner situated Chaikin's production in the modern theatre that "allows for the presence in Nature of the palpable manifestions of divine intelligence; it upholds firmly a visible communion between two realms of existence — the eternal and the mortal"(149). Chaikin and Rafalowicz pared down the script and deleted naturalist details to create an atmospheric production focused on the central image of the dybbuk and the process of its "epiphany." According to Giner, the emphasis of the production is on the "summoning, the bringing forth, the facticity of the *presence* of the foreign spirit in the mortal body: something which, standing as a counterpoint to the appearance of the *dybbuk*, reflects an instability in the frameworks of reality set by the play, and further contributes to the shattering of the divisions that separate Chanon [*sic*] and Leah" (150). The dybbuk is always visible with Leah, and the director combines the actors playing Leah and Chonen to express the dybbuk in sounds, cries, or movement. In other words, Chaikin fuses the spiritual and mortal and negates the boundaries between these realms as well as between the lovers.

The 1990s witnessed several incarnations of Ansky's rendering of a dybbuk narrative. In 1992 three theatrical productions experimented with different approaches to situating and staging the haunting quality of the tale. Katie Mitchell's production for the Royal Shakespeare Company relied on Rafalowitz's script (used by Chaikin). As a director known for her extensive research around her dramatic subjects, Mitchell brought in wedding guests with their formal attire "caked in Ukranian mud." Even in the scenes that take place in candlelight to evoke an aura of the mystery in a universe where the dead inhabit the living, Iving Wardle sees Mitchell's achievement in presenting such beliefs as part of "humdrum reality" (1). Two other productions appeared in London in 1992: Bruce Myers (Peter Brook's associate) staged "A Dybbuk for Two People" using a framing device of a Sabbath dinner to tell the story enacted by two performers morphing into different roles; and Julia Pascal framed another telling of the tale within a World War II ghetto, where secular Jews recount the story as they hide from Nazi stormtroopers. Clearly, these framing devices signal to audiences the need for this story to be retold in different contexts.[8]

The 1990s also produced renderings of dybbuk narratives informed by feminist and queer theory. "Retellings" of Jewish tales in novels, such as Judith Katz's *Running Fiercely Toward a High Thin Sound* (1992) and Ellen Galford's *The Dyke and the Dybbuk* (1994), might be read productively alongside theatrical adaptations of this period in terms of re-conceiving the gendered dimensions of the tale. They create dybbuks who are female and lesbian. They speak in their own voices, transform lives of the possessed in alternate scenarios, and, as Ruth Bienstock Anolik observes, inject the notion that women can share a love as intense as that experienced by the young male Yeshiva students (49) as well as Khonen and Leah. Agnieszka Legutko observes in dybbuk novels by women a focus on the possessed woman, as much as on the female dybbuk, while the exorcist, the legendary character of traditional narratives, is given a secondary role (7).[9]

These novels provide intriguing intertexts to perhaps the best-known contemporary theatrical adaptation of *The Dybbuk,* entitled *A Dybbuk,* by celebrated playwright Tony Kushner in 1997. Both Bienstock Anolik and Legutko cite Kushner's interpretation of *The Dybbuk* in terms of his depiction of restrictions on women in Hassidic communities and the "homosexual subtext" in the relationships between the young Yeshiva scholars as well as between the fathers in Ansky's play, first alluded to in the 1937 film. For Kushner, as for Legutko, the dybbuk itself is a transgressive image of gender ambiguity in a culture with seemingly fixed gender distinctions, and a metaphor for the consummation of the fathers' love for each other through the union of their children. (Schifrin 35 qtd. in Bienstock Anolik 49; Legutko 12). All of these interpretations engage the construction of masculinity and femininity by the patriarchal community of the synagogue and the village, and suggest the potential of the dybbuk to deconstruct the masculine/feminine dichotomy represented by Khonen and Leah's fusion. Indeed, Alisa Solomon observes in Kushner's "complex vision" several "opposing ideas [that] require and reproduce each other: death resides in life, male in female, the spiritual in the carnal, religious doubt in devotion, evil in goodness, social well-being in private acts, Hasidism in modernity, the holy in the profane" (121).

Tony Kushner's A Dybbuk

Tony Kushner was already in the process of writing *Angels in America* when Mark Lamos, artistic director of the Hartford Stage Company, suggested that Kushner adapt Ansky's *The Dybbuk,* given Kushner's interests in adaptation as well as Yiddish Theatre. Kushner had already adapted several prior works, and Lamos directed his adaptation of Corneille's 1636 comedy *L'Illusion comique* (1636), which Kushner entitled *The Illusion* (1989).[10] His version of Ansky's play resonates with issues that James Fisher has identified throughout Kushner's oeuvre: the "collisions of history, literature, art, spirituality, race and ethnicity, gender and sexuality, and politics..." (*Tony Kushner* 3). It is apparent that Rabbi Azriel confronts an issue (albeit in very different terms) that torments the characters in *Angels in America*: the "difficulty to understand God's harsh ways, seeming indifference to human suffering, and abandonment of his creations," and at the same time the need to seek out the potential in the universe for redemption and justice (Fisher, *Theater* 142–143). These issues seem particularly urgent during periods of enormous social change: for Ansky, industrialism, mass immigration, pogroms, and World War I; for Kushner, the ravages of modern warfare, continued oppression for marginalized communities, and the AIDS epidemic that had decimated the gay community (Alekson 168). In the final scene of Kushner's dybbuk play, Rabbi Azriel tells the Messenger that the "more cause He gives to doubt Him ... [t]he deeper delves faith. Though His love become only abrasion, derision, excoriation, tell Him, I cling.... We will always find Him, no matter how few there are ... [t]o deliver our complaint" (act 4, 106).

Lamos ultimately directed Kushner's *A Dybbuk* in 1995 for the Hartford, and Brian Kulick directed Kushner's revised script for the play's premiere at the New York Public Theater in 1997. At the outset of the process, Kushner asked Joachim Neugroschel to produce a new translation from Ansky's Yiddish text that Kushner would then adapt. Kushner's change in title from *The Dybbuk* to *A Dybbuk* suggests that his dybbuk adaptation is one among many and that the dybbuk that haunts Kushner's play is one among many "dybbuks" that might be "lurking" in the world (Rizzo qtd. in Alekson 155). Although Kushner has stated that his adaptation is "fairly straightforward" and that he retained Ansky's plot and structure, critics have observed changes in dialogue, inserted scenes, a tightening of specific sections of the structure, and most importantly his poetic verse in rendering the mystical moments in the play (Alekson 155, 161).

In both Ansky's and Kushner's plays chanting establishes a world that suggests both religious and erotic yearning. The dramas open with a passage from a nigun (a religious song), chanted in the dark before the curtain rises, and also at the end of the final act. The passage poses a question and offers a response pondered by the characters throughout the play: why does the soul fall from the "highest height'" to the "deepest end"? The answer? The fall contains the upward flight. As Seth Wolitz asserts, the chant establishes the theosophic and cosmic vision of Hasidism. A "spark of the divine has been cast down into the gross animal world," and "the interrogative sentence expresses human incomprehension if not despair facing this catastrophic cosmic event." However, "dross can be purified," and as a result of the process, the purified soul can rise even higher (191–192).

Perhaps most salient in Kushner's published version as well as in his 1995 production is that the soul in the chant belongs immediately to Khonen, at once the spiritual seeker and the lover who, in a sense, finds redemption, his kind of purification, in his union with Leah. In Ansky's opening scene in act 1, the audience is in darkness, and hears a "soft, mystical chanting in the distance." The chant is disembodied, though as the play unfolds it becomes associated with Khonen's plight. In Kushner's opening scene the audience sees (and hears) Khonen, also in darkness, chanting as he bathes himself in a ritual cleansing. Critic Richard Dyer of the *Boston Globe* describes this tableau in the Hartford production as Khonen rising "moon-pale and dripping from the waters of the ritual bath" (Dyer qtd. in Alekson 166), foreshadowing Khonen's transgressive claim (uttered to the more conventional scholar Henech, who fears Khonen's inquiries into kabbalistic mysteries): "We should not try to banish sin, but to make sin holy" (act 1, 25) Later in act 1 of both Ansky's and Kushner's texts, Khonen begins to chant a verse from the erotic "Song of Songs" just prior to seeing Leah and after she leaves the temple having kissed the Torah passionately in Khonen's presence. Leah's amorous embrace clearly signals her desire for Khonen, and Khonen's chanting in this context might be interpreted as enacting passion in both erotic and religious terms. Or it may be that Khonen cloaks his yearning for Leah in his recitation of "The Song of Songs," a Biblical text often read metaphorically as describing the love between humankind and God (Wolitz 194).

However individual, existential, and erotic Khonen's plight might at first seem in Kushner's version, Khonen, too, is quickly absorbed into an intensely homosocial community of men cloistered behind the curtain — the synagogue inhabited by young scholars studying Torah and the "Batlonim"— idlers waiting to be called upon (and paid) for ritual prayers that require the minyan of ten men. As in Ansky's play, we are invited into an intensely homosocial setting where men debate philosophical questions, such as the dangers of kabbalistic inquiry into the mysteries of the cosmos versus the more traditional Talmudic study of laws governing ethics and religious practice. Furthermore, although they are poor in comparison to Leah's father, Sender, these men comprise the social order that lauds arranged marriages for economic survival, stability, and procreation within the community. Beyond idle gossip, they are eager to learn news of the marriage contract Sender is in the process of arranging for his daughter, and they rejoice when Sender arrives with news that he has finally come to an agreement with another family. Because he is a prosperous member of this poor village, Sender's dealings with a family of means from another village becomes a central event in consolidating these communities, and this union trickles down to the most impoverished — hence, the choreographic attention to the "beggars' dance" in renderings of the wedding feast. However, beggars' clawing at the bride for good luck and Sender's attempt to ward off bad luck by entertaining the beggars also suggest class conflict in a community that celebrates the bartering of the bride for financial gain.

When women appear unexpectedly in the synagogue, they are seen as intruders, imploring the men to pray for sick daughters or those suffering in childbirth. One old woman bursts through the temple doors, wanting to "shove" her head into the Holy Ark holding the sacred Torah scrolls, imploring the men to pray for her ill daughter. In Kushner's version, the beadle of the temple explicitly tells the woman to leave because women are not "permitted here." In response, the woman tells them that she wants to "shriek at the Torahs," "douse" the flickering light with her tears, and rail against the King of the Universe for taking her child (act 1, scene 1, 19). When Leah arrives (presumably because she knows that Khonen is there), she is only admitted to view the ancient embroidered curtains of the Ark so that she can sew new ones in honor of her dead mother. Even Khonen describes the Torah scrolls inside the Ark "like dark men engulfed in shadow, draped in velvet shawls, bent over mysteries" that presumably do not concern the women (act 1, scene 1, 21). In act 2, Kushner inserts a scene in which Leah is instructed by her old nurse Fradde on the "three sins" for which a woman might die in childbirth, and the first is "not keeping separation when we are bleeding" (act 2, scene 1, 41). When the young and inept bridegroom arrives, he withdraws in terror from the arranged marriage, alluding to the morning prayer when he says, "no one is more grateful than I am" when we "thank God ... he didn't make us women" (act 2, scene 2, 59). Kushner is explicit in rendering the restrictions on women in holy worship, which then makes the union between Khonen's and Leah's souls all the more transgressive. Indeed, Leah's reclamation of Khonen's spirit might be seen as instrumental agency as well as an escape from her (second) arranged marriage.

Alisa Solomon observes that Kushner has "levitated to the surface" the homoeroticism of Ansky's text and that he adds a feminist perspective "for ballast." She argues that in Kushner's version, "the play's intensely homosocial world vibrates with erotic implication: the students' orgiastic dancing in the synagogue, the displaced marriage between the two fathers who have promised to betroth their children to each other, the son's sensual recitation of the 'Song of Songs'"(121). In interviews about his adaptation, Kushner has spoken directly to the transgressive dimensions that he sees in Ansky's rendering of the story: "I would really like to have people see A Dybbuk as a gay play, not because I've done things to make it gay, but because there are all sorts of ways this is a play about gender transgression and the refusal of love to obey moral strictures. But also I want homosexuals to come watch Rabbi Azriel the exorcist, wrestling with God, because I feel that's part of the gay project" (Goldstein 59).

Kushner's interpretive stance toward the homoerotic subtexts he reads in Ansky's play resonates with recent queer studies interpretations of The Dyb-

buk and underscores the fertile ground between theory and theatre. In an article entitled "The Ghost of Queer Loves Past," Naomi Seidman argues that Ansky presents two pairs of lovers: the two fathers, Sender and Nissin, "whose bond has the force of fate," and the young couple who "reenact" their love. "The key to understanding [Khonen and Leah's] otherworldly power lies in the homoerotic friendship that refuses to remain relegated to the past or to the background. In *The Dybbuk* homosexual and heterosexual love are mutually dependent, and as a combined system, act as the very engine of the social order rather than operating at its margins"(243). One of the rabbis dreams of the broken vow between Sender and Nissin that then calls forth the rabbinic trial. And when Sender is reminded that he has betrayed Nissin, he quickly acknowledges his betrayal and agrees to mourn for Nissin and, as penance, to give charity to the poor. Sender even admits that he was always drawn to Nissin's son but never asked his parentage because he was poor. In addition to the homoeroticism that Seidman reads in this play, she sees the dybbuk as an expression of ambivalent heterosexuality, a "conflation of male and female in a single body," an "over determined figure" that mediates between life and death, male and female, the transcendent and the deformed, victimization and empowerment (236–237) — a perspective that Kushner clearly finds intriguing.

Kushner's revised production for the Public Theatre drew critics' attention to the historical dimensions of his play perhaps at the expense of the eroticism foregrounded in the first production.[11] He comes to the play with a profound awareness of the impending Holocaust that would destroy the world that Ansky knew so well, even in the midst of modernization and the assimilation that accompanied it. Perhaps to underscore this point, Kushner has inserted two scenes that speak to this historical transformation: the messenger travels on a train to Miropol, Poland where Rabbi Azriel resides, and his fellow travelers speak to him of modernization (the tempo of the trains, electricity) and the potential for Jews to assimilate. In act 4 Rabbi Azriel expounds on his uncertainty about his power to commune with God during these changing times. Even his scribe miraculously sees a page from the future unfolding itself in terms that resonate with the Holocaust and the destruction of his people.

I would argue, however, that the historical and erotic dimensions of the play are intertwined as the doomed couple resurrects their own faith in these changing times. They create a future that simultaneously refers back to the sacred and impassioned vow of their fathers and yet defies the elders in their community who have moved toward a materialist concept of arranged marriage. Historically their union evokes but opposes the image of the joint grave of a bride and groom in the village square, said to be murdered in the Khmieltnitsky massacres of the Jews (1648) and their ghosts invited to each wedding ceremony in perpetuity. When Leah goes to the gravesite to invite the couple to her arranged marriage, however, she summons Khonen's spirit as well. Unlike the buried couple, Khonen and Leah survive in more than memory. They are forever entwined in a hybrid spirit that ascends. When Khonen and Leah finally merge in what Leah calls a "Holy fire," their mystical union becomes intensely erotic precisely because they have endured separation in life. As Leah calls out to him: "Come to me my bridegroom, enter my heart, let me bear you there, my dead man, till in dreams at night I can deliver you, in dreams at night we can cradle the children we will never have..." (act four, scene 1, 104). Perhaps to the elders' dismay, they have made sin holy.

Conclusion: Twenty-First Century Dybbuks

The dybbuk legend has continued to intrigue writers and directors in the twenty-first century, giving rise to productions that use experimental staging, original music, and inventive choreography to foreground aspects of the scenario that seem most compelling to a particular artist. These adaptations include intercultural as well as feminist orientations. In 2002 director Zvika Serper and co-adapter Carol Fisher Sorgenfrei staged an intercultural production influenced by the style of Japanese theatre, particularly Noh theatre and elements of Kabuki, by finding the resonance in the surrealism of Kabbalah and elements of Japanese drama. Also in 2002, adapter and director, David Zinder staged *White Fire/Black Fire* (*The Dybbuk*), performed by the Hungarian State Theatre of Cluj, Romania, and nominated for the Romanian Theatre Union's Best Production Award for that year. The title alludes to the warning by the nurse Fradde to Leah when, in Khonen's presence, she kisses the Torah passionately: the Torah is made of black and white fire, and it will burn her if she lingers. Clearly Leah does not fear the fire, and in his comments on the play, Zinder tells his audiences that he has created "a very different, pro-active Leah, who wants to possess Hannan [*sic*] no less than he wants to possess her." Zinder's enigmatic character of the Meshulakh figure acknowledges that even though in retelling the story he has not been able to "change its tragic outcome," he will come back at some point in time and try again.[12]

We might conclude that contemporary theatre artists have, in a sense, acted as the most compelling messengers for this mythic story as they interpret it for new audiences, posing questions informed by their respective historical moment, ideological perspective, and aesthetic style. As theatre artists they show us the performative aspect of storytelling that makes things happen in ways that we might not anticipate even when we think we know what happens at the end.

NOTES

1. Alexander notes that the term *dybbuk* appears for the first time in a Yiddish pamphlet in Volhnia around 1680 (309). She maintains that the first known narrative refers to a case from 1563 in which the exorcist was R. Joseph Karo. Later exorcists in the kabbalistic tradition of the sixteenth and seventeenth centuries were R. Isaac Luria and his disciple R. Hayyim Vital (315), who conceptualized and described the rituals related to the dybbuk. Also note the distinctions between concepts of *gilgul, ibbur,* and *dybbuk.* Alexander cites, among her sources, Gershom Scholem's *Elements of the Kabbalah and Its Symbolism* (in Hebrew) (Jerusalem: Mosad Bialik, 1977).

2. Goldish offers several explanations for the development of possessions in Judaism, among them the evolving conception of the human soul in kabbalistic ontology, an increase in intellectual discourse among Jews, Christians, and Muslims in a period when Christians, especially, were witnessing a proliferation of possession events, and rapid changes during this period when accepted beliefs about God and the universe were being "challenged" by humanism, the Protestant Reformation, the scientific revolution, geographic exploration, and the military successes of the Muslim Ottomans. Goldish speculates that possessions might be symptomatic of an era of uncertainty and "identity displacement" (25–26). For other interpretations of possessions in Judaism, see Dan, 27–40; Chajes; Neugroschel, xiii.

3. For further discussion of Habimah's production, its theatrical aesthetics, and Nathan Altman's set and costume designs, see Fishman. The Yiddish version of the play *Tsvishn tsey veltn (Der Dibek)* was published in 1919 and was first staged on December 9, 1920 in Warsaw by the Vilna Troupe at the end of the 30-day period of mourning after Ansky's death. Also see Wolitz for a fully developed history of the play in the context of Ansky's life experience and his attempt to target two audiences — Russians and Jews.

4. See Gedaliah Nigal, *Dybbuk Tales in Jewish Literature* (1994); Yoram Bilu, "The Dybbuk in Judaism: Mental Disturbance as Cultural Resource," *Jerusalem Studies in Jewish Thought,* 2:4 (1983): 529–563; Chajes; Alexander; and Elior.

5. *A Dybbuk or Between Two Worlds* received its world premier in February 1995 at Hartford Stage Company, Hartford, Connecticut (Mark Lamos, Artistic Director). In November 1997 a revised version of the play was produced at New York City's Joseph Papp Public Theater/New York Shakespeare Festival (Brian Kulick, Director). Both productions incorporated original music composed by The Klezmatics. This paper will focus on the published play and will reference reviews of the 1995 and 1997 productions.

6. My discussion of Ansky's *The Dybbuk* relies on Joachim Neugroschel's translation published in *The Dybbuk and the Yiddish Imagination* (2000).

7. See Manor's analysis of the Beggars' Dance in Vakhtangov's Habimah Theatre production of *The Dybbuk.*

8. Bruce Myers' *A Dybbuk for Two People* (originally presented in 1989 by the Traveling Jewish Theatre) was produced at Hampstead Theatre, London NW3 on January 9, 1992; Julia Pascal's *The Dybbuk* was produced by New End Theatre, London NW3 on June 25, 1992.

9. Legutko presents a comparative analysis of the motif of dybbuk and spirit possession in E.M. Broner's *A Weave of Women,* Francine Prose's *Hungry Hearts,* Pearl Abraham's *The Romance Reader,*and Ruth Knafo Setton's *The Road to Fez,* and notes that these feminist dybbuk stories address issues such as arranged marriage, sexual difference, domestic violence, or mother-daughter relationships, and give less attention to the religious aspects of possession.

10. See Fisher's discussion of Kushner's adaptations in his chapter "Transformations and Convergences" in *The Theater of Tony Kushner*, 111–168. Also see Alekson's discussion of director Mark Lamos's interest in Ansky's *The Dybbuk* (152–153).

11. For a detailed comparative analysis of both productions and the distinctive directorial visions of Lamos and Kulick, see Alekson, who delineates the many ways in which Lamos's production stressed the love story related to Leah's possession by her lover and a more erotic concept of possession than Kulick's production. She also cites several reviewers (e.g., Ben Brantley, Charles Isherwood) who perceived the second production as more focused on historical collisions rather than on individual relationships.

12. Svika Serper's *The Dybbuk/Between Two Worlds* was originally produced at Tel Aviv University in 2002 using Bialik's Hebrew translation; David Zinder's *White Fire/Black Fire (The Dybbuk)* opened on May 13, 2002 at the Hungarian State Theatre of Cluj, Romania. See commentary at www.davidzinder.com/Production_2.htm. Also note that Theater J and Synetic Theater collaborated to produce a theatrical dance performance of *The Dybbuk*, with text written by Hannah Hessel and Paata Tsikurishvili in Washington, DC, 2006, and in that same year Eve Leigh adapted and directed *The Dybbuk* at the King's Head Theatre in Islington, London.

WORKS CITED

Alekson, Paula T. "When Worlds Collide, The Kushner-Lamos *A Dybbuk* at Hartford Stage." In *Tony Kushner: New Essays on the Art and Politics of the Plays*. Ed. Fisher. 149–171.

Alexander, Tamar. "Love and Death in a Contemporary *Dybbuk* Story: Personal Narrative and the Female Voice." In Goldish, 307–345.

Ansky, S. *The Dybbuk or Between Two Worlds*. Trans. Neugroschel. *"The Dybbuk" and the Yiddish Imagination: A Haunted Reader*. Ed. Neugroschel. 3–52.

_____. *"From* A Letter to Khaim Zhitlovsky." *"The Dybbuk" and the Yiddish Imagination: A Haunted Reader*. Ed. and Trans. Neugroschel. 1–2.

Ben-Amos, Dan. Introduction. *Folktales of the Jews*, Vol.2. Ed. Dan Ben-Amos. Philadelphia: Jewish Publication Society, 2007, xvii–xxxix.

Bienstock Anolik, Ruth. "Appropriating the Golem, Possessing the Dybbuk: Female Retellings of Jewish Tales." *Modern Language Studies* 31:2 (Autumn 2001): 39–55.

Brantley, Ben. "Theater Review; A 'Dybbuk' Foresees 'The Martyred Dead.'" *New York Times* 17 November 1997.

Chajes, J.H. *Between Two Worlds: Dybbuks, Exorcists, and Early Modern Judaism*. Philadelphia: University of Pennsylvania Press, 2003.

Dan, Joseph. Introduction, *Spirit Possession in Judaism*, Ed. Goldish. 27–40.

Elior, Rachel. *Dybbuks and Jewish Women in Social History, Mysticism and Folklore*. Trans. Joel Linsider. Jerusalem: Urim Publications, 2008.

Fisher, James. Preface. *The Theater of Tony Kushner, Living Past Hope*. New York: Routledge, 2001.

_____, ed. *Tony Kushner: New Essays on the Art and Politics of the Plays*. Jefferson, NC: McFarland, 2006. 1–4.

Fishman, Pearl. "Vakhtangov's *The Dybbuk*." *The Drama Review* 24:3 (September 1980): 44–58.

Giner, Oscar. "Mark Me: *The Dybbuk*." *Theatre* 9:2 (Spring 1978): 149–152.

Goldish, Matt. Prologue. *Spirit Possession in Judaism*. Ed. Matt Goldish. Detroit: Wayne State University Press, 2003. 25–26.

Goldstein, Richard. "A Queer Dybbuk: Tony Kushner Dares to Speak the Name." *Village Voice* 2, December 1997, 59.

Hoberman, J. *Bridge of Light: Yiddish Film Between Two Worlds.* Hanover: Dartmouth College Press, 2010.

Isherwood, Charles. "Review of *A Dybbuk or Between Two Worlds* by Tony Kushner." *Daily Variety*, 18 November 1997, review section.

Keller, Mary. *The Hammer and the Flute: Women, Power and Spirit Possession.* Baltimore: Johns Hopkins University Press, 2002.

Kushner, Tony, *A Dybbuk*, adapted from S. Ansky, *The Dybbuk.* Ed. and Trans. Joachim Neugroschel. *"A Dybbuk" and Other Tales of the Supernatural.* New York: Theatre Communications Group, 1997, 1–107.

Legutko, Agnieszka. "Feminist Dybbuks: Spirit Possession Motif in Post-Second Wave Jewish Women's Fiction." *Bridges: A Jewish Feminist Journal* 15:1 (spring 2010): 6–26.

Manor, Giora. "Extending the Traditional Wedding Dance: Inbal's *Yeminite Wedding* and The Beggars' Dance in Habimah's *The Dybbuk.*" *Dance Research Journal* 17/1(Autumn 1985–Spring 1986): 71–75.

Neugroschel, Joachim, ed. and trans. *"The Dybbuk" and the Yiddish Imagination: A Haunted Reader.* Syracuse: Syracuse University Press, 2000.

Roskies, David, ed. *The Dybbuk and Other Writings by S. Ansky.* New York: Schocken Books, 1992.

Schifrin, Daniel R. "A Play for All Seasons." *Hadassah Magazine* 78 (May 1997): 32–35.

Seidman, Noami. "The Ghost of Queer Loves Past: Ansky's 'Dybbuk' and the Sexual Transformation of Ashkenaz." *Queer Theory and the Jewish Question.* Eds. Daniel Boyarin, Daniel Itzkovitz, and Ann Pellegrini. New York: Columbia University Press, 2003. 228–245.

Solomon, Alisa. *Re-Dressing the Canon: Essays on Theater and Gender.* London: Routledge, 1997.

Wardle, Iving. (www.independent.co.uk/...theatre-high-culture-sits-on-its-morals-1).

Wolitz, Seth L. "Inscribing An-sky's *Dybbuk* in Russian and Jewish Letters." *The Worlds of S. An-sky: A Russian Jewish Intellectual at the Turn of the Century.* Eds. Gabriella Safran and Steven J. Zipperstein. Stanford: Stanford University Press, 2006. 164–202.

Yassif, Eli. *The Hebrew Folktale: History, Genre, Meaning.* Trans. Jacqueline S. Teitelbaum. Bloomington: Indiana University Press, 1999.

Martin McDonagh's Fractured Fairy Tales

Representational Horrors *in* The Pillowman

Anthony Ellis

Martin McDonagh's *The Pillowman* (2003) is a challenging play that, at its core, asks questions with a long intellectual pedigree — about the functions of storytelling, and also the anxious relations between artists and the society that produces and, later, appraises them, often unkindly. Its challenge to audiences derives from McDonagh's method of raising these familiar issues to a violent, feverish pitch, while rejecting the easy path of didacticism. Unremitting in its portrayal of horrors, which get alternately narrated and enacted onstage, *The Pillowman* probes the power of stories by distorting and amplifying the darkest elements in popular folktales — specifically, fairy tales and legends. While the exact purpose of McDonagh's adaptations is hard to pin down, his experiments with folk narrative can be seen as vehicles for testing the limits of art in a putatively free society. Furthermore, these adapted tales, considered as a group, help form a psychological portrait of an artist, one whose claim to imaginative autonomy the action of the play proves to be false.

McDonagh's principal teller of tales is an aspiring writer named Katurian Katurian, citizen and now prisoner of an unidentified totalitarian state, who composes short stories featuring the ritual abuse and murder of children. Several of these fictional murders, the audience learns early in the play, have been re-enacted by somebody in real life, down to their goriest details. An obvious suspect, Katurian has been arrested and gets interrogated in act 1, scene 1, by two sadistic detectives, Tupolski and Ariel. The police have also seized all his stories. Elsewhere in the police station, Katurian's slow-witted brother, Michal, remains imprisoned as well. The truth emerges later in act 1 that it was Michal, captivated by his brother's lurid stories, who conceived and carried out the copycat murders of innocent children. When Katurian is reunited with Michal in the prison and learns the truth, he smothers Michal with a pillow, this means of execution serving as an important motif for McDonagh. In committing fratricide, Katurian intends a mercy killing that evokes one of his own fictional characters, the Pillowman, a creature composed entirely of pillows who travels back in time to convince children to commit suicide so that they need not go on to lead what have turned out to be miserable lives. But in addition to sparing Michal the anguish of further detention and state-sponsored capital punishment, Katurian kills his brother — and confesses to that murder and, falsely, those of the children — in a bid to negotiate the preservation of his four hundred unpublished stories after his own death. By all accounts a failed writer, Katurian still wants his work to outlive him. And despite his stories' flaws, the play's other major characters — Michal, Tupolski, Ariel — are aware of, if unable to articulate, a kind of affective energy in them. I contend that much of this energy derives from their incorporation of fairy-tale elements, which McDonagh subverts in ways that mystify not only his characters, left to grapple, mostly unsuccessfully, with philosophic questions of narrative, but also his audiences, who must struggle to reach their own coherent interpretations of *The Pillowman*.

As compelling as this play is on both stage and page, McDonagh's obliqueness of purpose has preoccupied many critics since the premiere at the Royal National Theatre, London, in November 2003. To cite just two examples, Toby Lichtig, writing in the *Times Literary Supplement*, acknowledged the clear thematic significance of the role of fiction in our lives yet concluded that, while *The Pillowman* is not meaningless, "its messages do not come neatly wrapped" (20). Reviewing the New York premiere at the Booth Theatre in 2005, Richard Hornby offered that the drama "floats in a lake of indeterminacy" and that amid all the uncertainty, the playwright remains, ultimately, uncommitted to a central purpose. Hornby notes the bizarre quality of so many of the stories narrated at various points in the play for audiences both on- and offstage —"fairy tales for grownups," he rightly dubs them, and, as such, they are highly "unfashionable" as commercial high-literary endeavors in the contemporary age (472).[1] The contention that adults no longer want fairy tales may be dubious; in any event, Katurian's most serious defect as a writer is not choice of genre but lack of skill, as his sensational, bloodstained prose recalls nothing so much as the excesses of now-defunct serial horror comics. In his career, he has been able to publish only one story, meaning that the significance his work possesses during his incarceration, within the insular circle of the play's cast of characters, far outstrips its import in the larger dramatic world outside the police station, where it has been ignored. Yet his vivid stories can appeal to a childlike mentality, like that of Michal, who receives them with all the trust and candor expected in children, but also, tragically, cannot differentiate between reality and the life of the imagination.

Katurian's stories' resemblance to fairy tales — the likely source of their seductiveness to Michal — is both thematic and structural, and, as a starting point for analysis, can be perceived in the play's title story. Katurian retells "The Pillowman" from memory, by request, to his brother while they are incarcerated in act 2, scene 1. As mentioned earlier, the Pillowman's calling is to travel back though time and persuade the childhood selves of now wretched adults to end their lives prematurely, only in a manner that resembles an accident, not suicide, so as to spare their parents' feelings. In a surprise twist, the Pillowman, welcoming retirement after a lifetime spent urging minors to their deaths, decides for his final task to visit his own child self, the Pillowboy, and arrange his own early demise. As a result of this last job, his adult existence — along with his entire life's work — is expunged; the Pillowman finds relief only at the cost of ensuring that the widespread misery he had formerly eradicated will now persist.

By considering a story like "The Pillowman" in the context of Stith Thompson's *The Folktale* (1946), we can trace some distinguishing features of fairy tales in Katurian's art. (Thompson notes the imprecision of the English term *fairy tale* for stories that normally do not include fairies; Verna Foster echoes this point in the introduction to this volume. Despite his adoption of the somewhat broader term *folktale*—in his view, a nearer equivalent to the German *Märchen*—Thompson does distinguish this category of stories from myth, which has even wider parameters.[2]) First, Katurian's fiction "moves in an unreal world without definite locality" (Thompson 8). "The Pillowman" takes place in the never-never land of "once upon a time," the classic phrase he uses to launch every story, affording it an initial, false patina of innocence. His stories also feature the episodic structure evident in *Märchen* (Thompson 8). These qualities — one, the lack of any delimiting historical context and, two, the author's liberal use of improbable or supernatural elements, such as a nine-foot-tall time-traveling pillow creature — bestow on the stories the high degree of "creative freedom" which Foster discusses as characteristic of fairy tales. Katurian's stories focus on children, in situations of duress, as do fairy tales. They also possess many of the qualities Max Lüthi has posited for the genre: "depthlessness, one-dimensionality (the otherworldly not perceived as another dimension), linearity, isolation ... and the abstract style" (44). In fact, it may be just these open-ended qualities that captivate Michal's imagination. The characters and settings are portrayed so broadly that Michal seems able to project them easily onto his own perception of reality.[3]

In addition, the *manner* in which Katurian narrates his material is noteworthy. His stories are marked by a blunted emotionality, a deadpan delivery that, contrasting with their litany of horrors, winds up augmenting one's revulsion. Modern fairy tales, too, such as those collected by the Grimm brothers, present their acts of violence matter-of-factly, as if all their grotesqueries represented completely normal behavior. Cinderella's sisters cut off their toes in order to fit their feet into a glass slipper; a witch burns to death in an oven in "Hansel and Gretel"; the evil queen in "Snow White" must dance in hot iron shoes for her sins: the Brothers Grimm (and others) narrate these atrocities with a decided lack of affect. Although there is occasional emotion in Katurian's stories, such as the Pillowman's crying from all the years of assisting suicides, the violence itself tends toward the cold-blooded. For instance, the Pillowman, during his self-immolation, "sat there watching him[self] burn, and as the Pillowman gently started to fade away, the last thing he saw was the Pillowboy's happy smiley mouth as it slowly melted away, stinking into nothingness" (47). A diet of such stories seems to have anesthetized Michal to violence, as he becomes in effect a real-life Pillowman, extinguishing at least two children in gruesome fashion, only without the self-awareness of Katurian's title character.

Michal's extreme impressionability points up longstanding debates about the effect of fictional violence in childhood development, a consideration the play counterbalances against Katurian's imperiled right to artistic autonomy. For as much as fairy tales exist as aesthetic products, their status as ideologically loaded texts engages McDonagh here as well. Bruno Bettelheim, in his analysis of fairy tales, identifies some of the same structural properties as Thompson, including the tales' succinctness and their simplicity in terms of level of detail. (Katurian's tales are much briefer than standard published short stories, unless he abridges them when he tells them to his brother and the detectives.) But Bettelheim's interests in *The Uses of Enchantment* run deeper, to the psychological work performed by fairy tales. For him, the tales are of paramount importance as tools of human socialization. They allow listeners (or readers) to process at a subconscious level a variety of hopes, fears, and anxieties, some involving sexuality, others concerning basic questions of belonging and identity construction. The very strangeness of their fictional worlds may distract us from their central function of illustrating and resolving basic inner conflicts roiling within their young audiences. As Bettelheim puts it, encountering fairy tales, "the child fits unconscious content into conscious fantasies, which then enable him to deal with that content. It is here that fairy tales have unequaled value, because they offer new dimensions to the child's imagination which would be impossible for him to discover as truly on his own" (7).

Critical to the psychological benefits offered by fairy tales is their promise of a positive resolution: at the culmination of the imaginative "battle to achieve self-realization," the tale "guarantees a happy ending" (Bettelheim 39). Katurian's stories, however, after exaggerating the worst violence found in classic fairy tales, reject any such happy endings. In this aspect, their content belies their structure, which would appear to hold out hope for a reassuring finale, the kind in which the hero overcomes obstacles and achieves a reward (Thompson 23). Instead, Katurian's stories, by withholding such satisfactions, wind up as interpretive problems, for Tupolski and Ariel, certainly, and no less for us. Whereas conventional fairy tales and their adaptations, according to prevailing theories on their functions, may be seen either to inculcate a society's traditional values or, more radically, to revise canonical stories so as to call attention to the limitations, hypocrisy, or outright falseness of those values, neither function describes what goes on in Katurian's stories. They are *not* socially useful, in either a conservative or liberatory sense. For one thing, the stories cannot promote the healthy self-realization postulated by Bettelheim, for they are not themselves products of a nurturing environment. Rather, they betray the lingering effects of the author's torturous childhood.

Katurian narrates his fictionalized treatment of his and Michal's upbringing, titled "The Writer and the Writer's Brother," in act 1, scene 2. While he tells this story, which goes on for some five pages, the stage directions call for actors playing his family members to re-enact the events onstage. According to the story, their parents encouraged the flowering of literary artistry in Katurian while, unbeknownst to him, they tortured Michal daily on the other side of his bedroom door. The young Katurian could hear horrific sounds from behind that door, which caused his fiction to turn darker and, based on some early success in short-story competitions, artistically promising. The parents convinced him, when pressed, that they had been simulating the sounds of drills and screams as part of a bizarre artistic experiment designed to feed his developing imagination. Only in young adulthood, according to the story, does Katurian return to the house and discover not only his brother's corpse, with the evidence of years of torture marked upon it, but, improbably, a short story written by that tormented brother, a true masterpiece the likes of which he never could write. The difference between Katurian's fictionalizing of this boyhood experience and what actually happened, revealed soon after, is noteworthy: we learn, soon after witnessing the enactment of "The Writer and the Writer's Brother," that, in fact, Katurian managed to murder his parents and escape with Michal, rescuing his mentally and emotionally damaged brother from further abuse. Since that day, Katurian's life has consisted of working in a butcher shop, writing short fiction, and caring for Michal.

"The Writer and the Writer's Brother" differs from Katurian's other stories in being, in my view, unconnected to popular fairy tale or myth. It is instead, unique, and in an important sense: it is *explicitly* autobiographical, a quality he stresses to the detectives. It is possible that in the story he altered details of his childhood trauma in order to avoid incriminating Michal and himself in their parents' murder. But Katurian seems to have added a further embellishment: in the tale, his boyhood self wins short-story competitions and early adulation for his work, whereas the adult author, toiling in obscurity, has had almost no success placing his work in literary journals. Thus Katurian represses the truth of parricide as he fantasizes about literary recognition, which he then displaces onto Michal (the supposed true genius), whose sufferings inspired all Katurian's dark prose that issued forth in later years. Raised as the favored son while his mind was being imprinted with the sounds of the abuse of his sibling, Katurian goes on to imagine numerous variations of the tortured child in his short stories. His anti-hero, the Pillowman, ministers to each of these young victims individually, in the story that figures euthanasia as personal salvation. Meanwhile Michal has become not only Katurian's responsibility, but his only legitimate fan, someone who reads all of his stories with an over-literalism that eventually leads him to begin abducting children and subjecting them to the same physical abuses his brother describes so graphically. As Michal explains, he has killed the children because he believes his brother's stories have instructed him to do so:

> KATURIAN: What did you do it for?
> MICHAL: *You* know. Because you told me to.
> KATURIAN: *(pause)* Because I what?
> MICHAL: Because you told me to. [...] And I wouldn't have done anything if you hadn't told me, so don't you act all the innocent. Every story you tell me, something horrible happens to somebody [49, 50].

Much of the dialogue among the play's four main characters contains questions which are implicit in this fraternal exchange. These questions are related to the intrinsic power of stories and the struggle over who gets to control their interpretation — authors, readers, or institutions. As one example, Katurian professes to his interrogators, either naively or disingenuously, that his stories mean nothing, while Tupolski disagrees:

> KATURIAN: I'm not trying to tell you anything. It's supposed to be just a puzzle without a solution.
> TUPOLSKI: And what *is* the solution?
> KATURIAN: *(pause)* There isn't one. It's a puzzle *without* a solution.
> TUPOLSKI: *I* think there's a solution. But then, I'm really clever.
> KATURIAN: Well, I mean, you're right, the idea is you should wonder what the solution is, but the truth is there is no solution, because there *is* nothing worse, is there? [17].

Here the alienated artist embodies one of the play's central paradoxes. On the one hand, Katurian believes in the worth of his art, even if he cannot ever quite justify why it merits his high opinion. Again, his single condition, before he will falsely confess to his brother's murder of the children, is that the authorities preserve his stories after his death. Katurian also tells Michal in no uncertain terms that saving his stories is more important to him than either his own life or the life of his brother (53). But, on the other hand, he attests publicly to those stories' inconsequentiality: he asks his interlocutors, as if in disbelief, "What, are you trying to say that I'm trying to say that the children represent something?" (12). Earlier, Katurian has attempted to assure Tupolski, "You read these things, these 'stories,' supposedly, 'The police are all this,' 'The government is all this.' All these political...what would you call 'em? You know what I say? I say if you've got a political axe to grind, if you've got a political what-do-ya-call-it, go write a fucking essay, I will know where I stand. I say keep your left-wing this, keep your right-wing that and tell me a fucking story!" He concludes simplistically, "That's what I do, I tell stories. No axe to grind, no anything to grind. No social anything whatsoever" (7).

In these exchanges, Katurian and the detectives argue about whether the characters and events in his stories refer to anything beyond themselves, the author denying their connection to anything outside the fiction, political or otherwise, while the officers allege a strict correspondence between narrated events and the recently committed atrocities against children. It would seem that both sides overstate their case. Art never mirrors life completely, but Katurian denies the mimetic nature of the fictional enterprise when he claims that he has "[n]o axe to grind" and that his work contains "[n]o social anything whatsoever." His repeated mantra, which he uses as a form of self-defense, is "The first duty of a storyteller is to tell a story" (7). (Significantly, he cannot remember if this dictum as remembered is accurate or whether the storyteller's *only* duty is to tell a story, a distinction whose serious theoretical implications he waves off.) However, such self-dismissal contradicts his fervent wish that his stories outlive him. This conviction itself attests to Katurian's belief that the stories represent something other than mere entertainment. And still more, despite the work's unmistakable preoccupation with child abuse — the very category of trauma that figured so predominantly in his own family life — Katurian is blind to how much autobiography exists in the tales *not* set in his parents' home.

This subtextual quality, privileging emotional over literal truth, accounts, according to historian of folklore Jack Zipes, for much of the socializing power of fairy tales, which depend on a bending of reality to fulfill their function as "initiation myths" (3). Zipes explains that myths change over time to reflect historical developments, but their constructedness — as well as their ideological content — remains hidden from most people who hear them.[4] As fantastical tales not bound by natural law, they may appear to exist in a separate realm from real-life affairs; but as Susan Sellers clarifies, in her discussion of Bettelheim, "the truth of fairy tale is the truth of the imagination and not that of ordinary causality" (11). This imaginative form of truth is what Katurian ignores when he claims not to write autobiographically. So, although we may not be able to understand the workings of Katurian's dark imagination as fully as we would like, he himself is a poor guide to that project, whether his utter denial of representation in his work derives from a wish to mislead the detectives or, more likely, from insufficiently cultivated powers of introspection.

Threatened with execution, Katurian tries to justify the relentlessly morbid content of his stories — and the violation of children at the core of almost all his work — by freeing the artist's imagination from the shaping power of personal context: "Well ... I kind of hate any kind of writing that's even vaguely autobiographical. I think people who only write about what they know only write about what they know because they're too fucking stupid to make anything up" (76). Literature should derive from make-believe, not personal experience, according to Katurian, but attempts by writers to deny the imprint of autobiographical influences are clearly false in most instances. Thus, the series of tales that run through the play, and by extension *The Pillowman* as a whole, accomplishes more than Katurian would allow art to do. First, the tales act as a window into Katurian's psyche. Second, they invite the act of interpretation, precisely when they are at their most inscrutable, for the human urge to understand compels this activity. The sheer absurdity of McDonagh's sequence of stories disorients the audience, which is challenged to reflect on the relationship between source narratives, where they are discernible, and Katurian's dark subversions of them.[5] I would like to move now to consider three other stories, all of which evoke aspects of well-known fairy tales. The first, "The Tale of the Town on the River," Katurian tells to his interrogators in act 1, scene 1. The second, "The Little Jesus," is narrated by Katurian while actors perform its action onstage in act 2, scene 2. The third, "The Little Green Pig," is the story Katurian tells Michal before he smothers him with a pillow in his cell.

Katurian reads "The Tale of the Town on the River" to Tupolski and Ariel in response to their demand to hear his one published story. In this tale, a retelling of the Pied Piper legend,[6] a young boy, the son of drunkard parents, is bullied by his peers but nonetheless manages to maintain a happy and generous disposition. When he encounters a mysterious wanderer, hungry from his travels, he readily offers the stranger half of his sandwich. Following this act of charity, the stranger says, "I would like to give you something now, the worth of which today you may not realise" (22), whereupon he pulls out a meat cleaver, severs the boy's toes, and rides away. In an instance of peripeteia, the injury winds up saving the boy later. When the stranger, who is actually the Pied Piper of Hamelin, returns to lure away all the children of the town as punishment for the citizenry's reneging on its debt, the boy's disability prevents him from keeping pace. In Katurian's version, the Piper wanted the children, not the money, from the beginning. He simply exploits the town's greed; he anticipates Hamelin's refusal to pay him for solving its rat infestation problem and uses it as a convenient excuse for abduction. The story is, at every level, grim but, despite the amputation, the boy is spared — his singular virtue, which contrasts with the depravity of his fellow townspeople, is obliquely rewarded.

Here we see, as with "The Pillowman," a number of elements visible in folktales. Once again there is their formulaic beginning, "Once upon a time." The story is very brief, about five hundred words; it takes place in an unnamed location, described only as "on the banks of a fast flowing river" (21); it contains elements of the supernatural or, at least, utter improbabilities (such as the Pied Piper's powers, foreknowledge of which is essential for the story's audience); and it features both childhood trauma and a shocking moment of violence. (The toe amputation recalls Cinderella's sisters' grisly self-mutilation.) In addition, the fact that many of Katurian's tales are told orally in the play, often to Michal, a childlike listener, helps produce the impression that we are in a fairy-tale-like realm, if an infernal one. Because we hear the tales as they unfold, while Michal is doing the same, we in a sense occupy his position, that of the child listening to an adult tell a favorite story. Certainly, this dynamic reminds us that drama and fairy tale are both performative genres, which demand to be *heard* as well as read or seen. Both genres, though eventually having been written down and deemed "literature," developed in aural contexts, in early theatre and preliterate folk cultures, respectively.

Regarding storytelling and oral performance, *The Pillowman* encourages us to consider the extent to which these concepts have been adulterated in modern Western culture. Part of the change can be attributed to how many art works — e.g., stories and plays — get produced and disseminated today, as a result of their by-now thorough commodification. Zipes has argued that the late-twentieth century represented something of an ideological nadir when it comes to fairy tale adaptation: "It would appear that the fairy tale in the 1980s became nothing more than a decorative ornament, designed to titillate and distract readers and viewers, no matter how it was transformed," in any genre (142). It may be that McDonagh intends some type of critique of such dilution of the storytelling function in our society. Katurian's stories are not high art, by any means, and his attempts at selling them in the literary marketplace have failed. They produce only the most baleful effects in their limited audience. As such, they are hardly a model of socially useful adaptation. But they do achieve one productive end: they force the principals of the play (and by extension, us) to consider the real, potential uses of art, beyond the commodifying impulse and beyond its status as mere entertainment ("The only duty of a storyteller is to tell a story"). Stories can and do produce tangible effects in audiences, which artists may disclaim and governments seek to alter and eradicate via censorship. In Katurian's stories, a disturbing level of violence is done to children. But in the realm of mass entertainment (which *The Pillowman* is decidedly not), cultural products can be seen as performing a kind of metaphoric violence on children — and the rest of us —, coarsening our sensibilities in the name of profit.

The profit motive and the business side of art, though not explicit themes in *The Pillowman*, do find expression in the dialogue that follows "The Tale of the Town on the River." The tale interests Tupolski so much largely because it is the one piece Katurian has managed to publish, so we may ask ourselves what it is about this tale that causes it to be the one commercial exception. A hint is provided in the type of publication that accepted it: the *Libertad*, which would have to be a left-wing journal, by the connotations of its name and by the fact that Katurian, fearful of charges of undermining the government, denies ever having read it. Had its editors discerned some underlying meaning in this story that might fit a progressive agenda, maybe one that Katurian himself is not aware of?

On this possibility, it is useful to note that another writer, the novelist Christopher Wallace, has also adapted this legend in his novel *The Pied Piper's Poison* (1998), a text discussed by Julie Sanders in a chapter on fairy tales and folklore in her study *Adaptation and Appropriation*. In Wallace's case, unlike McDonagh's, the political nature of the adaptation is quite evident: the novelist substitutes Spanish soldiers, besieging Hamelin during the Thirty Years War, for the rats plaguing the town in the legend (Sanders 84–85). Wallace wishes to situate the Piper figure as an outsider historically, indicating, according to Sanders, that "many fairy tales exhibit a deep rooted anxiety about the figure of the incomer, the outsider, the person or creature from elsewhere"; it would be easy to imagine, she speculates, a further adaptation of the Pied Piper tale that would explore European resistance to the recent influx of foreign "migrant workers and asylum seekers" (85). Sanders reminds us that at its core, the Pied Piper narrative is about the powers-that-be refusing to relinquish the town's wealth, to redistribute it to someone who performs the most vital work of the city. As a result, the Piper absconds with "the symbolic economic future of the community" (84). Presumably, the editors of the *Libertad* perceived the radical dimension of Katurian's adaptation, the subtext that lack of charity and heavy-handedness by a central government can result in a society's degeneration. Meanwhile, the children emerge as the foremost victims, bearing the burdens of the older generation's sins as surely as Katurian and Michal cannot escape the consequences of their parents' mistreatment of them. We notice that the unnamed boy in "The Tale of the Town on the River," though preserved, is at the same time scarred for life, as is Michal.

Another young victim of adult violence appears in "The Little Jesus," a kind of modern-day parody of the biblical Crucifixion story, in which a six-year-old girl takes the place of the adult male Jesus. As for the story's roots in myth and fairy tale, it combines a corruption of the most sacred aspect of Christian mythology with a recurrent figure described by Vladimir Propp, in *Theory and History of Folklore*, as "the persecuted stepdaughter" archetype (69–70).[7] This type of persecution often takes place at the hands of a step-mother, as is the situation in "The Little Jesus." Eamonn Jordan has detected a specific connection between the girl in "The Little Jesus" and Snow White, who both suffer interment in the late stages of persecution (187). This story is narrated in act 2, scene 2. Like "The Writer and the Writer's Brother," this is one of the stories we not only hear, but watch performed as a type of play-within-a-play. It focuses on another isolated child, one who lives a life of virtue in the home of abusive foster parents. The unnamed heroine believes that she is the second coming of Jesus and costumes herself accordingly, with sandals and a fake beard. She wanders about the town, caring for the sick and trying to provide solace for beggars, drug addicts, and the like. These actions cause the townspeople to shun her and her parents to ramp up their abuse. When nothing can deter her from acting like Jesus, her foster parents ulti-mately ask her, "So you want to be just like Jesus, do you?" (70). They give her what they take to be her wish when they torture, crucify, and bury her alive. She does not manage to rise on the third day, but the story implies that she might have, if a blind man walking by her gravesite had heard her faint scratching on the coffin lid.

This story, too, poses interpretive challenges. Its plot significance derives from the fact that Michal informs Katurian elliptically in act 2, scene 1, that he has killed three children following methods described in his brother's sto-ries. The bodies of two of these have already been found by the police. Their fates were inspired by "The Tale of the Town on the River" and another tale called "The Little Apple Men," in which a girl dies after feeding her abusive father carved "applemen" with razors hidden in them; the night after his mur-der a group of animate "applemen" visit the girl and force their way down her throat, ostensibly to avenge their consumed "brothers" (12–13). (One is put in mind again of Snow White, forced to eat a poisonous apple in the Grimms' version.) According to Michal, he crucified and buried the third girl, Maria, to match the denouement of "Little Jesus." Because Michal divulges that he has buried Maria by a wishing well — the same location where, years ago, Katurian secretly interred their parents — the police rush to this site expecting to find the little girl, perhaps even still alive in her grave like her fictional predecessor.

It turns out, however, that the police do not find a crucified girl at the wishing well, either dead or alive. Instead, Michal, for whatever reason, has lied. He has re-enacted the only story of Katurian's that ends happily — "The Little Green Pig." The title calls to mind "The Three Little Pigs," and for once, the evocation of a fairy-tale element is true to the story's basic charm and clear moral purpose. In this story, the last one Katurian tells Michal before killing him, a pig is green-skinned and thus very different from all the other normal, pink-colored pigs on a farm. The farmers paint the green pig with pink indelible ink, so that he will fit in with the rest of the pigs. However, one evening after a heavy "green" shower (the supernatural occurrence audiences of fairy tales accept as plausible), all the pink pigs turn green, except of course the once-green pig, whose now-pink color cannot be erased. Thus, the green pig retains his uniqueness, though now as a pink pig. In this latest of Katurian's surprise endings, the persecuted hero again celebrates individuality, which gets challenged but, in the end, cannot be eradicated, despite all efforts to repress it. The repressive agent here, the farmers, might be seen to stand in for various agencies of social control of young people, including the state, the family, religion, and the mass media, all of which tend to promote an ideal of uniformity. A rather innocuous fable on its surface, "The Little Green Pig" still manages to explore the challenges faced by outsiders, although more cheerily than the other, darker stories.

Michal's decision to re-enact this happy story — little Maria is led into the interrogation room painted green and beaming with happiness — stands as one of only two bright spots in a play marked otherwise by misunderstanding, cruelty, oppression, and police brutality. The other, which follows Katurian's execution in the final scene, involves another reversal: despite having sworn to burn the author's manuscripts, Ariel decides instead to preserve them in Katurian's case file. As the final act has revealed Ariel himself to have been a victim of childhood sexual abuse, it becomes clear that in some way these stories speak to him, too, on some deep level that, like the author, he could not be counted upon to articulate. Thus, in a play that may strike some as nihilistic, we have, by the third and final act, "the possibility of redemption, a possibility grounded in Katurian's compulsive act of writing" (Cliff 139).[8]

Leading up to his final change of heart, Ariel embodies the effort of the state to appropriate narrative and use it for its own ends. In act 3, he conjures up his own story in which, at some point later in his career, children will follow him around; in his words, the children "are gonna give me some of their sweets in thanks and I'm gonna take those sweets and thank them, and tell them to get home safe, and I'm gonna be happy." Although Ariel does not hesitate to torture people like Katurian who have not yet been convicted, he is convinced, he claims, that "I stand on the right side. *I* may not always be right, but I stand on the right side. The child's side" (78). This claim, perhaps more explicitly than any other in the play, suggests the battleground upon which the struggle for the control of representation is waged. The battle occurs, here, between the wild, unruly, potentially transformative impulses of radical art (of which Katurian's fractured fairy tales are shocking, if not always aesthetically successful examples) and a state apparatus that would quash resistant voices and write itself in as its own story's hero, as personal liberties ebb in the name of law and order.

Before concluding that McDonagh's patchwork adaptation of myths and fairy tales resists interpretation, that the search for greater meaning in *The Pillowman* is a lost cause, we should recall Katurian's disingenuousness on the issue of representation and not confuse his denial of signification with the playwright's practice. Katurian himself gives us the clue to his own unreliability as literary critic in the exchange that occasions his claim that his work is "a puzzle without a solution," quoted above. At that moment, the detectives are asking him about another short, unpublished story titled "The Three Gibbet Crossroads." In this tale, the very first one we hear in full, which Tupolski this time reads aloud, a prisoner awakes in a cage where he has been condemned to starve to death. He is sure of his guilt but cannot recall the nature of his offense. Near him are two other criminals, also trapped in cages, one dead and one alive, with placards in front that record their crimes: one reads "Rapist," the other "Murderer." The main character, however, cannot read the placard placed outside his own cage. When an old man appears, he first weeps for the fate of the dead rapist, then manages to free the murderer, but when the old man reads the placard by the cage of the wakened criminal, he shoots the condemned man in the chest. "Just tell me what I've done?!" the dying man asks his killer, but he — and thus we, the audience — never learn the answer (18).

Tupolski insists that "The Three Gibbet Crossroads" is what he terms a "pointer," by which he means it suggests something beyond its literal content, an allegation as to which Katurian, as is his wont, professes ignorance (18–19). Katurian's meager analysis stops at the momentary summoning of a literary-critical term, before he dismisses such inquiry as irrelevant where his work is concerned: "That's a good story. That's something-esque. What kind of 'esque' is it? I can't remember. I don't really go in for that 'esque' sort of stuff anyway, but there's really nothing wrong with that story" (18). Despite the author's protests, though, the mystery of this story does have a solution — one that becomes all but indisputable as the sequence of horror stories nested within *The Pillowman* runs unremittingly on. Given Katurian's personal history and its transmutation in narratives describing the murder and mutilation of innocents, the third criminal's placard can only have written on it one unforgiveable transgression: "child abuser."

If Katurian's other tales resist interpretation even more than does "The Three Gibbet Crossroads," their difficulty may have something to do with the indeterminacy of the fairy tales and legends from which they are — not always so straightforwardly — adapted. That stories can mean different things to different people, and at different times, with results that range from the explosive to the banal, is part of what underlies the agonizing verbal exchanges in *The Pillowman*. Pushing the boundaries of adaptation far beyond the comfortable, McDonagh forces his audience to confront the core elements of fairy-tale worlds — children and violence, fear and isolation — in unfiltered form. The experience reminds us that we are defined by the stories we tell, including the most distressful of them.

NOTES

1. Eamonn Jordan agrees that "Katurian's stories are almost anti fairy tales" (180). He detects in McDonagh's play a carnivalesque sensibility, evident in its surreal aspects and overall sense of Bakhtinian misrule.

2. Thompson anticipates many later thinkers in calling myth the "most confusing" class of narrative to define because it "has been used in too many different senses" (9). Foster's introduction, however, reviews some helpful differences between myths, fairy tales, and legends, including the tendency of myth to be taken as true by the culture that produces it and its traffic in gods. In addition, Ülo Valk, defining myth in *The Greenwood Encyclopedia of Folktales and Fairy Tales*, explains that while fairy tales typically exist as written artifacts, myths are more free-floating: "Myths do not come as single texts; instead they usually belong to an identifiable textual tradition, a set of interrelated myths that is called 'mythology'" (652).

3. The extent to which Katurian's stories depend on the reader or listener's imagination to fill in concrete details, in response to their abstraction, may be suggested by a detail in Caryn James's discussion of two previews at the Royal National Theatre. In these productions, an actor came onstage dressed as the Pillowman, even though there is no textual cue for his appearance. The disappointment of many audience members, who reported having imagined the Pillowman as looking quite different, despite the director's attempt to remain faithful to McDonagh's description, led to the rejection of this staging concept (James).

4. Although Jack Zipes believes that most fairy tales, in their commercialized form, fulfill a largely conservative function, he does remain open to the possibility that rewritings of the tales can act as critiques and thus help effect social change. In the introduction to *Fairy Tales as Myth /Myth as Fairy Tale*, he distinguishes between the uncritical duplication of a story (or its co-optation by mass media) and a fresh adaptation: "As a result of transformed values, the revised classical fairy tale seeks to alter the reader's views of traditional patterns, images, and codes" (9). While revision may in some cases be uninspired or even wrongheaded, "the premise of revision is that there is something wrong with an original work and that it needs to be changed for the better" (9–10).

5. McDonagh wrote Katurian's stories as separate pieces, well before he started *The Pillowman*, with the idea of their being filmed; see James. This fact may contribute to the

opinion of some critics that his stories fail to cohere well together. Thus, an element of disjointedness has been seen by some to characterize the play itself. For instance, Ondřej Pilný observes "an incessant switching of themes" in *The Pillowman*, leading him to maintain that "there is no consistency of genre and theme" in the play (216).

6. The *Oxford English Dictionary* distinguishes a *legend* from other folk tales in its being mistakenly given historical credence: the word is defined as "an unauthentic or non-historical story, esp. one handed down by tradition from early times and popularly regarded as historical." The Brothers Grimm were influential in asserting such a distinction based on the legend's ostensible basis in fact: "The fairy tale is more poetic, the legend is more historical" (1:1). While the Pied Piper story is sometimes discussed in terms of its fairy-tale qualities, as in Sanders 84–86, its origins in German history, murky though they may be, mark it as a legend. According to the town's website, "Hameln became known worldwide by the exodus of the 'Hämelschen Kinder' (children of Hameln) in 1284 from which later on the Pied Piper's Legend developed" (Rattenfängerstadt Hameln). Theories attempting to account for the disappearance of one hundred thirty young people range from a children's pilgrimage to the Holy Land, to a decision by town leaders to sell unwanted dependents to foreign recruiters, to a plague brought on by a rat infestation (Harty 89).

7. The fullest analysis of the gamut of "persecuted heroine" tales, following Propp, has been undertaken by Steven Swann Jones. Jones identified twenty-six tales in this subgenre, from famous examples like "Sleeping Beauty," "Rapunzel," and "Cinderella," to lesser known tales such as "The Princess Confined in the Mound." The overlap between myth and fairy tale is significant with "The Little Jesus Story." As a retelling of the Christ narrative, "Little Jesus" adapts a religious myth that serves as the foundation for the spiritual lives of millions of people. Valk reminds us, "Religion and ritual have always served as the basic context of mythologies," and Christianity may be seen as no exception (655). It is surely important that Katurian assigns names to none of his characters, except for the Pillowman, if we consider that a proper name. This fact strengthens the impression that McDonagh is working with archetypes.

8. Brian Cliff, who confronts successfully the charge that McDonagh has little substantive to tell us in *The Pillowman*, concludes, "Katurian's art has proven transformative, not because of its content or beauty," qualities it is surely lacking, "but instead ... because of the redemptive impulse it fosters despite its content, limited and contingent though that impulse might be" (143).

WORKS CITED

Bettelheim, Bruno. *The Uses of Enchantment: The Meaning and Importance of Fairy Tales.* New York: Knopf, 1976.

Chambers, Lilian, and Eamonn Jordan, ed. *The Theatre of Martin McDonagh: A World of Savage Stories.* Dublin: Carysfort, 2007.

Cliff, Brian. "*The Pillowman*: A New Story to Tell." In Russell 131–48.

Grimm, Wilhelm, and Jacob Grimm. *The German Legends of the Brothers Grimm.* Ed. and trans. Donald Ward. 2 vols. Philadelphia: Institute for the Study of Human Issues, 1981.

Harty, Sheila. "Pied Piper Revisited." *Education and the Market Place.* Ed. David Bridges and Terence H. McLaughlin. London: Falmer, 1994. 89–102.

Hornby, Richard. "Beyond a Reasonable Doubt." *Hudson Review* Autumn 2005: 469–75.

James, Caryn. "Critic's Notebook: A Haunting Play Resounds Far Beyond the Stage," *New York Times* 15 April 2005.

Jones, Steven Swann. "The Innocent Persecuted Heroine Genre: An Analysis of Its Structures and Themes." *Western Folklore* 52 (1993): 13–41.

Jordan, Eamonn. "War on Narrative: *The Pillowman*." In Chambers and Jordan. *The Theatre of Martin McDonagh: A World of Savage Stories*, 174–97.

Lichtig, Toby. "It Must Be the Way He Tells Them." *Times Literary Supplement* 28 Nov. 2003: 20.

Lüthi, Max. *The Fairy Tale as Art Form and Portrait of Man*. Trans. Jon Erickson. Bloomington: Indiana University Press, 1984.

McDonagh, Martin. *The Pillowman*. London: Faber and Faber, 2003.

Pilný, Ondřej. "Grotesque Entertainment: *The Pillowman* as Puppet Theatre." In Chambers and Jordan 214–23.

Propp, Vladimir. *Theory and History of Folklore*. Ed. Anatoly Liberman. Trans. Ariadna Y. Martin and Richard P. Martin. Minneapolis: University of Minnesota Press, 1984.

"Rattenfängerstadt Hameln." http://www.hameln.com/info/history.htm.

Russell, Richard Rankin, ed. *Martin McDonagh: A Casebook*. London: Routledge, 2007.

Sanders, Julie. *Adaptation and Appropriation*. London: Routledge, 2006.

Sellers, Susan. *Myth and Fairy Tale in Contemporary Women's Fiction*. Houndmills: Palgrave, 2001.

Thompson, Stith. *The Folktale*. 2nd ed. New York: Dryden, 1951.

Valk, Ülo. "Myth." *The Greenwood Encyclopedia of Folktales and Fairy Tales*. Vol. 2. Ed. Donald Haase. Westport, CT: Greenwood, 2008.

Zipes, Jack. *Fairy Tale as Myth/Myth as Fairy Tale*. Lexington: University Press of Kentucky, 1994.

Food, Sex and Fairy Tales

Wallace Shawn's Grasses of a Thousand Colors

SHEILA RABILLARD

> To some people, folk tales, fairy tales, and myths seem like the most realistic narratives
> — Dedication, *Grasses of a Thousand Colors.*

Wallace Shawn's *Grasses of a Thousand Colors*, which had its world premiere at the Royal Court Theatre, London, in May 2009, draws upon the power of myth and fairy tale to challenge contemporary mores. Shawn reworks elements of Marie-Catherine D'Aulnoy's tale "The White Cat" along with touches of Charles Perrault's "Sleeping Beauty" to create a fantastic drama which has been described by some critics as a depiction of the war between the sexes ("The play, after all, is a wry account of the sex war" Sierz unpaged) and seen by others as a vision of spiritual and ecological sickness.[1] I argue it is both, and the relationship between these two aspects — a relationship achieved largely through adapting fairy tales and adopting something of their logic — is my focus.

The dramatic strategy of the play recalls the folk art of story-telling: the protagonist, Ben, addresses the audience directly for much of the play while his three human sexual partners, Cerise, Robin, and Rose, also narrate events to the audience. As in a number of sophisticated literary versions of the wonder tale (to use Marina Warner's useful term), the teller is subtly implicated in the tale; and as Ben's erotic reminiscences take on the contours of myth or nightmare, the drama itself assumes an oneiric (as well as onanistic) form. By virtue of a transformation as strange as those in wonder tales, usually taboo aspects of sexuality are discussed openly while the provenance of food, especially its genetic manipulation by the scientist Ben, for the most part is elided politely only to erupt with the force of the repressed when it becomes evident that the food chain has been horribly damaged. In D'Aulnoy's "The White

Cat"(and in other wonder tales such as "Beauty and the Beast," and "Don-key-skin") the erotic involves transactions across species boundaries; in Shawn's play such boundaries are transgressed, and in the alimentary realm as well. Via such transgressions the play binds critique of ecological hubris and satire of heterosexual male self-involvement by suggesting a like underlying consumerism.

The play's resolution presents a series of disturbing analogies between non-human animals and women as the ostensibly exploited prove unexpectedly powerful. "Nature" takes its revenge when the unintended consequences of genetic manipulation unfold; the White Cat of Ben's erotic dreamland, although killed, migrates into the everyday as a mysteriously powerful pet; and his estranged wife, Cerise, is revealed as herself Blanche the Cat, overseer of his erotic adventuring. Yet if these analogies appear to reinforce historically damaging associations between women and "Nature," the plot also mocks "masculine" technocratic self-assurance and the repressed fears such assurance denies. Comparison with the fairy-tale source suggests that Shawn has developed D'Aulnoy's sly depiction of men's almost infinite capacity to accept what women give them as if it were theirs by right into a contemporary cautionary tale with wide implications regarding many kinds of assumed dominion.

This quick sketch of the drama's themes and Shawn's debt to D'Aulnoy captures neither the play's elusiveness and capacity to disturb — John Lahr calls it "a model of the grotesque," a play which "like all dreams, resists interpretation"(88) — nor the complexity of Shawn's work of adaptation. These crucial aspects of the play are closely bound together. For the elusiveness of the play and its capacity to disturb derive not only from its peculiar sexuality, dreamlike plot, and dystopic vision of future ecological disaster but also from the history of the fairy tale, its past subtleties of tone and address. *Grasses of a Thousand Colors* does not simply adapt a prior literary work, though Shawn's play can certainly be analyzed, using Linda Hutcheon's terminology, as an "indigenizing" adaptation.[2] Rather, Shawn responds as well to aspects of the fairy tale mode per se.

Shawn's broader interest in the discourse of the fairy tale (its history of expressing the fears and sly subversions of the marginalized as well as the views of those in power; the complex relationship of teller, tale, and audience)[3] is signaled by his "Author's Note" acknowledging not one but two versions of the story. He refers to "The White Cat" of Mme. D'Aulnoy (1650/51–1705), translated by John Ashbery, which appeared in Warner's collection *Wonder Tales* (1994); and the version, based on D'Aulnoy, published by Andrew Lang in *The Blue Fairy Book* (1889). Indeed, Shawn's note ("Let's be frank — I've taken a few elements of this play from the story 'The White Cat' by Madame d'Aulnoy" *Grasses* 90) itself assumes the stance of the teller of wonder tales for, as he is surely aware, the aristocratic, predominantly female authors who invented the modern fairy tale openly declared the origin of their stories in tradition (Warner *Wonder Tales* 12). They also shared the anonymous wonder tale culture, so that motifs echo among the stories of D'Aulnoy, Marie-Jeanne L'Héritier, and the Comtesse de Murat. As Warner further notes, "The White Cat" "recognizably combines the plots of 'Rapunzel' and 'The Three Feathers,' two of the best-known Grimm Brothers' tales published much later, in 1812" (Warner *Wonder Tales* 13). If one takes Shawn's note as a signal that he borrows openly just as D'Aulnoy herself did, then one might infer that Shawn adopts to some degree the strategies of her genre. The discussion which follows, then, will consider both Shawn's adaptation of his source and his use of the resources of the wonder tale.

I consider Shawn in relation to D'Aulnoy under the influence of Warner's magisterial *From the Beast to the Blonde*, which, along with more recent volumes such as *Signs and Wonders*, establishes an historicized reading of fairy tale and myth against the approach of a Bettelheim or a Jung who seeks eternal psychological verities. James Lasdun comments in a review of Warner's *Fantastic Metamorphoses*:

> Far from being reductive or merely debunking, this recovery of "circumstance" has an invigorating effect on the myths Warner examines. It may be that historical time is richer in the contradiction and instability that keeps myths vital than the unchanging Dreamtime or Time of Origins ("*illo tempore*") designated as the true locus of myth by Mircea Eliade. Or perhaps it is simply that Warner is able to keep both perspectives in play [Lasdun 24].

Given Shawn's reference to Warner's *Wonder Tales*, and the fact that the essay introducing this collection presents some of her central ideas about the political and cultural meanings of such tales, she seems an appropriate guide to the possibilities Shawn discovers in the tradition and in the specific tale he plunders. Further, Warner's emphasis on the transformations which fairy tales undergo as different tellers put them to different historical uses accords with Hutcheon's analysis of the indigenizing force of adaptation and suits the play's concern with pressing questions of our times: the growing global need for food, impending ecological disaster.

To begin, then, a brief description of Shawn's play and its staging at the Royal Court, where Shawn played Ben, the protagonist, and his long-time collaborator, André Gregory, directed.[4] *Grasses of a Thousand Colors* opens as if it is a public reading by Ben, a scientist, from his memoirs. The set is simple — a large white sofa, behind this a huge screen, and a back wall comprising "a field of tall, waving grass through which the characters vanish" (Lahr 88). Ben greets the audience dressed in a black dressing-gown, black monogrammed slippers, and black cravat. He reads a few lines and talks with enormous self-satisfaction about his "lucky" life and his success as a scientist and businessman. He and his colleagues have solved the problem of food (the time appears to be the near future) by altering animals so that frogs, cows, his own dog, Rufus, and, by implication, *Homo sapiens* (this becomes clear only later in the play) can feed on their own kind as well as on the corpses of other animals. He touches a button, and on screen appears Rufus, "the very first large mammal ever to be raised entirely on the meat of members of his own species" (*Grasses* 12).

Shortly after his activation of the screen, an unbidden image of his wife, Cerise, appears with a popping sound, and from this point on his talk is interrupted intermittently by her screen appearances. She looks ill, and she reads passages from a letter describing heaps of dead squirrels, a wolf crawling like a worm, dogs in death-agony. Her screen appearances seem like memory flashes, the images "brilliantly designed by Bill Morrison to resemble surrealist Rayographs" (Lahr 88). The play here departs from what had seemed a realistic representation of an author on a book tour and moves into the dreamlike; perhaps Ben is haunted by the consequences of his intervention in the food chain, though he speaks of his work with unapologetic self-approval.

Cerise (Miranda Richardson) then appears on stage in person, looking *"younger and healthier than in the bits of film"* (*Grasses* 16). Legs and face lightly brushed with glitter, "flirty as a cat," she "slithers over the back of the sofa onto Ben's lap" (Lahr 88). She may be Cerise objectified by Ben's memories and desires, but she is also curiously powerful, and her dialogue hints that she may be controlling him or even stage-managing the whole fantastic drama, and hence controlling the imaginations of the audience as well. She addresses the audience:

> All right. Now can you take this? I'm going to be very frank with you and tell you something true rather than being euphemistic about it: (*she speaks the next sentence very slowly and distinctly*) Cats like to tease mice. They *like* to tease mice. They like to play with them a little. Are you with me so far? Cats like to tease mice. In other words, I'm saying, it's not something that happens by accident when they're pursuing some other more respectable purpose. No. They *like* to do it. And I'm a bit of an expert on cats, you see. (*she looks around at the audience*) And of course everyone knows that cats punish mice [*Grasses* 17].

Cerise has her own memories of events which undercut Ben's self-congratulation. She reads passages from her diary indicating they had a disturbing and difficult sex life. She implicitly reproaches him for the disastrous results of his science, recalling the good old days when you didn't need to worry about what you ate: "People ate and digested the same foods for their whole lives" (*Grasses* 20).

Cerise leaves, but Ben is disconcerted enough to discard his entire manuscript, and begin a different tack. He now focuses on the present, and the scale of his self-report shrinks from a life span to the past twenty-four hours: his condition at breakfast yesterday, ill and taken care of by "my sweet friend Rose"; staring at the tablecloth; receiving an invitation. He counters Cerise's regrets about the loss of the good old days when people could eat asparagus with his own preference for the present unrestricted consumption of sex in contrast to "the old, old days when I was growing up" and "people simply didn't think very much about their genitals" (*Grasses* 23). He dwells on this theme, taking his self-satisfaction and diminished range of subject matter to their logical, ludicrous conclusion:

> I really only mention my dick as frequently as I do because, to be absolutely frank, it interests me, and to be perfectly honest, it's just about the only thing that interests me now, and so I'm bound to talk about it. It boils down to the fact that, to put it simply, my dick happens to be, when all is said and done, my best friend, and in a certain way, it's my only friend [Grasses 24].

There follows a paean to his "friend," a preparation for the two Parts to follow in which a veritable Iliad of the penis (Lahr's phrase) will be recounted. Robin appears on stage briefly before the end of Part One, to complete the trio of women with whom Ben had sex: Cerise the wife, Robin the mistress (cheating on her own spouse), and the gentle, maternal-seeming Rose, who first took care of the cat, then became Ben's sexual partner, and ended as his nurse. The classic triad of wife, mistress, and nurse/mother is clearly an aspect of the fairy-tale patterning; there are strong suggestions that the three are aspects of one woman deriving from myth and nightmare.

The second of the three Parts presents Ben's affair with Robin, chiefly via their alternating narrations. Ben recalls that he met Robin at a party, and they made love in a park: "I could see my face as a dog's face. Then her face became a dog's face, too" (*Grasses* 32). It's not clear at this point whether the canine comparison refers to their use of mouths and teeth during sex, which is mentioned, or indicates a creeping erasure of species boundaries due to the alterations Ben's science has produced. Later that same night Ben returned to the park, mounted a horse, and rode through a forest to a castle where he dined on mice and became the lover of a beautiful white cat. Thereafter, every few weeks Ben rode at night through the forest to the White Cat. He began to experience some odd physical symptoms: "bleeding lines" (like cat scratches?) appeared on his skin (*Grasses* 40). Taking up the narrative, Robin tells how she discovered his secret excursions and followed him one night. At the castle she joined a banquet attended by men and asses, a motif alluding to Apuleius' *The Golden Ass* and its transformation of man into animal. Ben here interjects his own account, recalling that he banqueted as usual with the cats; the dishes presented this night (the heads of mice, and of human penises) suggest in dream-fashion that Ben's science has made cannibals of humanity. Robin recounts that she found her way to the White Cat's chamber, cut off her head, and rode home with the body in a bag, the cat's head re-growing en route. Ben, on his return, saw this "totally fucked-up version of a domestic pussy" and retreated to the bathroom vomiting (*Grasses* 47). Robin recollects: "Yes, he was one of the first to feel in his gut that the tricks certain people had played on frogs and cows in regard to their ability, for example, to eat their own kind, had not gone unnoticed by that whole population of smaller creatures, the bacteria and viruses whose sensitivity had perhaps been under-appreciated" (*Grasses* 47).

At the end of Part Two we are told that Ben has grown sicker and is incapable of doing much more than masturbate in front of Robin; Robin has reunited with her husband, attempted suicide, and tried to kill Ben (her weapon in both cases a knife). Ben interprets her behavior as a reaction to his inability to perform sexually, and explains that he was terribly tired because he could not sleep at night due to the prowling of Blanche, the resurrected white cat. The transfer of cat and Ben to Rose is then arranged by Robin. Cat and sexual partner remain closely identified. While Blanche is with Robin, both animal and woman are associated with aggression and knives. Once Blanche is established in Rose's domain, cat and woman alike seem to Ben sweetly affectionate and Blanche appears to him to collaborate in his sexual activities.

In the play's final, third, Part the peculiar illness vividly described by Cerise in Part One afflicts all humans as well as animals: people are in great pain, can digest ever fewer foods, and die when they reach the point where they vomit continuously. Ben's sexual journey from partner to partner begins to collapse in upon itself as the partners conjoin and overlap in various ways. Robin and Cerise dally with a lesbian relationship; Cerise resumes sexual relations with Ben ("I liked to have his dick inside me — it gave me something to think about" *Grasses* 68); Robin, displaced by Cerise's return, kills Blanche (seemingly substituting cat for wife); and Cerise ends up fondly caring for sick Rose. In the dream-like circular structure of the play — evocative of the truncated food cycle Ben has created, in which eaters consume their own kind — the close of the play returns to the situation of Part One, and the invitation to a party. It has been issued by Blanche, who according to Ben "is now a sort of ordinary, bourgeois middle-aged woman" (*Grasses* 85). She is also Cerise (Ben notices that "the dress Blanche was wearing, which I found awfully nice, was actually a dress I'd once bought for Cerise" *Grasses* 85). And she is clearly the magical White Cat, as Cerise appears on screen in an image combining Richardson's face with a cat's green eyes, red collar, and whiskers (Lahr 88) and says to the camera: "Of course you have to understand that

over the centuries we all took turns wearing that bright red ribbon and decid-
ing things. Every decade or so, we'd pass the ribbon on to the next cat, so
each of us knew that if we made terrible decisions, they'd probably be corrected
later" (*Grasses* 84). Hostess of the party, powerful controller of the plot,
Blanche "took pity on me" in the midst of a painful bout of vomiting, Ben
recalls. She showed him "a somewhat nicer way out," an enormous meadow
filled with buttercups, "across which one could walk until one pleasantly fell
asleep, with no vomiting at all." "Most things aren't alive in the first place,"
she reminded him, and death would feel "no different from a dreamless sleep."
So Ben walked, lay down, and in the last words of the play reports that dying
"felt quite nice" (*Grasses* 88).

     The central motifs of Shawn's play — animals, food, and sex — derive
from "The White Cat" and from the discourse of the modern fairy tale
D'Aulnoy helped to shape. As in Shawn's play, a beautiful, magical white cat
is the central figure in D'Aulnoy's *conte*. Her queenly cat is discovered (like
Shawn's) in a castle in a forest, presiding over feline courtiers who engage in
all of the activities one would expect to find at a human court, albeit on a
smaller scale — in particular, music and dining, likewise prominently mentioned in the play. The protagonist of D'Aulnoy's story is a young prince
engaged in a competition with his two older brothers to be named sole heir
to their father's kingdom. However, as Warner points out, the witty, aristocratic women who put their mark upon the first literary versions of European
wonder tales could deftly indicate that their sympathies as authors lay with a
figure other than the protagonist of a tale (whether passive princess or active
prince) and this seems to be the case with "The White Cat." ("Fairy tales are
not told in the first person of the protagonist. [...] the voice of the storyteller
may be issuing elsewhere" *Beast* 215.) It is the powerful, wise cat who provides
the prince (otherwise unsuccessful) with the three winning treasures to present
to the king: the world's tiniest dog, the finest cloth, and (once a spell is broken)
herself as the most beautiful woman to be the prince's bride. Here, too, we
find a pattern Shawn has adapted: by the close of his drama, it is discovered
that Blanche/Cerise has been toying, cat-like, with Ben throughout the play;
in a certain sense he is not the true author of his story of sexual conquests
and certainly the end of the tale, his death, is stage-managed for him.

Humans and Animals

     The theme of animal-human transformation has a long history in myth
and fairy tale prior to D'Aulnoy, of course, but her handling of the material
points to some of the subtleties of Shawn's treatment and comparison clarifies

how Shawn uses the motif to create an ecological grotesque. In D'Aulnoy's tale, the boundaries between human and animal are quite plain, even though the young prince is attracted to the beautiful White Cat, shares the courtly pastimes of his "Blanchette," and is appalled by her instruction that he cut off her head and tail. The latter action will, of course, break the spell and return White Cat to her human self; the prince's horror at the prospective deed indicates that (although he does not yet know her story) he responds to her animality as superficial; he reacts as if asked to murder a dear friend. In the logic of the plot, the animal guise is an enchanted exterior in which she is imprisoned, just as she was once imprisoned in a tower. And if we read Queen White Cat as in unchanged essence a woman, then we can see that the tale slyly teaches the wisdom of trusting in a woman's advice. The prince wins his bride, the contest, and several kingdoms (White Cat turns out to be enormously wealthy) by submitting to a woman. As Warner suggests, this interpretation which puts the male to the test and emphasizes the happy results of obedience to women might well have amused D'Aulnoy's circle of intelligent women on the margins of power, especially those who knew that D'Aulnoy herself had been married against her will to a dominating, uncongenial spouse. There is little suggestion of a blurring of boundaries between species here, despite the ready conversation of cats, a dog, and a parrot. (Or perhaps one suggestion: there is an interesting complexity to the prince's dilemma, as he must intuit the woman imprisoned in a cat's fur in order to obey her superior wisdom and yet must also bring himself to the point of slaying the animal as animal, as a mere killing not a murder.)

In Shawn's play, this distinction between human and animal is sustained in order to shock the audience with bestiality, and by dint of that shock of the taboo to suggest that the practice of manipulating animals so that herbivores become carnivores and eventually all can be fed their own kind is likewise a terrible transgression of boundaries. Shawn is surely aware that consumers of food produced by contemporary agribusiness have already accepted into their diets genetically modified corn, chickens fed upon dead chickens, and so on, so that the logical development of such food production in the future must be made more shocking in its practices as well as its unintended consequences in order to horrify. Hence he gives us a society in which humans engage in cannibalism and (seemingly a corollary) bestiality. The practices in a sense go together because they refuse the concept of humans as in any way distinguished from other beasts. Shawn's curious play thus invites the audience to consider society's practices and principles in a manner that owes a good deal to D'Aulnoy's covert challenge to the assumed inferiority of women in the eyes of complacent aristocratic males, and the inferiority of fantastic stories and folk culture in the view of rising rationalist philosophers.[5] On what philosophical grounds might our revulsion or tolerance be based? Is there an ethical principle operant, or simply deeply ingrained cultural imprinting? As a Socratic provocation Shawn's play bears some relation to Edward Albee's *The Goat, or Who Is Sylvia?* (first produced New York, 2002). Like *Grasses of a Thousand Colors*, which it predates by a few years, Albee's play works with genre, chiefly pastoral and tragedy, the latter concern indicated in the subtitle "notes toward a definition of tragedy." As in Shawn's play, a plot involving bestiality opens to question a series of unexamined assumptions about the divide between human and animal and hence the ethical relationship of humans to animals and to the whole environing planet. Perhaps Shawn and Albee also have some fun at the expense of right-wing extremists who at times have asserted that tolerance of homosexuality leads inevitably to tolerance of bestiality; both dramatists appear to have taken such remarks not as stimuli prompting horrified avoidance, but as topics for thought experiments in the fictional worlds of drama.

Shawn's play shocks as well because the human/animal transformations refuse to stay within the distancing context familiar from fantasy tales such as those of D'Aulnoy. "The White Cat" nests tale within tale: after she is restored to human form, Queen White Cat tells the prince how her mother lost her to the fairies when she was an infant; and how, imprisoned in a tower by these fairies, she defied them and tried to wed a young knight of her own choosing, resulting in his death and her own transformation into a cat. But none of these delightful inset tales returns the reader from fantasy to a mundane reality.

In contrast, Shawn's White Cat does not stay in the realm of castles visited at night in the mysterious forest but migrates as a domestic pet into the ordinary world of apartments, adulterous affairs, and party invitations. Further, in this world of science and business Blanche the pet cat exerts disturbing power over the human characters, so that Ben, as mentioned, is distressed by her night-time prowling and Robin, seemingly jealous of the cat rather than Cerise or Rose, steals Blanche back from Rose and chops up the cat (for the second time) with a knife. Strange transformations continue in the more "realistic" world: the cat becomes a suburban woman according to Ben's account, and also melds into Cerise in the projected screen image seen near the close of the play; and, of course, Ben's science has achieved its own transformations of food and digestive processes — transformations which turn humans into the ethical equivalent of animals, creatures for whom cannibal foods are mere sources of protein.

There is some loss of the inimitable lightness of D'Aulnoy with this element of realism; instead of simply following the turns of an inventive tale, one feels obliged to try to account logically for these transformations, deeming some the unexpected consequences of scientific interventions by Ben and his ilk, others perhaps the hallucinations of minds diseased as a result of the disruption of every organism. One's sense of the horrifying unnaturalness of the world Ben has brought about depends to a certain extent upon Shawn's handling of the fairy tale, his transgression of the conventions of the genre; that is, the transformation from animal to human, or the reverse, is not meant to occur in a world governed by science, only in a world of magic. Even in D'Aulnoy's magical tale, however, there is a hint of humankind's potentially dangerous desire to explore and perhaps manipulate the limits of the animal world: the king sets his sons to discover the world's tiniest dog, and the youngest son produces a dog which fits in an acorn.

Food

Many a myth contains the motif of forbidden fruit which is dangerous to eat; in the story of Adam and Eve, as in Shawn's play, the wrong kind of eating results in the coming of death. In D'Aulnoy's story, interestingly, food appears prominently twice. The first demonstrates the importance of foodstuffs appropriate to one's species, but in a playful way which implies the role played by custom as well as nature in the human diet. The prince, at his first meal in the White Cat's castle, sees two bisques placed on the table, the one of pigeon, the other of well-fattened mice. "The sight of one prevented the prince from tasting the other, for he supposed the same cook had prepared them both; but the little Cat, who guessed his thoughts from the face he made, assured him that his meal was cooked separately, and that he could eat what was served him, in the certitude that there would be neither rats nor mice in it" (D'Aulnoy 25). There are many cues for Shawn's invention in this brief scene, and it clearly relates to Ben's account of the meal he made of mouse and penis heads. Although it is absurd for a cat to assure a man that a meal is appropriate for human consumption, and it seems a small step from conversing with a feline hostess to dining on mice in what is after all a bizarre fantasy world, nonetheless the scenario evokes a sense of decorum which by contrast makes Ben's blithe unconcern all the more appalling. When Ben recalls that he laid his own penis on the table at the end of the meal (in a gesture suggesting the inward turn of sexual and nutritional appetites), the breach of table manners still carries its own small shock value, and the audience is teased with a glimpse of the strange assortment of unexamined laws governing behaviors of great and small import. Considered together, the two passages suggest that Shawn is exploring a failing civilization and its loss of the habits of thought and action upon which ethical behavior is founded (according to Aristotle).

The second appearance of food in D'Aulnoy's tale adds a note of danger and suggestively links eating with uncontrolled desire and with sexual reproduction. The White Cat's mother, while she was pregnant with her, succumbed to a longing for magical fruit that grew in a fairy's garden and in order to eat it promised the fairies her unborn child. When he discovers this bargain, the King is furious with his Queen for depriving him of the offspring he wants and rages against what he sees as an injury to him: "Obviously you love me not at all" (D'Aulnoy 45). Keeping in mind the feminist sympathies D'Aulnoy and her circle inherited from the previous generation of *précieuses*, it is not hard to see that her tale alludes to the use of women within a patriarchal structure to reproduce. Covertly the tale suggests that mothers may not want their children; they may desire something as different as magical fruit, although if they act upon such desires they will be shunned and imprisoned like the unhappy Queen. This story concerning food is more tangentially related to Shawn's drama, yet it hints at the yoking of food and sexuality which Shawn exploits so thoroughly in pursuing the ethics of a consumer society to their absurd extreme. And it also provides a model for the satiric effect which can result when a writer subtly shifts between masculine and feminine perspectives, indicating the gap between them, as Shawn does in counterpointing the views of Ben and Cerise/Blanche.

Actor and Audience, Teller and Tale

If one reads D'Aulnoy as subtly shifting between gendered perspectives, subversively implying alternatives to the patriarchal point of view, then one reads her under the guidance of Warner's historicizing analysis as a writer whose work bears particular meanings in her own time for a coterie of like-minded writers and readers who formed part of her immediate social world.

> The writers of the *contes* during the new fashion for the elaborate, literary fairy tale were [...] women (and men) like D'Aulnoy, of high status, creators and frequenters of the *ruelles*, worldly, even influential, related to the independent women of the earlier generation who had taken a leading role in the Fronde uprising of the nobles against the king and then, after its defeat, developed the social ideals of préciosité as a polite revolt against the dominant culture. Fairy tales became part of this position of protest [Warner, *Beast* 168].

In several respects, Shawn's play — at least in its Royal Court production, in which he performed the role of Ben — likewise invites interpretation in the light of his previous work and career. Just as D'Aulnoy's tale rewards those who keep in mind her feminist stance and unhappy personal history, so Shawn's play produces some of its effects by dint of its use of Shawn's public persona.

The implied author of D'Aulnoy's tale diverges amusingly from patriarchal perspectives, for example, when the narrator of the tale remarks of her heroine, "It is true that White Cat had a pleasant, good-natured and almost omniscient mind. She was more learned than a cat is permitted to be" (33). Surely, the reader is meant to smile at the word "permitted," as it seems to imply that other cats might become educated and conversational were it not for prohibitions. And one recalls arguments against women's education based upon their supposed inferiority, their "natural" status as virtual domestic animals. The twists of the plot provide similar moments of amusement. For if one expects a story focused upon the desires of a questing youth, it is surprising to discover that the prince wins the attentions of White Cat because he resembles exactly her first, dead, beloved. According to the fairies' decree, a duplicate youth is required to undo the cat-guise spell, and this plot device diminishes the individual importance of the prince at the same time as it throws emphasis upon White Cat's emotions and desires expressed in her original choice of partner.

In Shawn's case, he addresses a coterie audience in the sense that *Grasses of a Thousand Colors* premiered at the Royal Court Theatre as part of a festival of his work. The Shawn festival featured revivals of his one-man play *The Fever* (1990) and *Aunt Dan and Lemon* (1985), as well as five staged readings and two of his films: *My Dinner with André* (1981), which he co-wrote with André Gregory, the director of *Grasses*, and *Vanya on 42nd Street* (1994). The Royal Court management evidently anticipated an audience acquainted with Shawn as a playwright, and presumably *Grasses* met with an audience prepared for the way in which his works, in Lahr's phrase, "prey on both consciousness and conscience" (Lahr 88). If "coterie" suggests exclusivity too strongly, it is worth noting that Shawn as playwright is admired in England but "a relatively unknown quantity" in the United States (Lahr 88). Shawn himself remarks that "most people have disliked my writing and paid no attention to it whereas as a humorous actor and cartoon voice I have found some measure of popular approval" (Interview by Animashawun).

Those acquainted with his work would recognize more readily that Ben's bizzarre, pornographic reminiscences bear upon the preoccupations of the audience's world. As in *The Designated Mourner*, Shawn presents a talkative protagonist who word by word reveals an appalling self-centeredness and a desire for self-preservation which unwittingly calls into question not only what he, but what societies or governments, are willing to do in order to survive. And in *Grasses* Shawn uses the physical illness of the protagonist metonymically, as he did in *The Fever*. In this earlier play, in which Shawn himself played the sole character, the violence and injustice of the world seemingly induce bouts of violent vomiting. (This is the only play, he has said, that "I pictured myself being in" when he wrote it, although it could also be played by someone else. Interview by Animashawun). Vomiting functions both literally and metonymically in *Grasses*: as a symptom of an illness caused by disruption of the relationship among the earth's biota and as microcosmic equivalent of the spiritual dissolution of the society that has brought about the disaster.

Shawn's public persona adds disturbing comedy to the tale his protagonist tells, much as D'Aulnoy's saloniste figure implies an ironizing, sophisticated frame to her faux-naif tales. Even though Shawn tells an interviewer that he did not write the role of Ben with himself in mind — "I offered it to someone else but he turned it down" (Interview by Animashawun) — it seems clear that he and director Gregory made the most of the contrast between Shawn's popular image as a beloved, comedic actor (featuring, for example, in the film *The Princess Bride*) and the self-absorbed, sex-obsessed, scientist without a trace of conscience who is Ben. Much of the comedy comes, of course, from Shawn's writing, which gives Ben a succession of delightfully self-damning speeches. But the costuming — Shawn's black silk robe with matching black slippers, striking against the white sofa — begins the process of undermining the protagonist as it calls to mind Hugh Hefner's habitual garb, and creates a comic suggestion that Ben (as impersonated by an actor who usually plays impish, lovable, slightly naïve characters) has bought into the most readily available, simplistic version of sexual power in the mass marketing of desire.

Shawn, as implied author, engages in a certain amount of teasing of the audience which might be compared to that of Cerise/Blanche or to the fairy tale author's teasing. These figures, enjoying various modes of figurative or literal authorship, disconcert in part because they themselves are elusive, shape-shifting: the audience does not know quite how to get hold of them, if we think of ourselves as consumers and of them as our cultural prey.[6] For a moment at the opening, for example, consumption patterns are inverted and the audience glimpses itself as consumable. "I'm deriving a great deal of pleasure from each and every one of you, as if you were chocolates I was eating," Ben says to the audience (*Grasses* 7). Shawn's teasing includes some playful and estranging literalizations of concepts popular in eighties literary criticism. In this play, the Foucauldian notion that sexuality became not what was repressed but what had to be discussed[7] takes on an astonishing reality: Ben talks of the old days when children did not masturbate in front of their parents, nor vice-versa, nor did parents copulate with offspring (*Grasses* 23); Rose's business card features a picture of her vagina (*Grasses* 57).

Similarly, the following passage in which Ben recalls his first erotic encounter with the White Cat seems to allude to Derrida's meditations on self, on human and animal, occasioned by the gaze of his cat,[8] and resonates beyond Derrida to a variety of thinkers who respond to the current ecological crisis by trying to articulate the limitations of conceptual oppositions between human self and non-human other[9]:

> When I turned towards her, all of a sudden she stared into my eyes, penetrating me so deeply and fully that I turned inside out. My God — finally. Finally, to be known, I thought, as hot sperm flowed out of me, flowing over her paw as if it would never stop [*Grasses* 35].

Truly, human and animal find no boundaries here as they unite sexually in a conjunction Ben describes in language more often used for the experience of being fully known by God. On the one hand, Ben's seemingly unwitting use of the language of Christian belief — like the title of his memoir about genetically engineering food, *Loaves, With Fishes, For Dinner* — seems an irony directed against the unrepentant self-absorption of the protagonist. But perhaps a measure of decadence belongs to the audience too if we have taken comfort (perhaps even pleasure?) in deep ecological thoughts critiquing conceptual divisions between human and non-human and yet taken no action to deter the "optimistic," the "lucky," the people like Ben who see the planet in terms of a series of human supply and demand problems to be "fixed" not incidentally for their own profit.

Sex, Gender and Ethics

The consumption of food, and of sex, are twinned in Ben's pseudo-pornographic memoir and the extremity of his ethical blindness and self-absorption reveals the destructiveness of treating either a lover or the productive capacity of the earth as mere instruments for one's own satisfaction. Shawn's play seems to presuppose a capitalist society much like our own, in which vast systems work to arouse and provide for desires, so that the consequences of an individual, even solipsistic, range of awareness and action are writ large upon the planet as a whole. The gender politics of the play find a place within this larger perspective. While it is true that Ben speaks of his sexual partners without notice of their needs, and the transfer of his sexual attentions from human to feline implies the familiar objectification of women as "pussy," nevertheless Shawn has a larger concern. In fact, I suggest that the apparent gender war — the tables turned upon Ben, who becomes the prey toyed with by cat/woman — has as much to do with the play's overall project of undermining the ethical attitude of a Ben by showing his misunderstanding and misevaluation of well nigh everything, as it does with engineering an interesting reversal of gender domination. Madame D'Aulnoy unfolds a tale in which the handsome prince journeys forward to his happy fate but slyly indicates he is helpless without a wise woman, and may be playing a useful role in someone else's story (White Cat's) of which he is scarcely aware. Similarly, Shawn allows us to enjoy Ben's amazing self-absorption and his comeuppance. The self-absorption is not necessarily that of the heterosexual male, though the Hugh Hefner costume implies that the monogrammed slipper sometimes fits. But at root, Ben's tale is that of a man and his only "friend," his penis; of self-satisfaction in every sense. And if this is true, then the plot's apparent alliance of women with nature becomes itself a product of Ben's perspective, the consequence of an ethical isolation which creates a seeming opposition between self and everything and everyone else.

Sex

In an essay called "Writing About Sex" (originally published as an afterword to *Our Late Night* and *A Thought in Three Parts: Two Plays* 2007), Shawn presents a view of sexuality which illuminates the satire of this play and what may seem at first glance his odd linking of sexuality and ecological concerns. For Shawn asserts, first of all, that he writes about sex because he picks up the pervasive preoccupations of society. To write about sex is to address a topic which concerns the audience often, and in many ways; thus, Ben's bizarre narrative of sexual exploits concerns us, even as it induces uneasy laughter, or disgust, or boredom.

> When I try to define the voice, I say, weakly, "Oh, that's the unconscious," but I'm eventually forced to conclude that, if the unconscious has thoughts, it has to have heard these thoughts (or at least their constituent fragments) from human beings of some description — from the people I've met, the people I've read about, the people I've happened to overhear in the street. So it's not just a theory that society is speaking itself through me ["Writing About Sex" 155].

Writing about sex, then, is writing about the attitudes of our society.

Further, Shawn proposes that he writes about sex because it is "shocking" in a very particular way. If, as Shawn says, "most bourgeois people, including me, still walk around with an image of themselves in their heads that doesn't include — well — that" (157), then writing about sex can bring his audiences into an awareness of "mammalian processes" (Shawn's term) which they share with many species, an awareness with significance for ecological ethics. "Writing about sex is really a variant of what Wordsworth did, that is, it's a variant of writing about nature, or as we call it now, 'the environment.' Sex is 'the environment' coming inside, coming into our home and apartment and taking root inside our minds" (157). "No part of the self is unconnected to it," Shawn declares (158). If Ben's account of his sex life has shocked the audience because of its utter lack of self-censorship and complete want of any ethical sense, it has also reminded us of our mammalian nature. On the basis of this sexual, mammalian, nature Shawn implies a clear analogy between exploiting other living beings for one's sole sexual pleasure and exploiting the environment for the sole benefit of human kind.

Our mammalian sexuality "has taught us to love the meaningless and thereby turn it into the meaningful" and this love of the arbitrary could be described alternatively as "the love of reality" (158). Indeed, he sees sex properly regarded as a "humbling, equalizing force" and "a symbol of the possibility that we might all defect for one reason or another from the obedient columns in which we march" (161). In a queer way, then, the upside-down, dystopic fantasy world of Shawn's play is a reminder of our real sexual, appetitive, nature; of our being in Nature; of our human capacity to value the world, to act ethically. It is an invitation to step out of the march towards ever more convenient, unthinking, acts of consumption.

So it is appropriate that Ben's nightmarish account ends in a way that allows us to hope it has all been a dream. His last words announce that he lay down in a grassy meadow to die and found dying pleasant. If he is dead, how can he address us in the present, as giving a reading from his memoirs? Perhaps Ben is meant to be a ghost; perhaps Ben has presented his dreams and fantasies rather than his life story. In any event, the audience must re-adjust its sense of the governing premises of the fiction since no memoirist is allowed to describe his own death. And spurred by Shawn's ethical satire, perhaps we are meant to feel relief and hope that this play turns out to be governed by dream logic rather than the inexorable logic of consequences, that it is more nightmare than vision of the future. The closing moments of the play suggest that we are offered a chance to wake ourselves from nightmare, to step out of the march. The poetic description read by Ben at the opening of the play as an epigraph to his memoirs, and seemingly echoed by his dying moments recounted at the play's conclusion, is attributed to "Count D'Aurore":

> When I finally awakened after a long, long sleep with many dreams, I was surprised to find that I was lying on a battlefield and holding a sword. It was just after dawn, the air was cold, and the ground was damp with my own blood. As I wondered what circumstances could have brought me here, I looked across the vast expanse of the plain on which I lay, and it seemed that I could see grasses of a thousand colors, in which many rabbits, in absolute silence, were leaping and running like small horses [*Grasses* 8].

The language of the passage reminds us of the Biblical teaching that all flesh is grass; the bounty of colors suggests the joy of valuing the variety which, arbitrarily, exists. And the name of this apparently fictive author makes him the male counter-part of Sleeping Beauty ("Aurore," in Perrault's *conte*), implying we can hope that awakening is still possible.

NOTES

1. Lahr describes the protagonist, Ben, as "one of the barbarians who has devoured the planet" and comments that the field of high, waving grass which forms the back wall of the minimalist set in the Royal Court production "plays as a coda of hope. If we leave nature alone, Shawn seems to be saying, regeneration and beauty may still be possible" (Lahr 88).

2. See Hutcheon's *A Theory of Adaptation*, especially pages 148–153.

3. Throughout, my discussion of the form and history of the fairy tale is indebted to Marina Warner's work, especially *From the Beast to the Blonde*.

4. Gregory and Shawn co-wrote the screenplay of *My Dinner with André*, and Gregory has previously directed Shawn.

5. See Warner for a brief description of the context in which D'Aulnoy wrote. Although Rousseau would "proscribe fairy tales from children's education in *Émile*," and scorn the salons "for their effeminacy," the practice of storytelling which had grown up in the salons of the *précieuses*, the feminist writers of the generation before D'Aulnoy, was "part of an open campaign about equality and intelligence in conversation" (Introduction, *Wonder Tales* 8).

6. It may seem excessive to describe spectatorship as predation, but see Brecht's critique of "culinary" opera designed for consumption. His *Mahagonny* suggests an interesting parallel to Shawn's play, for Brecht's opera similarly makes pleasure the object of inquiry and in section thirteen a glutton "stuffs himself to death" while others are going hungry and "his pleasure provokes, because it implies so much" (Brecht 36).

7. "What is peculiar to modern societies, in fact, is not that they consigned sex to a shadow existence, but that they dedicated themselves to speaking of it *ad infinitum*, while exploiting it as *the* secret" (Foucault 35).

8. Throughout *The Animal That Therefore I Am* Derrida returns to the cat which observes him naked in his bedroom or bathroom (9 and passim).

9. See, for example, deep ecology inspired by Arne Naess, and interrogations of the human/animal divide by theorists such as Agamben, Calacro, and Chaudhuri.

WORKS CITED

Agamben, Giorgio. *The Open: Man and Animal.* Trans. Kevin Attell. Stanford, CA: Stanford University Press, 2004.

Albee, Edward. *The Goat, or Who Is Sylvia?* Woodstock & New York: Overlook Press, 2005.

Apuleius, Lucius. *The Golden Ass.* Trans. P.G. Walsh. New York: Oxford University Press, 1994.

Billington, Michael. Review of *Grasses of a Thousand Colors. The Guardian.* The Guardian, 20 May 2009. Web. 20 Dec. 2011.

Brecht, Bertolt. "The Modern Theatre is the Epic Theatre." *Brecht on Theatre.* Trans. John Willett. New York: Hill and Wang, 1964. 33–42.

Calacro, Matthew. *Zoographies: The Question of the Animal from Heidegger to Derrida.* New York: Columbia University Press, 2008.

Chaudhuri, Una. "Animal Geographies: Zooesis and the Space of Modern Drama." *Modern Drama* 46.4 (2003): 646–62.

d'Aulnoy, Marie-Catherine. "The White Cat." Trans. John Ashbery. *Wonder Tales.* Ed. Marina Warner. New York: Farrar, Straus and Giroux, 1996. 19–63.

Derrida, Jacques. *The Animal That Therefore I Am.* Ed. Marie-Louise Mallet. Trans. David Wills. New York: Fordham University Press, 2008.

Foucault, Michel. *The History of Sexuality Volume I: An Introduction.* Trans. Robert Hurley. New York: Random House, 1990.

Hitchings, Henry. "Seduced by Sex in *Grasses of a Thousand Colors.*" *Evening Standard.* Evening Standard, 19 May 2009. Web. 15 Sept. 2011.

Hutcheon, Linda. *A Theory of Adaptation.* New York & London: Routledge, 2006.

Lahr, John. "Catnip." *The New Yorker.* 1 June 2009: 88–89. newyorker.com. Web. 4 Mar. 2012.

Lang, Andrew, ed. *The Blue Fairy Book.* Longmans, Green, 1890.

Lasdun, James. "Hatching, Splitting, Doubling" (review of Marina Warner, *Fantastic Metamorphoses, Other Worlds*). *London Review of Books.* 25.16 (21 August 2003): 24–25.

Naess, Arne. *Ecology, Community and Lifestyle.* Cambridge: Cambridge University Press, 1989.

Perrault, Charles. "La Belle au bois dormant." *Contes du tems* [sic] *passé de Ma Mere l'Oye. Avec des morales. Par M. Perrault. Augmentée d'une nouvelle, viz. L'Adroite princesse.* New York: J. Rivington, libraire, 1795. 39–67.

Shawn, Wallace. *The Designated Mourner.* New York: Farrar, Straus and Giroux, 1996.

_____. *The Fever. Wallace Shawn: Plays One.* London: Faber and Faber, 1997. 157–202.

_____. *Grasses of a Thousand Colors.* New York: Theatre Communications Group, 2009.

_____. Interview by Ola Animashawun. Video. Royal Court Theatre. You Tube, 10 June 2009. Web. 20 Dec. 2011.

_____."Writing About Sex." *Essays.* Chicago: Haymarket Books, 2009. 153–161.

Sierz, Aleks. Review of *Grasses of a Thousand Colors. The Stage.* The Stage, 19 May 2009. Web. 20 Oct. 2011.

Warner, Marina. *From the Beast to the Blonde: On Fairy Tales and Their Tellers.* London: Chatto and Windus, 1994.

_____. *Signs and Wonders.* London: Chatto and Windus, 2003.

_____. Introduction. *Wonder Tales.* New York: Farrar, Straus and Giroux, 1996. 1–17.

Turning Komachi Legends, Gender and Noh *Inside Out*

Remaking Desire in Timberlake Wertenbaker's Early Play

MAYA E. ROTH

Longings darker than the flowers at night, when these press too close, I wear my robe turned inside out...
— Poem by Ono No Komachi as cited in *Inside Out*

A highly intertextual, sexy play premiered at Stoke-on-Trent in 1982. Timberlake Wertenbaker's *Inside Out* crafts a hybridic encounter with Komachi legends for Anglophone audiences. Inspired by the (presumably) ninth-century Japanese court poet who perfected an evocative, erotic precursor to the haiku, *Inside Out* sheds light not only on the widely acclaimed British dramatist's early work, but also on Wertenbaker's ambitious cross-cultural transformations of myths, legends, and fairy tales throughout her playwriting. Presenting a complex instance of international feminist storytelling, *Inside Out* adapts legends about the historic Ono no Komachi — heralded as one of the "immortals" of Japanese classical culture and the most widely represented female character in *Noh* theatre. In so doing this mesmerizing work creates space for women's subjectivity, desire, and creativity as well as Buddhist perspectives.

Using a fairy tale framework familiar to Western audiences, where The Girl encounters a Crone (who here transforms into her own lover), the play reflects on life passages: sexual coming-of-age, partnering, aging, death. Meanwhile, *Inside Out* adapts iconic variations of Komachi legends to actively re-imagine pernicious binaries of male/female, mind/body, and East/West in surprising ways. On every level, Wertenbaker experiments with turning elements of the play and of culture (identity, desire, gender, representation) "inside out," evoking a feminist erotics — and poetics — of transformation.

178

Wertenbaker's hybridic adaptation connects the transformational ethos of *Noh*, feminist praxis, and Komachi's poetry to reimagine desire and mor(t)ality.

Of the Komachi-Shosho legend, Wertenbaker says, "It seems to have all the elements: a woman who writes, the cruelty of love, the haunting, the transformation of guilt and something more mysterious" (Personal Correspondence 2011).[1] Wertenbaker rewrites one prominent Komachi legend: that she was a proud beauty who challenged a suitor to return to the palace garden on 100 nights before accepting him as a lover — only to revisit that journey herself when old and haggard, haunted by the suitor who never arrived on the final night. *Inside Out* revisits this legend through cross-dressed reenactments that stage mutual desire and discovery.

Originally conceived as one of a trilogy of plays about female cross-dressing, *Inside Out* was intended to partner with *New Anatomies*, Wertenbaker's widely discussed play about Isabelle Eberhardt, the Russian-Swiss-Armenian journalist who cross-dressed as an Arab man in French colonial Africa (premiered in 1981, published in 1984), as well as her lesser-known monologic play *Variations* about George Sand, the protofeminist nineteenth-century novelist (unproduced, but published in the Friends of George Sand Newsletter in 1981).[2] Although in the Preface to *Plays: One* Wertenbaker refers to these quite different works as a "trilogy [...] about women who cross-dressed in different historical periods," what best connects them is that their protagonists are female writers. (Indeed, no historical accounts suggest Komachi was a cross-dresser; rather Wertenbaker was first inspired by a painting of Komachi as represented in famous *Noh* plays, possessed by a male ghost.) Through her unnamed focus on women writers, Wertenbaker experiments with her own artistic voice, too, probing women's attempts to, in her language, "de-objectify" themselves (*Rage and Reason* 139).

Wertenbaker's trilogy manifests the playwright's early theoretical and creative interest in discovering women's complex articulations of self, subjectivity, sexuality, and language in cross-historical array and contemporary dialogue. By framing her trilogy about women writers through cross-dressing, however, she rhetorically both refutes and honors "women's writing." Certainly within her wide-ranging oeuvre *Inside Out* stands out for its explicit exploration of what Wertenbaker has referred to as "women's imagination," dealing as the play does with dreams and desire (*Rage and Reason* 136–37).

More broadly, the play reveals what Sara Freeman calls Wertenbaker's "translatorial consciousness," participating in what I have theorized as Wertenbaker's rigorous praxis of dialogic translation and creative transformation (Roth and Freeman, 275, 12–13). Certainly it is Wertenbaker's most complex, sustained treatment of legend, as differentiated from myth (e.g., the Philomela myth for *The Love of the Nightingale*, 1989), fairy tales (e.g., "Cinderella" for *The Ash Girl*, 2001), adaptations of classic plays (e.g., *The Theban Plays*, 1984), and history (e.g., Australian colonial history for *Our Country's Good*, 1988). If *Inside Out* presents the playwright's most rigorous *adaptation* of legend — particularly the 100 Nights variant — legend also features in several Wertenbaker plays, including *After Darwin, Three Birds Alighting on a Field, Dianeira*, and *Credible Witness*. Indeed *The Grace of Mary Traverse* (1985), written just four years after *Inside Out*, cross-fertilizes with the Faustian legend more rigorously than the Gordon Riots, boldly morphing narrative structures to probe human nature (and social atrocities) in Mary's quest for power, knowledge, and — finally — grace, traversed through female subjectivities. Similarly, *Inside Out* transforms the gendered narratives and moral codes of medieval Japanese Komachi legends to reimagine desire, agency, courtship, and aging for pluralist audiences in an increasingly global West. Equally, this play decenters Euro-American sexual politics and poetics by engaging a classical legend from Asia.

Komachi, the Poet

In Ono no Komachi, Wertenbaker finds profound inspiration for feminist and meta/physical exploration. A highly esteemed Heian court poet, Komachi came to lasting prominence through Japan's first Imperial Anthology of Poetry, the *Kokinwakashü*, published in Japanese and Chinese editions in the tenth century.[3] Of the six then-recent Sages of Poetry, or "poetic geniuses" distinguished alongside ancient masters, Komachi was the only female — one of only two in the whole volume. Historically, only her 18 poems included in the *Kokinwakashü* are certain; however, she is widely assumed to have been a ninth-century court consort, a great beauty and wit.

Her extant poems, still popular, are erudite and accessible, erotic and philosphical. Since refined court culture revered poetry, deemed a gift from "the age of the gods," perhaps it is unsurprising that Komachi's life and work would become shrouded by legend. For over a millennium, her poetry has been beloved, but also defined, as an example of "women's writing," and specifically Japanese poetics. In the twentieth century, Komachi's writing was widely classified as "passionate" and, in recent decades, also often as feminist (Parker 271).

One of a cadre of famous women writers during the Heian period, Komachi stands out for the immediacy of her poems, their creative wordplay, and their sophisticated layering of allusions, classical intertexts, and disparate first-person personae, voicing bold desire, intense if subtle emotion, and dream imagery (Kawashima, Keene, Teele). She specialized in Japanese-language *waka* (or *tanka*), distilling sensitive, profound perceptions of nature, experience, and *yugen* ("grace") into 31 syllables, an icon of Heian court/ship culture.

Various literary and historical practices shaped Komachi legends from her poetry (Kawashima, Parker, Strong). In particular, the Imperial Anthology's brief Preface disparages Komachi's female body: "[H]ers is the poetry of a beautiful woman who is ill and suffering" (Trans. Teele). Written as though Komachi's gender infects the poetry, the editorial frame sought to promote male poets newly writing in Japanese, versus Chinese, in the tenth century (Parker 273). Meanwhile, Komachi's "passionate" immediacy of language and inventive use of sometimes female, sometimes male personae were subsumed into a singular voice framed as Komachi herself, read as memoir (Kawashima 152). Over time, the body of poetry attributed to Komachi grew with her legends, reinforcing femme fatale, aging beauty, and exile tropes, which proliferate in the *Komachishu* (Anthology of 100 "Komachi" poems), likely published in the eleventh century.

The comparatively cloistered lives of women at court, the historical practice of recording women by family name and gender only, and the erotic vitality of the poet's work created fertile ground for imagination and rumor to shape the storied life, rather than biography, of Komachi. Annually celebrated in a festival at one of her (four) alleged burial sites, Komachi became — and remains — the most frequently represented female figure in the *Noh* repertory, a testament to her poetry and legends, both.

The Komachi Legends

The Komachi legends are varied and ubiquitous in Japan. Frequently Komachi stands in for Woman, whether a young beauty, a haggard crone, or a re-incarnation of the bohissattva of compassion. Yet she is also cast as exceptional — an unparalleled beauty and/or talent. Legends often figure her as the agent of men's downfall as well as, paradoxically, their enlightenment (Pandey, Strong). Associated with cherry blossoms, she represents a Buddhist exemplar of impermanence and fleeting beauty — of the body, of love and desire. Indeed, Buddhist morality tales in the Muromachi Period leveraged the Poet's recent prestige and storied beauty to lure diverse audiences — peasants and court, male and female (Kimbrough 1–7). As the cultural centrality of Buddhism and samurai culture grew, *Noh* representations shaped Komachi legends most prominently, beginning in the fourteenth century. Visual artists subsequently used Komachi imagery to represent bodily decay after death (Chin 300–01, Kawashima 190–92, Pandey 203), ostensibly to neutralize desire by showing beauty as illusory; meanwhile the Komachi paintings (costumed as in *Noh*) epitomize Japanese Buddhism's ambivalent teachings on *fujo* (impurity), increasingly gendered female, accenting evanescence and aestheticized longing (Pandey 197).

The association of Komachi with the pre-existing 100 Nights Legend arose largely through the Imperial Anthology's (re)contextutalization of a Komachi poem as a heartless rejection of a worthy suitor's appeal poem (Kawashima 159–60, Strong 393–4). That trope merged with Buddhist morality tales, which cast Komachi as leaving court suddenly due to, alternately, her wealthy parents' deaths, a patron banning her from court life, or punishment (self- or other-imposed) for the death of a suitor who she insisted return to her on 100 nights "through rain, snow, hail and wind" before embracing him (Waley 148). It is this last legend which *Inside Out* reworks, triggering the playwright's explicit interaction with Elder Komachi *Noh* plays.

The 100 Nights Legend refracts across Komachi's life-cycle, hinging on duality: a great beauty in youth, a penniless beggar in old age. The classical plays display her verbal mastery over men, while also revealing her vulnerability or "madness" marked female. All three Elder Komachi *Noh* plays present her as too ashamed to acknowledge her identity, a shame that stems partly from her ugliness and poverty, her fall. Yet too, Komachi's shame presents poetic retribution for her sexual agency and rejection of Shosho in her youth; this foregrounds *his* indignities suffered, his just suit (not only his emotional duress) in plaguing her. Typically *Noh* plays develop sympathy for Komachi through her wisdom and poetry, and by her making peace with a male whom she has wronged (e.g., Shosho in *The Nightly Courting of Komachi* and *Komachi on the Stupa*) or a male who has wronged her (e.g., Kuronushi in *Komachi Clears Her Name*). All *Noh* Komachi plays provide ample inspiration for Wertenbaker's feminist interaction.

Legends have an after-life. They also have a prior-life, inspired by previous sources, people or events, generated within existing cultural frameworks and values. Skeletal details about Ono no Komachi and the editorial commentaries about her were laid onto pre-existing stories. The fundamentally adaptational, intertextual aesthetics of Asian literature (both fiction and non-fiction) contribute to the vitality and plurality of Komachi legends. Equally, the legends' movement across the life cycle (from youth to after-death) and Komachi's iconic status as Woman multiplies the legend (casting her as youth's flower, crone, goddess, desiring lover, Buddhist nun, courtesan). Like most legends, Komachi legends engender a deeper commitment to specific, even if changing, cultural values (Oring 145): Komachi's connect to gender and desire. Since the Edo Period, her name has been a sobriquet for beautiful women. Komachi's legends endure and mutate, exemplifying the ongoing co-creation of legends.

Wertenbaker's variation is but one of a chain of revisionings steered to the values of their makers and audiences. What differentiates Wertenbaker's is that it emerges in a different cultural tradition and draws audience attention to its acts of revisioning, as I will explain. Written during the second wave of feminist theorizing and theatre, when Komachi's poetry was first being translated into English by women (e.g., Jane Hirshfield and Mariko Aratani, Helen Craig McCullough), Wertenbaker's play articulates sensuous philosophy and cultural commingling.

Inside Out

On a narrative level, Wertenbaker's *Inside Out* follows an aged itinerant poet (Elder Komachi) who appears to a contemporary Girl seeking love on the Mountain of Desire. Energized by desire and memory, Elder Komachi speaks as though she is her dead lover — Shosho — yearning for Komachi, counting the nights until they can consummate their love; three times she murmurs snippets of Komachi's poetry, which enables the Girl's recognition, eventually, that the old crone *is* the famous beauty, now haggard and haunted. As the Male Chorus enters, announcing "the story," Elder Komachi removes her tattered rags to reveal Shosho, a young warrior in fine robes, underneath; together Young Komachi (performed by another actor) and Shosho re-live their courtship. She is sophisticated and cultured, a Poet; he blunt and confident, a Warrior full of desire; although she initially refuses him, they joust, trade roles briefly, and develop love. Shosho agrees to visit her garden on 100 nights, unseen, to prove himself. He experiences the world through his nightly journeys; meanwhile, cloistered at court, Young Komachi makes art, meditates on desire, shares intimacies with her companion Li, dreams (even visiting Shosho's dreams in the play's center). On the 100th night, when she will finally embrace him, he does not arrive. Wertenbaker presents four variations of the legend as to why not. At play's end, Elder Komachi is again on the Mountain of Desire, as if infinitely replaying memories, revitalized. The contemporary Girl steps out of her role as Li, Young Komachi's companion — without a lover but newly attuned to sexuality, love, and the legend. Amid ensemble counting to the 100th night, Elder Komachi speaks the play's last non-numbered word: "Desire."

Inside Out draws most vividly on four sources for its understanding of the legend: the two *Noh* plays about the 100 Night Legend, *Komachi Sotoba* (*Komachi on the Stupa*) and *Kayoi Komachi* (*The Nightly Courting of Komachi*), both by Kan'Ami with possible revisions by his son Zeami; specific poems by Ono no Komachi; and Wertenbaker herself, whose close listening to those sources is matched by her creative interactions with them. Of the five Komachi *Noh* plays still actively in the repertory since the fourteenth century, *Komachi Sotoba* and *Kayoi Komachi* are most often translated, having reached Anglophone audiences in the twentieth century via translations by Ezra Pound and Ernest Fenellosa (1916–17), much-anthologized more "faithful" versions by Arthur Waley (1921) and Donald Keene (1993), and alongside all active Komachi plays as translated by Rebecca and Roy Teele, respectively (1993).[4] Presenting Komachi late in life (or as a wraith), *Komachi on the Stupa* and *The Nightly Courting* enjoy prominence in anthologies due to their climactic scenes of ghost/possession, complex focus on Buddhist enlightenment, dramatic riffs on the legend, and performance challenges.

Whereas classical *Noh* interact with poems by Komachi that meditate on loneliness and felt-exile after the blush of youth and Buddhist lessons, Wertenbaker leverages Komachi's erotic poetry, dream imagery, and meditations on life passage; both draw on the poet's sophisticated wordplay and wit. By interacting with the medieval legends, sometimes redressing them, *Inside Out* participates in a deeply contemporary, cross-cultural dialogue, not only a cross-historical one: for the medieval legends endure in the living tradition of *Noh* performance (passed on generationally), replayed in critical introductions and preserved in classical paintings such as the Seven Komachi cycle.

In the unpublished script used for the 1983 Edinburgh Festival performance, *Inside Out* calls for "a stage, bare except for two benches, three blinds." With her stage vocabulary evoking an Asian playing space and presentational style, Wertenbaker signals her inspiration in *Noh*, the traditional dance-theatre form steeped in Buddhism, Japanese legends, and classical poetry. In form, as well as theme, Wertenbaker's play engages the central Buddhist principle that all life and identity are transient, in flux. Further, the play cites and resituates female impersonation in traditional Asian theatre — or rather, the dynamic fluidity of sex/gender, the not male/not female of *Noh* performance theory.

Wertenbaker brings the legend into the present day West via contemporary frames and figures. Translational bridges include The Girl, who speaks to the audience before unwittingly summoning Komachi, and the Male Chorus. The latter functions as a contemporary storyteller, guiding us into the legend from here and now: "Where are we? Ninth century Japan. Or anywhere, anytime... In the rules of this play, past and present intermingle: no prejudice." These figures anticipate Wertenbaker's frequent later use of translational characters who mirror audiences, moving us reciprocally inside and outside of action — as in *Love of the Nightingale, Dianeira,* and *The Ash Girl.* More striking is the image of Elder Komachi living in the present — the beggar appearing to the "modern girl" at the Mountain of Desire. This provocative image translates *Noh* hierophanies where figures encounter the legendary Komachi, initially unrecognized; or, as in *The Nightly Courting of Komachi*, a Buddhist monk stirs her spirit by passing the field where Komachi's talking skull lies. A theatrical icon of the legend, Wertenbaker's Elder Komachi surviving centuries later in the West also functions as a talisman of the legend's afterlife and migration. Less than reading as a miraculous event, Elder Komachi's appearance in the here/now registers as the legend's endurance, "the story" traveling — and the poet's polymorphic influence. Which is to say, Wertenbaker participates in the Komachi legends.

Inside Out enwraps the audience in Komachi's poetry and the 100 Nights Legend, reframed. Folding layer upon layer, the dramatic structure conjures images of interactive embrace and revelation. Closing her eyes to summon a handsome, educated lover she has never met, the contemporary Girl, on one level, dreams the entire play that follows — as if we are together dreaming with the legend and Poet's ideas. The Girl functions like a credible storyteller whose suspicion of "superstition" — what she dismisses as "dream logic" — makes the legend more credible and transformative. Drawing on tropes of realism no less than legend and fairy tale, this contemporary frame draws *us* into the Komachi world, even as the *Noh* Komachi appears onstage. The Girl concisely summarizes the duality perpetuated across anthologies and arts, which *Inside Out* ultimately revisions: "Komachi was very beautiful when she was young. Then she was old and ugly and died in rags." Yet even before we explicitly enter Komachi's story, Wertenbaker rebuts the sexist debris that has infused the reception of Komachi's poetry and fueled the 100 Nights Legend.

Before the Girl recognizes Komachi, Wertenbaker foregrounds the female body as the crucial site of provocation in this legend. As in Western fairy tales, the Girl, our contemporary surrogate, fears the old woman's ragged, blistering body. First, she tells the audience: "[a] handsome man, seeing her, will run as fast as he can and he won't notice me." Second, the elder woman's body frightens her because it is so mortal, so messy: "Sores on her flesh. I hope I never grow that old." She fears that diseased body as an object, but also a signifier of what she will become: "Can that cluster of boils and cancers ever have been young. Like me?" Though the play focuses on embodied lives, Elder Komachi is performed by a man, citing *Noh*; in this way, Wertenbaker keeps audience focus more on Western cultural fears of aging than staging disease or a visceral body. At play's start, Wertenbaker highlights cultural anxieties internalized by women, no less than projected by men, about female bodies. Threateningly mortal — smelly, abject, transient — Elder Komachi's body reminds the Girl, too, of her own inevitable death, as Komachi's old age and corpse do in the Japanese Buddhist tales (redirecting desire). It reminds her that she *is* a body, not feminine youth in perpetuity. Those fears in turn economically, socially, psychologically disenfranchise, isolate the "offending" body-person: "Drop bread in her basket, but make sure I don't touch her. In case age is contagious after all." The playwright offers an effective feminist reframing of the crone trope — and the extent to which Komachi has been equated with her body, that body cast as "sick" by the *Kokinwakashū*'s Preface, a site of decay and demise in Buddhist paintings and fables. Yet this Elder Komachi resists the iconic shame of her age and faded beauty, for she is still full of desire, like the poetry; she murmurs for Komachi (as Shosho), counting the 99th night. "Let me go to her, let me go to her...."

Whereas the traditional Komachi *Noh* focus on her dead lover's fury, his need for retribution and, typically, priestly intervention to achieve transcendence, this version focuses on Komachi's ongoing desire for him and re-performance of their overlapping journeys until his death, which left her as both of them, *and* as only her. It is as though she becomes him in order to fulfill the poetic action through to the 100th night so that they might change the tragic story, keep him from having died. She transforms into her shadow self, her desired lover; thus in a way fulfilling her own desire. Although most Komachi-Shosho legends emphasize Shosho's desire as central, this play focuses on their mutual desire — and even more fully on hers for him in the play's outside frames. Instead of Buddhist Priests, who facilitate Komachi and Shosho's enlightenment in *Noh*, finally exorcising their emotional and spiritual turmoil, *Inside Out* stages a moral framework that presents enlightenment arising from relationship, imagination, and inquiry.[5]

Unlike *Noh*, Wertenbaker's cast is coed in a six-character play performed by two women and two men. Wertenbaker casts Komachi across two performers, with discrete roles for Young Komachi (performed by a female) and Elder Komachi (performed by a male). By having the same (male) actor play Elder Komachi and Shosho, the legend's poetic force gains emphasis. "That's the story: lovers become one." This choice sustains the Elder Komachi/Shosho transformation as theatrically and thematically integral; it also allows (Elder) Komachi to perform her own lover, while resisting clear sex/gender roles — or clarity about who is ghosting whom here. Structurally, Wertenbaker's casting layers feminism — four female roles to two male in her story, refusal of sex/gender binaries — with equality, the play opening to democratic impulses by the significance of male roles and performers (the plum role of Elder Komachi/Shosho, a Male Chorus). The casting reinforces how *Inside Out* works as a complex feminist perspective thinking *through* the legend and poetry, engaging Buddhism and sensuous philosophy.

Inside Out returns to its beginning at its end, as if an ongoing spiral, or a single moment's complex memory opened infinitely. Using structural inversions — Elder Komachi as Shosho, later Shosho as Komachi, male performing female performing male, the inner play beginning at the 99th night — the play enacts cyclic, transformational storytelling. This move is both seductive and productive; we are lured into the legend, even as the play transforms — remakes — the legend. In the midst of drawing us in, Wertenbaker's hermeneutic dramaturgy also intervenes critically, drawing on yet another trope of feminist theatre: the Girl's disruptive encounter with the ragged crone interrogates fear of aging and disgust with women's bodies; the Male Chorus comments on the action and playwriting, often wryly; Komachi challenges the sexism of the legend when Shosho and she first meet — and again when at 33 nights he casts her as a body more than person. Nowhere are Wertenbaker's critical interventions more visible than when the play presents four different versions of the 100th night, their ideologies exposed, as I discuss later. In myriad ways, the play moves us both inside and outside the received legend, inside and outside the playworld, engaging us emotionally and critically at once.

In the creative, theatrical dream logic of this play, here is the crux of Wertenbaker's redress: she uses Buddhist principles to undo the gender-coding unquestioned in prominent romance/narratives, sex/desire metaphors, social and performance spaces — to undo the chauvinism of legends which punished Komachi for having refused a male, girding the "woman's play," in relation to her shame and his (arduous) journey, in relation to her contagious female body and his productive male one (a warrior infected with desire for her).

In contrast to the male-dominated publication and framing of Komachi's poetry for the first millennium of its influence and the all-male tradition of classical *Noh* performance, Wertenbaker creates women-centered frameworks for the reception of the 100 Nights Legend. *Inside Out*'s scene titles — *The Young Woman; Courtship; Waiting; Dreams; The Ninety-Ninth Night; The Old Woman* — thread the play's imaginary to women's lives, framed as cyclic, archetypal, cross-generational. The titles spring from Komachi's poetry as much as the legend, engaging the philosophical depth that characterizes the poems and Elder Komachi plays. Intended to be performed without intermission, *Inside Out*'s dynamic staging of interaction between the playwright, tradition, the actors, audience members, and the characters-as-interlocutors activates awareness of how we co-create legends and can engage cultural dialogues with and through them. Like the play's transformational tropes, this dynamic interactive web of co-creation poses an invitation for audiences to together transform the cultural frameworks of our lives.

Nodal Moments of Redress

Wertenbaker writes three scenes that visibly remap the Komachi-Shosho love story. First is their scene of encounter, particularly how the 100 Nights

Challenge arises. Second she writes an erotic dream/dance that Komachi invents to sustain mutual desire, inspired by Komachi's famous poem of journeying to a lover's dreams. Third, Wertenbaker remaps the legend's ending — replaying why and how Shosho does not return the last night. Drawing on classical and contemporary sources, Buddhist and feminist praxis equally, these three scenes critically and creatively engage the legend. Each theatrically re-shapes the action by imagining interventions in gender hostitilies embedded in the legend, but also according to character dilemmas; marked visibly for audiences, these theatrical transformations build on Komachi's poetry and the motif of cross-dressing.

In the most famous Komachi play, *Komachi on the Stupa*, Komachi defends her rights to the Buddha's (metaphoric) body, the sacred gnarled tree stump, by debating Buddhist priests and winning. In Wertenbaker's re-visioning the Young Poet defends rights to her (sexual) body — and subjectivity. The traditional *Noh* plays elide focus on Komachi's perspective by giving emphasis instead to Shosho's desire and arduous journeys. In Wertenbaker's contemporarization, Shosho is unsettled by her refusal, partly because she has so many lovers — and partly because he desires her; she checks his presumption of her diminished rights if sexually active by witty assurance that her "garden," her body, is made more colorful, not cheapened, by a range of seeds — positioning herself, not him, as gardener. She seeks some "place for me," for *her*, in his wooing, claiming subjectivity. Here, Wertenbaker suggests the psychic and political stakes for transforming the legend today — to change the ways cultural narratives shape our desires and constitute rights.

Komachi improvises a theatrical solution to what has become for her an offensive cliché (and for audiences an incisive parable for sexual politics): she wraps Shosho in the silk he gave her and circles him, he now embodying her. At that pivotal juncture the scene transforms from gender conflict to discovery. Each playfully imagines the other's perspective, while seeing simultaneously, intermittently, from their own: "Lady open your legs," she-as-he commands Shosho-performing-Komachi. "But I only open my legs to the poetic," he responds as she, wryly. By trading roles and corporeal perspectives, they arrive someplace surprisingly new. Unexpectedly, this move transforms their impasse of his unrequited desire and her savvy critique, keeping the play from escalating into violence, as in *The Love of the Nightingale*, or getting mired in the legend's chauvinism. In performance, their switching roles and replaying action lead them to re-imagine their relationship, just as actors find that by performing others their sense of self and the world expands. "How strange it was to be you for a moment, Komachi. Is that what you want?" Their role reversal, *and layering*, facilitates altered consciousness for audiences no less than characters.[6]

Inside Out complicates techniques used by the Women's Movement (and feminist theatre) by drawing on models of transformation and cross-gender impersonation in *Noh* and Komachi's poetry. The example above epitomizes how Wertenbaker recurrently problematizes sex/gender identity and stable bodies in *Inside Out*. Identity is multiply blurred: Young Komachi — performed by a young woman — performs Shosho; meanwhile Shosho, performed by Elder Komachi, enacted by a man, performs Young Komachi. It is in this complicated performance moment — a play of sorts, within a play in a play, where sex and gender cross multiply — that Shosho agrees to prove his love by coming to the palace garden for 100 nights. In Wertenbaker's version, the challenge arises as a poetic action meant to match her skill at poetic verse; his challenge is to make the journey 100 nights, hers (as she later explains to Li) to wait. As Ned Chaillet suggests, "Because it is by imagining himself as Komachi that Shosho has invented the idea of the poetic action, it is forever unclear who really suggested the task" (697).

The next nodal moment in Wertenbaker's inventive "collaboration and confrontation" with the received legend, to invoke Mark Fortier's shorthand for critical adaptation (340), arises with the erotic dream encounter shared by Komachi and Shosho. After 33 nightly visits without seeing her, Shosho's commitment dissipates and his antagonism toward her grows (hostility staged in *Noh* years later). As if anticipating Susan Bordo's premise in *Unbearable Weight*, this Shosho yearns for sex, then departure from the dark otherness of women: "Need for fresh air, solidity, light, the opposite of a woman." Retorting across the elastic narrative space, Komachi critiques the simultaneous danger and anonymity ("bottomless pit") assigned to women's bodies in the sexist rendering to which Shosho reverts. To re-ignite their desire and teach him "the anatomy of a woman," Komachi turns her sleeves inside out, bringing her to his dreams. ("Dream, Shosho, dream," urges the Male Chorus.) Based on Komachi's famous poem, this scene deepens their love, creating intimacy shared. Moreover, Wertenbaker stages the poet talking back — as her poems so often did — to tradition and men, here directly challenging the sexist residue associated with the Komachi legend, here voiced by Shosho. Functioning as the *kuse* in *Noh* terms — the central narrative event accented with dance, poetry, and subtle choral layering — this scene exemplifies Wertenbaker's rigorous collaboration with the legend's form, not only its content.

In "Dream," Young Komachi and Shosho enact a stylized "restrained" dance of love; they come together and apart, slowly stopping short of a kiss, while Li and the (Male) Chorus speak as if they too were the lovers. Imagining how to love "without force" and "at the speed of conversation rather than battle," they discover where "my skin's turned inside out under your touch." Interchangeably they share lines, enacting *Noh's* fluid character and narrative stance, using words to dress and undress desire. Instead of male and female bodies or "the imagined void," here bodies and spirits intermingle, the lovers (and storytellers) an intersubjective one.

> LI: Hands and parts intermingle. I don't know which are mine and which are yours.
> CHORUS: I'm inside out, you sink inside me.
> LI: You're inside me.
> CHORUS: Fold after fold, not the imagined void.
> LI: All distances covered.

This scene is sexy and mutual, subverting gendered differentiation in erotic intimacy, teaching Shosho how to encounter Komachi as lover rather than desired, dangerous other. By summoning Komachi's poem into the legend, the playwright transforms the emphasis on spurned love (first by her, then by him) into reciprocal love, re-making a cautionary tale of destructive desire into an erotic tale of love grown through desire creatively sustained and sustaining.

While this play focuses most of all on remapping a (traditionally traumatic) love story, it equally creates social and psychic space for bodied and female subjectivities, as Komachi's poetry is understood to do. Here, one of Francophone Wertenbaker's key guides for reworking the Komachi legend was surely Luce Irigaray's influential collection of essays, *Ce sexe qui n'est pas un* (1977), later translated into English as "This Sex Which Is Not One."[7] Irigaray's precise phrases layer with classical Japanese sources as part of the intertextual dialogue in "Waiting" and "Komachi's Dream." Like Irigaray, *Inside Out* explicitly transforms an erotic imaginary based in male penetration and/or mastery to a feminist erotics of mutual touch, imaginative discovery, and interfolding bodies (and lips), here multiplied in lesbian and autoerotic as well as heterosexual encounters. "I have four lips, perhaps you have two," says Li when narrating the desire dream, in effect speaking as Komachi describing her experience (poetically evoked) of oral sex: "You touch them, they touch each other: reverberations of feeling."[8] Here each subject gives and receives (a "double sensation" in phenomenological terms), self-touching and other-touching, with overlapping boundaries and fluidity between one and two (and more). Drawing on *écriture féminine*, Wertenbaker rebuts and transforms the denigration of the female body transported via the Komachi legend; she stages "jouissance"—connecting writing and bodily pleasures—to help audiences dream with Komachi's poetry.

The play's title, *Inside Out*, derived from Komachi's famous poem quoted to start this essay, suggests dynamic inter-relations that stir profound insight. Like Taoism's yin and yang, where reciprocal boundaries spill one into the other, each aspect transforms and carries its seeming opposite to create a fluid whole, conjuring corporeal subjectivities.[9] *Inside Out* also checks Irigaray's tactical essentialisms by sharing the imagery across women and men, spinning layers of cross-casting and choral exchange, leveraging *Noh*. If with Young Komachi Wertenbaker re-claims what has been constituted as feminine, imagining female bodies as sites of subjectivity, language, performance, and desire, *Inside Out* equally multiplies and destabilizes gender representations. In creating a dramatic structure that folds inside out, one character multiplying into another, times and cultures intermingling, Wertenbaker embraces a "new anatomy," to quote her most famous cross-dressing play, of desire, courtship narratives, and the Komachi legend.

Partly situated as Buddhist and partly as feminist, this play proposes that imagination and interconnection, not consummation and conquest, best enlighten — awakening the spirit-body. Whereas Li earlier argued for "the real moment" as the source (and consummation) of desire, Komachi (as in the poems) suggests that anticipation, imagination, and memory are more persuasive and lasting than the actual moment of contact, for they together make the body come alive in the "real" moment, if it does, turning one's world inside out.

After "Komachi's Dream," Wertenbaker remakes journey and narrative structure explicitly, including for newcomers to the legend. This story never arrives at The Climax — the 100th night — just as it does not in the legend; nor, however, does a vengeful ghost haunt Komachi years later as in *The Nightly Courting of Komachi* and *Komachi on the Stupa*, both of which stage their most dramatic moments at the precise juncture of Shosho's haunting/possession of (Elder) Komachi. By explicitly transforming *and transposing* the received Komachi-Shosho legends' events for and with the audience, Wertenbaker transforms a bad death to a good (if poignant) one, a trope of absence and disgrace (for Shosho or Komachi, depending) to a passage observed with intimacy.

In the "Ninety-Ninth Night" scene, Shosho continues his nightly visits, his experience of self, desire, and the journey more perceptive and mature. Disguising himself many nights — as beggar, woman, courtier (thus inviting the possibility that the beggar woman might be yet another of Shosho's disguises) — lest rumors wreck their reputations, he experiences his journey in its rigor and simplicity, its variety and repetitions. Like Prince Siddhartha's discovery that all experiences and people interweave in the river of life, so does Shosho's journey accent the transience, multiplicity, and flow of time. It is as if his whole life transpires over the courtship: the 66 days after the "Dreams" scene reading equally like 66 years. On the 99th night, Shosho's energy is gone; he is an old man. "I've come to love this journey. I can find the garden by the smell of the jasmine. No need to look." Imagining that his fatigue arises from that night's journey rather than, as the Chorus's ironic interruptions reveal, time running out — death — Shosho dreams of peeling off the tattered rags of life experience, or his beggar's disguise, imagining that underneath he will again be young. The Chorus interrupts Shosho's dying to stage four variations on how/why Shosho does not arrive on the 100th night, including two of Wertenbaker's own. These alternate endings disrupt the narrative necessity of any of them, buttressed by the (male) Chorus's blunt, sometimes wry, critiques for audiences of the different sex/gender/social systems they enact.

The first traditional version has Komachi receiving a note from her lover that his father died, an ending Wertenbaker's play critiques as Freudian ("the father denies his son pleasure"). As he had to miss the 100th night, Shosho forever lost his chance at Komachi's favor. The Chorus attributes the second to the Chinese and "in it we see a creeping dislike of women"; having demonstrated his ability to endure the challenge, building her desire, Shosho leaves Komachi forever awaiting his return. Such an ending flaunts his control, as traditional versions show Komachi earlier flaunting hers by insisting on a lengthy, grueling period of wooing (which Wertenbaker complicates, as I have discussed). The third ending, which Wertenbaker quickly adds, comedic in contrast, features Shosho writing Komachi to visit him the last night: "Equal Rights Amendment," summarizes the Chorus. This ending recalls Li's earlier stance that when Shosho wearied at 33 nights, Komachi should trade travel to him for a while, regardless of gender taboos. "But in 1982," the Chorus continues, locating the premiere's year (re-framed to whenever performed), "our evidence points to this...."

In a last, moving, and extended variation, Wertenbaker writes for Komachi to join Shosho on the bench at night 99. Together they wait for the last night, she trying to inspire him to keep breathing, to hold on for their long-awaited consummation, he wondering why it had to be so hard. By the 100th night, Shosho has died. Struggling with whether to blame herself or him — for he had volunteered 100 nights, or was it she, Komachi wonders — she offers her death in exchange. The narrator refuses, for that would not only reframe the story, but forget it. Instead, as in Japanese ghost stories and the traditional *Noh* versions, she is haunted by her long-dead suitor, both of them blaming her; at this, Young Komachi runs off. Yet it is not Shosho, nor his vengeful ghost, that haunts Komachi: rather, we see, it is Komachi's own self-doubt, grief, and desire which pummel her. The Male Chorus clarifies this distinction, refusing for the play to re-play those phallocentrisms which so infiltrated the 100 Nights Legend. Wertenbaker writes for Shosho to rise and put Elder Komachi's tattered robes back on as at the beginning.

Here as elsewhere, *Inside Out* is always already Komachi's story, even when it is Shosho's: for the whole courtship is framed within her complexity and aged wanderings, in her feminist and Buddhist path, travelling and performing him. Once again, *Inside Out* spirals, transforming back to the first setting where the Girl and Elder Komachi, a bit crazy in age with fewer filters between past and present, talk. "I don't always know who I am," she laughs, still the beggar woman who disrobes to a young man, the beautiful courtesan who turns into "an old ugly clusters of boils and bones," the one who receives and who gives, the one who journeys and who waits, the one who is many at once.

More important than contemporizing the legend's framing, Wertenbaker contemporizes its mores. The playwright creates a moving love story, mutually felt. In *The Nightly Courting of Komachi*, Shosho's ghost ascends to the Buddhist Path of Enlightenment, when as he and the wraith of Komachi re-visit their courtship, he chooses not to fulfill the 100th night visit, detaching from obsessive love — suffering and desire. In Wertenbaker's play Shosho's enlightenment comes through experiences in this world, instead. By deferring his peaceful dying, interrupted by alternative endings for the legend, Wertenbaker attunes her audience to developing critical perspectives as well as empathy, juxtaposing different modes of engagement to involve and challenge us, a technique she differently harnesses to pointed effect in *The Love of the Nightingale* (Roth 49). Desire, mortality, women's bodies, enlightenment: these pivot points illuminate the Komachi legends, both traditionally and in Wertenbaker's rendering. What changes is the moral and gendered perspective. In *Inside Out* the danger associated with desire transforms into a creative life-renewing force.

Contemporary Perspective

Characteristically, the well that Wertenbaker draws from for *Inside Out* runs deep — manifested in a rigorous critical and creative journey with classical culture, contemporized. Linda Hutcheon suggests that the power of adaptations comes in their simultaneous appeal to the human desires for repetition and innovation. The Komachi legend variations, infused as they are with paradoxes of *human life*—youth begets old age, desire consumes or dissipates, riches can turn to rags, dreams reveal more than reality, change is constant, two become (like) one — enable different audiences to reflect on love and loss, self and other, death and metaphysical journeys. Wertenbaker's adaptation moves in two directions at once, both retelling a prominent strand of the Komachi legend in its complexity, and changing it with new cultural perspectives (and ideologies) at play. This accounts for its success as adaptation: It is both new and old, familiar and foreign. It reaches to disparate audiences with particularity, and connects them, opening through metaphor and symbolic reworking of legend, layering *Noh* and fairy tale, *écriture féminine* and storytelling theatre with subtlety and self-conscious markers, alike.

Although new to most Western audiences, the Komachi legend's classical prominence, its plural spins (and sources) contextualized, and its symbolic significance for audiences halfway across the world (*and* for Asians living in the West) increase its allure and meaning, surely, for contemporary audiences in the ever-more Asian West. Moreover, Wertenbaker's layering of repetition, citation, and transformation enacts not only a dramaturgy of adaptation, but a poetics of legend migration (across cultures as well as generations). Wertenbaker's dialogic complexity provides ample means to excavate Komachi's legacy for intercultural and Western audiences, alike — and differently.

Most specifically, *Inside Out* excavates and transforms legends of desire and women's danger, cast in transcultural dialogue. Like Brecht's use of Asian legends to displace commentary on Western values, so does Wertenbaker's *Inside Out* speak to Anglophone audiences by estranging their cultural and historical locations to intervene in specific ideologies — here of desire, agency, and femininity. Meanwhile these variations of Asian legends open more consciously to international webs of concern, moving beyond the ethnocentric assumptions that so often fuel legends. While the play was written for an Anglophone audience, the perspective of 2012 suggests this play — which casts a specifically transcultural imaginary and theatrical practice — might equally intrigue audiences in the Asian diaspora, including in Japan, Korea, and China, where scholarly interest in Wertenbaker is growing. Provocatively, *Inside Out* encourages cross-cultural imagination, critical inquiry, and creative experimentation that move reciprocally from the West to Asia and back.

NOTES

1. I am indebted to the playwright for the rights to quote her and the unpublished play (archived in the British Library). I would also like to thank Gay Cima and Bill Talcott for their responses to an earlier draft of this essay, as well as my colleagues on the Comparative Literature Committee at Georgetown.

2. For a discussion of *New Anatomies*, see my chapter on Wertenbaker's history plays in *International Dramaturgy.*

3. This edition, also referred to as the *Kokinshū*, consisted of roughly 1100 poems total and was a household classic for centuries.

4. There were ten additional Komachi plays no longer active in the repertory.

5. The twentieth-century master onnogata Yukio Mishima also wrote a striking Elder Komachi *Noh* play; in his, a young man desires Young Komachi, an enchantment projected by Elder Komachi, on encountering her in a park. Likewise, Tsumura Kimiko, a female *Noh* performer specializing in Komachi roles (who founded the Ryokusen-kai kanze troupe for female performers), wrote *The Love Letters*, which gracefully echoes the traditional repertory's rendering of Elder Komachi's shame, purified by a Buddhist priest.

6. Like consciousness-raising exercises for men during the early women's movement designed to demonstrate how "female subjectivity is trained and subordinated by the everyday bodily requirements and vulnerabilities of "femininity" (Bordo 19), Wertenbaker stages a role reversal that lets each character experience the other's embodied perspectives — and gender scripts.

7. Irigaray counters "phallocritic" discourses by envisioning *écriture féminine*, an experimental poetic language and sexual-social cultural imaginary that can transform the denigration of "the feminine."

8. "Woman 'touches herself' all the time [...] for her genitals are formed of two lips in continuous contact. Thus, within herself, she is already two — but not divisible into one(s) — that caress each other" (Irigaray 24).

9. Like Merleau-Ponty, Irigaray rebuts Cartesian boundaries between subject and object, using touch to theorize corporeal subjectivity and, thus, embodied knowing. Yet her model insists on women's sexual experience and difference. See Grosz's chapter "Lived Bodies" (esp. 101–7).

Works Cited

Bordo, Susan. *Unbearable Weight: Feminism, Western Culture, and the Body.* Berkeley: University of California Press, 1993.

Chaillet, Ned. "Wertenbaker, with Comments by Timberlake Wertenbaker." *Contemporary Dramatists: Contemporary Writers of the English Language.* Ed. K. A. Berney. 5th ed. London; Washington, DC: St. James Press, 1993. 696–8.

Chin, Gail. "The Gender of Buddhist Truth: The Female Corpse in a Group of Japanese Paintings." *Japanese Journal of Religious Studies* 25.3/4 (1998): 227–317.

Fortier, Mark. "Undead and Unsafe: Acting Shakespeare (in Canada)." *Shakespeare in Canada: A World Elsewhere?* Eds. Diana Brydon and Irena Makaryk. Toronto: University of Toronto Press, 2002: 339–352.

Grosz, E. A. *Volatile Bodies: Toward a Corporeal Feminism.* Bloomington: Indiana University Press, 1994.

Hirshfield, Jane, Ono, and Shikibu Izumi. *The Ink Dark Moon: Love Poems by Ono No Komachi & Izumi Shikibu.* New York: Scribner, 1988.

Hutcheon, Linda. *A Theory of Adaptation.* New York: Routledge, 2006.

Irigaray, Luce. *This Sex Which Is Not One.* Trans. Catherine Porter. Ithaca: Cornell University Press, 1985.

Kawashima, Terry. *Writing Margins: The Textual Construction of Gender in Heian and Kamakura Japan.* Cambridge, MA: Harvard University Asia Center: distributed by Harvard University Press, 2001.

Keene, Donald. *Seeds in the Heart: Japanese Literature from Earliest Times to the Late Sixteenth Century.* 1st ed. New York: Henry Holt, 1993.

Kimbrough, R. Keller. *Preachers, Poets, Women, and the Way: Izumi Shikibu and the Buddhist Literature of Medieval Japan.* Ann Arbor: University of Michigan Center for Japanese Studies, 2008.

Oring, Elliott. "Legendry and the Rhetoric of Truth." *Journal of American Folklore* 121.480 (2008): 127–166. Web.

Pandey, Rajyashree. "Desire and Disgust: Meditations on the Impure Body in Medieval Japanese Narratives." *Monumenta Nipponica* 60.2 (2005): 195–234.

Parker, Joe. "Dreaming Gender: Kygoku School Japanese Women Poets (Re)Writing the Feminine Subject." *Tulsa Studies in Women's Literature* 27.2 (2008): 259–289.

Roth, Maya. "The Philomela Myth as Postcolonial Feminist Theater: Timberlake Wertenbaker's *The Love of the Nightingale.*" *Feminist Theatrical Revisions of Classic Works.* Ed. Sharon Friedman. Jefferson, N.C.: McFarland, 2009. 42–60.

_____, and Sara Freeman, Eds. *International Dramaturgy: Translation & Transformations in the Theatre of Timberlake Wertenbaker*. Brusells, Belgium; New York: P.I.E. Peter Lang, 2008.

Strong, Sarah M. "The Making of a Femme Fatale. Ono No Komachi in the Early Medieval Commentaries." *Monumenta Nipponica* 49.4 (1994): 391–412.

Teele, Roy E., Nicholas J., and H. Rebecca. *Ono No Komachi: Poems, Stories, No Plays. World Literature in Translation*. New York: Garland Pub., 1993.

Waley, Arthur, and Oswald Sickert. *The No Plays of Japan*. New York Grove Press, 1957.

Wertenbaker, Timberlake. *Inside Out*. Unpublished manuscript. London: British Library Special Archives, 1983. Accessed November 2007.

_____. "Interview." *Rage and Reason: Women Playwrights on Playwriting*. Eds. Heidi Stephenson and Natasha Langridge. London: Methuen Drama, 1997. 136–45.

_____. Personal correspondence. Message to the author. 29 July 2011. Email.

_____. *Wertenbaker: Plays One*. London and Boston: Faber and Faber, 1996.

Romancing "La Corriveau" and Marguerite de Nontron

Anne Hébert's La Cage *and* L'Île de la demoiselle

GREGORY J. REID

In *Anatomy of Criticism*, Northorp Frye's seminal work on mythopoeic criticism, the concept of romance cuts an enormous swath, covering whatever falls between pure myth and naturalism. Frye's description of the tendency of romance "to displace myth in a human direction and yet, in contrast to 'realism,' to conventionalize content in an idealized direction" (137) aptly describes Anne Hébert's treatment of the histories and myths of Marie-Josephte Corriveau, convicted in 1763 of murdering her husband, and Marguerite de Nontron, castaway on the deserted "Isle of Demons" by the Sieur Jean-François La Roque de Roberval in 1542. Neither Frye nor Hébert has shown much interest in the concept of history as a record of actual events.[1] Frye's definitions of myth, legend, and romance are closely aligned and frequently overlap or tend toward one. In his glossary for *Anatomy of Criticism*, Frye defines myth as "A narrative in which some characters are superhuman beings who do things that 'happen only in stories'; hence, a conventionalized or stylized narrative not fully adapted to plausibility or realism" (366). In his "Theory of Modes," Frye associates romance with "legends, folk tale, *märchen*, and their literary affiliates" (*Anatomy* 33), and defines it as a narrative in which "the ordinary laws of nature are slightly suspended" and the hero, who is a human being, is nonetheless capable of marvelous actions (*Anatomy* 33). Romance, then, is the mode of literature closest to and frequently overlapping with myth, but in romance, according to Frye, we move out of myth proper into the slightly more recent and human realm of legend (*Anatomy* 33). In her plays, *The Cage* and *L'Île de la demoiselle*, Hébert humanizes the witch and the ingénue of legend but resists verisimilitude in favor of idealizing and romanticizing the stories of these young women. Hébert celebrates these women and rewards them with heroic, poetic destinies, in a style bordering on myth, thereby providing alternatives to established mythologies and resisting the prosaic restrictions of historical realism.

Northrop Frye achieved world renown as "one of the twentieth century's pre-eminent English scholars and literary critics" ("Northrop Frye Centre"), and Anne Hébert, writing in French, is equally recognized internationally "as a pre-eminent literary figure of the twentieth century" (Forsyth ix). Both were born in the province of Québec within four years and 200 miles of each other: Frye in Sherbrooke, Québec in 1912 and Hébert in 1916 in Sainte-Catherine-de-Fossambault. The propinquity of their origins invites speculative observations about the over-determination of their mutual interest in romance and their specific alignment of romance with liberation and freedom. A preoccupation with overcoming local constraints and inequities in favor of the imagined, the other-worldly and idealized runs throughout their work, and can be substantiated from even a cursory view of their personal biographies.

As Frank Lentricchia points out in his critique of *Anatomy of Criticism* in *After the New Criticism*, "The real desideratum of Northrop Frye's world is freedom, the shredding of all constraints, and the pecking order of the modes is structured according to the fullness of freedom each mode is thought to image forth" (16). The "modes," as Frye explains, are determined by "the hero's power of action" (*Anatomy* 33). Additionally, each of the modes — "myth," "romance," "high mimetic mode," "low mimetic," and "ironic mode" — correspond to the shifting "center of gravity" of "European fiction, during the last fifteen centuries" (*Anatomy* 34). Although Frye's criticism and Hébert's drama were written during the period which, in Frye's schema, was dominated by the ironic mode and corresponding anti-hero in narrative fiction, roughly the era of late modernism, they both privilege romance; that is, the form of narrative where human action and human desires have the highest potential for achievement. This vision of romance as the freedom of human desire overcoming history and experience runs throughout Frye's work and informs his understanding of all culture, which he generally describes as giving form to human desire. While popular imagination might construe romance as sentimental love stories, it is also revolutionary in its impetus toward democratization[2] and overcoming impediments to the aspirations of individuals.

In *The Cage* and *L'Île de la demoiselle* we can see the continuity between the popular idealization of romantic love and the politics of liberation, specifically as applied to women and the desires of women. In these plays Hébert transforms sentimental love stories, which literary critics have traditionally denigrated as trite, superficial, and clichéd, into poetic allegories. Hébert accomplishes this transformation through what is best described as "romantic irony"; that is, by adopting a distanced, ironical stance in relation, not so much to romantic love, which remains the affective core of both dramas, but to the mythical and historical narratives she is dealing with and, to some degree, the dramatic forms she herself employs.

While the plays contain relatively few instances of the verbal, situational, or dramatic irony that we would typically identify as sophisticated examples of irony, an ironic attitude runs throughout the dramatic works. In other words, the plays reveal a constant parabasis, a sense of the author deliberately undermining her own discourses as she stands back, detached from the work, and we find ourselves imagining her with a wry grin, or consternated, or mocking the very work which she is at the same time producing. Recognizing the posture of the dissembling, ironic romantic poet goes a long way in facilitating our understanding of the paradoxes and contradictions which seem to run throughout the plays. As Clyde Ryals observes, in *A World of Possibilities: Romantic Irony in Victorian Literature,* romantic irony was seminally dictated by "the perception that various and even contradictory views might be alike true" (3). In this context the artist recognizes that the "work is not a representation of reality but an *artistic* re-presentation" (8). Viewing them from the perspective of romantic irony, we can begin to understand the how and why of Hébert's choosing to write plays about *La Corriveau* and Marguerite de Nontron, two figures who had already been the subjects of numerous literary works, and were among the most mythologized in the entirety of Québec history. Hébert's re-presentation of these figures, rather than effacing existing myths, legends and history, encourages us to reconsider them against the foils that she has created for the occasion. Rather than challenging the credibility of earlier presentations, Hébert's plays encourage us to notice the incredibility which all versions of these stories, including Hébert's, share.

In *The Legend of Marguerite de Roberval,* Arthur Stabler lists a dozen different versions of the Marguerite story in at least four different literary genres over four centuries: from "How the Sire de Roberval, granting a traitor his life at the prayers of the man's wife, set them both down on a desert island, and how, after the husband's death, the wife was rescued and brought back to La Rochelle," the 67th short story in Marguerite de Navarre's collection *Heptameron* (meaning "eight days," a nod to Boccaccio's *Decameron*) written in 1558, to John Clarke Bowman's swashbuckler novel, *The Isle of Demons,* published in 1953. Stabler's overview of historical mentions and analyses of the legend extends to 1971 and Samuel E. Morrison's *The European Discovery of America: The Northern Voyages A.D. 500–1600.* To Stabler's list from 1972 we can, of course, also add Anne Hébert's *L'Île de la demoiselle,* first presented as a radio play on *France-Culture* in 1974, then published in *Écrits du Canada français* in 1979 and in book form with *La Cage* in 1990, and published in English translation in 2010. There are also numerous current web sites, and a recent novel — Rosette Laberge's *La Noble sur l'île déserte*, published in 2011 with the subtitle *L'Histoire vraie de Marguerite de Roberval, abandonnée dans le nouveau monde.*

From his analysis of the three sixteenth-century versions of the story, all of which were said to be based on direct contact with the protagonists (either Marguerite or de Roberval or both), Stabler concludes that

> the bare outlines of the "authentic" story may be stated as follows. During his voyage to Canada in 1542–43, Roberval maroons a noblewoman, who is probably a close relative of his, on one of the Harrington Islands in the Gulf of St. Lawrence, as punishment for a clandestine love affair. Sharing her exile is her lover. Roberval leaves them with guns, ammunition, food, and clothing. Their diet is supplemented by edible plants and products of the hunt. A child may have been born to them; but if so, it dies, and so does her lover. The woman defends the grave from wild animals which seek to devour the corpse. After about a year the bereaved woman, emaciated and haggard from her ordeal, is rescued by a French vessel and returned to France [31].

While Stabler's analysis amply demonstrates why he might reach these conclusions, his review also shows that these conclusions are speculative and why he must judiciously enclose the word "authentic" in quotation marks. The three earliest versions of the story are at odds about the woman's age, marital status, social class, and the reasons for her being marooned. The location of the Isle of Demons, purportedly renamed L'Île de la demoiselle by sailors in Marguerite's honor, as one of the Harrington Islands in the Gulf of Saint Laurence is modern conjecture. The record of events which took place during her abandonment is simply the result of choosing to believe one version of the details over another, and there is no documentation indicating how the woman was rescued outside of the stories themselves.

In terms of the relationship between Hébert's version of the Marguerite de Nontron story and earlier variations, Hébert's play seems, at first glance, to fit Linda Hutcheon's definition and descriptive parameters of an "adaptation" in *A Theory of Adaptation*: "An acknowledged transposition of a recognizable other work or works. A creative *and* an interpretative act of appropriation/salvaging. An extended intertextual engagement with the adapted work" (8). In fact, the case seems to exemplify Hutcheon's conclusion that "In the workings of the imagination, adaptation is the norm, not the exception" (177). The many uses and re-uses of Marguerite's story parallel the many versions of Carmen, whose multifarious re-uses hold a privileged position in Hutcheon's theory of adaptation. The cases of Marguerite and Carmen, and even more obviously, *La Corriveau*, fit Hutcheon's evolutionary, "natural selection" theory of adaptation in which "each adapts to its new environment and exploits it, and the story lives on ... (167). Although Hutcheon does refer to "the adapted work" in her definition, what seems to be consistently missing from her theory is a concept of an original work. The absence of such a concept is predictable since the objective of her monograph is to challenge the hierarchical evaluations of adaptations as inferior, "secondary, derivative" (2), and so on in relation to an original, and "the critical orthodoxy in adaptation studies" which she identifies as "fidelity criticism" (6–7). The risk of Hutcheon's theory is that all adaptations become originals and conversely all *soi disant* originals adaptations, rendering both terms moot. Hutcheon seems to recognize the problem when, for example, she distinguishes adaptation from intertextuality "with the added proviso that they [adaptations] are also acknowledged as adaptations *of specific texts*" (21). However, this stressed insistence on "*specific texts*" fades as her evolutionary theory of adaptation as "adaptation to" rather than "adaptation from" takes hold. Hutcheon's notion that adaptations, like biological entities, must adjust to new environments is applicable to Hébert's plays. However, our inability — more to the point, the impossibility — to specify the "*specific texts*" upon which Hébert's version of *L'Île de la demoiselle* and *La Cage* are based argues against analyzing the plays as adaptations per se.

Nonetheless, as Robert Stam points out in his essay, "Beyond Fidelity: The Dialogics of Adaptation," Gérard Genette's transtextual notions of hypertext and hypotext are both practical and promising in dealing with cases typically labeled as adaptations. It will serve our understanding of the plays (the hypertexts) to note what Hébert has added or changed as well as repeated and re-used of these stories relative to established myth and legend and the historical record (the hypotexts), to whatever degree we can make such determinations, and to recognize each hypotext and hypertext "as a situated utterance produced in one medium and in one historical context, then transformed into another equally situated utterance that is produced in a different context and in a different medium" (Stam 68).

As Verna Foster outlines in the introduction to this volume, before judiciously arriving at the conception of "re-vision," numerous terms have been suggested and adopted to frame the hyper/hypo relationship between texts. Ryals's notion of "re-presentation" and Frye's theories of literary displacement offer additional means of elucidating a refined reading of *La Cage* and *L'Île de la demoiselle*. In fact, in many respects, Hutcheon's theory of adaptation is itself an adaptation of the mythopoeics of her predecessor and professor at the Centre for Comparative Literature at the University of Toronto, Northrop Frye. For it is Frye who most emphatically argued that all literature is the adaptation and reassembling of earlier literature and myth thus creating the archetypes, the symbols which move from one work to another and are the objects of study in mythopoeic criticism. Our understanding and appreciation of *La Cage* and *L'Île de la demoiselle* will be served by recognizing the literary displacements, the intertextual and stylistic choices which Hébert makes, the archetypes and themes which she adopts in both plays, and how these plays might be situated in terms of changing contexts and what we know about her life and work.

The historical basis of the myths of *La Corriveau* is more solidly established in part because the case is more recent, but also because there was an official garrison court martial and consequent documentation, including her signed confession which reads:

> Maria Josephe Corriveaux Widow Dodier declares she murdered her husband Louis Helene Dodier in the night, that he was in bed asleep, that she did it with hatchet; that she was neither advised to it, assisted in it neither did any one know of it; she is conscious that she deserves death, only begs of the court she may be indulged with a little time to confess, and make her peace with Heaven; adds, that it was indeed a good deal owing to the ill Treatment of her husband, she was guilty of the crime [qtd. in Lacoursière 162].

However, her confession has raised numerous questions about her trial as it is speculated that she could not read, could not have understood English, and that she was a victim of violent spousal abuse. Like Marguerite de Nontron's story and Hutcheon's example of Carmen, Marie-Josephte Corriveau's case has spawned numerous variations. *La Corriveau*'s is a distinctly, almost exclusively, Québec story and, as a result, is a particularly clear example of Hutcheon's focus on how stories change to fit a new social and cultural environment as well as changing media. As illustrated in Nicole Guilbault's *Il était cent fois La Corriveau* and elsewhere, in keeping with the cultural and political climate of the times *La Corriveau* was portrayed as a witch, who is said to have poisoned seven husbands, in texts from the nineteenth century, in oral tradition, and in popular culture, but was recuperated as a symbol of English oppression with the rise of Québec nationalism in the 1960s and 1970s, and most recently as an icon of women's victimization and liberation. Although Hébert's "feminism" has been questioned,[3] the play's themes are in keeping with basic feminist preoccupations, the liberation of women from the traditional constraints of gender and patriarchy.

In comparing *La Cage* and *L'Île de la demoiselle* to each other, the consistency in both detail and archetype stands out. Both plays incorporate what Frye identifies as a typical plot of comedy, "an erotic intrigue between a young man and a young woman which is blocked by some kind of opposition, usually paternal..." (*Anatomy* 44), which we would today associate with Shakespeare's tragedy of *Romeo and Juliet*. In *La Cage*, Ludivine Corriveau (as Hébert rechristens her heroine) shares a Platonic love with the young painter, Hyacinthe, who repeatedly visits the river near her home in the months and "entire years" (Hébert 29) her husband Elzéar Corriveau is away in the north. Elzéar is a brute who is described as taking his young wife by force, but his abuse is given a distinctly symbolic tenor. In the stage directions he is described throwing a "long green grass snake" (26) in his wife's face, and when she runs off, screaming, he soliloquizes: "Just wait, Ludivine, my wife, I'm coming. Yes, here I come, the big green snake, and I like to hear you scream with terror in the night, shut up in the house" (26). The biblical and phallic imagery is clearly intended here, and the phallic symbolism is once again invoked in the manner in which Ludivine kills Elzéar. Contrary to the historical record that Marie-Josephte killed her husband with an axe, and the legend of *La Corriveau* as a witch using poison, in *La Cage*, Ludivine Corriveau shoots her husband accidentally when he arrives home unexpectedly and unidentifiable after years of absence in the bush, using the rifle he had left her with instructions to shoot "any man comes prowling around you" (26). Ultimately, the paternal figure who stands between Ludivine and Hyacinthe, and their idealized love, is Judge John Crebessa, "the richest and most powerful man in this savage land" (36), who condemns Ludivine to death by "hanging in chains" or gibbeting, not for any crime that she might have committed but because he has lusted after her and been refused.

This pattern of figures and events is paralleled in *L'Île de la demoiselle* with the Sieur de Roberval, like John Crebessa, in a position of absolute power, the patriarchal guardian of justice and morality in a circumscribed universe — in this case the ship of which de Roberval is "master onboard after God" (67). Hébert first invokes the ambiguity of de Roberval's relationship with Marguerite de Nontron through the passengers' elliptical discussion of whether Marguerite is his niece or his ward, "or both at once, or perhaps..." (71). When an onboard love affair develops between Marguerite and the young carpenter, Nicolas Guillou, de Roberval condemns Marguerite to a near-certain death by abandoning her on a deserted island (presumably in the Gulf of St. Lawrence) for their tryst — just as Crebessa condemned Ludivine for immorality, accusing her of fornication and adultery with Hyacinthe (56). In both plays then, the guardian of morality proves an unrelentingly evil villain, as it becomes apparent that de Roberval's real motivation is jealous rage and his lust for his ward.

Despite the fabulousness of events as recounted in both history and legend, Hébert hyper-romanticizes the resolutions of the conflicts between protagonist and antagonist in both plays, moving the climaxes still further from verisimilitude and realism. In most accounts Marguerite's lover, her maid, and the infant she gave birth to on the island all died, but Marguerite survived and returned to live in France. In *L'Île de la demoiselle*, Marguerite kills the black bird which symbolizes death and dresses herself in its feathers, becoming like one of the "savages" alluded to early in the play by a "Gentleman" passenger: "...red from head to toe, their bodies covered with feathers..." (69). She leads the sailors who come to rescue her into her grotto and shows them a drawing on the wall which magically shows de Roberval as he had died thousands of miles away "in an alley in Saint-Malo, after his return from Canada: the eyes put out, stabbed through the heart [...]" (130–131).

The historical record is well established that Marie-Josephte Corriveau was hanged by a military tribunal, during the period immediately following the British Conquest of New France, and her body was left hanging on display in an iron cage at a crossroads in Levis (across the Saint Lawrence River from Québec City) for 40 days. Although Annabelle Rea, in her discussion of the play in her article, "Living with the Cultural Legacy of La Corriveau: *La Cage*," describes John Crebessa's death as "a heart attack" (31), the context makes it clear that his death should be understood as a magical event, comprehensible only on a secondary, allegorical level. When Hyacinthe pleads for Ludivine's life, the Judge responds: "...that damned word. Love, love, love you say so intensely, between clenched teeth. I hear it like a cry that offends me. No, no, I cannot stand it. It's too much to bear. I have but the time to die. I hear, from afar, a song of love in a foreign language soaring on the wind like the tolling of brown bells above my head..." (61). Crebessa slumps in his chair and is immediately pronounced dead, a victim, in the play's allegorical structure, of the evil he was fated to personify and his repudiation of love. Ludivine Corriveau is consequently saved from execution and any further persecution. The First White Fairy takes up a key which has fallen from Crebessa's pocket, the play's third explicitly phallic symbol, and Ludivine's entourage of supporters departs to free the judge's wife, Rosalinde Crebessa, from the manor where he has imprisoned her.

In addition to the deliberate use of naive allegory, both plays employ a narrator — Babette, Ludivine's daughter, in *La Cage* and the "Narrator" in *L'Île de la demoiselle*—linking the episodes and the plays' rhapsodic, lyrical verse. Key dramatic, revelatory scenes in both plays are presented as dream sequences. Despite the experiences that the female protagonists go through, Hébert keeps their inner, youthful innocence intact, and their rancor and rebelliousness are only expressed in dreams. In the surreal sequence, Ludivine presents her husband with a stillborn fetus and tells him, "Had you not taken me by force, my husband. Now I can speak to you in the freedom of my dreams, and I am talking to you as if to a stranger. I do not love you" (29). In a feverous delirium Marguerite exchanges dialogue with the voice of an Augustinian Nun, a figure from her childhood in an orphanage. She tells the

Nun, "I want to curse the captain in my dreams. Let me sleep" (123). To which the Nun responds: "Curse no one, not even in a dream, God forbids it" (124). Continuing to play out a scene as if from childhood, Marguerite draws a picture of de Roberval as she would wish him, his eyes put out, stabbed through the heart, "his blood there on the wall" (124).

The plot structure of both plays, then, is basic melodrama: a good, innocent victim as protagonist against an evil, all-powerful villain, with strict moral justice served in a final, last-minute reversal against all probability. Rather than supplying a compelling intrigue, the narrative structure supplies a frame within which to display Hébert's verse. The emotional core of both dramas is very much centered on the fate of the fifteen-year-old girl, a very specific and repeated icon in Hébert's work. *L'Île de la demoiselle* includes repeated mention of Marguerite's age, ultimately specifying that she was "aged fifteen years and four months" (105). Fifteen is further specified as the age when a young woman comes of age when, in conversation with a "Lady" onboard ship, Marguerite explains that she first began menstruating some four months ago (74). In *La Cage*, Ludivine's alter ego, Rosalinde Crebessa, is given in marriage at the age of fifteen to John Crebessa, who, to celebrate the marriage, carries his bride into a "cage which is adorned with white ribbons" (17). The cage conceit is repeated in *L'Île de la demoiselle* as Marguerite is confined first to a cabin on the ship, and then to a cave on the island. In Hébert's work the fifteen-year-old girl is an icon of sexual, creative, and personal awakening, of the joyous discovery of independence and desire, but that burgeoning independence and desire is the cause of confinement, danger and pain as much as it is a source of liberty, pleasure and fulfillment, as we see in the cases of both Rosalinde and Marguerite.

Hébert's symbolism of caves and cages would seem to reflect the "garrison mentality" which Northrop Frye famously claimed typified Canadian literature (Frye, *Bush Garden* 225ff). The story of *La Corriveau* takes place in a garrison, but we must be wary of a tendency to either take the expression too literally or to generalize the metaphor too broadly. Frye's use of the expression should be understood within the context of his valorization of "an individual separated in standards and attitudes from the community" (Frye, *Bush Garden* 237), and his view of literature as "an autonomous world that gives us an imaginative perspective on the actual one" (Frye, *Bush Garden* 235). Writing, from Frye's perspective, in order to be literature must emerge from the world of literature, not the "actual world," and writing which remains closely connected to the social concerns of the world and community of the author is consequently labeled as displaying a "garrison mentality." The basis of literature, Frye argues, is "myth," not "history" (Frye, *Bush Garden* 231).

In *The Bush Garden*, Frye asks, "Why do Canadians write so many historical romances...?" (Frye, 235). In this instance, by romance Frye has in mind "'Popular' literature, the kind that is read for relaxation and the quieting of the mind..." (235). Frye's answer is that popular romance is basically conservative, therefore concerned with the past, and, in keeping with the "garrison mentality," works "within a framework of established social values" (Frye, *Bush Garden* 235–36). The key in Frye's analysis to distinguishing between writing that is fully literary from other forms is "detachment" (Frye, *Bush Garden* 237) from the actual world, the community, prevailing social values, popular expectations, and so on. This detachment, which is particularly conspicuous in romantic irony, is evident in Hébert's writing, including her drama. In performance, her plays have typically been criticized for their lack of realism. In a 1963 interview, Hébert herself confessed to having "four or five unpublished scripts stored away in boxes which were too literary to be played" (qtd. in Lasnier 74, my translation).

A parallel reading of Frye's criticism and Hébert's drama confirms the shared values from which their work emerges. The shy, awkward, uncoordinated Frye, out of place, as his biographer John Ayer reports, in both Sherbrooke, Québec and later Moncton, New Brunswick, would eventually flourish as a seventeen-year-old in the removed and culturally rich environment of and around the University of Toronto. We can well imagine, from this biography, how Frye would come to conclude that literature was a world of its own, removed from the far less interesting and satisfying actual world.

Until her late twenties, Anne Hébert lived with her parents primarily in the rural ambience of Sainte-Catherine de Fossambault in a house by the Jacques Cartier River, a setting which would figure prominently in much of her work, in particular, *La Cage*. Hébert moved to Ottawa in the early 1950s where she eventually had the distinction of being the first francophone woman ever hired by the National Film Board of Canada as a scriptwriter (Watteyne 24). In the mid 1960s she moved to Paris where she would live for the rest of her career, writing primarily about her native Québec. Anne Hébert was a great beauty all her life, and is reported to have been the object of many unrequited loves. Despite the sensuality and sexual insights and frankness in her work, she never married and was never known, in the public domain, to have had a lover. When Hébert was fifteen, we know that she spent her summers with her nineteen-year-old cousin Hector de Saint-Denys Garneau, the poet and painter, who died at the age of twenty-two. The great influence of Saint-Denys Garneau and this period of her life notwithstanding, Hébert's biography and her oeuvre display the "detachment" from the subject of her writing which Frye claimed as essential to the creation of literature. While we might well speculate that her teen years in rural Québec were a source of inspiration for Hébert, much of her writing derived from this time and place was done in Paris, decades later. Additionally, in her literature we can see a belief in another, imagined, romantic, idealized world which gives us a new perspective on the world of actual events.

Although we might imagine the influence of real-life events in her life, the empirical source of her writing is myth and literature — which as Frye would claim is the case with any significant literary writer. In analyzing *La Cage*, critics have typically pointed to the play's "fairy tale" form (O'Meara 165–166, Rea 28, 32, Slott 156, Marchese, 96, Rousselot 165–166). The play's opening "Prologue," with Black Fairies and White Fairies arriving pregnant (literally) with magic wishes to bestow, evil and beneficent, on the infants, Ludivine and Rosalinde, certainly seems a parody of "Sleeping Beauty." However, the dramatic forms of the play are those of the morality play and the masque.[4] To fully appreciate the romantic irony and satiric thrust of this play, we must recognize that in order to challenge patriarchy and British imperialism, Hébert has chosen the masque and the morality play: exactly the forms traditionally designed to reinforce patriarchy and imperialism. Moreover, if we stop to consider the intentions of the British garrison when they condemned Marie-Josephte Corriveau to "hanging in chains," a punishment typically reserved for the most heinous of crimes, we can quickly recognize that this execution was a theatrical performance designed to intimidate, in fact, horrify the French population. *La Cage* creates an imagined world where love and liberty triumph, and from which we can begin to see that patriarchy and imperialism are also imagined, arbitrary constructs which, though capable of perpetrating horrific acts, are ultimately destined to failure and being turned against themselves.

Religious and biblical intertextuality, in addition to its fairy-tale elements, are ample in *La Cage*. Biblical allusions are frequent in the phraseology of the dialogue — particularly in the speeches of John Crebessa. Hébert's choice of names in this play has been the source of much scholarly discussion.[5] John Crebessa appears as a supernumerary in Hébert's novel *Kamouraska*, but the motivations behind Hébert's choice of this particular name remain unclear. Maureen O'Meara speculates that John Crebessa's initials, J.C., confirm that he "becomes a true anti–Christ" (169). In the "Prologue," the infant Ludivine with her parents form a tableau which is described as a "living nativity scene" (7), and Ludivine's trial is an explicit imitation of a morality play as the "Seven Deadly Sins" are called to testify falsely against her, and Judge Crebessa, in the role of Everyman, is invited to repent and save himself from damnation, which he refuses. Ludivine, though a young woman, is cast in the role of a saintly, surrogate mother who shelters and nourishes the orphans and pariahs of the village. Her only moment of hubris in the play is when she parades her surrogate family in the village, capturing Judge Crebessa's malign attention.

In each of these intertextual gestures we see Hébert turning the moral order and its overweening constraints against itself. As Vera Calin points out, "the essence of Romantic irony lies in the tendency towards the re-creation and re-dimensioning of the universe" (190). In *The Cage* and *L'Île de la demoiselle* these gestures seem deliberately excessive, romantic to the point of being mythic, as if to display through a competing mythology that the prevailing social and moral order is ultimately arbitrary.

Contrary to Frye's description of historical romances in *The Bush Garden* as conservative and written to accommodate "established social values," Hébert's romantic treatment of *La Corriveau*, Rosalinde, and Marguerite de Nontron contests established values by displaying the strength, passion, and humanity of women's desires. In these plays, as in all of Hébert's writing, we can witness her turning to the untamed, uncivilized, bucolic or apocalyptic setting, stripping away what Nietzsche called "the mendacious finery of that alleged reality of the man of culture" (61), in order to reveal the truth and peril of female desire against the lie and menace of puritanical patriarchy. However, in keeping with literary detachment and romantic irony, Anne Hébert recognizes that the experience of desire cannot be represented directly in language. Language, or more precisely the experience of language, can never be equivalent to non-linguistic experience. Moreover, a language can only say what the lexicon at its disposal permits. On a broader, analogous scale, literary and dramatic texts depend on and must use the texts at their disposal. Thus Hébert uses the personification of Lust, the Fourth Deadly Sin from religious instruction and the morality plays, to describe "poor [...] dry" Ludivine who became "hot and wet" after meeting Hyacinthe (53). Using the well-established figure of the miser from both French and Québec literature, the Third Black Fairy announces to the infant Rosalinde that "your husband will be a miser" in all things including "the pleasures of love" (8). And the Seventh Black Fairy tells Rosalinde, "A prisoner of good manners, you will be crushed in corset too tight, as day and night parade their wonders around your cage, to which only your husband will hold the key" (9). In *L'Île de la demoiselle* it is not simply the story of Marguerite de Nontron that is being revivified and rewritten, but Shakespeare's *Romeo and Juliet* with Charlotte, Marguerite's maid, playing the role of Juliet's Nurse. However, in Hébert's version Charlotte complains, "Ah 'tis a fine thing, this republic of yours, Marguerite de Nontron! The holy family basks under fur while out in the cold the servant freezes to death" (114), until she is invited under the covers with Marguerite and Nicolas. As in *La Cage*, biblical imagery is invoked, as Nicolas is laid to rest in the grotto, a Christ-like figure, and a stone rolled in place to cover the entrance, and bells are given a mysterious, mystical and ultimately magical significance. Hébert imagines unique, primordial worlds where the struggles of desire, of life against death, can be played out and reveal themselves.

As Clyde Ryals points out, romantic irony is the posture that a thinking individual is forced to adopt when faced with "a world of change" (3). Rather than attempting to directly contradict, erase, or overwrite previous myths and legends, Hébert's strategy in her romancing of *La Corriveau* and Marguerite de Nontron has been to re-use, re-present and re-vision those myths and legends, and offer not only an alternative, but a conspicuously better alternative for the times. From the inclinations of romance Hébert creates literary, poetic worlds which are counterpoints to patriarchal myths, and foils to the repression and folly of the worlds in which women have actually lived. The result is an indirect, detached and subtle satire on the prevailing moral and social order inscribed in established mythologies, and a celebration of independent women who have the courage and determination to pursue their desires.

NOTES

1. Hébert's attitude toward history is best illustrated in her epigraph to *Kamouraska* which reads: "'Although this novel is based on real events which took place in Canada, a long time ago, it remains nonetheless a work of imagination. The real characters of this drama have lent to my story only the most public, in a sense, the most official, of their gestures. For the rest, in the course of a slow, interior passage, they have become the creatures of my imagination. (A.H.)'" (my translation).

2. The word "romance" derives, of course, from the translation of literary works from Latin into the Romance languages and consequently implies popularization, vulgarization, and democratization.

3. In her article "La Corriveau et Anne Hébert: état d'études," Janis Pallister concludes: "One could suggest that the author, who leaves the protagonist of *Kamouraska* in her cage, shows herself to be more and more a 'femalist,' that is to say focussed on women, or 'parafeminist' for, in my opinion, one cannot really see in Hébert, at least in her early works, a true feminist. The portraits of terrible mothers from 'Le Torrent' to *Les Fous de Bassan*, and of women drowned in the vortex of their desires seem to me to prohibit inclusion of Anne Hébert in the category of radical feminist [...]" (108, my translation).

4. For further discussion of the play as a satire on the morality play and the masque see Reid, "Anne Hébert's *La Cage*: A Masque of Liberation."

5. For a summary of this discussion of Hébert's choice of names in the play see Reid, "Anne Hébert's *La Cage*: A Masque of Liberation."

WORKS CITED

Ayre, John. *Northrop Frye: A Biography*. Toronto: Random House, 1989.

Calin, Vera. "Irony and World-Creation in the Work of Mihai Eminescu." *Romantic Irony*. Ed. Frederick Garber. Budapest: Akadémiai Kiadó, 1988.

de Navarre, Marguerite. *Heptameron*. Translation and Comments by Walter K. Kelly. 3 August 2011. Web.

Forsyth, Louise. "Introduction." *Two Plays:* The Cage *and* L'Île de la demoiselle, by Anne Hébert. Trans Pamela Grant, Gregory J. Reid, and Sheila Fischman. Toronto: Playwrights Canada Press, 2009.

Frye, Northrop. *Anatomy of Criticism: Four Essays*. Princeton, NJ: Princeton University Press, 1957.

_____. *The Bush Garden: Essays on the Canadian Imagination*. Toronto: House of Anansi, 1971.

Genette, Gérard. *Palimpsests: Literature in the Second Degree*. Trans. Channa Newman and Claude Doubinsky. Lincoln: University of Nebraska Press, 1997.

Guilbault, Nicole. *Il était cent fois la Corriveau*. Québec, Québec: Nuit Blanche, 1995.

Hébert, Anne. *Kamouraska*. Paris: Éditions du Seuil, 1970.

_____. *Two Plays:* The Cage *and* L'Ile de la demoiselle. Trans. Pamela Grant, Gregory J. Reid, and Sheila Fischman. Toronto: Playwrights Canada Press, 2009.

Hutcheon, Linda. *A Theory of Adaptation*. New York: Routledge, 2006.

Laberge, Rosette. *La Noble sur l'île déserte: l'histoire vraie de Marguerite de Roberval, aban-donée dans le Nouveau Monde*. Marieville, Québec: Les Éditeurs Réunis, 2011.

Lacoursière, Luc. "Le Triple Destin de Marie-Josephte Corriveau (1733-1763)." In Guilbault, 147-180.

Lasnier, Michelle. "Anne Hébert la magicienne." *Châtelaine* (avril) 1963. 28-29, 74 et 76.

Lentricchia, Frank. *After the New Criticism*. Chicago: University of Chicago Press, 1980.

Marchese, Elena. "Le projet de réécriture historique dans *La Cage* et *L'Île de la demoiselle* d'Anne Hébert." *Les Cahiers Anne Hébert 4: Anne Hébert et la critique*. Ville Saint-Laurent, Québec: Fides, 2003: 91-101.

Nietzsche, Frederic. *The Birth of Tragedy and the Case of Wagner*. Trans. W. Kaufman. New York: Vintage Books, 1967.

"Northrop Frye Centre." Victoria College, University of Toronto, 3 August 2011. Web.

O'Meara, Maureen. "Living with the Cultural Legacy of La Corriveau: *La Cage*. *The Art and Genius of Anne Hébert*. Ed. Janis L. Pallister. Madison, NJ: Fairleigh Dickinson University Press, 2001: 161-178.

Pallister, Janis L. "La Corriveau et Anne Hébert: état d'études." In *Les Cahiers Anne Hébert 4: Anne Hébert et la critique*. Ville Saint-Laurent, Québec: Fides, 2003: 103-109.

Rea, Annabelle. "Marie-Josephte Becomes Ludivine: The Family Reformed in Anne Hébert's *La Cage*." *Doing Gender: Franco-Canadian Women Writers of the 1990s*. Eds. Paula Ruth Gilbert and Roseanna L. Dufault. Madison, NJ: Fairleigh Dickinson University Press, 2001: 23-35.

Reid, Gregory J. "Anne Hébert's *La Cage*: A Masque of Liberation." *Text & Presentation 2008: The Comparative Drama Conference Series*. Jefferson, NC: McFarland, 2008: 141-155.

Rousselot, Elodie. *Re-Writing Women into Canadian History: Margaret Atwood and Anne Hébert*. Diss. University of Kent, 2004.

Ryals, Clyde. *A World of Possibilities: Romantic Irony in Victorian Literature*. Columbus: Ohio State University Press, 1991.

Slott, Kathryn. "La Remise en question de la Corriveau dans *La Cage* de Anne Hébert." *The Art and Genius of Anne Hébert*. Ed Janis L. Pallister. Madison, NJ: Fairleigh Dickinson University Press, 2001: 140-149.

Stabler, Arthur. *The Legend of Marguerite de Roberval*. Pullman: Washington State University Press, 1972.

Stam, Robert. "Beyond Fidelity: The Dialogics of Adaptation." *Film Adaptation*. Ed. James Naremore. Piscataway, NJ: Rutgers University Press, 2000: 54-78.

Watteyne, Nathalie, et al. *Anne Hébert: Chronologie et bibliographie*. Montréal: Les Presses de l'Université de Montréal, 2008.

Bloody Relations of Exchange

Sharon Pollock's Revision of Legend and Feminine Myth in Blood Relations

LAURA SNYDER

Over the past thirty years, Feminist Revisionist Theatre has attained genre status. Playwrights and Theatre Companies as diverse as The Women's Theatre Group, Timberlake Wertenbaker, Suzan-Lori Parks, Caryl Churchill, Split Britches, Mabou Mines, Anne-Marie MacDonald, and Paula Vogel have turned their talents to adapting well-known stories, myths, and legends. In such Revisionist Theatre, the purpose is not simply to re-present the source, but to illuminate, interpret, and *re-vision* it from a feminist perspective (Friedman 1–7). Often, these plays highlight, critique, and deconstruct archetypal visions of femininity that pattern cultural perception,[1] and so it is with Canadian dramatist Sharon Pollock's 1980 *Blood Relations*. Pollock's drama is a metatheatrical re-enactment of the events surrounding the sensational and highly publicized 1892 murders of Andrew and Abigail Borden. In *Blood Relations*, Pollock rewrites the legend of American Lizzie Borden to create a complex contemporary statement. As almost every analysis of the play clearly recognizes, Pollock critiques the limited scripts for women within patriarchal culture, limitations perpetuated by archetypal, even mythic, visions of femininity. More importantly, however, Pollock's metatheatrical revision of the story highlights those limited scripts for women also as products of a materialist economic system, in which all relations are of exchange and competition, in which all people are commodities and adversaries. Ultimately, Pollock's choices as a dramatist and revisionist deny the supposed reward system in a materialist economy and highlight the individual as trapped within bloody relations of exchange and competition.

Before an in-depth analysis of *Blood Relations* can begin, however, an overview of the legend of Lizzie Borden, and its historical basis, is in order. The *Oxford English Dictionary* reveals that the word "legend" has a rather contradictory set of definitions, from a "story, history, account," to an "unauthentic or non-historical story, esp[ecially] one ... popularly regarded as historical." As Verna Foster's introduction to this collection of essays suggests, there is a "continuing conflation of history and legend in popular consciousness" (8). For the purpose of this discussion, legend will be defined as a fictional story that is generally held to be true, a tale that has taken on the appearance of history. Certainly, "history can ... easily turn into legend" (8) when a famous figure becomes the subject of popular imagination, and such is the case with the tales surrounding the Borden murders. The consistent facts are clear: on August 4, 1892, Andrew and Abigail Borden were murdered in their home in Fall River, Massachusetts. Abigail was battered with a sharp instrument 19 times, Andrew 10. Lizzie Andrew Borden, Andrew's daughter and Abigail's stepdaughter, was charged with the crimes. No blood was found on the suspect or her clothes. No murder weapon was identified. Lizzie Borden was acquitted. No one was ever brought to justice for the crime.

But these facts are not the stuff of legend. For the majority of Americans, a childhood rhyme constitutes the sum of their knowledge of the Borden murders: "Lizzie Borden took an axe/ And gave her mother forty whacks/ And when the job was nicely done/ She gave her father forty-one." The rhyme is legendary, not historical; the murder weapon, number of blows dealt, and guilt of the accused do not tally with the factual accounts. It is the legend of Lizzie Borden that is alive and thriving in the twenty-first century. In the classes I teach, I am hard pressed to find a student who does not know some variation of this same rhyme that I jumped rope to in grade school. Many people do know more concerning the Borden case, but much of that knowledge is also legendary, based on imagination and speculation. For example, people my parents' age often remember the song "Fall River Hoedown" by Michael Brown that was first performed in the Broadway production *New Faces of 1952*, starring such talents as Paul Lynde, Mel Brooks, and Eartha Kitt. The Chad Mitchell Trio, a folk group, went on to popularize the tune as "You Can't Chop Your Poppa Up in Massachusetts" in 1961. While gruesome, the song is also quite funny, as one of the choruses shows: "But you can't chop your momma up in Massachusetts/Not even if you're tired of her cuisine./No, you can't chop your momma up in Massachusetts,/You know it's almost sure to cause a scene" (lines 21–4). However, the Borden legend goes far beyond a macabre tune or two. A simple Google search will proffer a bewildering array of reading. There are non-fiction texts purporting to have the "real" story of the Borden case (from William Masterton's *Lizzie Didn't Do It!* to Victoria Lincoln's *A Private Disgrace: Lizzie Borden by Daylight*), historical fiction novels (like Elizabeth Engstrom's *Lizzie Borden* and Evan Hunter's *Lizzie*), and even a graphic novel by Rick Geary (*The Borden Tragedy*).

Such tales are not limited to print sources. Lizzie can be found on myriad web sites. *The Lizzie Andrew Borden Virtual Museum and Library, Famous Trials: The Trial of Lizzie Borden 1893,* and truTV's *Crime Library: Lizzie Borden* are some of the most all-encompassing. Film and television documentaries continue to debate the case; the History Channel produced *History's Mysteries: The Strange Case of Lizzie Borden* in 2001 and in 2008 A & E's *Biography* released *Lizzie Borden: A Woman Accused.* Lizzie is also the central figure in a series of movies. In 1975 Elizabeth Montgomery starred in the television movie *The Legend of Lizzie Borden.* Dark Morgue's film *Lizzie,* featuring Gary Busey, is scheduled for release in 2011, and HBO is currently planning a miniseries showcasing Chloe Sevigny (Andreeva).

For those left unsatisfied by the blitz of print, web, and visual media, there are more interactive methods of assaying the Borden legend. The story has promulgated a variety of theatrical productions, including a ballet (*Fall River Legend*), an opera, and an array of musicals and docudramas. In 1992 a Centennial Conference on the Lizzie Borden Case was held in Fall River, and the Fall River Historical Society maintains an archive and features exhibits concerning the Borden trial. Of course, for the ultimate Borden experience, aficionados can pay to sleep in the "haunted" rooms of the Lizzie Borden Bed and Breakfast/Museum, located in the 92 Second Street house in which the murders were committed.

So why did this particular case capture the North American imagination so thoroughly, both in 1892 and today? One reason is the brutal, gruesome nature of the killings; as all accounts agree, the skulls of the Bordens were chopped into pieces. Another equally compelling reason is that the murders remain unsolved, a mystery begging for a detective to close the case, and mysteries, especially gory ones, are an American national pastime rivaling baseball. Our popular television shows — *CSI, NCIS, Criminal Minds, The Glades, Law and Order: Special Victims Unit, Dexter*— all reveal our somewhat perverse fascination. Nevertheless, the strongest reason the Borden case has continued to fascinate seems to lie in the nature of the main suspect: a female ... a daughter. Men commit the vast majority of murders (U.S. Department of Justice); for a woman to have killed is, in a friend's word, "titillating." For a daughter, by gender stereotype the tender caregiver to aging parents, to have brutally smashed in their skulls crosses over into spectacle. Russell Aiuto sums up Americans' fascination with the legend well:

> Along with the gruesome nature of the crimes is the unexpected character of the accused, not a hatchet-wielding maniac, but a church-going, Sunday-school-teaching, respectable, spinster-daughter, charged with parricide, the murder of parents, a crime worthy of Classical Greek tragedy [truTV *Crime Library*].

Clearly, the grisly murders of Andrew and Abigail Borden in 1892, the subsequent trial and acquittal of their daughter Lizzie Borden, and the fact that no one was ever brought to justice for the crimes, provide a sensational basis for a story that continues to fascinate well over 100 years later. It has been told and retold, refashioned and reshaped, and thus the story has become legend, with the majority of audience members knowing little of the historical facts and drawing what they do know from the proliferation of tales circulating in broadcast media and popular culture ... all in an attempt to answer the fascinating question: Did Lizzie take an axe? It is not surprising, then, that Sharon Pollock chose to examine the legend surrounding Lizzie Borden, to tell the story yet again, to revision it through her own critical lens. While her first theatrical musings resulted in the play *My Name Is Lisbeth*, a play focused on answering whether Lizzie did or did not kill her parents, Pollock's 1980 play *Blood Relations* instead explores *why* someone like Lizzie Borden might commit parricide (Pollock "Afterword" 123–4).

Pollock's play is set in two different time periods. The actual setting is in 1902, in the home of Lizzie Borden and her sister, Emma, ten years after the murder of their father, Andrew, and stepmother, Abigail Borden. The sisters are still living in the same house in Fall River in which the murders occurred. The primary action of this frame setting is a visit by a friend of Lizzie, generically titled "The Actress," who, like Emma and everyone else, wants to know if Lizzie "did it," murdered Abigail and Andrew Borden, despite Lizzie's acquittal for those murders. Although Lizzie argues that The Actress knows her well and thus should already know the answer, The Actress persists in her questioning until Lizzie suggests a "game." In the game, The Actress will play Lizzie and Lizzie will "paint the background" (Pollock 13), will begin directing the action as Bridget, the Bordens' maid and cook. This metatheatrical reenactment, designated the "dream thesis" (4), is set on the days prior to and of the murder of the Bordens.

The series of actions which unfold in the dream thesis suggests that, as Madonne Miner argues, "daughters in nineteenth-century patriarchal households read from scripts that allow them only two options — to be killed or to kill" (12). As portrayed by The Actress, Lizzie Borden is to be ladylike and obey her father. She is to be a "good girl" like her sister, Emma (Pollock 32). She is to marry, at her father's directive, a local widower with two children, a marriage Lizzie finds repugnant. When she fails to behave as ordered, various punishments are enacted, both physical and economic. Her father beats her and kills her beloved pigeons, the only beings that Lizzie feels accept her as she is. Her stepmother spells out that Lizzie must obey, or she will be disinherited. Abigail and her brother, Harry, will convince Andrew to sign over much of his property to them. As Susan Stratton describes, "The trap tightens around Lizzie, as her prospects for further freedom are cut off by the transfer of her father's property to her stepmother" (70). The Actress/Lizzie considers suicide, but decides that her own "life is precious" (Pollock 63) and that she is too "strong" (58) to take her own life. She chooses to be the victimizer rather than the victim, and murders Abigail, and then Andrew when he comes home before The Actress/Lizzie has had the chance to hide her crime. Stratton argues that "Lizzie's murder of the senior Bordens can be taken as an attempt to destroy blind male authority and female acceptance of it" in the form of Mrs. Borden's complicity in Lizzie's oppression (70). In fact, every analysis of *Blood Relations* recognizes Pollock's critique of patriarchy and sees Lizzie as trapped within patriarchal expectations of femininity.

Many of those critiques further reference two archetypal patterns of femininity that limit Lizzie: the angel and the monster. As feminist theorists from Simone de Beauvoir to Sandra Gilbert and Susan Gubar have delineated, in a patriarchal culture, visions of femininity fit within an angel/monster pattern: the angel who serves patriarchy, and the monster who refuses to serve. The dichotomy of the pattern can be clearly seen in the opposition of the Furies/Eumenides. The Furies are monstrous when loose in the *polis* but are transfigured to the beneficent Eumenides once they are bound to a subservient position within the *oikos*. But, of course, rebellious female monsters are *rampant* in myth: Eve and Pandora, whose uncontained sexuality can destroy entire cultures; Clytemnestra and Medea, women whose power, when no longer contained within traditional marriage, destroys their entire families.

Ironically, an article in the *New York Sun* on June 5, 1893, part of the media frenzy surrounding the opening day of the trial, described Lizzie Borden as "either the most injured of innocents or the blackest of monsters" (qtd. in Rehak, frontmatter). As the legend grew, subsequent versions tended to play off this archetypal dichotomy. When Lizzie is not a hatchet-wielding fiend or cold-blooded killer (as she is portrayed by Elizabeth Montgomery in *The Legend of Lizzie Borden*), she is Andrew's loving daughter, the spinster victim of trial-by-media, her judgmental neighbors, or an alternate killer. Lizzie's sister, Emma, her stepbrother, William Borden, her uncle, John Morse, and the family maid, Bridget, are some of the more popular murderers skulking in the background, capitalizing on Lizzie's vilification. As Herb Wylie points out, in traditional tellings of the story, "Lizzie must be either innocent or monstrous" (203), must be either the persecuted angel or the rebellious killer who destroys the family.

Such societal expectations for females script The Actress's portrayal of Lizzie. The Actress, as Lizzie, describes herself as "unnatural" for not wanting to be a wife and mother (Pollack 34). She recognizes herself as "different" (47), and Miss Lizzie/Bridget herself steps in to pronounce herself "defective" (32). In a haunting scene, Miss Lizzie steps out of the role of Bridget to describe the soul-destroying effect of having to play the "angel" role as donning a mask that slowly erases the wearer (43). After creating Lizzie as a role within the dream thesis, The Actress enacts the murders, pronouncing that Lizzie did indeed "do it," was trapped into murdering her parents. According to Stratton, the Actress's "murders can be seen as an act of strength, an assertion of Lizzie's own value, of the repressed woman's right to life" (Stratton 70). Clearly, the Actress's dream thesis re-enactment of the murder of the Bordens critiques the limitations placed upon women by archetypal, even mythic, visions of femininity.

However, when at the end of the play the Actress turns to Lizzie and says, "Lizzie, you did" commit the murders, Miss Lizzie answers, "I didn't ... You did" (73). In production and in the 1981 and 2002 scripts, the Actress looks to the murder weapon in her hand and out to the audience (Wylie 195; Pollock 73). The ending highlights the play-within-the-play, the metatheatre, and broadens the critique of patriarchy. It implies that the audience — representative of contemporary culture — is complicitous in the murders.[2] Pollock is suggesting that The Actress, and by extension the audience, would have chosen to murder in Lizzie's place, would have elected to be the monster rather than binding themselves within the role of angel. Because everyone in this culture accepts these limiting archetypes of femininity, society is as guilty of the murders as is the Actress. As Wylie points out, in *Blood Relations* the Actress's performance of Lizzie "widens the notion of complicity and undermines the traditional construction of Lizzie Borden as a monster" (Wylie 196). Because the murders were expected by the Actress, and probably most of the audience, we have to look at the acts not as an aberration, as monstrous, but as a condition of a societal script.

Yet Pollock's revision of the Lizzie Borden legend goes further to highlight those limited scripts for women not simply as part and parcel of patriarchy, but also as products of a materialist economic system, in which **all** relations are of exchange and competition, in which all people are commodities and adversaries, victims and victimizers. According to Wylie, "contemporary Canadian literary treatments of historical subjects" such as *Blood Relations* have a "view of history as the product of story-making" (197). Such "[h]istoriography ... becomes the ongoing process of *re*-making history ... as fiction and myth" (Richard Paul Knowles 229; qtd. in Wylie 197). Sharon Pollock heavily researched the history of Lizzie Borden (Pollock "Afterword" 123), which, because it does tap into our archetypes of the monstrous woman, has become an "underworld myth" in Michelene Wandor's terms (X). What becomes interesting for us, therefore, is not simply the historical details of the play, but what Pollock does with those details — her additions and deletions, her *remaking* of history, her *revision* of a legend with archetypal or "mythic" resonances. Feminist Revisionist playwright Naomi Iizuka makes the point more eloquently:

Myth is a story we tell. So is history. So is science. The story determines our perception of reality. Which is to say: The story determines our reality.... We have a
choice of how to tell the story. We have a choice of whom to make the hero, how
to name the demon, how to chart the journey. And the choice matters more than
I can say [19].

The most obvious, and most controversial, choice Pollock makes is to
add the character of The Actress, who is, quite clearly, Lizzie Borden's lesbian
lover. According to Erin Striff, while famous actress Nance O'Neill was a
well-known friend of Lizzie Borden, "Pollock's choice to cast Borden as a lesbian has no basis in historical record" (97). Pollock herself has said that histories aren't definite, that they tend to deny that O'Neill was more than a
friend, but at the time, lesbianism certainly would not have been practiced
openly (qtd. in Wylie 200). As for the legend, mainstream discussion of Borden as lesbian has burgeoned recently among internet groups concerned either
with lurid details or with gender and sexual equity, and relatively recent books,
Evan Hunter's 1985 *Lizzie*, for example, portray Borden as lesbian. However,
whether Lizzie Borden was or was not a lesbian is not the question; why Pollock chose to make Borden's relationship with Nance O'Neill homosexual *is*
the question. After all, in 1980, before the internet buzz had begun, while
Borden aficionados may have been aware of the possibility that Borden might
have been a lesbian, her homosexuality was *not* a part of our North American
legend. Further, as Striff reports, the portrayal is problematic because the
audience may assume that Pollock intends the murders to be seen as the acts
of the "deviant" monstrous homosexual, a deplorable cultural stereotype that
can be seen in *The Silence of the Lambs* and any other number of films or television shows. However, Striff further argues, Pollock is probably just highlighting how difficult our culture makes life for homosexuals (97–8), and that
reading is supported by all of the references of The Actress and Miss Lizzie
to their own sense of difference and defect.

This judgement of the female who does not accept her normal place as
sexual producer for the male hierarchy is as old as patriarchy. When excess
accumulated wealth is passed from father to son, the maintenance of clear
lineage becomes important. As Marxist and materialist feminists argue, in
trade- and conquest-based cultures, procreation is subsumed in service to the
family and state. Economies geared to the acquisition of capital turn all relationships, even family, into relations of exchange. Wives are not partners but
producers of heirs. Daughters are not heirs but products to exchange for heirs.
In this way, patriarchy and the system of exchange are complicitous, designed
to keep wealth within the family unit. As Miner explains, there is no place
within patriarchal culture for a female whose sexuality is not in service to that
culture. "In patriarchal culture, wives serve as conduits between fathers and

sons; wives are responsible for producing male heirs so 'the family' may continue" through inheritance, in particular (Miner 15). Of course, such a claim is only true if patriarchy is part and parcel of a materialist/capitalist culture.

This theme seems complicated somewhat by Emma. Although she is not portrayed as a lesbian, she, too, is unmarried and does not seem destined to marry. This means that her sexuality is not in direct service to the economy, raising the question: Why is Emma not a threat? Why is not Emma seen as monstrous, defective, unnatural, as is Lizzie? The answer is fairly simple, if disturbing. Emma is a pathetic "good girl" in her late 30s who accepts her place. In patriarchal materialist culture, there is a use for an old maid. She serves as a warning to other women to be pretty and compliant, to desire marriage at any cost. As even the supposedly liberated, unconventional Actress tells us, she is not sure what is worse, "To have murdered one's parents, or to be a pretentious small-town spinster" (13). While she is referring to Lizzie when she says this, the Actress reveals a deeply held, almost unconscious revulsion for the unmarried woman that she herself *is*. The cat lady, the old maid, the pathetic solitary woman living on the charity of her relations, "the spinster," are all useful threats for patriarchal capitalist culture that make women not simply accept but *compete* for the chance to *sell* their procreative ability.

This competition is another factor that is quite obvious in *Blood Relations*, particularly in the constant battles in the dream thesis between The Actress/Lizzie and Lizzie's stepmother, Abigail Borden. A second addition by Pollock is a plan by Abigail and Andrew to force Lizzie to marry a local widower, Johnny MacLeod, and become the stepmother of his two children. Even if there were negotiations between Andrew Borden and a local widower (and no account I have read has advanced such speculation) they are, once again, not part of the legend. However, in Pollock's skillful revisioning, the increasing threat that Lizzie will be disinherited due to refusing MacLeod becomes a central factor in The Actress/Lizzie's decision to kill Abigail and Andrew. Theoretically, we would assume that Abigail would have some empathy and sympathy for Lizzie. Lizzie finds the proposition repugnant, an attempt to force her into the role of "housekeeper" (36), and Abigail was similarly trapped into marriage and motherhood with Andrew, Lizzie, and Emma. Nevertheless, Abby fights for the marriage more strongly than Andrew Borden. Abby's actions are driven by strong motives. First, there is a long history of bitter aggression between Abigail and Lizzie, and Lizzie's loathing of her stepmother, and not her father, is a constant. Even after her father kills her beloved pigeons in a threatening gesture to make her accept MacLeod, Lizzie still claims to love her father, yet she reviles her stepmother. As Miner explains, "Power dynamics within patriarchal cultures ... encourage daughters to deflect anger away from fathers [the power figure, and] toward mothers" (15). "To hate the father and to provoke his hatred places the daughter in an extremely perilous position; she risks being disinherited ... rendered homeless" (16). Therefore, Lizzie must have, for years, displaced all of her frustration onto her stepmother, Abigail, who could not have been particularly happy about that dubious honor.

Nevertheless, such a power dynamic is not true simply of patriarchy, but of a patriarchal capitalist ideological system. Competition in a capitalist system pits workers against workers. For example, in contemporary American culture blue-collar workers often hate immigrants for "taking our jobs." Why is such hatred not aimed at the owners, at the employers who manipulate the workers to compete against each other for increasingly lower rewards? We can see the same dynamic between Abigail and Lizzie. If Lizzie is married off to Johnnie MacLeod, more of the money will come to Abigail. Instead of cooperating to better both of their situations, they compete for Andrew's favor and money; this is materialism and patriarchy working hand in hand.[3]

Further, another key revision by Pollock strengthens the idea that *Blood Relations* is not simply a critique of patriarchy but of patriarchy that is complicitous with a capitalist economy. According to Wylie, one of the "most prominent departure[s] from established details of the Borden case ... involves the character of Harry" (199). In the dream thesis, Harry Wingate, Abbie's brother, is staying with the family. The purpose of his visit is to convince Andrew Borden to put his farm in Abigail's name, presumably so that Harry can run a rental stables on the property without fear of Lizzie's interference should Andrew die and Lizzie inherit the property. In fact, Andrew Borden did not have a brother-in-law named Harry Wingate. He had a brother-in-law named John Morse, who was Lizzie's uncle by her biological mother. Morse was staying with the Bordens at the time of the murders (Brown, Arnold 41; Wylie 199). Andrew Borden also had brother-in-law named Hiram Harrington, the brother of Abigail, who may have paid a visit the day before the murders. According to Wylie, Harry is a fictional "composite" of John Morse and Hiram Harrington "who gives a little more substance to the conspiracy between Abbie and Andrew to consolidate Andrew's wealth and property in Abbie's hands in the event of Andrew's death, and thus to the oppressiveness of The Actress/Lizzie's situation, as she faces being under the thumb of her despised stepmother" (Wylie 199). As Miner points out, Harry is the male heir that the first Mrs. Borden failed to provide, and that Lizzie and Emma refuse to provide, but that the second Mrs. Borden brings to the marriage (15). Clearly, the battle that rages focuses on money and property. Lizzie, Harry, and Abigail all want to own the farm, and land ownership is a class symbol. Owners are the bourgeoisie, the privileged class. Non-owners, the proletariat, are the workers, the servants. Lizzie is in competition with Harry and Abby for property ownership, for inheritance, for class position. Without ownership, she is the Bordens' maid; she is Bridget.

Ironically, Lizzie directs the dream thesis in the character of Bridget, and this to me seems Pollock's most important and most overlooked revision. Why choose Bridget to direct the dream thesis? The ending of the play highlights this question. Throughout *Blood Relations* Lizzie's sister, Emma, is described as her mother, the one who raised Lizzie. In the final scene of the play, part of the 1902 frame play, when once again Emma asks, "Lizzie did you?" Lizzie rounds on her in a fury and says, "if I did, then you were guilty too.... I was like a puppet, your puppet ... your hand working my mouth, me saying all the things you felt like saying, me doing all the things you felt like doing" (73). Her statements clearly suggest that Emma has always directed Lizzie's speech and actions, yet Pollock has Lizzie choose to play Bridget to direct the Actress in the dream thesis. Why? I would argue that, once again, Pollock's revision shows us that the conflicts we are viewing are not simply the consequence of patriarchy, but of a materialist, capitalist culture as well.

By having Lizzie step into Bridget's character, and having the Actress, who would be considered of a lower social class at this time, become Lizzie, Pollock deftly shifts the class scales and places familial conflict in the broader context of class conflict. The opening scene of the dream thesis focuses on Bridget, a lower-class Irish maid and cook, introducing her as a strong and intelligent woman, but as a servant who has to live with her place in the system. As Lizzie becomes Bridget, she draws the Actress into the dream sequence by enacting a scene in which Bridget is being man-handled by a crude, vulgar Harry. He "*grabs her ass with both hands*" (14). She screams and pushes him away, but he grabs her again and attempts to kiss her, to which she responds by dumping a glass of water on his head, which derails his attack. We discover through their arguing that this is Harry's traditional treatment of Bridget and that she is "pinched black and blue" each time he visits (97). Bridget is, thank goodness, no fainting Pamela, but she obviously has little choice but to play this lewd, boorish game each time Harry, her employers' brother/brother-in-law and thus her social superior, visits.

This strong woman who is making the best of her limited position within the class system is Pollock's choice of director for the Actress, and while Bridget/Lizzie eventually loses all control of The Actress/Lizzie, her early direction of the Actress is telling. Bridget/Lizzie coaches The Actress/Lizzie, providing her prompts on dealing with her family conflicts:

> Smile and get round them ... I'll tell you a story.... before I worked here I worked up on the hill and the lady of the house ... she loved [her] cook [Mary]. Out in the kitchen, Mary'd be spitting in the soup! ... These two eyes have seen her season up mutton stew when it's off and gone bad ... and the next day they was hit

with ... *stomach flu!* ... I daren't tell you what she served up in their food, for fear you'd be sick!! ... You should try bein' more like cook, Lizzie. Smile and get round them.
LIZZIE: It's not ... fair that I have to.
BRIDGET: There ain't nothin' fair in this world
LIZZIE: Well then ... I don't want to! [41–2].

As Miner has argued, "Lizzie is right: it *isn't* fair that she should *have* to perform, to run the risk of losing herself in the performance. The more often one dons the mask, the more likely the mask will shape one's features, will affect one's vision of the self and world" (20). However, this moment in the play is highly metatheatrical. Lizzie is not the one who says that it is not fair that she should have to perform. The Actress says it, a professional performer, and she is at that moment performing voluntarily. As Stratton points out, metatheatrical productions highlight "the fact that role-playing is essential to existence"(78).

Simply put, no one wants to have to prepare a subservient face for the faces that we meet, although we often enjoy putting on the face of power. We live within a materialist culture in which everyone is placed within a hierarchy, everyone is pitted against everyone else for money and position, and there are times when we are forced to accept that we do not have the higher position. In this scene, in the class context, Lizzie's response seems naïve, perhaps the response of a pampered child. Particularly, the metatheatre highlights The Actress/Lizzie's denial of the web of power relations that extend far beyond the family, a family that is highly privileged, that has servants and property.

There is one further choice that Pollock makes in her creation of Bridget that may prove relevant to Pollock's critique of class. Bridget Sullivan was the legal name of the Bordens' Irish maid, but according to Bridget Sullivan, Lizzie often referred to her as "Maggie" (qtd. in Linder; "Crime Library"). However, Pollock retains Bridget's legal name for the character, and, as those of us who are highly aware of our Irish heritage tend to know, a popular term at the turn of the nineteenth century for a maid was a "Bridget." After the Irish diaspora, when so many of the Irish-born fled to America to escape poverty and starvation, Irish women regularly performed what were considered the menial household duties as cooks and maids in upper-middle-class American households. Much as contemporary Americans have the stereotype of the Mexican maid, nanny, and gardener, in 1900 Irish immigrants and their descendants were stereotyped as police force "flatfoots," drunken day-laborer "Paddys," and "Bridgets": maids and cooks. By maintaining Bridget Sullivan's legal name, rather than using the name by which Lizzie and Emma actually referred to her, "Maggie," Pollock again seems to be highlighting Bridget's class in comparison to that of her employers.

While Pollock is placing the patriarchal familial conflicts within the larger context of class conflict, she is not attempting to deny the limiting archetypes of femininity — the angel and the monster — that she delineated as integral to patriarchal control of women; she is simply highlighting them for what they are: archetypes of upper-middle-class femininity. And the roles that upper-middle-class women are forced to play in order to maintain or obtain property, money, and position are simply variations on the roles that we see everyone else in the play "playing." Abigail took on the role of wife and mother for social position and financial security. Harry puts on the "concerned brother and uncle" role whenever he visits with Andrew so that Andrew will sign over property to him. Bridget "smiles and gets around them" to keep her job. Emma pretends to be the angel, the "good girl" who will care for her parents in their old age, so that she in turn will be financially cared for. And The Actress/Lizzie chooses to be the monster, like us, the audience, chooses to kill for the money and property. After the killings, The Actress/Lizzie tells Bridget: "[Papa] would never leave me the farm ... but now ... I will have the farm, and I will have the money, yes, to do what I please! And you too Bridget, I'll give you some of my money but you've got to help me" (119). In *Blood Relations*, all people are commodities and adversaries trapped within bloody relations of exchange and competition.

Intriguingly, Pollock's Afterword to the 1982 edition of *Blood Relations* highlights a seeming ambiguity. After Pollock had been in an abusive marriage for many years, she writes that she

> spent a great deal of time devising ... murderous schemes to rid me of [my abusive husband]. I implemented none of them... Eventually, I crept, with my children, into the night... Had I been more inventive and less irresolute, I might now be the beneficiary of a large insurance policy, and the owner of quite a nice house in the country. I would not have killed for money and real estate... I would have killed to maintain my sense of self... And so it is with Lizzie (123–24)

The quote suggests that Pollock's character Lizzie "would not have killed for money and real estate." Neither Pollock nor her play, however, makes clear whether Lizzie (either the character or the "real" historical figure) killed Abigail and Andrew; Pollock's play only shows how the Actress, following a societal script, kills for the farm and the money, for property ownership and capital.

Ultimately, however, Pollock refuses to validate the supposed reward system in a materialist economy. According to history, Lizzie Borden did inherit her father's farm and money. She bought a new, beautiful house named Maplecroft and threw extravagant parties for her friends (Brown, Arnold 280). However, in Pollock's revisioning, Lizzie does not receive the farm.[4] The murders come too late and the farm has been signed over to Harry. Lizzie and Emma have only inherited enough money to get by and are still living in the claustrophobic atmosphere of Abigail and Andrew's home ten years after their deaths. Lizzie is still no society belle, she still lost her beloved farm, and she is still trapped with her sister, Emma, asking perpetually, "Did you Lizzie? Lizzie did you?" As a result, *Blood Relations*, Pollock's revision of the legend of Lizzie Borden, is a strong metatheatrical exposé of our societal scripts; a critique of the capitalist system and the roles that all individuals are forced to play in order to maintain or obtain property, money, and position; an attack on oppressive myths of the feminine and gender and the economic ideologies that limit all of our lives.

NOTES

1. See Sharon Friedman's *Feminist Theatrical Revisions of Classic Works*, Lizbeth Goodman's *Mythic Women/Real Women: Plays and Performance Pieces by Women*, Alisa Solomon's *Re-Dressing the Canon: Essays on Theatre and Gender*, and Marianne Novy's *Women's Re-Visions of Shakespeare* series (see Works Cited).

2. As Alisa Solomon delineates in her introduction to *Re-Dressing the Canon*, metatheatre is a particularly useful technique to highlight the constructed nature of gender. Since "femininity" is a performance inscribed and demanded by social conventions and cultural institutions, self-reflexive theatre can call attention to the social enactment of femininity: "On stage there's a radical synergy between theater that displays its performance conventions and makes the fact of theater part of its subject, and the real-life, theater-like conventions of gender roles. In such works, theater and gender take shape as critical images of one another, as mimetic ... twins" (5).

3. Intriguingly, Pollock also changes another detail that highlights the competition between mothers and daughters. According to history, Sarah A. Borden died when Lizzie was two years old (Brown, Arnold 2). In Pollock's play, Lizzie's mother died giving birth to her, prompting Lizzie to feel that she "killed" her mother (115). I did not discover this revision. A student in my Women's Theatre class in 2009, Adrianna Furgison, did, to my great delight. The revision highlights how mothers and daughters must victimize each other ("kill" each other) to maintain or gain place within the system.

4. Whether Pollock's audiences are aware of this significant revision, or of any revisions she makes, is uncertain. My own knowledge of Lizzie Borden prior to reading and researching *Blood Relations* was limited to the comically grotesque hatchet murderer from the school rhyme. However, no matter what knowledge an audience brings to a production of Pollock's play, the text's critique of the patriarchal capitalist system remains clear.

WORKS CITED

Aiuto, Russell. "Lizzie Borden." *truTV Crime Library*. Turner Entertainment Networks. 2011. Web. 17 June 2011.

Andreeva, Nellie. "HBO Developing Lizzie Borden Miniseries with Chloe Sevigny and Playtone." *Deadline Hollywood*.14 Mar. 2011. Web. 27 Mar. 2011.

Brown, Arnold R. *Lizzie Borden: The Legend, the Truth, the Final Chapter*. Nashville: Rutledge Hill, 1991.

Brown, Michael. "Fall River Hoedown." *Lizzie Andrew Borden Virtual Museum and Library: Mondo Lizzie*. PearTree Press. 15 Aug. 2006. Web. 27 May 2011.

"Crime Library: Cast of Characters." *Lizzie Andrew Borden Virtual Museum and Library*. PearTree Press. 29 Sept. 2008. Web. 27 May 2011.

Friedman, Sharon, ed. *Feminist Theatrical Revisions of Classic Works: Critical Essays.* Jefferson, NC: McFarland, 2009.

Goodman, Lizbeth. *Mythic Women/Real Women: Plays and Performance Pieces by Women.* London: Faber and Faber, 2000.

Hunter, Evan. *Lizzie.* New York: Dell, 2005.

Iizuka, Naomi. "What Myths May Come: Can We See the Future in the Mirror of Our Storied Past?" *American Theatre.* (Sept. 1999): 18, 19, 75, 79, 80.

Knowles, Richard Paul. "Replaying History: Canadian Historiographic Metadrama." *Dalhousie Review.* 67 (1987): 228–43.

"Legend." *Oxford English Dictionary.* Oxford University Press. 2010. Web. 9 June 2011.

The Legend of Lizzie Borden. Dir. Paul Wendkos. Perf. Elizabeth Montgomery. Paramount Television. 1975. Film.

Linder, Douglas. "Testimony of Bridget Sullivan in the Trial of Lizzie Borden. June 7 1893." *Famous Trials: The Trial of Lizzie Borden 1893.* University of Missouri Kansas-City School of Law. 2004. Web. 31 May 2011.

Miner, Madonne. "'Lizzie Borden Took an Ax': Enacting *Blood Relations.*" *Literature in Performance.* 2.6 (1986): 10–21.

Novy, Marianne, ed. *Cross-Cultural Performances: Differences in Women's Re-Visions of Shakespeare.* Urbana: University of Illinois Press, 1993.

_____.*Transforming Shakespeare: Contemporary Women's Re-Visions in Literature and Performance.* New York: St. Martin's Press, 1999.

Pollock, Sharon. "Afterword." In Micheline Wandor, ed. *Plays by Women: Volume Three.* London: Methuen, 1982. 123–24.

_____. "Blood Relations." *Blood Relations and Other Plays.* Ed. Anne Nothof. Edmonton: NeWest Press, 2002. 1–73.

Rehak, David. *Did Lizzie Borden Axe for It?* Wilmington: Just My Best, 2005.

Solomon, Alisa. *Re-Dressing the Canon: Essays on Theater and Gender.* London: Routledge, 1997.

Stratton, Susan. "Feminism and Metadrama: Role-Playing in *Blood Relations.*" *Sharon Pollock: Essays on Her Work.* Toronto: Guernica, 2000. 68–80.

Striff, Erin. "Lady Killers: Feminism and Murder in Sharon Pollock's *Blood Relations* and Wendy Kesselman's *My Sister in This House.*" *New England Theatre Journal.* 8 (1997): 95–109.

United States Department of Justice-Federal Bureau of Investigation. "Expanded Homicide Data." *Crime in the United States 2009.* Sept. 2010. Web. 9 June 2011.

Wandor, Michelene, ed. *Plays by Women: Volume Three.* London: Methuen, 1982.

Wylie, Herb. "'Painting the Background'; Metadrama and the Fabric of History in Sharon Pollock's *Blood Relations.*" *Essays in Theatre.* 15.2 (1997): 191–205.

Beth Henley's *Abundance*

The Cinematic Myth
of the Wild West Revised

Verna A. Foster

In *Abundance* (1989) Beth Henley revises America's national myth of the Wild West, long familiar to the general public from movies and television series. Over the first half of the twentieth century Westerns provided us with a compelling, if scarcely factual, story of America's growth and development comprising various assortments of wagon trains moving westward, conflict on the range, the coming of the railway, rugged, individualistic heroes, civilizing heroines (often school marms), new brides, Indian attacks and captivities, romance, shoot-outs, and lots of cows and horses. By the 1960s, however, Westerns were in decline and those Westerns that were made, notably the Italian Westerns of Sergio Leone, had become more cynical and dystopic, their male protagonists more hard-boiled and self-serving, and their women more negligible (Lusted 187). These Westerns also incorporated commentary on the genre itself (Lusted 191).

The myth of the American Frontier, or the Wild West, is a political myth, a secular myth of origin, that has theorized, interpreted, and transformed historical events into a romantic national story and turned real people into heroic legends. The origin, history, diffusion, and reception of the myth have been narrated and explicated many times, notably in Henry Nash Smith's classic *Virgin Land: The American West as Symbol and Myth* (1950) as well as in numerous subsequent works. The mid-nineteenth-century concept of manifest destiny (the idea that it was the destiny of Americans of European descent to control the entire continent from the Atlantic ever westward to the Pacific) provided the ideological context for the representation of the West that developed in popular literature from James Fenimore Cooper's Leatherstocking stories to dime novels that focused on such heroes as Daniel Boone, Kit Carson, and Buffalo Bill (historical figures who became legends). In 1893 Frederick

Jackson Turner's frontier thesis, presented to a World's Congress of Historians in Chicago, gave this mythic version of the West scholarly respectability. Turner argued that the advance of American settlement westward into the wilderness explains the development of distinctively American institutions and American character. At the frontier, "the meeting point between savagery and civilization" (38), traditional European culture ceases. Popular culture's classic take on this American creation myth is the recurring motif of marriage between a civilizing Eastern woman and a rough, individualistic Western man (as in Owen Wister's *The Virginian* [1902], made into a play in 1904 and into a film four times from 1914 to 1946). From the eighteenth century to the twentieth, as Smith observes, "the popular imagination had constantly transformed the facts of westward movement in accord with the requirements of myth" (102). Or, in the words of more recent commentators, "dime literature reflected and participated in a mass fairytale" (Jones and Wills 77).[1] In the twentieth century American cinema inherited the myth and disseminated it ever more widely: "No medium has done more to promote and popularize the Western frontier myth than the movies" (Maynard 55). David Lusted notes that even today this "popular representation of the West *is* The West to most people" (9).

Like any political myth, then, the myth of the Wild West has been conflated with history. During the nineteenth and much of the twentieth century and to an extent still today the Western myth is true "for the social group which believes it" (Flood 8). However, from the 1930s on as a representation of history the myth was also subjected to criticism, and by the late 1980s revisionist (or "new") Western historians had undermined its historical underpinnings, in particular the Turner thesis (Jones and Wills 41–45). The revisionist turn, responding to contemporary social circumstances and more enlightened attitudes to Native Americans and women, affected popular as well as scholarly representations of the West. The movies themselves presented revisionist versions of the myth of the Wild West. In the late-twentieth century especially a number of film directors made parodic or revisionist Westerns, ranging from Mel Brooks's satiric *Blazing Saddles* (1974), which makes affectionate fun of Western motifs, to Clint Eastwood's much-praised *Unforgiven* (1992), which more seriously interrogates the ethos of gunfighting. Both of these films are self-reflexive. *Blazing Saddles* ends up exploding into the film studio in which it is being made, while *Unforgiven* includes an author who is writing a book about gunfighters.[2]

Curiously, perhaps (since modern stage drama is not normally a genre that lends itself to the depiction of wide open spaces), in the same decades that the cinema was interrogating its own representations of the mythic West, several plays by important dramatists—notably Sam Shepard's *True West*

(1980), Marsha Norman's *The Holdup* (1983), and Beth Henley's *Abundance* (1989) — similarly questioned the popular cultural representations of the classic Western movie.[3] And, using more or less domestic settings, they did so, in particular, by foregrounding both the literary and cinematic constructedness of the Western myth and, in Henley's case, by rewriting it from the point of view of women. All three plays present the opposition between the Western myth as embedded in various forms of popular culture, especially the movies, and a purported, if problematized, "true" reality. Shepherd's title implicitly enshrines his play's interrogation of the Western myth; Norman's italicizes her play's use of a typical Western motif; and Henley's alludes (ironically, it transpires) to the plenitude associated with the construction of the Frontier myth in American historiography.[4]

Henley chooses to interrogate the myth of the Wild West perpetuated in the movies both by undermining some of its romantic tenets through the incorporation of unpleasant facts and by retelling the myth from the perspective of women. By working with several kinds of historical sources and incorporating into her play multiple popular motifs, Henley, in an even more complicated way than Shepard and Norman, exposes and explores the constructedness of the Western myth as it appears in popular culture. *Abundance* contains numerous references to popular representations of the West: dime novels ("penny dreadfuls"), melodrama, Buffalo Bill's Wild West shows, as well as the novel that Macon, one of the play's two heroines, had wished to write, and the captivity narrative that Bess, the other one, does write. In particular, *Abundance* works against motifs popular in classic Westerns. In a 1993 interview with Mary Dellasega, Henley indicated that she wrote *Abundance* in part to show "the harsh reality of the West ... which was not portrayed in the cowboy movies or the westerns of the time" (256). Unfortunately, Henley does not indicate what "time" she means so that it is difficult to determine just which Westerns she had in mind. But, given her assumption that Westerns do not depict "the harsh reality," she may have been thinking of classic mid-century versions of the genre such as John Wayne movies. More specifically, however, she is referring, not to the extraordinary dangers and hardships of the trail or of life on the frontier that certainly are depicted in numerous Western movies, but to the harsh realities of "everyday" domestic life that would have been particularly burdensome to women. I will return to this point below.

Though she was concerned to set the record straight in respect to the difficulties of frontier life, Henley personally seems to have retained a more optimistic view of what the West might mean than do Shepard and Norman. Shepard depicts the bankruptcy of the mythic West, while Norman presents its demise. Henley, however, seems to have placed more stock in the West as symbol. She explained to Mary Dellasega, "After living in California for so many years, I like the idea of having the West symbolize hope and new things and danger — you know, you can move West and change things" (256). Henley's relative optimism derives from the fact that she is rewriting the Western myth from a female perspective, that she is concerned to explore specifically the hopes and dreams that women might have had. But as the play progresses, *Abundance* hardly bears out its heroines' optimistic view of Western possibilities. According to Henley, Macon and Bess "each betray their own dreams" (Dellasega 256). But it would be equally accurate to say that their hopes and dreams are misplaced from the beginning.

Bess and Macon travel to the Wyoming Territory in the late 1860s as mail order brides. Both enter into loveless marriages that destroy their dreams of a better life. Bess, the romantic would-be homemaker, lives in poverty with an abusive husband, while Macon, who wanted to have adventures and write a novel, allows her talents to be absorbed in prosperous farming ventures.[5] The two women, like the brothers in *True West*, eventually change places. After being kidnapped by Indians, Bess becomes rich on the profits of her captivity narrative and lecture tour; Macon has settled for material success but, after a liaison with Bess's husband that alienates both her own husband and Bess, she dwindles into poverty and ultimately contracts syphilis, implying that, like Bess, she has sold herself, but less profitably.

Henley, as noted above, has said that she wanted to show "the harsh reality" of Western life. She researched her subject for several years (Plunka 26). Bess's story of her captivity, for example, may be based on several captivity narratives, particularly that of Olive Oatman (Laughlin 102–03).[6] One further inspiration for the play was Michael Lesy's book *Wisconsin Death Trip* (1973), which presents photographs taken by Black River Falls, Wisconsin photographer Charles Van Schaick and cuttings from the town newspaper, the *Badger State Banner*, along with excerpts from the state asylum record book, chronicling in a matter-of-fact way the ordinary but extraordinary occurrences in the lives of ordinary people from the last half decade of the nineteenth century. The cuttings selected by Lesy give brief accounts of suicides, dead children, self-mutilation, arson, diptheria epidemics, and insanity. Henley was strongly impressed by Lesy's book: "I saw this book, and I was just stunned because of the harsh reality of the West it showed, which was not portrayed in the cowboy movies or the westerns of the time. I was fascinated by the specifics of everyday life and how brutal they were" (Dellasega 256). Obviously, events that occurred in the last decade of the nineteenth century in Wisconsin, which had been admitted to the Union as a state as early as 1848, could not provide an adequate historical basis for a play about the Wyoming Territory in the mid-nineteenth century. What Henley drew upon in Lesy's book, however, were the quotidian hardships of an agrarian region in the nineteenth century that might not make much of a film script but that could determine the happiness or misery of ordinary people, especially women. As Jane Tompkins notes in her feminist study *West of Everything*, Westerns focus on the hero's confrontation with death and thus place "unnatural emphasis on a few extraordinary moments — the holdup, the jailbreak, the shoot-out" while ignoring "nearly everything" else (31). Some of the happenings in Black River Falls make their way into *Abundance* to constitute the daily "nearly everything" that is otherwise usually left out of the record.

Taken together, the occurrences chronicled in Lesy's book, especially given the matter-of-fact tone of their reporting, sound rather like some of the grotesque incidents that occur and the stories characters tell one another in a Beth Henley play: such as the horse killed by lightning in *Crimes of the Heart* or the numerous diseased and mutilated characters who appear throughout Henley's work. Perhaps Lesy's book "triggered" Henley's imagination (Dellasega 256) because it cohered so well with what was already in that imagination. By focusing on suffering — poverty, hunger, drought, parched wheat, dead livestock, repossession, brutality, loveless marriages, a dead baby — *Abundance* certainly corrects the popular romantic view of the Wild West, though its excess partially anaesthetizes the audience's feelings, enabling laughter and reflection. There are plenty of instances of the quirky and the grotesque in the play, some of which may have been inspired by incidents related in Lesy's book: Macon's husband lost an eye in an accident with a mining pick; after the death of her baby, Bess dresses her dog in a bonnet and shawl and talks to it; Jack's brother, Michael, whom Bess was supposed to have married, choked to death on cornbread while riding bareback over a swinging bridge; Jack sets fire to their cabin; and so on. But *Abundance* does more than rework the myth of the Wild West from the perspective of black comedy and Lesy's *Wisconsin Death Trip*. The play exploits from a Henleyan perspective the mish-mash of motifs and ideological concepts that comprise popular representations of the Wild West in American culture. Henley revises these popular representations, especially those enshrined in the Western movie, in order to focus on themes and interpretations of events that emphasize women's rather than men's experience, expectations, and motives in shaping the mythic narrative of American history. Henley's particular brand of black comedy assists in her project of demystification.

Henley introduces many of the motifs of the popular Western, especially as they apply to women, to underscore how the lives of Bess and Macon do not fit any of the available stereotypes. Macon and Bess are neither saloon girls, representing temptation, nor schoolmarms, representing the Eastern cultural values that will ultimately "civilize" the "savage" West. Nor are they competent and loving helpmates. And certainly they are not the kind of spunky women (their strength authorized by a powerful male protector) who can stand up to and even with their men — the Barbara Stanwyck role, as in, for example, *The Furies* (1950).[7] When Henley evokes conventional Western female roles, it is only to dismiss them. Attempting to clean their cabin, Bess, the would-be homemaker, is ordered by her husband not to "start messing with things around here" (9); she cannot bake and is too poor to create a domestic haven; she resorts, sadly and ridiculously, to picking shreds of wheat out of the straw mattress in an attempt to find enough to eat.[8] The more practical and intelligent Macon does make her home cozy with material objects — a copper kettle and so forth — but she is not a faithful wife; she is instead an inadvertent temptress who indulges her newly discovered sexuality with her friend's husband. Henley's most overt dismissal of the Western's classic female stereotype occurs early in the play when Bess tries to read a letter to her illiterate husband and Jack tells her roughly, "You ain't no schoolmarm" (10).

The two main tropes of the Western that Henley uses to structure her play are also those that place women in stereotypical positions: the new bride narrative, in which the heroine is typically the romantic civilizer, dominates act one, and the Indian captivity narrative, in which the heroine is typically the victim, governs act two. Henley connects these two apparently disparate actions through her presentation of the complex and changing relationship between Macon and Bess, which is itself a female variant of a third classic trope: that of the male bonding and/or rivalry that often takes precedence over any heterosexual relationship in Western movies. Henley overturns the conventions of all three of these classic Western narratives by telling the first two from the point of view of the women and by choosing women as the central characters of the overarching friendship story.

The apparently female perspective of films that feature new or mail order brides — I am thinking of the largely female cast of William Wellman's *Westward the Women* (1952) — is, of course, actually contained within a male perspective. The women in Wellman's film are led westward to their welcoming new husbands by the male lead (Robert Taylor). On the side, this hero roughs up the heroine (Denise Darcel), who falls in love with him. The two are set to marry at film's end. Bess and Macon, by contrast, travel alone to meet their husbands. Left for several days to fend for herself, Bess has to trade the buttons from her suit for a night's lodging. Macon provides Bess with food, and the two women bond with each other, not with their husbands.

Henley certainly debunks the romantic myth of the civilizer and the savage in which the bride and her handsome if rough husband fall in love with one another. Bess's unpleasant husband, Jack Flan, as Karen L. Laughlin notes

(92), physically fits the stereotype: "*He is handsome, with an air of wild danger*" (7). But he abuses Bess, is useless as a provider, and instead of falling in love with his own wife, lusts after Macon, who succumbs to his good looks despite his lack of charm. Macon acclimates better than Bess to her new life as a farmer's wife, but her success in choosing the right crop, in buying more land, or in winning a baking contest creates personal satisfactions that undermine her original dreams of adventure without providing the traditional alternative of a happy marriage. Macon's conventional feminine civilizing influence is entirely superficial. Her husband learns to admire the "delicate" (20, 21) way she pours a drink and to recognize that "[s]carlet plush sofa pillows" "cheer up the place" (34). But Will Curtis, a decent man, though ugly, boring, and a bit ridiculous (he gives Macon as a present a glass eye intended for himself), hopes in vain for some wifely affection.

While female characters are perforce central to films about new brides, films about Indian captivities are generally presented almost exclusively from the point of view of the male rescuers, as in John Ford's *The Searchers* (1956) and *Two Rode Together* (1961). In such films the perspective of the female victims, like that of their captors, is all but erased. In *Two Rode Together* the rescued heroine (Linda Cristal) tells her story to her rescuer, McCabe (James Stewart), but it is he who provides the public account of her captivity along with a defense of her moral character. But at least this is better than what happens in *The Searchers*, in which Ethan (John Wayne) is prevented only by a last-minute change of heart from killing his "tainted" niece (Natalie Wood), whose own story is not told at all. While Ethan's obsession is presented at least somewhat negatively, mid–twentieth-century filmmakers dealing with captivity were generally much more retrograde in their views of miscegenation than were many of the historical captives themselves. A number of female captives were happy with their Indian husbands and wanted to return to them if forcibly removed, as Bess wishes initially to return to her Indian family (Derounian-Stodola and Levernier 5–7).

Henley's dramatization of the captivity motif, despite its fanciful elements, revises cinematic versions by more accurately representing the content and use made of historical captivity narratives and by presenting Bess's captivity, not from the perspective of her rescuers, but entirely from her own point of view. Bess's five years' absence occurs between the first and second acts of *Abundance*, and her captivity is not staged in any way, except that when she returns she bears its outward marks, a tattoo on her chin (like that of Olive Oatman). The audience in the theatre, like Bess's audiences on her lecture tour, has only Bess's word for what happened. Further, Bess's captivity ultimately empowers her, not the men who rescued her, who remain offstage and distant. Her new status as the famous and wealthy "author" of her captivity narrative turns her bullying husband into her fawning servant and enables her to pay back Macon for stealing him in the first place. In revenge Bess steals Macon's voice, taking images and phrases Macon used in act one — "I'd chew constantly on a small stick to help prevent parching, or I'd hunt for wild fruits that grow all in abundance" (42) — to write the book that Macon herself would have wished to write.

Bess's use of Macon's language to write her book suggests, as Robert Andreach has argued, that Bess's account of her life with the Oglala Indians may be in some respects imaginary. In support of this view Andreach notes, too, that some parts of Bess's story clearly compensate for her unhappy marriage — her singing, for example, which Jack would not permit, enchanted the Indians — and seem thus to be embellishments (144). Not only does Bess borrow words and images from Macon, she also collaborates in writing her book with Professor Elmore Crome, the entrepreneur who arranges its publication and Bess's subsequent profitable tour. Bess reports to Crome what he clearly wants to hear about the hardships of her life and the savagery of the Indians: "I'll tell you all about how the horrid hell hounds tattooed my face with sharp sticks dipped in weed juices and the powder from blue mud stones" (43). Later in the play, however, she acknowledges to Macon that she had a "[b]eautiful time" (52) with the Oglala — "I saw rivers that were so clear you could see every pebble and fish. And the water was any color you could dream: pink and turquoise, gold and white, lime green" (52) — exchanging the cliché of savagery for the cliché of idyll. Laughlin compares Bess's description of the rivers to the imagery of Disney's *Pocahontas* (98), reminding us again of the role of cinema in the construction and mediation of American myth.

However, if the status of Bess's account of her captivity (which we learn about only in fragments) is problematic, historically, too, by the nineteenth century especially, the problem of authenticity in captivity narratives had become almost irresolvable. In such works it is often hard to distinguish fact from fiction and authorial from editorial contributions (Derounian-Stodola and Levernier 10–11). As Macon comments, Bess's story is "the real factualized version" of contemporary popular "atrocity stories" and "penny dreadfuls" (47). Curiously, too, Bess's appropriation of Macon's voice, which seems, as Laughlin notes (91), one of the least realistic, most literary of the play's devices, may have, if not a basis, at least an analogue in history. In 1864, while journeying West on a wagon train, two women, Fanny Kelly and Sarah L. Larimer, were captured by Oglala Sioux in Wyoming. Both wrote accounts of their captivity. Though Larimer's account appeared first, it seems to have been plagiarized from Kelly's manuscript, which was published a year later (Derounian-Stodola and Levernier 12).

The inauthenticity of Bess's captivity narrative, then, is itself historically authentic, though Henley shapes the components of and influences on Bess's book and lectures to foreground feminine rather than masculine motives and concerns. Robert Brustein in a condescending review of *Abundance* objected to the way in which Henley "has domesticated a savage episode of American history into a story of broken hearts and damaged hearths" (108). This simplistic dismissal of specifically women's concerns dramatized in *Abundance* underscores the need for Henley's revisioning of the myth of the Wild West from a feminine perspective in the first place. Bess's captivity narrative offers a peculiarly female perspective on events in a number of ways. First of all, Bess is herself the heroine of her own narrative: she creates a strong image of herself, albeit by "pictur[ing]" Macon (42) and using her voice; she survives, is honored by the Indians for her singing, marries their chief, Ottawa, whom she believed to be her "true one" (37) in place of Jack and by whom she had two children, replacing the baby who died. Even if Bess fictionalizes her captivity narrative to some extent, such "fictionalization," as Christopher Castiglia argues, allowed white women to overcome the boundaries of gender and to transform captivity into "agency and pleasure" (110–11).

Traded back to white people by Ottawa for two horses, a blanket, beads, and bullets, Bess is transformed from heroine to heroic victim who seeks and gains revenge on those who have wronged her. Transculturated for a second time, Bess is motivated to write her narrative not only for the financial rewards it brings but also as an opportunity to expatiate on "treachery" (41). Her anger against her friend Macon for treacherously having an affair with Jack informs her attitude to Ottawa for (as she sees it) treacherously selling her back. (Actually, he was threatened with the massacre of his people, though Bess may not know this.) Clearly Macon serves for Bess as Ottawa's immediately available emotional surrogate. But it seems that equally the unseen Ottawa is Macon's surrogate in Bess's mind. When Elmore Crome asks Bess to "expound certain philosophical beliefs" on behalf of the promoter of her lecture tour, a land speculator "who is deeply devoted to western expansion and the concept of manifest destiny," that is, Bess is to "demand the immediate extermination of all Indian tribes," Bess has "no problem with that" (45–48).[9] She is happy to comply with Crome's request as an act of personal vengeance against Ottawa. Her motive is made clear in that her decision is fuelled by the heated confrontation she has just had with Macon, Ottawa's stand-in. Henley herself has confirmed the personal nature of Bess's motive for calling for genocide: "But she feels *he* betrayed *her*, and so that's her revenge. She agrees to that, and it's really kind of blood-curdling. It's amazing what people will do when they've been hurt, how they will strike out viciously" (Dellasega 256–57).

In her depiction of the motives behind Crome and his promoter's use of Bess's captivity narrative, Henley debunks the myth of westward expansion, showing it up for what it was: unbridled masculine greed and theft of land belonging to others. She also, however, invents and incorporates women's motives into her revision of the myth. Jealousy and desire for revenge certainly are no more excusable motives for projected genocide than greed or racist ideology. But as Henley rewrites women into the story, at least Bess does not hide her motives under some fancier name. Her bitter sense of Ottawa's betrayal underscores how ugly personal motives, not destiny, direct historical courses.

In its use of historical material, both mythic and factual, and its Western setting, *Abundance* was a new departure for Henley, whose previous plays had been set in the twentieth century and in her native South. What does remain familiar is the play's presentation of the central complicated relationship between women, recognizable from Henley's earlier depictions of the three sisters in *Crimes of the Heart* or the two sisters in *The Wake of Jamey Foster* or the two cousins (quasi-sisters) in *The Miss Firecracker Contest*. Bess and Macon are not literally sisters, but Macon recognizes the kinship between them as soon as they meet — "You're like me" (5) — a kinship that is affirmed when they discover their mutual status as mail order brides. Their homosocial bonding lasts longer and is more important to them and satisfying to the audience than any of the play's heterosexual relationships. In this way *Abundance* reverses one of the classic gender configurations of male-oriented Westerns, apparent in films about Wyatt Earp and Doc Holliday or Butch Cassidy and the Sundance Kid and many others — Howard Hawks's *Red River* (1948), John Ford's *The Searchers*, and Peter Fonda's *The Hired Hand* (1971) come to mind — in which one or both of the bonded heroes invest more in male friendship or male rivalry and certainly male adventure than in romantic love.[10]

Like many of the male duos of Western films, Henley's female protagonists consist of a stronger and a weaker friend, a mentor and a pupil. For much of the play Macon is the stronger character. Symbolic of their relationship, Macon teaches Bess to whistle, a masculine activity (in contrast to Bess's feminine singing) that signifies freedom, self-confidence, and the courage to do what one wants. As a woman, Macon obviously is not called on to stand by Bess in some extreme situation such as a gunfight; rather she supports her friend through long-term domestic hardships, "the harsh reality" of everyday life that Henley had set out to dramatize in her play. Macon stands up for Bess when Jack abuses her, feeds Bess when she has nothing to eat, takes her into her own home when Jack burns down their cabin, and inspires in her a desire for adventure to replace her lost dream of domestic bliss; later, even when impoverished herself, she acquires a dress and shoes for Bess after she returns from her captivity. Will cannot understand what Macon sees in Bess. To him she is "not special. Just some joyless creature with sawdust for brains"

(17). Macon, however, insists on the same kind of unconditional loyalty to her friend because she is her friend as any male hero has for his partner: "I gotta look out for Bess. She's a friend of mine" (17). At first Bess values the friendship as much as Macon does: "I realize now — now that you're brushing my hair, that I love you so much more — so much more than anyone else" (23). The only true and reciprocal intimacy we see in the play is that between the two friends.

Though rivalry over Jack tears the women apart, theirs is not a conventional female jealousy. Neither of them in the end actually wants Jack, and their actions are motivated by their feelings for each other. Bess's pain at her friend's betrayal leads her to refuse to help Macon to save her homestead and to call for genocide because her Indian husband's "treachery" reminds her of Macon's. Macon, in turn, succumbs to Jack against her will and tries to give him up as soon as Bess returns from captivity. At the end of the play, fifteen years later, the women still care for each other more than for any of the men in their lives. When Jack reports seeing Macon, now poor and syphilitic, at a tent show, Bess obliquely expresses her anger at his callous attitude towards her friend: "Your cigar is foul. Put it out. Get it out" (51).

The last scene of *Abundance*, like the first, focuses on Bess and Macon. When Bess visits Macon in her tent, the women look back sadly over their lives. Neither has fulfilled the dreams with which she came West. Yet the women are pleased to see each other. Macon finally has someone to tell that she is dying, and Bess says, "I'm glad you looked my way" (53). Their friendship with each other has been perhaps the only real thing in their lives. Everything else — their marriages as mail order brides, Bess's captivity — has been no more than "the real factionalized version" (47), as Macon might have put it, of Western fictions. If *Abundance* begins by offering a female version of fantasies of life on the frontier, it concludes by sharing in the nostalgia and skepticism of late versions of the Western genre. Bess and Macon whistle together, remembering their early hopes and asserting perhaps a kind of resilience, but then, as the play ends, they share a deep-felt laugh that wryly comments on the failure of their fantasies.

Like *True West* and *The Holdup*, in numerous ways *Abundance* foregrounds the problematic relation between fact and fiction. Henley's play revises neither history nor historiography but already mythic representations of history. When Macon tells Bess that her book is "the real factualized version" of the fictions people have been reading in "penny dreadfuls" (47), it is as if fiction preceded fact rather than the other way around. And, of course, often it does, as recent revisionist Westerns such as *Unforgiven* as well as Henley's play are at pains to point out. *Abundance* itself both shares in and reflects metatheatrically upon the problematic status of Bess's book. Crome tells Bess that Dion Boucicault wants to "adapt" her book into "a hit play" (44). This reference to Boucicault at the beginning of Bess's professional career serves to establish Bess's story as more "real" than any future melodramatic adaptation could be. However, fifteen years later history catches up with Bess, and her story, according to one review, now seems "excessive and outdated like a worn-out melodrama one would read in a dime novel" (50). Consumers no longer wish to see Indians as "untamed savages" but, Crome says, as "beloved circus performers" (50), a reference to Buffalo Bill's late-nineteenth-century Wild West shows. These popular spectacles, including Native American performers such as Chief Sitting Bull and scenes supposedly depicting events on the frontier, themselves contributed to the creation of "the triumphal myth of western conquest" (Wattenberg 2011: 47) that Henley's play debunks.

Clearly representation is determined to a great extent not only by what artists want to create but by what audiences want, at least superficially, to believe. In the middle third of the twentieth century the conventions of highly popular classic Western movies gave us a macho Wild West in which men heroically bonded and fought with other men to civilize the frontier and women were assigned stereotypical supporting roles. Revisionist films of the late-twentieth century, like Shepard's, Norman's, and Henley's plays, revise the mythic Wild West while simultaneously commenting upon the nature of their own storytelling. With a handful of exceptions, however, few Westerns of any sort have seriously revised women's roles.[11] Beth Henley's *Abundance*, by contrast, shows us a West as it might have been dreamed about and experienced by rather ordinary women looking for their own kinds of success, facing their own kinds of familial disappointments, and writing their own stories, all the while conscious that it is itself a revision of a representation of a myth.

NOTES

1. On the nature of political myth see Flood, *Political Myth*. Flood argues that political myth exists at the intersection of sacred myth and ideology (5). He cites the American Frontier myth as an example of political myth (68). Segal, also citing the American Frontier, notes that a myth can be based on a belief to which illustrative stories are attached (*Myth* 4). On the development and popularization of the Frontier myth see Smith, *Virgin Land*; Jones and Wills, *The American West*; Wattenberg, "Challenging the Frontier Myth: Contemporary Women's Plays about Women Pioneers." On the dramatic representation of the marriage between savagery and civilization as the marriage between a man and a woman see Wattenberg, *Early-Twentieth-Century Frontier Dramas on Broadway*, passim.

2. While I have examined several of the recent spate of books on the Western, in my discussions of the conventions of and historical trends in Western movies I have drawn especially on John G. Cawelti's now classic *The Six-Gun Mystique* and David Lusted's *The Western*, as well as on my own viewing of Western films. I have also found useful Peter C. Rollins and John E. O'Connor, ed. *Hollywood's West: The American Frontier in Film, Television, and History*, especially the editors' review of the literature in the Introduction (1–

34). On revisionist films and other revisionist representations, especially literary, of the West see also Johnson, *Hunger for the Wild* (352–62).

3. On revisionist frontier plays by women, including *Abundance*, produced between 1982 and 1990 see Wattenberg, "Challenging the Frontier Myth." Useful essays on *True West* and *The Holdup* include Wattenberg, "Feminizing the Frontier Myth: Marsha Norman's *The Holdup*," Erben, "The Western Holdup Play: The Pilgrimage Continues," and Laughlin, "Abundance or Excess? Beth Henley's Postmodern Romance of the True West," which includes a comparison of *Abundance* and *True West*.

4. See the chapter "Abundance and the Frontier Hypothesis" in David M. Potter, *People of Plenty: Economic Abundance and the American Character*, in which Potter revises Turner's Frontier thesis ("The Significance of the Frontier in American History") to emphasize the importance of economic surplus rather than the frontier per se in forming the American character.

5. In *The Land Before Her: Fantasy and Experience of the American Frontiers, 1630–1860* Annette Kolodny demonstrates that most women's fantasies of the West during the period covered by her book were of an "idealized domesticity" (xiii) that was in its own way heroic in view of the hardships women faced. In the years after the Civil War, however, American women's fantasies included adventure as well as domesticity (240). Bess and Macon would appear to represent these two types of fantasy.

6. Like Bess, Oatman was tattooed on the chin, restored to white society against her will, initially wished to return to her Indian family, and told her story to an editor (Derounian-Stodola and Levernier 122, 163–64).

7. On women's roles in Westerns see Sandra Kay Schackel, "Women in Western Films: The Civilizer, the Saloon Singer, and Their Modern Sister." Schackel notes that since almost all Westerns have been directed by men, "women's roles tend to reflect a male perspective" (196). See also Lusted, *The Western*, 250–62; R. Philip Loy, *Westerns in a Changing America 1955–2000*, 271–303.

8. Quotations from *Abundance* are taken from Beth Henley, *Collected Plays*, Vol. II. Page numbers will be noted in the text.

9. Castiglia notes that captivity narratives were often edited to "propagandize westward expansion and Indian extermination"(82). See also Derounian-Stodola and Levernier 31, 35.

10. See Tompkins, *West of Everything*, 38–41; Lusted, *The Western*, 150, 234; Springer, "Beyond the River: Women and the Role of the Feminine in Howard Hawks's *Red River*." In *The Hired Hand* the protagonist (Peter Fonda) chooses to save his friend at the cost of abandoning his wife for a second (and final) time.

11. While there have always been some strong or unusual female characters in Westerns (Calamity Jane or Belle Starr, for example), conventional versions of women predominate even in recent examples of the genre. Exceptions that do present the human and physical difficulties of living in the West from the perspective of women include *Heartland* (1979) and *The Ballad of Little Jo* (1993). In *Heartland*, based on Elinore Pruitt Stewart's autobiographical account, produced by Wildernesss Women, and directed by Richard Pearce, a mail order housekeeper, later wife (Conchata Ferrell), struggles heroically to make a living in a harsh country; in *The Ballad of Little Jo* (1993), directed by a woman (Maggie Greenwald), the female protagonist (Suzy Amis) survives in the West by cross-dressing as a man.

WORKS CITED

Andreach, Robert J. "The Missing Five Years and Subjectivity in Beth Henley's *Abundance*." *Southern Quarterly* 39:3 (2001): 141–150.

Brustein, Robert. "She-Plays, American Style." *Reimagining American Theatre*. New York: Hill and Wang, 1991. 104–108.

Castiglia, Christopher. *Bound and Determined: Captivity, Culture-Crossing, and White Womanhood from Mary Rowlandson to Patty Hearst*. Chicago: University of Chicago Press, 1996.

Cawelti, John G. *The Six-Gun Mystique*. Bowling Green, OH: Bowling Green University Popular Press, 1971.

Dellasega, Mary. "Beth Henley." *Speaking on Stage: Interviews with Contemporary American Playwrights*. Eds. Philip C. Kolin and Colby H. Kullman. Tuscaloosa: University of Alabama Press, 1996. 250–259.

Derounian-Stodola, Kathryn Zabelle and James Arthur Levernier. *The Indian Captivity Narrative 1550–1900*. New York: Twayne Publishers, 1993.

Erben, Rudolf. "The Western Holdup Play: The Pilgrimage Continues." *Western American Literature* 23:4 (1989): 311–322.

Flood, Christopher G. *Political Myth: A Theoretical Introduction*. New York: Garland Publishing, 1996.

Henley, Beth, *Abundance. Collected Plays* II. Lyme, NH: Smith and Kraus, 2000.

_____. *Crimes of the Heart. Collected Plays* I. Lyme, NH: Smith and Kraus, 2000.

_____. *The Miss Firecracker Contest. Collected Plays* I. Lyme, NH: Smith and Kraus, 2000.

_____. *The Wake of Jamey Foster. Collected Plays* I. Lyme, NH: Smith and Kraus, 2000.

Johnson, Michael L. *Hunger for the Wild: America's Obsession with the Untamed West*. Lawrence: University of Kansas Press, 2007.

Jones, Karen R. and John Wills. *The American West: Competing Visions*. Edinburgh: Edinburgh University Press, 2009.

Kolodny, Annette. *The Land Before Her: Fantasy and Experience of the American Frontiers, 1630–1860*. Chapel Hill: University of North Carolina Press, 1984.

Laughlin, Karen L. "Abundance or Excess? Beth Henley's Postmodern Romance of the True West." *Beth Henley: A Casebook*. Ed. Julia A. Fesmire. New York: Routledge, 2002.

Lesy, Michael. *Wisconsin Death Trip*. Albuquerque: University of New Mexico Press, 1973.

Loy, R. Philip. *Westerns in a Changing America, 1955–2000*. Jefferson, NC: McFarland, 2004.

Lusted, David. *The Western*. Harlow, Essex: Pearson Education, 2003.

Maynard, Richard A. *The American West on Film: Myth and Reality*. Rochelle Park, N.J.: Hayden Book Company, Inc., 1974.

Norman, Marsha. *The Holdup*. New York: Dramatists Play Service, 1987.

Plunka, Gene A. *The Plays of Beth Henley: A Critical Study*. Jefferson, NC: McFarland, 2005.

Potter, David M. *People of Plenty: Economic Abundance and the American Character*. Chicago: University of Chicago Press, 1954.

Rollins, Peter C. and John E. O' Connor. Eds. *Hollywood's West: The American Frontier in Film, Television, and History*. Lexington: University Press of Kentucky, 2005.

Schackel, Sandra Kay. "Women in Western Films: The Civilizer, the Saloon Singer, and Their Modern Sister." *Shooting Stars: Heroes and Heroines of Western Film*. Ed. Archie P. McDonald. Bloomington: Indiana University Press, 1987.

Segal, Robert A. Ed. *Myth: Critical Concepts in Literary and Cultural Studies*. Vol. 1. London and New York: Routledge, 2007.

Shepard, Sam. *True West*. London and New York: Samuel French, 1981.

Smith, Henry Nash. *Virgin Land: The American West as Symbol and Myth*. Cambridge, MA: Harvard University Press, 1950.

Springer, John Parris. "Beyond the River: Women and the Role of the Feminine in Howard Hawks's *Red River*." In Rollins and O' Connor, eds. 115–25. *Hollywood's West: The American Frontier in Film, Television, and History*. Lexington: University Press of Kentucky, 2005.

Tompkins, Jane. *West of Everything: The Inner Life of Westerns*. New York: Oxford University Press, 1992.

Turner, Frederick Jackson. "The Significance of the Frontier in American History." *Frontier and Section: Selected Essays of Frederick Jackson Turner.* Introd. Ray Allen Billington. Englewood Cliffs, N.J.: Prentice-Hall, 1961. 37–62.

Wattenberg, Richard. "Challenging the Frontier Myth: Contemporary Women's Plays About Women Pioneers." *Journal of American Drama and Theatre* 4:3 (1992): 42–61.

_____. *Early-Twentieth-Century Frontier Dramas on Broadway: Situating the Western Experience in Performing Arts.* New York: Palgrave Macmillan, 2011.

_____. "Feminizing the Frontier Myth: Marsha Norman's *The Holdup.*" *Modern Drama* 33:4 (December 1990): 507–517.

About the Contributors

Miriam **Chirico** is an associate professor of English literature at Eastern Connecticut State University. She received her Ph.D. from Emory University, specializing in dramatic literature. She has published numerous articles and reviews on drama, writing about playwrights including Eugene O'Neill, Sophie Treadwell, G.B. Shaw, Wendy Wasserstein, Beth Henley, John Leguizamo, José Rivera, and Mary Zimmerman.

Anthony **Ellis** is an associate professor in the English department at Western Michigan University. He is the author of *Old Age, Masculinity, and Early Modern Drama: Comic Elders on the Italian and Shakespearean Stage* (Ashgate 2009), and his articles on Renaissance drama have appeared in *Forum Italicum*, *Studi veneziani*, *Journal of Dramatic Theory and Criticism*, and *Ben Jonson Journal*. He serves as associate editor of the journal *Comparative Drama*, published in the WMU English Department.

Verna A. **Foster** is professor of English at Loyola University Chicago. She is the author of *The Name and Nature of Tragicomedy* (Ashgate 2004) and of numerous essays on Renaissance and modern drama, including Shakespeare, Ford, Ibsen, Chekhov, Williams, Beckett, Henley, Wertenbaker, and Parks. She is the book review editor of *Text & Presentation*, the Comparative Drama Conference Series.

Sharon **Friedman** is an associate professor in the Gallatin School of New York University. She is the editor of *Feminist Theatrical Revisions of Classic Works*, published by McFarland (2009), and her essays have appeared in such journals as *American Studies, New Theatre Quarterly, Women and Performance, Text & Presentation, TDR*, and *New England Theatre Journal*.

Karelisa **Hartigan** is a professor emeritus of classics at the University of Florida, where she taught Greek language, literature and history for 35 years. She has published extensively on Greek drama and the reception of the classical world in contemporary culture, and founded the Comparative Drama Conference, which she directed at the University of Florida from 1977 to 2000.

Amelia Howe **Kritzer** is a professor of English and theater at the University of St. Thomas in St. Paul, Minnesota. She has written *Political Theatre in Post-Thatcher Britain* and *The Plays of Caryl Churchill: Theatre of Empowerment*, as well as numerous articles on the work of Caryl Churchill and various aspects of contemporary British drama. She is also the editor of *Plays by Early American Women, 1775–1850* and has published a number of essays on early American drama and theater.

Jeffrey B. **Loomis** is a professor of English at Northwest Missouri State University. He holds a Ph.D. in comparative literature from the University of North Carolina at

Chapel Hill. He has written on O'Connor, Woolf, and Huysman and published many articles on dramatists, including Albee, Williams, Sondheim, Strindberg, Shakespeare, Goethe, Zindel, Sherman, and Tina Howe.

Sheila **Rabillard** is an associate professor of English at the University of Victoria, Canada. She has published on a variety of playwrights, and edited *Essays on Caryl Churchill: Contemporary Representations*. Her recent work includes a chapter on Churchill and ecology in *The Cambridge Companion to Caryl Churchill*, an article on Metis playwright Marie Clements, and "Theatre in an Age of Eco-Crisis," a co-edited special issue of *Canadian Theatre Review*.

Gregory J. **Reid** is a retired professor of English and comparative literature at the Université de Sherbrooke and a co-editor of *The Bibliography of Comparative Studies in Canadian, Québec and Foreign Literatures*. His work includes "Anne Hébert's *La Cage*: A Masque of Liberation" in *Text & Presentation* (2008) and "Wind in August: *Les Fous de Bassan*'s Reply to Faulkner" in *Studies in Canadian Literature*.

Maya E. **Roth** serves as program director of theater and performance studies at Georgetown University. She publishes on feminist playwriting, spatiality, civic poetics, and cross-cultural adaptations of history and myth. A leading scholar on the work of Timberlake Wertenbaker, she co-edited (together with Sara Freeman) *International Dramaturgy: Translation and Transformations in the Theatre of Timberlake Wertenbaker*.

Elizabeth W. **Scharffenberger** teaches in the Department of Classics at Columbia University. Her main area of specialization is ancient Athenian drama, and she has published on Aristophanes, Euripides, and Sophocles. She also works on the modern reception and translation of ancient texts.

Laura **Snyder** is a professor of English at Stevenson University in Stevenson, Maryland, where she specializes in modern and contemporary women's theatre. Publications include articles in *Modern Drama*, *Text & Presentation*, *The Encyclopedia of British Humorists*, and *College Teaching*. She is the director of the Comparative Drama Conference.

Christy **Stanlake** is an associate professor of English and director of theatre for the United States Naval Academy. Her book, *Native American Drama: A Critical Perspective*, develops a methodology based on Native intellectual traditions for the reading of Native plays. In summer 2012, she directed JudyLee Oliva's *Te Ata* for the Chickasaw Nation.

Kevin J. **Wetmore**, Jr., is an associate professor of theatre at Loyola Marymount University, the author of five books, and the editor or co-editor of five more, including *The Athenian Sun in an African Sky* and *Black Dionysus: Greek Tragedy and African-American Theatre* (both published by McFarland). He is also a working actor, director, and stage combat choreographer.

Index